MW01141785

Contributions To The Tertiary Paleontology Of The Pacific Coast: I. The Miocene Of Astoria And Coos Bay, Oregon...

William Healey Dall

Nabu Public Domain Reprints:

You are holding a reproduction of an original work published before 1923 that is in the public domain in the United States of America, and possibly other countries. You may freely copy and distribute this work as no entity (individual or corporate) has a copyright on the body of the work. This book may contain prior copyright references, and library stamps (as most of these works were scanned from library copies). These have been scanned and retained as part of the historical artifact.

This book may have occasional imperfections such as missing or blurred pages, poor pictures, errant marks, etc. that were either part of the original artifact, or were introduced by the scanning process. We believe this work is culturally important, and despite the imperfections, have elected to bring it back into print as part of our continuing commitment to the preservation of printed works worldwide. We appreciate your understanding of the imperfections in the preservation process, and hope you enjoy this valuable book.

DEPARTMENT OF THE INTERIOR

UNITED STATES GEOLOGICAL SURVEY

GEORGE OTIS SMITH, Director

PROFESSIONAL PAPER 59

CONTRIBUTIONS TO THE TERTIARY PALEONTOLOGY OF THE PACIFIC COAST

I. THE MIOCENE OF ASTORIA AND COOS BAY, OREGON

BY

WILLIAM HEALEY DALL, H. W.

WASHINGTON

GOVERNMENT PRINTING OFFICE

1909

CONTENTS.

3

ILLUSTRATIONS.

4

THE MIOCENE OF ASTORIA AND COOS BAY, OREGON.

By WILLIAM HEALEY DALL.

INTRODUCTION.

The object of the present memoir is not merely to describe and illustrate the fauna of a particular Tertiary horizon of the Pacific coast of the United States, although the larger portion of the work is devoted to that purpose. The literature of Pacific coast paleontology is scattered, much of it is inaccessible except in large libraries, and, though various worthy papers have appeared from time to time, no general revision of the nomenclature of the fossils has been made, and until recently the material for thorough monographic study has not existed anywhere. In the last few years large collections have been made under the auspices of the United States Geological Survey by members of its staff. These collections are now beginning to be sufficiently large for serious study, though, owing to the poor state of preservation so common in the Tertiary of the Pacific coast, this will prove a task much less easy and rapid than is possible with the well-preserved fossils of the Atlantic Tertiaries.

The work must proceed slowly and publication of the results will be possible only at intervals and, as it were, piecemeal. The present is the first of what I hope may prove a series of contributions to a better knowledge of the Tertiary faunas of the Pacific States.

I have aimed to describe and illustrate the Miocene fauna of the Empire formation of Coos Bay, Oregon, and the unfigured species of the Astoria group of Columbia River, and to revise and bring to date the systematic nomenclature of the species described or known from both localities. The description or illustration of a few species from other localities on the coast has been added when it seemed that these species would aid, by comparison or otherwise, in the elucidation of the fauna under consideration.

I have had the kind assistance of Dr. F. W. True, of the United States National Museum, in working up a remarkable fossil sea lion whose remains occur in the Coos Bay Miocene.

5

In view of the great difficulty in getting access to some of the early short papers on Pacific coast paleontology by T. A. Conrad and others, the text of a number of the more important of these papers has been included among the appendices to the main portion of the work. The student is thus enabled to consult a practically exact reprint of the originals. The text figures to the first paper ever printed on the invertebrate fossils of Oregon are also reproduced, as they have not been elsewhere refigured and the original paper is of great rarity.

In 1856 and 1863 the late Dr. Philip Pearsall Carpenter made reports to the British Association for the Advancement of Science "On the present state of our knowledge of the Mollusca of the northwest coast of America." These reports, published in 1857 and 1864, respectively, have been of the utmost value to students of the Tertiary and recent molluscan faunas of the coast. They not only analyzed the existing literature from the beginning, but systematized the data contained in it in a masterly way and at the cost of great labor. Since the death of Doctor Carpenter a large number of papers on the shells of this region, recent and fossil, have appeared, some of them in out of the way places. It was thought that a bibliography bringing the subject up to date—comprising all known papers issued since the publication of Carpenter's reports and including some titles omitted or imperfectly presented in the report of 1857 and the reprint of papers by Carpenter issued by the Smithsonian Institution in 1872—would be of value to students. Such a bibliography, gathering the titles to the output of some forty years of scientific activity, has been compiled and added to the series of appendices.

I have had the use of material and books belonging to the United States National Museum and of sundry specimens from the collection of Stanford University and the University of California; also the cooperation of Prof. W. B. Clark, of Johns Hopkins University; Dr. Ralph Arnold, of the United States Geological Survey, and many private correspondents on the Pacific coast, for which I desire to express my gratitude.

THE TERTIARY OF ASTORIA.

In Dana's report on the geology of the United States Exploring Expedition under Wilkes [a] he refers briefly to the Astoria Tertiaries as follows:

The Tertiary rocks were first seen on the Columbia in the vicinity of Astoria. They occur along the shores of this river for 20 miles from the sea, though occasionally interrupted by basalt as at the settlement Astoria. * * * These sedimentary deposits, according to the reports of the officers of the *Vincennes*, prevail to the north of the Columbia and upon the shores of Puget Sound. They were observed by the writer 10 miles north of the Columbia in a stream emptying near Gray's Bay.

*   *   *   *   *   *   *

We have already stated that the Tertiary formation of Oregon occurs in various places from Puget Sound to San Francisco, along the * * * Straits of De Fuca, the Cowlitz, the lower Columbia, the Willamette Valley, and the Elk. * * * The thickness of this formation on the Columbia and Willamette is in many places 1,000 or 1,200 feet. As * * * the rocks had evidently been much removed by denudation it is probable that 1,500 feet is even too low an estimate for the whole height above the present sea level. The rocks of the formation are soft sandstones more or less argillaceous and schistose, and clay shales, either firm or crumbling, besides basaltic tufa or conglomerate.

In many localities the argillaceous shale contains nodular concretions of limestone. These concretions are often very regularly spherical and vary from half an inch to 6 feet in diameter, though if

---

[a] Dana, J. D., Geology: U. S. Expl. Exped. 1838–1842, vol. 10, under command of Charles Wilkes, U. S. N., Philadelphia, 1849, pp. 626, 651, 652, 654, 657, 679.

exceeding a foot the form is more irregular. * * * They are often very abundant, and as they fall out from the crumbling precipice the plain at foot becomes covered with these balls of stone.

The concretions often contain a fragment of wood, a fossil shell, a crab's leg or bones of fish. * * * Fossils rarely occur in the shales where these concretions are found, except they are inclosed in some of the concretions. No solid layer of limestone was observed in any part of the sandstone formation. These nodules occur along the Columbia, east of Astoria, in sufficient abundance to be procured and burnt for lime. They were also observed in the shale of Elk River.

The layers of sandstone and shale are generally horizontal. The sandstone continues to the water's edge on the north shores [of the Columbia], while on the south banks of shale at least 200 feet thick border the river. Above this height the shale is covered by the soil. * * *

The shale in the vicinity of Astoria contains numerous fossils. Those to the eastward are embedded in calcareous nodules and are consequently well preserved, while those in the cliffs down the river lie unprotected in the shale and have suffered from compression. The specimens collected include numerous shells of Mollusca, minute Polythalamia, besides the legs of a crustacean, an echinoderm, the remainder of four species of fish, and some cetacean vertebræ. * * *

The fossils of Astoria have been examined and described for this report by Mr. T. Conrad, and the following are his conclusions with regard to the age of the deposits:

"From the investigation of the fossils previously received from Mr. Townsend, I had arrived at the conclusion that they were of the geological era of the Miocene, and the specimens you sent confirm the opinion. I do not recognize, it is true, any recent species of the coast of California or elsewhere, but neither is there any shell of the Eocene period, nor has the group any resemblance to that of the Eocene. On the contrary, the forms are decidedly approximate to those of the Miocene period which occur in Great Britain and the United States. *Nucula divaricata*, for instance, closely resembles *N. cobboldiæ* (Sowerby) of the English Miocene, and *Lucina acutilineata* can scarcely be distinguished from *L. contracta* (Say), a recent species from the Atlantic coast and found in the Miocene beds of Virginia. *Natica heros*, a shell of similar range, is quite as nearly related to the *N. sarea*. A similar number of species might be obtained from some of the Miocene localities of Maryland or Virginia, and yet no recent species be observed among them. In the Eocene, and also in the Miocene strata, there are peculiar forms which obtain in Europe and America, and although the species differ, yet they are so nearly allied that this character alone, independent of the percentage of extinct forms, is quite a safe guide to the relative ages of remote fossiliferous rocks. On this foundation I speak with confidence when I assign the fossils of the Columbia River to the era of the Miocene."

These observations of Conrad, however liable to criticism in minor details, afford good evidence of his acuteness in recognizing the salient features of a fossil fauna and in referring it approximately to its proper place in the geologic column. Nevertheless, some years later he modified his opinion, and in a paper issued in 1865 [a] he expressed himself as follows:

The fossil shells of the United States Exploring Expedition, collected at Astoria, and published in Dana's report on geology and paleontology, were referred by me to the Miocene period. A larger acquaintance with Tertiary fossils in general has led me to the conclusion that their position is in the older Eocene, and that they correspond in their horizon to the group of Shark River, Monmouth County, N. J., holding in common the *Aturia ziczac*. The shells of Shark River being in the form of casts, not sufficiently characteristic for comparison with those of Oregon, the *Aturia* is the only species that is certainly common to the two localities; but several of the Oregon species are almost identical with shells of the London clay of Bracklesham and Bognor.

This modification of Conrad's views in regard to the age of the Astoria group was doubtless due to his growing sense of the incongruity of the presence in an American Miocene formation of such forms as *Aturia*, *Miopleiona*, and *Trophosycon*. This feeling was to a certain extent justified, but the idea that the fauna of the miscellaneous concretions picked up at the foot of the Astoria bluff was not all derived from beds of a single age seems not to have occurred to him.

---

[a] Am. Jour. Conch., vol. 1, 1865, p. 150. See also Proc. Acad. Nat. Sci. Philadelphia, for 1865, p. 71.

That there was a modicum of uncertainty in the determination of 1849 was brought out by J. S. Newberry in his discussion of the Chico-Tejon problem of California[a] as early as 1857, and subsequently by C. A. White[b] in considering the same question. White observes:

There is apparently no reason to doubt that a large part of the species figured and described in the second work cited[c] are really of Miocene age; but it is the species which are published in the first-quoted work,[d] and in part republished in the second, concerning the Miocene age of which doubt is felt. The true Miocene fossils appear to have been collected by members of the exploring expedition, while the collection of those published in the American Journal [of Science] is credited by Mr. Conrad to J. K. Townsend. Mr. Conrad's descriptions of Mr. Townsend's fossils are brief and mostly unsatisfactory, but his woodcut figures are good, and they represent forms that have not to my knowledge been elsewhere recognized among the Miocene fauna of the Pacific coast.

Attention may be called especially to four or five of the species figured in the American Journal. For example, the *Nucula divaricata* differs, if at all, from *N. truncata* Gabb only in the asserted rounding, instead of the truncation, of the posterior ("anterior") extremity; and yet one of Mr. Conrad's figures shows such a truncation. The *Mactra albaria* of Conrad is exceedingly like *M. ashburneri* Gabb. The *Loripes paralis* [misprint for *parilis.*—W. H. D.] of Conrad recalls *L. dubia* Gabb. The *Pyrula modesta* of Conrad is possibly identical with *Ficus? cypræoides* Gabb, and the Survey collections contain specimens of *Solen* from the Tejon group of California, which closely resemble Conrad's figure of *S. curtus*. Besides this, the *Aturia angustatus* of Conrad, from Astoria, is much like *A. mathewsoni* Gabb, of the Tejon group of California, and the presence of that genus in Miocene strata seems out of place.

These similarities suggest at least the possibility that in the vicinity of Astoria both Miocene and Chico-Tejon strata occur.

In the last assertion White was undoubtedly close to the truth, especially if we read for "Chico-Tejon" the term "Oligocene," which, with our present knowledge, may be regarded as positively correct. The similarities pointed out by White can now in part be explained as of closely allied species of the Oligocene and Miocene, while others illustrate the fact that from the miscellaneous concretions both Townsend and Dana collected some Oligocene species as well as a majority of Miocene forms.

The fact that Astoria was a classical locality for Tertiary fossils on the Pacific coast led me, while engaged in studies for the United States Geological Survey, to visit the locality in August, 1890. The following is a summary of the observations made at that time.[e] Three distinct formations along the Columbia have been referred to the Tertiary period.

The first, named by Condon[f] the Astoria shales, consists of clayey or sandy shales of various colors and various degrees of consolidation. On weathering, they become soft and clayey, usually of a yellowish color, and so appear along the banks at Astoria. At the time of Dana's visit and until a few years ago numerous Oligocene fossil remains were obtained at the water's edge by collectors in the town of Astoria. These came from a single very thin stratum below the Miocene beds, which from the presence in it of the nautiloid *Aturia angustata* Conrad

[a] Pacific R. R. Repts., vol. 6, pt. 2. 1857, p. 25.
[b] Bull. U. S. Geol. Survey, No. 51. 1889, pp. 31 et seq.
[c] Conrad's appendix to Dana's report.
[d] Am. Jour. Sci., 2d ser., vol. 5, 1848. p. 432 (Conrad's descriptions of Townsend's fossils).
[e] See also Bull. U. S. Geol. Survey, No. 84. 1892, pp. 223–226.
[f] Condon, Thomas, Am. Naturalist, vol. 14, 1880, p. 457.

was named the *Aturia* bed by the writer in 1892. The age of the shales immediately above it, which are largely nonfossiliferous, is somewhat uncertain. That they are in part Oligocene and in part Miocene is probable, but the exact limits of each remain to be determined.

Owing to the fact that both the concretions in the *Aturia* bed and those from the Miocene shales above, released from the matrix by weathering, were mingled on the narrow beach and were more or less calcareous, and to the scarcity of limestone (already noted by Dana) in the region, it has happened that these concretions have been carefully collected by the settlers and burned for lime. The beach has been built over and entirely covered by dwellings and storehouses built on piles on account of the high and precipitous character of the river bank at Astoria. The supply of fossils from either source has thus virtually been cut off. Specimens inferior in preservation from the superincumbent Miocene beds may still be seen in the banks near Tongue Point, in the bluffs behind the schoolhouse, and at other localities about Astoria; yet the grading, wharfage, buildings, etc., have concealed nearly all the original exposures.

Fortunately, before this state of affairs had reached its present completeness, the late Dr. Thomas Condon had visited Astoria and made collections which are now preserved at the State University at Eugene, Oreg. In these collections the specimens from the Oligocene and Miocene horizons are carefully discriminated, and I had the privilege of examining them under the guidance of the venerable professor himself. This evidence explains the discrepancy which was so long a subject of controversy.

The second formation along the Columbia consists of a series of Miocene sandstones, which is represented on both banks of the river, but best developed on the north or right bank, while the shales above described are most prominent on the left or south bank. The sandstones are granular, brittle, or friable, in some places very compact and hard, usually of a brownish color.

The impression I gathered after my inspection of the exposures in August, 1890, though without the opportunity of examining any large district with care, was that the shales and sandstones form parts of a single series varying in the character of its beds or layers according to fluctuations in the sedimentation; the shales being more argillaceous, the sandstones more arenaceous, neither possessing an exclusive character; the fossils appearing to be the same species throughout the sandstones and the greater part of the shales; the lower portion of the shales being, however, almost destitute of fossil remains. The tendency seemed to be for the fossils to form concretions round them in the shales and to be represented chiefly by casts in the sandstones. The name, Astoria group, was adopted for the series in 1892.[a]

As the locality is classic, a few descriptive notes may be of use to future explorers of the geology.

No proper Eocene is exposed at Astoria, but the rocks may occur below the water level. The *Aturia* bed, of Oligocene age, in which *Aturia angustata, Miopleiona indurata, Marcia oregonensis, Trophosycon oregonensis,* and *Scapharca devincta* appear to be characteristic species, as already explained, is no longer accessible,

---

[a] Bull. U. S. Geol. Survey, No. 84, 1892, p. 225.

its outcrop having been close to the water's edge under the most elevated part of the high bluffs behind the town, which is strung along on a narrow talus or built out on piles over the river, there being hardly any level land between the bluffs and the water.

At Smiths Point, west of the town, the shales are very low, the vertical face not exceeding 15 feet. They dip about 16° in a southeasterly direction and are composed of thin layers of chiefly bluish-gray shale with numerous fractures lined with peroxide of iron which develop more numerously as the surface dries, while the iron causes the face to weather into a brownish color. Most of the layers contain a little sand, but some do not show any. The fluctuations seem to succeed each other with a certain regularity.

Here and there a little gravel is mixed in one of the layers, and in these gravelly layers are also small fragments of bivalve shells, the most perfect and numerous being valves of *Pecten (Pseudamusium) peckhami* Gabb, *Acila conradi* Meek, and fragments of a species of *Terebratalia*.

At some places in the upper layers of the shale the clayey parts form along a bedding plane lines of concretions, partly fossiliferous and containing most commonly specimens of *Macoma calcarea* in a bad state of preservation.

Above the shales at this point is a bed 8 to 20 feet in thickness of a yellowish clayey sand with irregular, mostly rounded fragments of a harder sandstone, maculated with peroxide of iron, with a few traces of marine fossils, and more or less gravel not regularly bedded and penetrating into fissures in the shaly rock below, in the form of dikes. The beach in this vicinity is composed of the pebbles, nodules, and small bowlders of the hard sandstone washed out of this layer mixed with a few fragments of volcanic tufa.

Near Tongue Point, at the other end of the town, 2 miles away, the same beds were recognized, but the gravelly layer seemed thicker and the shale much broken up. The same beds appear to compose the bluffs between Tongue and Smiths points, though owing to the way the town is built they are difficult of access. These bluffs at their highest point, near the high-school building, rise perhaps 150 feet. Here a fine section shows 30 to 40 feet of the shales exposed at an angle of 40° to 60°, dipping about 26° SE., though the dip is not invariable. The yellowish sandstone gravel overlies the shales to an equal thickness and descends into them in dikes here and there. The upper margin of the shales is in places indistinguishable, the clayey and sandy layers merging into each other and being similar in color.

It is notable that in the upper part of the shales some of the shells seem to have been fossilized in sandstone, washed out, and reembedded in the clays. Between the valves or on one side of a single valve of a bivalve shell, there will be a remnant of soft coarse sandstone, while the fossil is otherwise embedded in a dark waxy clay shale.

These sandstones and shales have much similarity to Miocene deposits occurring in various localities along the coast from California to Alaska and part of the fossils are of identical species.

The *Aturia* bed and the superincumbent Astoria group occur on the north bank of the Columbia in a good many places, apparently more elevated than on the

Oregon side. Condon obtained the *Aturia* also from Tillamook, and Oligocene beds exist near Port Blakely, on Puget Sound opposite Seattle.

The third member of the group regarded as Tertiary by Dana consists of basaltic rocks, either massive or broken into the form of tufa. Tongue Point itself is a basaltic mass, and according to Condon there is on the ridge behind the town an extensive layer of Pleistocene basalt, fragments of which appear on the beaches. At the time of my visit, a fire on the south side of the street leading from the Union Pacific dock, one block to the west, had destroyed some buildings and part of the planking of the roadway, exposing a fine solid basaltic rock 10 or 12 feet square and 15 feet high. The original beach at its base was abundantly strewn with fragments of the same material.

It is stated in the American Naturalist, from Condon's manuscript notes, that the backbone of the Coast Range in Oregon west of Eugene consists of argillaceous Miocene shale which contains fish remains and invertebrate fossils. These Condon identified with the shales of the Astoria group outcropping at the Columbia River. Above these lie extensive Miocene sandstones with beds rich in fossils, probably corresponding with the sandstones of the Astoria group.

The fauna of the Miocene sandstones of the Willamette Valley does not in all cases agree with the fauna of the beds at Astoria, but whether the distinction indicates a difference of horizon or only of distribution, more exhaustive study is requisite to determine.

From a preliminary examination of Miocene beds examined by Ralph Arnold under my instructions at Clallam Bay, Wash., it would seem that the species agree more generally with those of Astoria; but the difficulty of correlating in the present state of our knowledge is indicated by the fact that no trace of the Sooke Miocene fauna, profusely developed on the Vancouver Island shore of Juan de Fuca Strait, has yet been found after careful search on the opposite coast of Washington.

Less than one-third of the fauna of the Coos Bay Miocene is identical with the Astoria known Miocene fauna, and so far as our present very imperfect knowledge enables us to characterize these faunas, that of Astoria is more intimately connected with the Miocene forms which occur in beds to the north of Astoria, and the perhaps somewhat younger Empire formation of Coos Bay is more closely linked to the Miocene faunas known to exist farther south.

At present it is unsafe to regard the Astoria and Coos Bay faunas as strictly contemporaneous. They are doubtless both Miocene, and the Coos Bay fauna shows interesting parallels with the Chesapeake Miocene of Maryland, a certain number of representative and closely related species occurring in both. But to exactly what level in the Miocene column either of the Pacific coast horizons should be assigned it is yet too early to determine.

The following list of fossils collected at Astoria contains species referable both to the *Aturia* bed and to the Miocene above it. Before these can be finally disentangled from one another to form two distinct and accurate lists, the Oligocene and Miocene faunas of the region must be much more fully worked out than has hitherto been done. The species that have been recognized in other Oligocene horizons are indicated, and the general locality is stated in the list; but with regard to most of them we do not yet know whether they are exclusively Oligocene or not.   Unfortunately the beds at Coos Bay which may be referred with much probability to the Oligocene, and might have enabled us to solve the problem had they contained a fully representative fauna, are almost destitute of fossils.

Species collected at Astoria.

[The species followed by an O are probably Oligocene; if found elsewhere in Oligocene horizons the locality is added.]

Aturia angustata Conrad. O. Wash.	Scapharca microdonta Conrad.
Cylichnella petrosa Conrad.	Pecten propatulus Conrad.
Haminea petrosa Conrad.	Pecten peckhami Gabb.
Meiopleiona indurata Conrad. O. Wash.	Modiolus directus Dall.
Fusinus corpulentus Conrad. O.? Wash.	Venericardia subtenta Conrad.
Fusinus geniculus Conrad.	Diplodonta parilis Conrad.
Fusinus medialis Conrad.	Phacoides acutilineatus Conrad.
Fusinus nodiferus Conrad.	Thyasira bisecta Conrad.
Fusinus sp.	Macrocallista? vespertina Conrad.
Eudolium petrosum Conrad. O. Wash.	Venus ensifera Dall.
Ficus modestus Conrad.	Marcia oregonensis Conrad. O. Coos Bay.
Trophosycon oregonensis Conrad. O.?	Tellina oregonensis Conrad.
Trichotropis oregonensis Conrad.	Tellina emacerata Conrad.
Turritella oregonensis Conrad.	Moerella obruta Conrad.
Crepidula prærupta Conrad.	Moerella nuculana Dall.
Crepidula rostralis Conrad.	Angulus albaria Conrad.
Natica oregonensis Conrad.	Macoma arctata Conrad.
Natica consors Dall.	Macoma sp.
Polinices (Neverita) inezana Conrad. O. Cal.	Solen curtus Conrad.
Polinices (Euspira) galianoi Dall. O. Wash.	Spisula albaria Conrad.
Ampullinopsis mississippiensis Conrad. O. Wash.	Panopea estrellana Conrad.
Sinum scopulosum Conrad.	Xylotrya sp.
Solemya ventricosa Conrad.	Thracia trapezoidea Conrad.
Nucula townsendi Dall.	Dentalium conradi Dall.
Nucula (Acila) conradi Meek. O. Coos Bay.	Dentalium petricola Dall.
Leda penita Conrad.	Hemithyris astoriana Dall.
Yoldia oregona Shumard.	Conoclypeus? sp.
Yoldia impressa Conrad.	Toxopneustes? sp.
Malletia abrupta Conrad.	Galerites? oregonensis Dana.
Limopsis nitens Conrad.	Ophiurites sp.
Glycymeris (conradi Dall?).	Stephanotrochus sp.
Scapharca devincta Conrad. O.	

The total is 63 species, of which 33 are known as yet only from Astoria, 22 are common to the fauna of Coos Bay, 13 are also found in the Miocene of Washington, and 9 appear in California.

Nine of the species are known to be Oligocene, and most of these are thought to be exclusively Oligocene, leaving about 54 Miocene species, exclusive of Foraminifera, known from the Astoria beds.   Of these, not to exceed 7, and perhaps only 5, are known in the recent state, just about the same proportion as are found both recent and in the Empire formation; or, if we can venture in so small an assembly to make comparisons, about one in eleven of the Astoria species is found living at present, and from the Coos Bay fauna about one in nine.

THE TERTIARY OF COOS BAY.

The first reference to the marine Tertiary of Coos Bay which I have found is contained in B. F. Shumard's paper in the Transactions of the Academy of Science of St. Louis[a] where he describes a number of species from the Tertiary of Oregon, from Port Orford, Coos Bay, the Willamette Valley, and Columbia River above Astoria. These fossils, according to the title of Shumard's paper, were collected by Dr. John Evans, United States geologist, under instructions from the Interior Department.[b] Shumard confines himself entirely to the description of species and the only geologic details are given in connection with the locality of the several species, two of which—*Pecten coosensis* and *Venus (Chione) securis*—are stated to have come from "gray, fine-grained sandstone of the Miocene age at the mouth of Coos Bay."

I have searched the bibliographies for any reference to a published report by Evans on his work on the Pacific coast, but found none, and the inference is that his report was transmitted to the Interior Department at Washington and never published. The accident of his communicating some of the species he collected to Shumard has apparently led to the sole printed record of the existence of such an exploration.

The economic interest of the coal deposits near Coos Bay led to their investigation by J. S. Diller for the United States Geological Survey, and in 1897, at his request, I visited the locality and made a careful study of the section exposed on the south shore of the bay between Cape Gregory and the village known as Empire. Diller's results are published in the Nineteenth Annual Report of the Survey,[c] and in the Geological Atlas of the United States.[d]

The economic interest centering in the coal-bearing rocks, the minor details of the geology of the post-Eocene beds are but briefly referred to, as follows:[e]

Empire formation.—The Empire formation [see Pl. I] is composed chiefly of shales and sandstones, often containing an abundance of Miocene fossils. This is especially the case along Coos Bay toward Empire from the mouth of South Slough. Coos Head is a massive sandstone, and along South Slough the shales are light colored, closely resembling some of those associated with the coal, and yet readily distinguished from them under the microscope by the curious minute fossils which they contain.[f] The shales and thin sandstones along the coast south of Seven Devils are usually dark colored and much disturbed.

In the text of the Coos Bay folio Diller gives a more extended description of the Tertiary outcropping on the south shore of the bay, in which he divides the Eocene rocks (in their totality known as the Arago formation) into two subordinate formations, to which the names of Coaledo and "Pulaski" are applied. The lower or "Pulaski" beds comprise all the Eocene rocks of the Coos Bay quadrangle not included in the coal-bearing series. They contain few fossils except Foraminifera and remains of calcareous algæ and are laid down on the upturned edges of the Cretaceous Myrtle formation.

[a] Vol. 1, No. 2, 1858, pp. 120–123.
[b] See Appendix XI, p. 186.
[c] Pt. 3, 1899, pp. 309–376.
[d] Coos Bay folio, No. 73, U. S. Geol. Survey, 1901.
[e] Nineteenth Ann. Rept., pt. 3, 1899, p. 319.
[f] These fossils are Foraminifera, referred to later in this paper.—W. H. D.

The upper or Coaledo formation includes the coal-bearing rocks and follows conformably the soft yellowish sandstones of the "Pulaski" beds. Numerous changes of level occurred, so that the marine sandstones with a prolific fauna of marine invertebrates, which may be profitably studied near Cape Gregory, were at certain localities elevated above the sea and occupied by fresh-water swamps and forests, of which the presence is demonstrated by such fresh-water fossils as *Cyrena* and *Goniobasis*, and by the occurrence of important deposits of Tertiary coal.

With the close of the Arago epoch the rocks, originally horizontal, were elevated, compressed laterally into folds, and more or less broken and faulted. The upper portion of the formation, represented by about 2,200 feet of foraminiferal shales and 800 feet of sparsely fossiliferous rocks at Tunnel Point, being the youngest portion of the formation and occurring only, according to Diller, in the middle portion of the South Slough syncline, probably represents the Oligocene beds, which at other points on the coast are better characterized by a special invertebrate fauna, such as that at Restoration Point, Puget Sound, or that in the *Aturia* bed of the Astoria section. At all events, the strictly Eocene fauna of the beds near Cape Gregory, with *Venericardia planicosta*, *Ficopsis*, and other characteristic Eocene types, does not enter into the beds at Tunnel Point.

After the uplifts which closed the Arago epoch a general process of erosion was initiated, which, in the submerged portion of the Coos Bay basin and in a region on the outer seacoast south of Fivemile Creek, deposited a series of marine sandstones and shales containing a Miocene fauna, which has been named by Diller the Empire formation. These strata on the opposite sides of the shallow South Slough at its mouth incline gently toward each other as if forming a syncline (Pl. I.) According to Diller's observations—

These strata lie in the South Slough basin, and it is probable that the South Slough syncline continued as an axis of down-folding after the close of the Arago epoch and its terminating upheaval. A white shale lies in the middle of the syncline and rests upon the sandstones and darker shales which form the lower portion of the Empire formation. This white shale appears to be closely related in its general appearance and composition to that which occurs at Mist, on the Nehalem River, in Oregon, and to the Monterey shale of California. * * * The syncline in which these beds are comprised evidently rises southward. Similar beds occur on the coast 3 miles south of Bandon. * * * The Empire formation rests unconformably on the Arago, which had been previously folded and eroded. This unconformity may be seen on the shore a short distance west of Coos Head.[a]

After this clear account of the general features of the Empire formation it does not seem necessary to repeat from my own notebooks what would be merely confirmatory of Diller's observations. Some additional details as to the local outcrops, however, may not be useless, as well as a few geographic notes.

Coos Bay is the estuary of a number of streams of which Coos River is the most important, and, like all the estuary harbors of the coast, is obstructed by a bar at its mouth, through which a precarious channel is maintained by the aid of jetties. On the north side the harbor is formed by a broad sand spit more or less modified by dunes. Once inside the bar the harbor is safe and commodious. The chief settlement is Marshfield, at the head of navigation, but considerably

a Coos Bay folio, p. 3.

nearer the entrance is a village founded about the middle of the last century, with the ambitious title of Empire. This is situated on the southeastern side of the bay about 4 miles above a shallow inlet called South Slough and 6½ miles from Cape Gregory, a rocky point which is outside the narrow entrance and upon which a light-house is maintained. South Slough is about 10 feet in depth and is crossed a mile above its entrance by a ferry.

On this shore fronts a series of low bluffs above a muddy beach more or less variegated with flat rocky stretches. A mile and a half southwest of Empire the Miocene outcrops appear, at first capped by the Coos conglomerate and covered more or less deeply with alluvium. The bluffs become gradually higher until interrupted by South Slough, and are continued on the other side of the slough, culminating in Coos Head, a little west of which is an unconformity, partly marked by alluvial talus and indicated by a narrow ravine called Goldwashers Gully, where formerly the black sands of the beach were washed by the aid of a rill which trickled down the acclivity. This gully marks the end of the Miocene sandstones. Beyond it the bluff continues high, with rocky buttresses here and there projecting into the water and dividing the sandy beach into sections. Between the gully and one of these buttresses called Tunnel Point is a series of highly tilted, more or less contorted and faulted beds, dipping eastward 60° to 80°, largely fine-grained silts consolidated into an arenaceous shale and almost destitute of fossils. Except Foraminifera, which are sparsely disseminated through the shale, the only fossils observed in this stretch of beds were *Acila conradi* Meek, *Marcia oregonensis* Conrad, and *Saxidomus* aff. *giganteus* Deshayes. The numerous Miocene fossils so abundant in the rocks to the east of South Slough are here conspicuously absent.

At the base of the Miocene immediately east of Goldwashers Gully the Miocene rocks were observed to contain the following species, mostly inclosed in tough concretionary shales:

Miocene fossils found east of Goldwashers Gully. Coos Bay. Oregon.

Miopleiona oregonensis Dall.	Macoma calcarea Conrad.
Natica galianoi Dall.	Solen conradi Dall.
Nucula sp. (smooth).	Mactra albaria Conrad.
Pecten coosensis Shumard.	Saxicava aff. arctica Linné.
Macoma nasuta Conrad.	

The contrast in fossiliferous contents, as well as the conspicuous unconformity, indicates that the beds to the west belong to an earlier series, which, as the Eocene types are wholly absent, can only be of Oligocene age.

This series of beds was called by me the Tunnel Point beds[a] and was believed to represent in the Coos Bay section the unfossiliferous shales intervening at Astoria between the *Aturia* bed and the distinctively Miocene sandstones above.

Beyond Tunnel Point similar beds alternating with coarser sandy layers and with very irregular dips in the same general direction, running from 40° to 70°, may be followed to a small flat, called, after the proprietor, Millers Flat and watered by Miner Creek. This flat interrupts the bluff abruptly and doubtless indicates a wide fault. It is about an eighth of a mile in width and is occupied by a small

---

[a] Eighteenth Ann. Rept. U. S. Geol. Survey, pt. 2, 1898, p. 340.

ranch. The rocks abutting on the flat at the east contain Eocene fossils which gradually become sparser and fail entirely as we approach Tunnel Point, the dip on the average becoming constantly more steep, but no positive unconformity is visible, though a landslide in at least one place obscures the strata. On the western side of the flat there is first a sharply compressed anticlinal mass of shale without fossils, beyond which the Eocene sandstones vary in attitude from vertical to an easterly dip of 66°, the beach being interrupted by Yokam Point. Thence Eocene rocks of Diller's Coaledo formation extend to the light-house at Cape Gregory. These rocks maintain the high dip, but are interspersed with bodies of shale that are in many places greatly contorted. The fossils in this part of the exposure are uniform and comprise *Venericardia planicosta*, first collected here by Condon, and such types as *Cylichnella*, *Fusinus*, *Ficopsis penita* Conrad, *Dentalium*, *Acila truncata* Gabb, and species of *Paradione*. It is a distinctively Eocene fauna and may be compared to the "Lower Claibornian" of Alabama in its characteristics.

To return to the Empire formation, with the fauna of which this memoir is chiefly concerned, a few words on the condition and distribution of the fossils are in order.

Many of the fossils are surrounded with a zone of rock tougher and more resistant than the mass of the sandstone, owing perhaps to a partial diffusion of the lime into the adjacent matrix. This tough material renders it exceedingly difficult to extract the fossils in a satisfactory condition, as the substance of the fossil yields before the matrix and splits, leaving the collector without either a presentable fossil or a recognizable cast. Attempts in the laboratory to soften this shale by chemical means have not been successful, but the slow action of the weather on the exposed surface of the outcrops frequently performs the work in a manner much more satisfactory than any artificial method yet devised.

It happened that among the inhabitants of Empire was a retired merchant of German extraction and advanced age who, without any scientific training, books, or knowledge of paleontology, except such as he could extract from an old edition of Webster's Dictionary, seeking some occupation for his hours of leisure, became interested in the fossils he found on the beach during his strolls. He finally formed the habit of patrolling the beach between Empire and South Slough at regular intervals and especially after storms which might dislodge specimens from the bluff. This practice he had continued, according to his own account, for about fifteen years. During this time he had accumulated, in a disused warehouse, heaps of fossils. Of the commoner species, such as *Pecten coosensis* and *Chione securis*, he had literally gathered bushels, and amused himself when unable to go out by trying to clear them from the remaining adherent matrix. It naturally followed that it was possible to select from this accumulation a representative series of the Miocene fossils of this locality such as would have cost the ordinary geologist years of labor to bring together. I prevailed upon this person, Mr. B. H. Camman, to part with such a series, which was purchased by the Survey and rendered possible the preparation of this paper, which otherwise hardly could have been written.

One feature of the Camman collection was unfortunate; that is, the exact locality or horizon in the stretch of 3 or 4 miles of Miocene outcrops was not in any case determined, and I therefore endeavored to make up for this as far as possible by searching the rocks myself for indications of recognizable fossils, even when my efforts to extract them in presentable condition met with little success. The result of this was to show that in the whole series of outcrops the fauna appeared to be practically uniform, though its abundance varied greatly. The upper layers of the rock immediately under the Coos conglomerate and therefore nearly at the top of the Miocene series were very prolific. At a point on the south shore of Coos Bay due east (magnetic) from the extremity of North Spit (Pl. I) another favorable locality was found, and it is probable that from these two spots the majority of Mr. Camman's fossils were derived.

The second locality, just mentioned, is station 4073 of Diller's notes, and the dip of the beds is westward at 8° or 10°. This locality is somewhat protected from the direct wear of the sea in heavy storms by a small rocky prominence just south of it and by the submerged jetty which has been built to the north of it, extending to the southwest (magnetic) toward the main channel. Careful search was made here, and the following list enumerates the species positively identified:

Species noted at station 4073, Coos Bay, Oregon, in the upper Miocene sandstones.

Scaphander oregonensis Dall.
Olivella pedroana Conrad.
Chrysodomus imperialis Dall.
Liomesus sulculatus Dall.
Thais sp. (cf. mendica).
Thais lamellosa Gmelin?
Boreotrophon (like multicostatus Esch.).
Priene pacifica Dall.
Trochita inornata Gabb.
Polinices galianoi Dall.
Turcica gabbi Dall.
Acila conradi Meek.
Nucula sp. (smooth).
Leda sp. (like coelata).
Yoldia strigata Dall.

Yoldia oregona Shumard.
Pecten coosensis Shumard.
Modiolus directus Dall.
Diplodonta parilis Conrad.
Cardium coosense Dall.
Cardium corbis Martyn.
Chione securis Shumard.
Tellina obruta Conrad.
Macoma calcarea Gmelin.
Macoma nasuta Conrad.
Macoma astori Dall.
Solen conradi Dall.
Hemimactra albaria Conrad.
Hemimactra precursor Dall.

Before proceeding to enumerate the entire Miocene fauna recognized from the Empire formation I may add that vertebræ and other bones of fish were not uncommon, usually in concretions, but hardly affording a basis for recognizing the species. Dana mentions that at Astoria four species of fish were identified from similar material. No shark's teeth were obtained, this lack affording a marked contrast to the multitude of such teeth found in some of the Atlantic Miocene horizons.

Besides the cranium of the fossil sea lion *Pontolis magnus* True, Mr. Camman had accumulated a large number of fragments of cetacean bones of large size, chiefly vertebræ and fragments of ribs, that may have belonged to a fossil *Megaptera*, the skull of which was some years ago extracted from similar Miocene beds on the coast of California and which it is believed was sold to a European museum by the finder. However this may be, inasmuch as Mr. Camman's material contained nothing by which the species or even the genus might be positively recognized, no attempt was made to procure specimens from this part of his collection.

The rocks had also afforded him a number of small logs and fragments of fossilized wood, many of which were riddled by the borings of *Xylotrya* or other shipworms. Some of these pieces of wood retained the grain very perfectly, and Mr. Camman believed he could recognize the wood of *Sequoia* and *Abies* among them.

The following list includes the known invertebrate fauna of the Empire formation to date:

Fauna of the Empire formation at Coos Bay, Oregon. including the whole Miocene series there.

Scaphander conradi Dall.
Scaphander oregonensis Dall.
Turris coosensis Dall.
Turris cammani Dall.
Turris coli Dall.
Antiplanes perversa Gabb.   Also Pleistocene and recent.
Antiplanes impecunia Dall.
Bathytoma carpenteriana Gabb.
Bathytoma gabbiana Dall.
Cancellaria oregonensis Dall.
Olivella pedroana Conrad.   Also Pleistocene and recent.
Miopleiona oregonensis Dall.   Also Pliocene?
Fusinus (Buccinofusus) coosensis Dall.
Chrysodomus imperialis Dall.   Cal.
Chrysodomus bairdii Dall.   Cal.
Liomesus sulculatus Dall.
Purpura perponderosa Dall.
Arctoscala condoni Dall.
Gyrineum mediocre Dall.   Wash.
Gyrineum (mediocre var.?) corbiculatum Dall.
Fusitriton cammani Dall.
Fusitriton coosensis Dall
Prione pacifica Dall.   Cal.
Cymatium (Linatella) pacificum Dall.
Phalium (Bezoardica) turricula Dall.
Phalium (Bezoardica) æquisulcatum Dall.
Eudolium oregonense Dall.
Calyptræa (Trochita) inornata Gabb.   Cal.
Crepidula prærupta Conrad.   Cal.
Crepidula princeps Conrad.   Cal.
Natica oregonensis Conrad.
Cryptonatica consors Dall.
Polinices inezana Conrad.   Cal.
Polinices galianoi Dall.   Wash.
Amauropsis oregonensis Dall.
Sinum scopulosum Conrad.   Cal.
Astræa (Pachypoma) precursor Dall.
Tegula (Chlorostoma) stantoni Dall.   Cal.
Calliostoma cammani Dall.
Turcica gabbi Dall.
Margarites condoni Dall.
Nucula (Acila) conradi Meek.
Leda acuta Conrad.   Cal.
Leda whitmani Dall.
Yoldia strigata Dall.

Yoldia impressa Conrad.
Glycymeris grewingki Dall.
Glycymeris conradi Dall.
Glycymeris gabbi Dall.
Scapharca trilineata Conrad.   Cal.
Ostrea titan Conrad.   Cal.
Pecten coosensis Shumard.
Mytilus ficus Dall.
Modiolus directus Dall.
Modiolus inflatus Dall.
Venericardia (var.?) quadrata Dall.   Wash.
Phacoides acutilineatus Conrad.   Cal.
Diplodonta (Felaniella) parilis Conrad.   Wash.
Cardium coosense Dall.   Cal.
Cardium decoratum Grewingk.   Also Pleistocene, Alaska.
Cardium corbis Martyn.   Cal. Recent.
Chione securis Shumard.   Wash.
Chione staleyi Gabb.   Cal.
Chione bisculpta Dall.
Venus parapodema Dall.   Alaska.
Marcia oregonensis Conrad.   Also Oligocene.
Tellina aragonia Dall.
Macoma calcarea Gmelin.   Also Pleistocene and recent.
Macoma nasuta Conrad.   Also recent.
Macoma astori Dall.
Solen (var.?) conradi Dall.   Wash.
Hemimactra albaria Conrad.
Hemimactra precursor Dall.   Cal.
Mulinia oregonensis Dall.
Schizothærus pajaroanus Conrad.   Cal.
Mya truncata Linné.   Also recent.
Cryptomya oregonensis Dall.
Panomya (var.?) chrysis Dall.   Cal.
Pholadidea penita Conrad.   Also recent.
Xylotrya sp.
Thracia trapezoidea Conrad.
Dentalium conradi Dall.   Wash.
Dentalium petricola Dall.   Wash.
Discinisca oregonensis Dall.
Balanus tintinnabulum var. coosensis Dall.
Serpula? octoforis Dall.
Toxopneustes? sp.
Scutella oregonensis Clark.
Ophiurites sp.
Asterites sp.

This amounts to a total of 90 species, of which 41 are known at present only from Coos Bay, 22 are common to Astoria, and 10 to Washington, chiefly at Clallam Bay; 19 are reported from California, and 10 are known to exist in the recent state.

COOS CONGLOMERATE.

Fossil Point is a narrow, low, acute point about one-fifth mile long, extending in a northwest direction into the harbor (Pl. I). It is composed basally of Miocene sandstones with a southwesterly dip of about 10°; their upper surface is considerably waterworn. Upon this surface lies an unconformable layer of conglomerate, indistinctly bedded, and dipping with the Miocene sandstone below about 10° to the south and west. The conglomerate is only a few feet thick, and its upper surface has been brought to a level nearly uniform with that of the upper edges of the sandstones to the south and west, so that it gradually diminishes in thickness in that direction until it disappears entirely. At the end of the point, northward and eastward, it ceases abruptly, all except this patch, so far as now appears, having been removed by erosion. It contains many large, irregular pebbles derived from the underlying sandstone and shale; numerous Miocene fossils washed out of the sandstone and recemented; numerous small cherty pebbles; much quartzose sand filling the interstices; and a certain number of fossil shells which seem to have been of contemporaneous origin with the conglomerate.

The sand and fossils, together with the pebbles, are very solidly cemented together, and it is difficult to extract the fossils, which almost always splinter before the matrix does. The later fossils, on a careful inspection, may readily be distinguished from those derived from the preceding strata on account of the difference in the constitution and color of the matrix which most of them retain, the brown fine-grained sandstone or tough gray shale having no resemblance to the vitreous cemented sand which forms the genuine matrix of the conglomerate. The later fossils, as a rule, are also lighter colored and more chalky. They form, obviously, a shore deposit, with littoral shells like *Littorina* and *Thais*, *Bittium* and *Olivella*, some of which are extinct species. The small number of species noted renders the numerical method of estimating the probable age of this deposit unreliable, so I can only suggest that it may belong to the early Pleistocene or late Pliocene. With more information as to the Tertiary geology of the coast we may be able to find the same horizon repeated elsewhere and to determine positively its place in the column.

This conglomerate, of which a patch less than an acre in extent is all which remains after the erosion to which it has been subjected in this locality, was named by me the Coos conglomerate,[a] but to the patch exposed on the shore, forming a low bluff or bench and conspicuous by the white weathering of its contained fossils, the residents of the vicinity have given the name of Fossil Rock. According to Diller, after its deposition there was an upward movement of the land which raised it at least 200 feet above its present level, thus exposing it to energetic erosion. It has since been covered by more than 20 feet of sand and gravel, which at the exposure on the beach has been removed by the weather, leaving the upper surface of the conglomerate bare. At no point does it appear to be more than 30 feet in thickness,

---

a Eighteenth Ann. Rept. U. S. Geol. Survey, pt. 2, 1898, p. 336.

and the most accessible exposure, at the edge of the beach at the point, shows only 4 or 5 feet.

The species represented in the conglomerate and obtained by me are named below. They have been divided into adventitious species derived from the preexisting beds, and endemic species, or those which appear to have belonged to the living fauna at the time the conglomerate was in the process of deposition. The following Miocene species are regarded as adventitious:

Miocene fossils from Coos conglomerate of Fossil Rock, Coos Bay, Oregon.

Bathytoma gabbiana Dall.
Crepidula princeps Conrad.
Natica consors Dall.
Acila conradi Meek.

Leda whitmani Dall.
Venus parapodema Dall.
Scutella oregonensis Clark.

The following list includes the species believed to be normally present in the rock:

Pleistocene fossils from Coos conglomerate of Fossil Rock, Coos Bay, Oregon.

Turris (Antiplanes) perversa Gabb.
Olivella pedroana Conrad.
Thais lamellosa Gmelin.
Thais precursor Dall.
Fusitriton oregonensis Redfield.
Bittium (Stylidium) eschrichtii Middendorff.

Littorina petricola Dall.
Astræa inæqualis Martyn.
Cardium corbis Martyn.
Macoma calcarea Gmelin.
Macoma nasuta Conrad.
Pholadidea penita Conrad.

Of the above species, two, the *Littorina* and *Thais precursor*, are unknown in the recent state; the other 10 form part of the existing fauna.

DESCRIPTION OF THE INVERTEBRATE FAUNA OF THE ASTORIA GROUP AND EMPIRE FORMATION OF OREGON.

Subkingdom MOLLUSCA.

Class CEPHALOPODA.

Subclass TETRABRANCHIATA.

Order NAUTILOIDEA.

Suborder ORTHOCHOANITES.

Family CLYDONAUTILIDÆ.

Genus ATURIA Bronn.

ATURIA ANGUSTATA Conrad.

Nautilus angustatus Conrad, Geol. U. S. Expl. Exp., p. 728, pl. 20, figs. 5, 6, 1849.
Aturia ziczac Conrad, Am. Jour. Conch., I, p. 150, 1865; not of Sowerby.
Pelagus vanuxemi Conrad, Am. Jour. Conch., I, p. 150, 1865, in syn.; not of Conrad, 1848.
Aturia ziczac Gabb, Pal. California, II, p. 69, 1868; not of Sowerby.

Oligocene concretions from Astoria, Oreg., J. D. Dana; U. S. Nat. Mus. 3534, 3610 (Conrad's types); 3534, 3569, 3572 (cotypes). Also from the Oligocene of the right bank of the Columbia 30 miles above Astoria, and from Tillamook; and the Oligocene of Port Blakely, Wash., opposite Seattle on Puget Sound, Ralph Arnold.

This is a typical *Aturia* with funnel-shaped dorsal siphuncle and single loops laterally, the dorsal portion of the septum not concave. It should be compared with the upper Eocene *A. mathewsoni* Gabb, from Martinez, Cal., which from the figures seems very similar.

It may be mentioned here that the late Prof. Thomas Condon, at the State University at Eugene, Oreg., informed me that he had collected a fine specimen of true *Nautilus* from the Pliocene rocks of the coast due west from Eugene, the specimen being in his collection at the University.

Class GASTEROPODA.

Subclass ANISOPLEURA.

Superorder EUTHYNEURA.

Order OPISTHOBRANCHIATA.

Suborder TECTIBRANCHIATA.

Family SCAPHANDRIDÆ.

Genus SCAPHANDER Montfort.

Scaphander Montfort, Conch. Syst., II, p. 334, 1810; type *Bulla lignaria* Linné.

Two well-marked species of this genus are found in the fauna of the Empire formation.

SCAPHANDER CONRADI Dall, n. sp.

Pl. VI, fig. 3.

Shell of moderate size, rather broadly pyriform, the posterior end somewhat rapidly attenuated; apex imperforate, outer lip produced a little behind it and merging in the apical callus as usual in the genus; aperture narrow behind, wide in front, where it is evenly rounded, the pillar widely arcuate and moderately callous; exterior closely, finely, and sharply sulcate, the alternate sulci usually stronger and having a more or less punctate aspect; the sculpture faintly affects the outer surface of the internal cast, which also has a faint indication of a constriction about the posterior fourth of the shell. Altitude of shell, 19 mm.; maximum diameter, 12.5 mm.

Coos Bay Miocene, Empire formation, collected by W. H. Dall. U. S. Nat. Mus. 154137.

The types comprise two specimens, an internal cast which is figured in Pl. VI, and a less perfect specimen which, however, retains patches of the external surface of the shell, showing its sculpture.

From the following species this is easily distinguished by its shorter and more broadly pyriform profile, which also differentiates it from any of the known species.

The *Bulla jugularis* Conrad, from the lower Miocene beds of Kern River, near Ocoya Creek, has been referred by Anderson to *Scaphander*, but the constriction of the posterior part of the whorls is paralleled in several species of *Atys* and it seems as if the species might find a place more appropriately in the latter genus.

SCAPHANDER OREGONENSIS Dall, n. sp.

Pl. V, fig. 7.

Shell small, slightly attenuated behind, more swollen in front, the outer lip not thickened, the body without perceptible callus, the pillar arcuate; the outer surface spirally finely sulcate, the interspaces wider than the sulci; the interior polished, with a faint indication of the external sulci and of an obsolete constriction around the posterior third of the shell. Longitude 13.0 mm.; maximum latitude, 7.2 mm.

Coos Bay Miocene, Empire formation; U. S. Nat. Mus. 154136.

The type is an internal cast, retaining portions of the shell and filled with fine brownish sandstone matrix. Another specimen, apparently of a less mature individual of the same species, was obtained at station 2943. Both were collected by W. H. Dall.

This form recalls *S. punctostriatus* Mighels, though the specimens obtained are smaller than the adult of that species.

Genus CYLICHNELLA Gabb.

Cylichna Lovén, Öfv. K. Vet. Akad. Förh., 1846, p. 142, 1847; type *Bulla cylindracea* Pennant.
Cylichnella Gabb, Proc. Acad. Nat. Sci. Philadelphia for 1872 (February, 1873), p. 273; type *Bulla bidentata* Orbigny.
Bullinella R. Bullen-Newton, Brit. Olig. Eoc. Moll., p. 265, 1891.
Cryptaxis Jeffreys, 1883; not of Lowe, 1854.

CYLICHNELLA PETROSA Conrad.

Bullina petrosa Conrad, Am. Jour. Sci., 2d ser., V, 1848, p. 433, fig. 11.
Cylichna petrosa Conrad, Am. Jour. Conch., I, p. 151, 1865.

Miocene of Columbia River, Oregon, near Astoria; J. K. Townsend, fide Conrad.

This species has somewhat the aspect of *C. cylindracea*, but is more slender. Conrad's *Bulla petrosa* of the Wilkes exploring expedition report (1849) is a *Haminea*.

Family AKERIDÆ.

Genus HAMINEA Leach.

Haminea Leach, in Gray, Proc. Zool. Soc. London., for 1847, p. 161; type, *Bulla hydatis* Linné.

HAMINEA PETROSA Conrad.

Bulla petrosa Conrad, in Dana, Geol. U. S. Expl. Exp., p. 727, pl. 19, fig. 8, 1849.
Cylichna oregona Conrad. Am. Jour. Conch., I, p. 151, 1865.

Miocene of Astoria, Oreg., collected by J. D. Dana; U. S. Nat. Mus. 3607 (type) and 3558.

Bulla petrosa is not, strictly speaking, preoccupied by *Bullina petrosa*, as the two species belong to different families; so Conrad's substituted name *oregona* need not be used.

The types are in the national collection and there seems to be no reason to doubt that the species is properly referable to *Haminea*. The fine spiral sculpture, the general form, and the imperforate apex all combine to confirm this reference.

Superorder STREPTONEURA.

Order CTENOBRANCHIATA.

Suborder ORTHODONTA.

Superfamily TOXOGLOSSA.

Family PLEUROTOMATIDÆ.

Genus TURRIS Bolten.

Murex sp., Linné, Syst. Nat., 1758; Gmelin, 1792. etc.
Fusus Helbling, Abh. privatges. in Bohmen, IV, p. 116, 1779, ex parte: not of Lamarck. 1799.
Turris (anonymous). Mus. Calonnianum, pp. 34, 82, 1797: nude name, including *T. babylonius*.
Turris Bolten, Mus. Boltenianum, p. 123, 1798; first species *Murex babylonius* Gmelin, after *Turris babylonica* of Rumphius, 1704, and Argenville, 1757.
Pleurotoma Lamarck, Prodrome, p. 73, 1799; sole example. *Murex babylonius* Linné.
Turris Dall, Jour. Conch. (Leeds), XI, p. 291, April, 1906.

The name *Turris*, proposed by Rumphius and used in the same sense by Müller, Argenville, and other polynomial writers, was first used binomially in the anonymous Museum Calonnianum, where the names are all nude; but in a copy in my possession, under *Turris babylonia*, "*Murex babylonius* Lin." is written in Humphrey's handwriting. Cossmann is mistaken in supposing that *Turris* in this work is used to indicate *Turritella* Lamarck; that genus is called *Terebra* by the anonymous author. In the following year the genus was again adopted for the same type of shell in the Museum Boltenianum. In this work, of 22 species cited under *Turris*, 3 are nude names; of the 19 remaining which are furnished with references, 17 are *Pleurotoma*, 12 of which are referable to *Murex babylonius* (L.) Gmelin, 1 to *M. javanus* Gmelin, and 4 to *P. auriculifera* Lamarck. The other two references are to a pleurotomatiform Stromb, the *Strombus vittatus* Linné. The first species and type is *T. babylonius*.

It is always regrettable to part with an old and familiar name, but in the present case, if the rules of nomenclature be followed, there is absolutely no escape from the conclusion above indicated. We can only regret that Lamarck disregarded a century of usage and tradition when he adopted the new name *Pleurotoma* in place of the familiar old one *Turris*.

TURRIS COOSENSIS Dall, n. sp.

Pl. II, fig. 3.

Shell large, solid, with at least five well-rounded whorls markedly constricted at the sutures; the earlier whorls are axially sculptured with about 14 more or less flexuous rounded ribs extending from the shoulder nearly or quite to the suture in front, which is strongly appressed: these ribs are obsolete over most of the last whorl; the lines of growth are more or less perceptible and indicate a marked but shallow sinus between the shoulder and the suture; owing to the defective condition of this part of the shell, the figure does not show this sinuation on the side represented, but it is distinct in places on the opposite side of the specimen; the spiral sculpture is strong over the whole shell except just in front of the sutures and consists of strong cords separated by well-defined but narrower channels which sometimes contain an intercalary small thread; the larger cords are about a millimeter wide, and at the shoulder there is one that is a little wider and more prominent than the others, but does not carinate the whorls, which are gently excavated in the region of the anal fasciole: the aperture was short and wide, but is defective in the specimen. Altitude of shell, 67 mm.; maximum diameter of last whorl, 34 mm.

Coos Bay Empire formation, collected by W. H. Dall; U. S. Nat. Mus. 107783.

The type specimen is defective at the apex and about the aperture, but is evidently related to *T. cammani*, from which it appears to be differentiated by its more constricted sutures, coarse spiral sculpture, and the axial ribbing.

The condition of the family Pleurotomatidæ, so far as its subdivisions go, is admitted to be more or less chaotic, in spite of the attempts of several authors to clear up the confusion. This and the following species can certainly not be placed in any of the sections illustrated by Cossmann. It is evidently not a typical *Turris*, yet, for the present, it seems more prudent not to propose a new name until better-preserved specimens afford an opportunity to define with more precision its differential characters.

TURRIS CAMMANI Dall, n. sp.

Pl. IV, figs. 12, 13, 14.

Shell large, of five or more whorls, rather inflated, the whorl divided by an obtuse carina a little above the periphery; behind this carina the whorl is flattened, and closely appressed at the suture; in front of the carina the whorl is rounded, with a short, wide canal; the axial sculpture consists chiefly of the incremental lines, which are sinuous in conformity with the broad, shallow sinus of the immature shell; transverse sculpture comprising the carina and numerous spiral threads with narrower interspaces, the threads coarser on the base of the shell; aperture wide, ovate, short, without callosities on the body; outer lip blunt but not varicose or reflected, with a large, moderately deep sinus between the carina and the suture, the anterior part of the lip produced. Altitude of specimen showing upper whorls (fig. 12), 47 mm.; maximum diameter, 30 mm. Altitude of fragment showing last whorl (figs. 13, 14), 44 mm.; maximum diameter, 33 mm.

Coos Bay Miocene, Empire formation, collected by B. H. Camman; U. S. Nat. Mus. 153909.

The type specimens are both worn, which gives the spiral threads a duplex aspect. A portion of the apex and of the anterior end of the canal is missing in each, but the general form is sufficiently indicated as shown in the figures. No indication of any ribbing on the spire is visible. The spiral sculpture is fainter in front of the suture. A badly worn specimen from the same locality, which may possibly be a variety of this species, has rounded whorls, no carina, the shoulder rounded and excavated instead of flat, and indications of 10 or 12 obscure ribs on the penultimate whorl; it has a length of about 70 mm., and a diameter of half as much, with four and a half remaining whorls and a rather pointed spire. The condition of this specimen is so poor that I can not feel sure whether it is a variety of *T. cammani* or not, but I incline to think it might prove distinct if better-preserved specimens could be examined.

TURRIS COLI Dall. n. sp.

Pl. IV. fig. 2.

Shell rather large and heavy for the genus, of over five whorls; the apex defective, the fragment on which this description is based comprising somewhat less than four complete whorls; anterior portion of the shell with the canal missing; whorls swollen, except above the shoulder, where they are constricted and widely appressed to the preceding whorl; suture not conspicuous and rather sinuous; axial sculpture on each whorl of 9 or 10 robust rounded ribs with subequal interspaces, beginning below the constriction, on the upper whorls reaching the suture in front, on the last whorl hardly perceptible beyond the periphery of the whorl, and where a resting stage has coincided with a rib, showing traces of the sharp edge of the original margin; the lines of growth indicate a wide, shallow sinus having its maximum depth at the shoulder of the whorl; spiral sculpture of fine, numerous, rounded, low threads having sharply defined but usually narrower interspaces, which on the later whorls often carry a smaller intercalary thread; the spirals do not enlarge in passing over the ribs and toward the base are frequently crossed by fine slightly elevated incremental lines which give a certain roughness to the sculpture without being very conspicuous; the fractured end of the pillar is solid and heavy, and in the type there is no indication of any thickening of the outer lip or any callosity on the body. Altitude of specimen as figured, 35 mm.; maximum diameter, 22 mm.

Coos Bay Miocene, Empire formation, collected by B. H. Camman; U. S. Nat. Mus. 107783.

The sculpture of this form has some resemblance to that of the genus usually called *Fusus* (Lamarck, *Colus* of authors) but the outer lip is more sinuated than I have observed in any true *Fusus*, and as there are several undoubted pleurotomoid forms in this Miocene horizon with an analogous shallow sinus, I have thought it best to refer this one to that group until a more complete specimen enables us to determine its genus with certainty.

Section ANTIPLANES Dall.

TURRIS (ANTIPLANES) PERVERSA Gabb.

Pl. V. fig. 5.

Pleurotoma (Surcula) perversa Gabb, Proc. California Acad. Sci., III. p. 183. January, 1865.
Pleurotoma (Surcula) perversa Gabb, Pal. California. II, p. 6. 1866.
Drillia perversa Gabb. Pal. California. II, p. 73, pl. 1, fig. 10. 1868.
Pleurotoma (Antiplanes) perversa Dall. Proc. U. S. Nat. Mus., XXIV, No. 1264, p. 513, pl. 34. fig. 8. 1902.

Pleistocene of Fossil Rock, Coos Bay, Oregon, W. H. Dall; U. S. Nat. Mus., 110383. Altitude of specimen figured, 27.5 mm. Range: Miocene of the Empire formation, Coos Bay, Oregon; Pliocene of San Pedro and San Diego, Cal.; Pleistocene of the last-mentioned two localities and of the so-called Fossil Rock, Coos Bay,

Oregon; living in 40 to 60 fathoms, mud, in the Santa Barbara Channel and off the coast of Lower California.

This species is the type of the section *Antiplanes*. The figured specimen is more or less worn, but a fine recent specimen is figured in the Proceedings of the United States National Museum, No. 1264. There are at least half a dozen species in the California later Tertiary and recent faunas belonging to this group, some of which are dextral and others sinistral. A species collected from the Neocene of Humboldt County, Cal., below Bear River, near Humboldt Bay, and named *T. voyi* by Gabb, is dextral.

TURRIS (ANTIPLANES) IMPECUNIA Dall, n. sp.

Pl. IV, fig. 3.

Shell small, smooth, dextral, of five or six whorls; whorls flattish, sculptured only by faint incremental lines (the band at the suture in the photographic figure is due to weathering and is absent from the opposite side of the shell); suture indistinct; aperture obstructed by matrix; the anal sinus, as indicated by the incremental lines, rather wide and deep for so small a shell; canal short and well marked by the constriction over it at the anterior part of the whorl. Altitude, 18 mm.; maximum diameter, 7 mm.

Coos Bay Miocene, Empire formation, collected by W. H. Dall; U. S. Nat. Mus. 153912.

The type is rather weathered on the exposed side, but enough of the other side can be seen to show that the surface is almost perfectly smooth and the whorls but slightly convex. It obviously belongs to the peculiarly Pacific coast group which has been named *Antiplanes*, and, by its compact form and rather short canal, is sufficiently distinguished from any of the species already described.

Genus BATHYTOMA Harris and Burrows.

Dolichotoma Bellardi. Bull. Mal. Ital., I, p. 21, 1875; not of Hope (Coleoptera), 1839.
Bathytoma Harris and Burrows. Eoc. and Olig. Paris Basin, p. 113, 1891; type, *Murex cataphractus* Brocchi.
Surcula (sp.) Gabb, Pal. California, II, p. 72, 1868; not *Surcula* H. and A. Adams.

This group, so characteristic a member of the recent fauna of southern California, also appears in the Tertiary of successive horizons as low as the Miocene.

BATHYTOMA CARPENTERIANA Gabb.

Pl. IV, fig. 8.

Pleurotoma (Surcula) carpenteriana Gabb, Proc. California Acad. Sci., III, p. 183, 1865; Pal. California, II, p. 5, 1866; p. 72, pl. 1, fig. 8, 1868.

Shell ovate-fusiform, solid, of five or more whorls; sculpture chiefly with fine close-set spiral threads subequal in size, with linear interspaces, and almost obsolete above the shoulder; whorls moderately convex, above the rounded shoulder moderately excavated with a closely appressed suture; axial sculpture of rather inconspicuous incremental lines, most evident between the suture and the shoulder, where they are concavely arcuate in harmony with the wide, shallow anal sinus; aperture ovate-elongate, with a short canal and smooth pillar often obscurely thickened mesially. Altitude of figured specimen, 48 mm.; maximum diameter, 22 mm.

Miocene of Coos Bay, Empire formation, collected by W. H. Dall; U. S. Nat. Mus. 153911. Pliocene of San Pedro and San Diego, Cal.; Recent and Pleistocene of southern California.

This form differs from the next by attaining a larger size, by its simpler and less conspicuous sculpture, and by its wider and proportionately shallower anal sulcus. It is rather common in the Empire formation, but the specimens are, so far as yet observed, invariably worn and defective. It has been somewhat abundantly dredged by the United States Fish Commission off the coast of southern California in moderate depths of water.

BATHYTOMA GABBIANA Dall, n. sp.

Pl. IV, fig. 1.

Shell solid, short-fusiform, with five or more whorls; apex defective in the specimen figured; whorls moderately convex, excavated between the shoulder and the preceding suture; suture closely appressed; sculpture chiefly of coarse spiral cords, with shallow wider interspaces occasionally carrying a small intercalary thread; of the former there are in the figured specimen about nine between the canal and the shoulder, with a row of small subrectangular, rather distant sharply elevated nodulations on the spiral nearest the shoulder; above the shoulder are three to five small, less elevated, and more closely set spiral threads; on the earlier whorls the nodules come about midway between the sutures; the nodules on the last whorl of the figured specimen are about 2.5 mm. from center to center, the whole number being uncertain on account of erosion of the type specimen, which also prevents their appearance in the photographic figure; axial sculpture of coarse lines of growth, especially prominent above the shoulder, where they indicate a wide shallow sinus; aperture elongate-ovate, with a short canal and distinct siphonal fasciole; pillar smooth, probably with an obscure thickening on its middle part. Altitude of figured specimen, 33 mm.; maximum diameter, 16 mm.

Coos Bay Miocene, Empire formation, W. H. Dall; U. S. Nat. Mus. 153910.

This species is distinguished from the allied *B. carpenteriana* by its sculpture, which, unfortunately, is not well shown on the figure, but of which the description is made up from the uneroded patches remaining on the side opposite that which is figured.

Family CANCELLARIIDÆ.

Genus CANCELLARIA Lamarck.

CANCELLARIA OREGONENSIS Dall, n. sp.

Pl. II, fig. 7.

Shell heavy, with five and a half rather rapidly enlarging whorls; suture distinct, almost channeled; whorls full, handsomely rounded, apex small and blunt;

sculpture reticulate, strong, composed of (on the last whorl, about 14) strong elevated cordlike spiral ridges with wider interspaces (which on the last whorl frequently carry a small intercalary thread) crossed by axial riblets of very similar character (but without intercalaries) so spaced that their intersections with the major spirals form almost exactly square and equal reticulations, which are deeper and sharper on the upper whorls; the axial sculpture becomes gradually obsolete on the base, but the spirals, as usual, are somewhat coarser there; aperture ovate, narrow in front, forming a short curved canal which is followed by a well-marked siphonal fasciole, separated from the callus of the pillar in the adult by a very narrow chink; body with a mere wash of callus; pillar straight, with two strong middle plaits, a feebler posterior one, and, in the fully adult, the semblance of a fourth anterior plait laid on the edge of the pillar; outer lip moderately thickened, slightly reflected in the adult, probably internally lirate when full grown, though this is not shown on the specimens in hand. Altitude of figured specimen, 43 mm.; of adult, 49 mm.; maximum diameter of figured specimen, 23 mm.; of adult, 27 mm.

Coos Bay Miocene, Empire formation, collected by B. H. Camman; U. S. Nat. Mus. 107788 and 153901. The figured specimen wants about half a whorl of the adult stage, but shows, as the others do not, the form of the pillar.

This species obviously belongs to the same group as the recent *C. crawfordiana* Dall, of California, from which it differs by its larger size and greater proportional diameter. It may perhaps be regarded as the precursor of that species. While the shell does not strictly reproduce the group characters of the typical *C. reticulata*, it is sufficiently near to them to require no separate section and differs chiefly in the more posterior and oblique plaits and the absence of the furrow behind the siphonal fasciole.

Section MERICA H. and A. Adams.

CANCELLARIA ARNOLDI Dall, n. sp.

Pl. XIV, fig. 7.

Shell solid, with a short, acute, subtabulate spire and about five whorls, exclusive of the (lost) nucleus; last whorl much the largest, all are flattened, but hardly channeled for a narrow space in front of the suture; spiral sculpture of numerous rounded, little-elevated cords with shallow, somewhat wider interspaces, usually carrying a smaller intercalary thread; axial sculpture of 16 or more obscure riblets, most perceptible near the shoulder, but on most of the last whorl hardly evident, and numerous prominent, close-set incremental lines; the axial sculpture on the type specimen is not prominent enough to give a reticulate effect to the surface; aperture semilunar; outer lip slightly flaring, thickened, with about eight sharp internal lirations so disposed as to leave a wide smooth space near the posterior angle; body with a thick, smooth layer of callus; pillar short, obliquely truncate in front, with three rather blunt strong plaits and, on the left outer edge of the callus in front of them, several (in the type four or five) small pustulations; canal short, twisted to the right, forming a strong siphonal fasciole inclosing a funicular space terminating in a small perforate umbilicus. Altitude, 23.5 mm.; diameter, 12 mm.

Pliocene of the San Diego (Cal.) well, at a depth of 150 feet, collected by Henry Hemphill; U. S. Nat. Mus. 135038.

A near relation of this, though a much smaller shell, is the *C. modesta* Carpenter, of the recent fauna. *C. unalashkensis* and *C. circumcincta* Dall, of the Alaskan coast, also belong to the same group, though more elevated and proportionally more slender shells. The species is named in honor of Dr. Ralph Arnold, of the United States Geological Survey, who has recently published a monograph on the fossil fauna of the Pliocene and Pleistocene beds of San Pedro, Cal.

Section NARONA H. and A. Adams.

CANCELLARIA HEMPHILLI Dall, n. sp.

Pl. XIV, fig. 5.

Shell slender, solid, with about six subtabulate whorls, excluding the (lost) nucleus; whorls peripherally flattish, with a broad, deep channel at the suture, axially sculptured with (on the last whorl about eleven) sharp, nearly vertical, axial ribs, a little more swollen and prominent at the shoulder, extending over the whorl and separated by much wider excavated interspaces; spiral sculpture of (on the penultimate whorl five to seven) obsolete rounded, rather close-set spirals which override the ribs without nodulation at the intersections; apex of the spire rather acute; aperture narrow, canal long for the genus, strongly twisted, with a prominent siphonal fasciole; pillar slender, with two thin, sharp, prominent plaits, more or less glazed by a thin layer of enamel, but no umbilicus; outer lip defective, but apparently slightly thickened and somewhat flaring, without internal lirations. Altitude, 32 mm.; diameter, 14 mm.

Pliocene of the San Diego (Cal.) well, at a depth of 160 feet, collected by Henry Hemphill, in honor of whom it is named; U. S. Nat. Mus. 135050.

This species, though small, is distinctly of the type of *C. cooperi* Gabb, the finest representative of the genus.

I may add that what, on a cursory survey, appears to be a totally unnecessary number of names has been applied to subdivisions of the genus *Cancellaria;* but time fails me at present to review them in detail. Most of them are based on slight modifications of form which gradually merge into one another when a full series of species is considered.

The first species of the prior genus *Nucella* Bolten is *Cancellaria reticulata*, but by employing the method of elimination to the four modern genera represented in *Nucella* we are able to fix the name on the group usually called *Polytropa* Swainson, and thus avoid relegating *Cancellaria* to synonymy.

Superfamily RHACHIGLOSSA

Family OLIVIDÆ.

Genus OLIVELLA Swainson.

Olivella Swainson, Zool. Ill., II, pl. 58 and text, 1831; sole species, *O. purpurata* Sw. and *O. eburnea* Sw. (=*O. dama* Mawe and *O. nivea* Gmelin).

This genus was first published by Swainson in 1831, with the two species above cited as examples, one of which, necessarily, must be taken as type. It is not exact, therefore, to cite *O. jaspidea* as type, as has been done by several authors, unless, indeed, they regard *O. jaspidea* as a synonym of *O. nivea*. In the Malacology, Swainson defines his genus, and the essential part of the diagnosis is as follows: "Base of the pillar curved inward, and marked by two strong plaits; upper plaits obsolete or wanting." Of the two species above mentioned, the first—*O. dama* (*purpuratus*)—best illustrates these characters and, preceding the other in the text of 1831, should be regarded as the type. Of those referred to in the Manual, *O. biplicata* is the first mentioned and figured (p. 82), and the only species mentioned in the discussion. If it were not for the prior publication in the Zoological Illustrations, *O. biplicata* would doubtless be regarded as type of the genus. The distinctions between this and the other groups of species of *Olivella* which have been named are very trivial, and almost invariably of a transitional kind. Thus the anterior plication in one and the same species may be duplex or triplex, or single, according to the stage of growth attained by the same individual, while another species may be quite constant in the adult form of the same character. To take the California species, for example: *O. intorta* has the anterior plait single or duplex; *O. pedroana*, single, double, or triple; *O. dama* the same; while in *O. biplicata* the triple form is common. Too much stress should not be laid on the systematic value of such characters.

On a critical examination of *O. dama* we find it has, just within the aperture, one strong projecting plait, which, as it extends outward beyond the aperture, is divided almost always into two, sometimes into as many as five or six ridges; above these the pillar is excavated and callous. On the body the callus extends in the adult the whole height of the first whorl, and above the plaits above described there are in some shells five or six revolving ridges. The same is true of *O. nivea*, in which the anterior plait is less prominent and more oblique. *O. intorta* Carpenter has one plait divided by a groove, but within the aperture the plait is not sharp or projecting as in *dama*. *O. biplicata* is similar, but the plait may be divided by grooves until the number of intervening wrinkles is as high as nine; these last two species, however, appear to be always destitute of wrinkles or minor plaits on the body callus. Curiously enough, on *O. biplicata* it is comparatively rare to find exactly two plaits. The group of *biplicata* also includes, among western American species, *O. semistriata* and *O. columellaris*. Of the *dama* type are *O. pedroana, anazora, inconspicua, gracilis, tergina*, and *cærulea*.

O. volutella has the anterior callus flat, not raised into plaits, but with numerous subequal groovings, which are confined to the area of the siphonal fasciole or anterior band of enamel. The body behind the fasciole is not lirate. *O. undatella* and its variety *pulchra* have the grooved flat fasciole of *O. volutella*, but also have evenly spaced equal lirations on the body.   Differences in the thickness and extension of the body callus are of hardly more than specific weight systematically, and the species intergrade.   *O. undatella* is described by C. B. Adams as being entirely covered by the foot and propodia while active, just as are the species of true *Oliva*.   I do not know on what foundation rests Gray's statement[a] that this species has no operculum. His similar remark about *O. biplicata* Sby. is incorrect.   If, however, it is true that the former is inoperculate, on taking into consideration the character of the animal as observed by Adams and the characters of the shell, it is obvious that *O. volutella* and probably *O. undatella* belong with the true olives and not with *Olivella*.   Their differences from *Oliva* would hardly be generic.

The statement made by H. and A. Adams that in *Dactylidia*, which they hold to include *O. mutica*, the spire is concealed by a callous deposit is not literally correct. The body near the aperture in these species is coated with enamel, which extends to the suture but not over it, and the whorls are and remain perfectly distinct though the space between the sutures, as in nearly all the species of the family, is more or less coated with enamel.

The species of *Olivella* on the Pacific coast (assuming that *Lamprodoma* remains with this genus) may be grouped as follows:

A. Pillar concave. anterior fasciole with a few prominent grooved plaits.   *Olivella.*
    a. Body smooth. *Callianax* H. and A. Adams.
    b. Body lirate. *Olivella* s. s.
B. Pillar straight, anterior fasciole flat, with low similar numerous lirations.   *Lamprodoma* Sw.
    a. Body smooth. *Lamprodoma* s. s.
    b. Body lirate. *Strephonella* Dall, nov. sect.

The type of the section B*b* will be *Lamprodoma (Strephonella) undatella* Lamarck,[b] from the Gulf of California.

OLIVELLA PEDROANA Conrad.

Pl. VI. fig. 1.

Strephona pedroana Conrad, Pacific R. R. Repts., V, p. 327. pl. 6, fig. 51, 1856; H. Doc. 129, p. 17, 1855.
Olivella bætica Carpenter. Rept. Brit. Assoc. Adv. Sci. for 1863, p. 661. 1864: Keep, West Coast Shells,
    p. 42, fig. 21, 1892; Williamson, Proc. U. S. Nat. Mus., XV, p. 212. pl. 19. fig. 7, 1892.
Olivella pedroana Arnold, Pal. and Strat. San Pedro, p. 221, 1903.[c]

Shell small, smooth, bluntly pointed, with about six whorls; suture narrowly channeled; aperture narrow, outer lip sharp, simple; inner lip with a wash of callus; siphonal callus broad, smooth (the shell above its posterior edge slightly eroded in the figured specimen, which has also lost its apex); pillar short, twisted, with one strong plait sharply grooved in the middle, and thus presenting the aspect of two plaits; canal short and wide.   Altitude of decollate specimen figured, 13.0 mm.; maximum diameter, 6.7 mm.

Coos Bay Miocene, Empire formation, W. H. Dall; also Pliocene of California and Pleistocene of Fossil Rock, Coos Bay; U. S. Nat. Mus. 153918.   Recent, Kadiak Island, Alaska, to Lower California.

a Proc. Zool Soc. London, 1858, p. 47.
b Gray, in Zool Beechey's Voy., 1839, p. 131, pl. 36, figs. 23, 27.
c *Oliva alectra* Duclos, 1843, and *O. nota* Marrat, 1871, have also been united with this species by some authors.

This species occurs in masses in some portions of the sandstone (station 2950), but is invariably mutilated. Carpenter noted that a comparison between his *O. bætica* and Conrad's species was desirable, and Arnold has united them. Conrad's type is not preserved, his figure is poor, and his description is quite insufficient, but there is little doubt that *bætica* is synonymous with it, since it is a choice between three possible species, two of which can not be reconciled with *O. pedroana*, while topotypes from the original locality are undoubtedly identical with *O. bætica*.

Family VOLUTIDÆ.

Subfamily VOLUTINÆ.

Genus VOLUTODERMA Gabb.

Volutilithes? (sp.) Shumard, Proc. Boston Soc. Nat. Hist., VIII. p. 192, 1861 (*V. navarroënsis* n. sp., Texas).

Rostellites Conrad, Proc. Acad. Nat. Sci. Philadelphia, VII, 1855, p. 268; type, *R. texanus* Conrad; cf. Mex. Boundary Survey, I, p. 158, pl. 14, figs. 2a, 2b (?= *V. navarroënsis* Shumard), 1858. Not *Rostellites*, G. Fischer, Mus. Demidoff, II, p. 269, 1806. *fide* Deshayes in MS.

Volutilithes (*navarroënsis*) Gabb, Pal. California, I, p. 102, pl. 19, fig. 56, 1864; type, *V. navarroënsis* Gabb (non Shumard)= *Fulguraria gabbi* White, Bull. U. S. Geol. Survey No. 51, p. 23, pl. 3, fig. 1, 1889.

Volutoderma Gabb, Proc. Acad. Nat. Sci. Philadelphia, for 1876, p. 289; type, *V. navarroënsis* Gabb, non Shumard (= *V. californica* Dall, 1907, Cret. California); Holzapfel, in Zittel, Paleontographica, XXXIV, p. 87, 1888.

Fulguraria Stoliczka, Cret. Gastr. India, p. 85, 1868; White, Bull. U. S. Geol. Survey No. 51, p. 23, 1889; not of Schumacher, 1817.

Volutoderma Dall, Smithsonian Misc. Coll. (quarterly issue), L, pt. 1, No. 1704, p. 12, 1907.

Shell fusiform, rather thin, slender, few-whorled, with an acute apex consisting of a small shelly nucleus; suture conspicuously appressed; pillar nearly straight, with several (usually three) small, subequal, rather distant plications; canal hardly differentiated from the aperture; outer lip thin, slightly reflected when completely adult, with usually a small denticle where each spiral ridge intersects the margin; at the posterior commissure in the adult is a flaring sinus or channel with projecting margin; the outer lip usually a little patulous anteriorly; sculpture of axial ribs crossed by strong, narrow spiral ridges or cords, rather sparsely distributed; the surface without any superficial coating of enamel.

Type, *Volutoderma navarroënsis* Gabb, non Shumard (= *V. californica* Dall).

The genus has representatives in the middle (Turonian) and upper Cretaceous of North America, Europe, and India. Owing to the manner in which they have been and are likely to be confused with the Tertiary forms, it has seemed desirable to give the characteristics of these two volutoid genera, which have been more fully treated in a paper recently published in the Smithsonian Miscellaneous Collection for 1907.

Gabb referred his figured species to the unfigured species of Shumard, which appears to be identical with the earlier *Rostellites texanus* of Conrad, both having been described from the same horizon in Texas. Shumard's type, for which Doctor Stanton has made inquiries in the St. Louis Academy of Sciences, where it was deposited, appears to have been lost or destroyed, perhaps in a fire which injured the academy's collections. It was never figured, but Shumard's description is so full and precise, giving numerous measurements, that it is easy to produce diagrammatically a figure which can not be very unlike his fossil. On comparing this figure with the species from the region whence Shumard's type came, it is not difficult to recognize the form he described. A comparison of the types of Conrad, White, and Stanton, together with topotypes of Gabb's species and several of Conrad's forms from the Ripley (Cretaceous) of Alabama and Mississippi—for the opportunity to study which I am indebted to Dr. T. W. Stanton—has enabled me to clear up part of the confusion among the older species of this group. That there are more species than had been supposed, and that their characters are very similar, while few of the specimens are well preserved, explains why this has not been practicable sooner.

It seems reasonably certain that Shumard's name is a synonym of the earlier *texanus* of Conrad. Gabb's Californian species which he identified with the Texas form is certainly distinct from it; while the shell figured by White under the name of *gabbi*, and supposed by him to be the same as Gabb's *navarroënsis*, is again a different species. It follows that besides new forms, there are several which need distinctive names.

Volutoderma has been divided into several sections, as follows:

1. *Volutoderma s. s.*   Type, *V. californica* Dall.
2. *Rostellinda* Dall.   Type, *V. stoliczkana* Dall; Cretaceous of India and Colorado.
3. *Rostellana* Dall.   Type, *V. bronni* Zekeli; Cretaceous of Gosau, Austria, and Colorado.
4. *Rostellaca* Dall.   Type, *V. zitteliana* Holzapfel; Cretaceous of Aachen, North Germany.

Genus VOLUTOMORPHA Gabb.

Volutilithes (sp.) Gabb, Jour. Acad. Nat. Sci Philadelphia, 2d ser , IV, p. 300, 1860.
Volutomorpha Gabb, Proc. Acad. Nat. Sci. Philadelphia, for 1876, p. 290; types, *V. conradi* Gabb, Jour. Acad. Nat. Sci. Philadelphia, 2d ser., IV, p. 300, pl. 48, fig. 10, 1860; and *V. eufaulensis* Conrad, op. cit., pl. 47, fig. 18.

Shell elongate-fusiform, heavy, few-whorled; with a minute shelly nucleus; pillar straight, with one strong plait and sometimes a much feebler second plait behind the first; suture appressed, with a more or less conspicuous constriction of the whorl in front of it; outer lip simple, with a marked sinuosity behind near the suture; sculpture of axial ribs crossed by spiral ridges, the whole shell, when adult, covered by a thin coat of polished enamel which may obscure the sutures and minor sculpture. Types, *V. conradi* Gabb and *V. eufaulensis* Conrad, from the upper Cretaceous of New Jersey and Alabama, respectively.

The designated type is an internal cast which exhibits no characters except the fusiform shape and a single fold on the pillar. It has therefore been necessary to draw the characters largely from the second species included by Gabb, which has a faint second fold on the pillar and of which the external shell characters are known.

The coating of the shell with a layer of transparent enamel occurs in other groups of Volutidæ, as in *Scaphella* and *Aurinia*, to say nothing of *Zidona*, which has a permanent enlargement of the mantle capable of covering the entire shell.

This genus is related to the following one from the Tertiary, by its size, its general form, and its single (or duplex) strong columellar fold. But the sculpture, the presence of the coat of enamel covering the shell in the adult, and the geologic horizon separate them sufficiently.

Genus MIOPLEIONA Dall, nov.

Rostellaria (sp.) Conrad, Geol. U. S. Expl. Exp., p. 727, 1849. *R. indurata* Conrad, op. cit., pl. 19, fig. 12.
Volutilithes (sp.) Conrad, Am. Jour. Conch., I. p. 151, 1865; Gabb. Pal. California. II. p. 76. 1869.
Rostellites (sp.) Dall. Trans. Wagner Inst.. III, p. 71, 1890.

Shell large, heavy, fusiform, slender, with acute (? shelly) nucleus and few whorls; pillar straight, with one strong and one more posterior feeble plait upon it, not quite reaching the aperture and much more sharply defined in the early stages of growth; surface smooth or spirally striate, with small axial riblets; outer lip more or less channeled at the posterior commissure in the adult; the margin entire, slightly expanded; no internal lirations; the external surface not covered with enamel.

Type, *M. indurata* Conrad, sp., from the Oligocene Tertiary of Astoria, Oreg., and of the State of Washington.

MIOPLEIONA INDURATA Conrad.

Pl. XVIII, figs. 5, 6.

Rostellaria indurata Conrad, Geol. U. S. Expl. Exp.. p. 727, 1849.

From concretion at base of bluff at Astoria, Oreg., U. S. Nat. Mus. 5908 (type specimen); 112409, same locality, Condon; 110427, three-eighths of a mile northwest of Restoration Point, opposite Seattle, on Puget Sound, Arnold: 110428, 1½ miles southeast of Observation Point, Freshwater Bay, Juan de Fuca Strait, west of Port Angeles, Wash., Arnold. All are from the Oligocene sandstone of Oregon and Washington.

Shell rather thin for its size, slender, elevated, with six or seven whorls, the spire being longer than the aperture; sculpture of 15–17 narrow low arcuate axial ribs, extending over the periphery and separated by wider interspaces; the whole surface is sculptured by fine, close, subequal threadlike spirals, which are not swollen when they cross the ribs and do not produce denticles on the edge of the outer lip: suture appressed, not channeled except in internal casts, nucleus unknown; whorls moderately convex, aperture short, widely sulcate near the suture in the adult; pillar straight, with one strong and one feeble plait which are hardly visible at the aperture but stronger in the early whorls; outer lip arcuate, receding toward the suture, where there is a wide sulcus, the extreme margin slightly reflected, thin, not denticulate. Length, 102 mm. or more; maximum diameter, 40 mm.; length of spire above the aperture, 60 mm. The measurements are taken from an internal cast.

This species is much more slender and has a relatively much higher spire than the Miocene form, which also lacks the spiral striation.

MIOPLEIONA OREGONENSIS Dall, n. sp.

Pl. XVIII, figs 3, 7.

Tillamook Head, Washington, in Miocene strata, Chester Washburne; U. S. Nat. Mus. 154094, at station 2947, in Goldwashers Gully, Coos Bay, Oregon, Miocene sandstone, Dall; 153894 (types), Miocene of Coos Bay. Oregon, purchased of B. H. Camman; 110429, lower Pliocene at Point New Year (Año Nuevo), California, Arnold.

Shell rather thin for its size, subovate, with about six whorls, the apical whorls rapidly diminishing; nucleus small, its characters unknown; subsequent whorls with arcuate rounded ribs and wider interspaces, the ribs numbering about 14 on the penult and 20 on the last whorl; surface otherwise smooth except for incremental lines, the ribs feebler on the last whorl; body rather turgid, the suture distinct, not appressed, the whorl in front of it sometimes showing an obscure marginal ridge or slight tabulation; strength of the ribs variable in different specimens; aperture semi-ovate, sulcate at the posterior commissure; pillar straight, with one strong and one feeble plait about the middle of it, rather widely separated; outer lip thin, slightly reflected, produced in the adult at the posterior commissure. Length of largest (but imperfect) specimen, about 160 mm.; of restored smaller type specimen, 110 mm.; of aperture, 68 mm.; maximum diameter, 45 mm.

This is the species to which most of the citations of locality by J. G. Cooper and others in lists of California fossils are to be attributed. As previously shown, it is easily distinguished from *M. indurata*, but the amount of material belonging to the latter species has been small and badly preserved, so it is not unnatural that the related forms were taken to be one species, especially as nearly all the specimens were more or less decorticated. A fragment probably belonging to this species was found by Arnold at Fugler's asphalt mine near Gary, 12 miles southeast of Santa Maria, Santa Barbara County. Cal., in material which is referred to the lower Pliocene.

Family FASCIOLARIIDÆ.

Genus FUSINUS Rafinesque.

HISTORICAL NON-LINNEAN SYNONYMY.

Fusus Rumphius, Amboinische Rariteit·Kammer, pl. 29, figs. *F, G,* 1705.
Fusus (sp.) Klein, Tent. Meth. Ostr., p. 60, 1753; P. L. S. Müller, in Knorr. Del. Nat. Sel., p. 129. 1766.

SYSTEMATIC LINNEAN SYNONYMY.

Fusus Bruguière, Encycl. Meth., p. 15, 1789; nude name, not *Fusus* of Helbling. 1779.
Colus (anonymous), Mus. Calonnianum, p. 34, 1797, not of Bolten.
Fusus (ex parte) Cuvier, Tableau Elém., p. 403, 1798; not *Fusus* Helbling, 1779, nor of Mus. Calonnianum 1797; nor Bolten, 1798: cf. Dall, Jour. Conch. (Leeds), XI, pp. 289–297, April. 1906.
Syrinx (sp.) Bolten, Mus. Boltenianum, p. 121, 1798; not of Bohadsch, 1761.
Fusus Lamarck, Prodrome, p. 73, 1799; sole example, *F. colus* Linné (as *Murex*) Syst. des Anim. s. Vert., p. 82, 1801; Anim. s. Vert.. VII, p. 121, 1822; not of Helbling.
Neptunea (sp.) Link, Beschr. Rostock Samml., p. 117, 1807.
Fusinus Rafinesque, Anal. de la Nature. p. 145, 1815; new name for *Fusus* Lam.
Priscofusus Conrad, Am. Jour. Conch., I, p. 150, April, 1865; first species, *Fusus corpulentus* Conrad; Checkl. Eoc. Fos. N. Am.. Smiths. Misc. Coll. No. 200, p. 19, 1866.
Erilia Conrad, Jour. Acad. Nat. Sci., n. s., IV, p. 291, pl. 47. fig. 34, 1860; sole example, *E. pergracilis* Conrad, loc. cit.; not *Erilia* Mulsant (Coleoptera), 1863.
Erilifusus Conrad, Am. Jour. Conch.. I, p. 18, 1865; sole example, *E. thalloides* Conrad (as *Fusus*), Fos. Tert. Form., p. 56, pl. 18, fig. 12, 1835; not *Erilifusus* Gabb, 1876.
Erilifusus Gabb, Proc. Acad. Nat. Sci. Philadelphia, for 1876, p. 278; subgenus of *Fusus,* type *F.* (*E.*) *kerri* Gabb, op. cit., pl. 17, fig. 1; Cretaceous of North Carolina.
?Turrispira Conrad, Checkl. Eoc. Fos. N. Am.. Smiths. Misc. Coll. No. 200. p. 19, 1866: Tryon. Man. Conch.. III, p. 49. 1881: first species, *Fusus protextus* Conrad. 1855; but Tryon cites as example Conrad's other species. *F. salebrosus.* (Probably closely related to *Papillina* Conrad.)
Aptyxis Troschel, Gebiss d. Schnecken, II. p. 61. 1868; type. *Fusus syracusanus* Lamarck.

Mitræfusus Bellardi, Moll. Ter. Terz. Piem. e Lig., Mem. Reale Accad. Sci. di Torino, 2d ser., XXVII, p. 234, June, 1873; sole example. *Fusus orditus* Bell. e Mich., op. cit., p. 235, pl. 11, fig. 1; Miocene (= *Erilia* Conrad).
Euthriofusus Cossmann, Essais Pal. Comp., IV, pp. 6, 27, 1901; type, *Fusus burdigalensis* Basterot, Miocene.
Aptyxis Monterosato, Nom. Gen. e Spec., p. 116, 1884; first species. *Fusus syracusanus* Lam.
Pseudofusus Monterosato, Nom. Gen. e Spec., p. 117, 1884; first species, *Murex rostratus* Olivi.
Troschelia Mörch, Jour. de Conchyl., XXIV, p. 370, 1876; type. *Fusus berniciensis* King; not *Troschelia* Duncan, 1883, Corals.
Bucrinofusus Conrad, Am. Jour. Conch., III, p. 264, 1867; type. *Fusus parilis* Conrad.
Boreofusus Sars, Moll. Reg. Arct. Norv., p. 278, 1878; type. *Fusus berniciensis* King, var. *solida* Jeffreys (= *Troschelia* Morch).
Fusus Grabau, Smithsonian Misc. Coll., XLIV, No. 1417, pp. 7–72, 1904; type *F. colus* Lam.; not of Helbling, 1779, nor Dall, Jour. Conch. (Leeds), XI, No. 10, pp. 289–294, 1906.

I have shown elsewhere that the name *Fusus* can not be retained for the group typified by *F. colus*, Helbling having preceded all other authors in the binomial application of it. It remains, therefore, according to the rules of nomenclature, to raise to generic rank the oldest subsequent name of the Lamarckian genus, and apply it to the *colus* group.

A large number of names have been applied to the genus in question and its subdivisions, especially of late, but, as it is not my purpose to give in this place a complete revision of the group, but only to determine what name shall be used for the species of the Oregon Tertiary, it is not necessary to discuss all these later names, much information in regard to which may be had from the valuable Essais of Cossmann.

After eliminating from the Lamarckian *Fusus* those forms which are acknowledged to be of different genera, there is left a substantial remainder of species that can be divided only into subgenera or sections. Of these a large series have been shown by Grabau to have a uniform and distinctive protoconch and a similarity in other shell characters that warrants us in regarding them as a distinct group of species, of which Lamarck's *F. colus* is a typical exemplar. This is the group for which a name is necessary.

The first name available for the group is *Fusinus*, which was proposed by Rafinesque in 1815, as a substitute for *Fusus* Lamarck, and therefore would be regarded as having the same typical species.

From *Fusinus*, *Exilia* Conrad is separated only by its more delicate and less prominent sculpture, flatter whorls, small size, and particularly attenuated form. These characters are certainly not generic. The supposed plaits on the pillar, mentioned by Cossmann, are due to some misapprehension, as there is not a trace of any sculpture or plaiting on the pillar. With our present knowledge there is no sufficient ground for regarding *Exilia* as more than subgenerically different from *Fusinus* s. s. *Exilifusus* Conrad may be regarded as at least sectionally distinct, though *Exilifusus* Gabb seems to be merely a *Fusinus* with the canal a little more arcuate than usual. Cossmann has already pointed out that typical species of *Fusinus* differ in the straightness of the canal and that this character is of slight importance.

Troschel proposed a genus *Aptyxis* for *Fusus syracusanus* because of its fasciolaroid radula, he not having examined the dentition of a typical *Fusus*.

But later Schacko discovered that this kind of radula was typical of the true Fusi. *F. syracusanus*, however, will remain separated from typical *Fusinus* because it has a short canal, a long spire, and a protoconch which is of the type called fulguroid by Grabau, quite different from that of the true *Fusus* or *Fusinus*.

Some thirty years ago the types of Conrad's species were mislaid and supposed to have been lost, and with the obscure figure given in the atlas of the Exploring Expedition report it seemed as if it would be impossible to determine the character of the original. I expressed this opinion in a review of the Californian species of *Fusus*. However, by good fortune some years later the missing fossils were found, and I have had the opportunity of studying them carefully. Conrad had proposed a genus *Priscofusus* for the species from the Astoria group. By making careful casts from the rock molds the characters of the group can be pretty well determined, and it will form a discriminable section of the genus. Cossmann proposed later a genus *Euthriofusus* for *F. burdigalensis* Basterot, but he included with the latter another form, which is much more like *Priscofusus*. This is the *Fusus virgineus* of Grateloup. If the latter can be separated from *F. burdigalensis* it might find an appropriate refuge in *Priscofusus;* but if they can not be separated, then *Euthriofusus* must be regarded as a synonym of *Priscofusus*.

Mitræfusus Bellardi, as suggested by Cossmann and by Bellardi's figure, is apparently an exact synonym of *Exilia*.

Recently Monterosato, under the misapprehension that *Fusus colosseus* was the type of *Fusus* Lamarck, proposed for the obviously distinct group of *F. colus* the name *Pseudofusus*. This is the first exact synonym of *Fusus* Lamarck, since *Fusinus*, of which it becomes a synonym also.

For a Miocene fossil of Maryland, *Fusus parilis*, Conrad in 1867 proposed a genus *Buccinofusus*. The nucleus of this species is typically fusoid, as defined by Grabau, and its other characters are of not greater than subgeneric value as compared with those of *Fusinus*. With *Buccinofusus* Tryon was disposed to unite *Troschelia* Mörch (*Boreofusus* Sars), but an inspection of the protoconch and nepionic shell of *Troschelia* will show that this is quite inadmissible, inasmuch as the latter has a remarkably distinct form of nucleus, a character in which it is probable or certain that *Fusus nodosus* Jeffreys, *F. abyssorum* Fischer, *F. aquitanica, peregra,* and *ecaudis* of Locard, and several other species, agree with it. Mörch proposed the new name for *Troschelia* on account of its fasciolaroid radula, but later investigations indicate that this is true of the whole group in the wide sense, those species with a buccinoid radula being properly transferred to the Buccinidæ. Therefore the thin shell, delicate sculpture, and relatively short canal of *Troschelia* will hardly give it more than subgeneric rank under the restricted *Fusinus*.

The arrangement of the genus and its subdivisions with their type species will be about as follows:

Genus FUSINUS Rafinesque. 1815.

Subgenus FUSINUS s. s.

Section *Fusinus* s. s. Type. *F. colus* Lamarck.

Section *Euthriofusus* Cossmann. 1901. Type. *F. burdigalensis* Basterot.

Section *Heilprinia* Grabau. 1904. Type. *F. caloosaënsis* Heilprin.

Subgenus APTYXIS Troschel, 1868.

    Section *Aptyxis* s. s.   Type. *F. syracusanus* Lamarck.
    Section *Fulgurofusus* Grabau. 1904.   Type. *F. quercollis* Harris.
Subgenus EXILIA Conrad. 1865.

    Section *Exilia* s. s.   Type, *F. pergracilis* Conrad.
    Section *Exilifusus* Conrad. 1865.   Type. *F. thalloides* Conrad.
    Section *Falsifusus* Grabau, 1904.   Type. *F. ottonis* Aldrich.
Subgenus PRISCOFUSUS Conrad, 1865.

    Section *Priscofusus* s. s.   Type, *F. corpulentus* Conrad.
Subgenus BUCCINOFUSUS Conrad, 1865.

    Section *Buccinofusus* s. s.   Type. *F. parilis* Conrad.
Subgenus TROSCHELIA Mörch, 1867.

    Section *Troschelia* s. s.   Type. *F. berniciensis* King.

NOTE.—*Fulgurofusus* and *Aptyxis* have identical protoconchs. Of *Falsifusus* and *Exilia* the same is true. The nucleus of *Priscofusus* is unknown, but those of *Buccinofusus* and *Troschelia* are remarkably distinct. the former agreeing very well with that of typical *Fusinus* in this particular character.

Subgenus PRISCOFUSUS Conrad.

FUSINUS (PRISCOFUSUS) CORPULENTUS Conrad.

Fusus corpulentus Conrad. Geol. U. S. Expl. Exp.. appendix p. 728. pl. 20. fig. 4. 1849; not of E. A. Smith. Ann. Mag. Nat. Hist.. p. 344, fig., May. 1882 (=*F. pricei* Smith. n. nom. 1887). ,
Priscofusus corpulentus Conrad. Am. Jour. Conch.. 1. p. 150, 1865.

Oligocene or Miocene of the Astoria group, Astoria, Oreg., J. D. Dana; U. S. Nat. Mus. 3530, 3551 (type specimen), and 3552.

This species is represented by three internal casts, of which the best, framed in a concretion, is figured by Dana. The shell had five or six whorls, the apex being defective in the specimens. It was a thin shell, with rather rapidly increasing whorls, a relatively short and gently recurved canal, the suture distinct, hardly appressed; the aperture rounded; the outer lip thin, not lirate within, widely concavely sinuous behind; pillar smooth; sculpture of fine, close spiral threads, with about equal interspaces, covering the shell; the basal part of the last whorl somewhat abruptly contracted; the periphery of the earlier whorls subangular, with (on the penultimate whorl about 12) short, low axial riblets or nodulations, obsolete toward the sutures. Length of last three whorls, 41.5 mm.; of last whorl, 29 mm.; of the canal, 10 mm.; maximum diameter of last whorl, 22 mm.

Inasmuch as this species is the type of the subgenus, I have redescribed it in detail, the subgeneric characters seeming to lie in the delicate sculpture, the spire longer than the canal, the absence of lirations inside the aperture, and the short canal. Some of these characters might suggest *Chrysodomus*, but the sculpture has more the aspect of *Fusinus*. The next species agrees in these characters, though differing specifically. None of the recent species of this region show analogous characters. As this species does not appear in the undoubted Miocene of the Empire formation, it may be surmised that it belongs with the Oligocene species, which at Astoria were found mingled with other fossils of Miocene origin.

FUSINUS (PRISCOFUSUS) GENICULUS Conrad.

Fusus geniculus Conrad. Geol. U. S. Expl. Exp.. appendix, p. 728. pl. 20. fig. 3, 1849.
Priscofusus geniculus Conrad, Am. Jour. Conch., I. p. 150, 1865.
Priscofusus oregonensis Conrad. Am. Jour. Conch.. I. p. 150, 1865; Geol. U. S. Expl. Exp.. pl. 20, figs.
   10, 11, 1849 (no name proposed). Figures reversed on the plate. as are also figs. 1. 8, 12. and 13.
   Not *Fusus oregonensis* Conrad. 1848.

Miocene concretions derived from the Astoria group, Astoria, Oreg., collected by J. D. Dana; U. S. Nat. Mus. 3552 (type of *geniculus*); 3517 (type of *oregonensis*); 3530, 3535, 3543, 3559, 3565 (cotype of *oregonensis*); and at Clallam Bay, Washington, by Arnold, in the upper part of the lower Miocene sandstones.

F. geniculus is very much like *F. corpulentus*, but more slender and elongate, the axial ribs more elongate and persistent, appearing on the last whorl, where there would be 13 to 14; a specially prominent cord encircles the last whorl at the periphery, and one or two more are to be found on the base. The best specimen afforded a mold in gutta-percha, which shows seven whorls, the nucleus being small and prominent but furnishing no information in regard to its minor details except that it appears to have been smooth. The total length of the shell is 77.5 mm.; of last whorl, 30.0 mm.; of canal, 11.0 mm.; maximum diameter of last whorl, about 19 mm.

The figured specimen (scale 1¼) of *F. geniculus* shows the upper part of the spire only; the other specimens are casts and molds, mostly in small globular concretions. It is possible that Conrad's *Fusus devinctus* is identical with the present species, but the types are apparently lost, and the figures are from internal casts and very poor, so that it seems better to leave the name unused, at least until more information is available.

The Clallam Bay specimen retained the external sculpture and was positively identified.

FUSINUS (PRISCOFUSUS) sp. indet.

Shell small, short, whorls rapidly increasing (apex and outer lip wanting), with a subangular shoulder near the middle of the whorl, above which the surface is slightly excavated; on the angle of the shoulder is a series of (on the last whorl 10 or 12) short nodular riblets or projections, over which the fine sharp spiral threads which cover the shell pass without becoming swollen; the spirals are separated by subequal interspaces and are, for the most part, alternately larger and smaller; on the upper whorls a more prominent thread runs close behind the suture; the spiral sculpture is crossed by rather sharp, close, distinct incremental lines; pillar short, callous, twisted, obliquely truncate toward the extremity; canal moderately wide, slightly recurved. Length of last and penultimate whorls, 27.5 mm.; of aperture, about 18.0 mm.; maximum diameter just behind the aperture, 13.0 mm.

Miocene or Oligocene concretions at Astoria, Oreg., collected by J. D. Dana; U. S. Nat. Mus. 3544.

This species appears to be different from either of those named by Conrad, though its sculpture has the same general characteristics. The form is shorter than that of *F. geniculus*, and more angular than that of *F. corpulentus*, of which, however, it may be an extreme mutation. It seems best not to apply a name to it, pending the reception of better material. It does not appear among the forms collected at Coos Bay.

Fusinus (Priscofusus) medialis Conrad.

Cerithium mediale Conrad. Geol. U. S. Expl. Exp.. appendix. p. 728, pl. 20, figs. 1 (reversed). 1a. 1849.
Priscofusus medialis Conrad. Am. Jour. Conch., I. p. 150, 1865.

Oligocene or Miocene of the Astoria group, Astoria, Oreg., collected by J. D. Dana; U. S. Nat. Mus. 3532 (type).

This species is represented only by the type specimen, which has lost the lower half of the last whorl, with the aperture and canal, giving the specimen somewhat the look of a melanian or *Cerithium*. It is a distinct species from either of the others, with more prominent peripheral nodules (15 on the penult whorl), appressed and less constricted suture, and more broadly conical spire.

Fusinus (Priscofusus) nodiferus Conrad.

(No name) Conrad, Geol. U. S. Expl. Exp., pl. 20, figs. 12 (reversed). 12a 1849.
Priscofusus nodiferus Conrad. Am. Jour. Conch.. I. p. 150, 1865.

Astoria group, Astoria, Oreg., J. D. Dana.

The type specimen of this species has disappeared, but the figures indicate a much shorter and more inflated species than either of the others.

Subgenus BUCCINOFUSUS Conrad.

Fusinus (Buccinofusus) coosensis Dall, n. sp.

Pl. II. fig. 1.

Shell solid, strong, with about six rounded whorls; suture appressed, the whorl in front of it more or less excavated, and between the suture and the shoulder finely closely spirally threaded; whorl in front of the narrow excavated area strongly sculptured, with numerous straplike, crowded, moderately elevated spiral ridges with narrow interspaces; these spirals cover the whole shell in front of the shoulder and are not alternated, though somewhat irregular in width; they are crossed by short, rather strong, narrow, rounded riblets beginning near the shoulder and becoming obsolete on or near the periphery of the whorl; on the penultimate whorl in the figured specimen there are 11 of these riblets, and they are more conspicuous and with the sides more abrupt than the figure indicates; the other axial sculpture consists of the incremental lines, which are broadly flexuous on the posterior slope of the whorl and seem to have been visible as elevated lines in the interspaces between the spirals; the aperture was rather wide and apparently rounded, the anterior part of the pillar and the whole of the canal (as well as the apex of the spire) being defective in the figured type. Altitude of specimen, 62 mm.; maximum diameter, 31 mm.

Miocene of Coos Bay, Empire formation, collected by B. H. Camman; U. S. Nat. Mus. 107782.

This species being represented only by a worn and broken specimen, I have been somewhat in doubt as to the genus to which it should be referred. The flexuosity of the lines of growth does not show a sinus like that of the large Pleurotomas with which it is associated; in its present condition the aspect is somewhat like that of an elevated *Buccinum*, but no species of that genus has the excavated area in front of the suture; if we ascribe to the shell an elongated canal now lost, the characteristics fit in very well with the large species commonly referred to the genus *Fusinus*, the *Colus* of some authors, and to this group it is provisionally referred. The reference is to some extent confirmed by a very poorly preserved specimen from the same collection having a rather long canal, the whole of which is not preserved, and of which the surface characters, so far as they are recognizable, agree with those of the figured specimen. The second specimen alluded to has about three and a half whorls, the earlier part of the spire being defective as well as the anterior end of the canal. The last whorl measures 75 mm. in total length, with a maximum diameter of about 47 mm., a large part of the shell being densely incrusted with a heavy layer of fossilized polyzoon.

The specimen figured has much the aspect of *Turris coosensis*, and I was at first tempted to refer it to that species. On more mature consideration it was decided that the two were probably distinct, the present specimen having stronger ribbing, which persists on the last whorl, rather coarser spiral sculpture, and a general aspect decidedly more fusoid than the *Turris*. So far as the incremental lines can be made out on the upper border of the whorl, they do not show the characteristic sinus of the other species.

Family BUCCINIDÆ.

Subfamily CHRYSODOMINÆ.

Genus CHRYSODOMUS Swainson.

Chrysodomus Swainson, Malac., pp. 90, 308, 1840; type, *Murex antiquus* Linné; Dall, Proc. U. S. Nat. Mus., XXIV, No. 1264, p. 520, 1902.

CHRYSODOMUS IMPERIALIS Dall, n. sp.

Pl. VII, figs. 1, 3; Pl. XVIII, fig. 1.

Shell globose, very thick and heavy, with four or five well-rounded rapidly increasing whorls; last whorl comprising most of the shell; surface sculptured with obscure little elevated rounded axial ridges, irregular in size and distribution, from the posterior ends of which narrow, sharp, oblique, somewhat irregular laminæ extend across the suture to the preceding whorl, giving the effect of a rude fringe or series of "gathers;" posterior surface of the whorl otherwise smooth, the anterior surface in front of the periphery with little elevated, rather sparse spiral threads, which, as usual, grow coarser though not more crowded toward the canal; canal deep, very short, hardly recurved, with hardly any trace of a siphonal fasciole; aperture wide, ovate, the pillar short, thick, the body with a moderately short callus, the outer lip hardly reflected, somewhat thickened. Altitude of figured specimen, 52 mm.; maximum diameter, 42 mm.

Miocene of Coos Bay, Empire formation, collected by B. H. Camman; U. S. Nat. Mus. 153897. Lower Purisima formation, Santa Cruz County, Cal., Ralph Arnold.

Five specimens of this singular species were obtained. All had been somewhat worn before fossilization. They resemble a recent species now existing in Bering Sea, in some respects, but the latter is less heavy, has a more prominent and recurved canal, and is without the ribs or the curious sutural lamellation.

The California specimen is less worn than those from Oregon, and preserves the spiral sculpture over the whole shell, there being more than 20 spiral cords on the last whorl, pretty evenly distributed. These cords are flattened and separated by wider subequal interspaces.

CHRYSODOMUS POSTPLANATUS Dall, n. sp.

Pl. VII, fig. 5.

Shell large, solid, strong, with about 7 tabulated whorls; spire rather elevated, as in *C. liratus* Martyn, with a well-defined suture, in front of which the margin is somewhat appressed, then descends to a flattish tabulation bordered anteriorly by a conspicuous angle of about 90°, in front of which the whorl exhibits a moderate convexity extending to the base; the surface is more or less distinctly sculptured by flat straplike spirals, separated by much narrower interspaces, which are filled by a much smaller spiral of the same character in some specimens, while in others the intercalary spiral may be wanting or the whole sculpture, as in the figured specimen, more or less obsolete; the axial sculpture comprises only more or less conspicuous incremental lines; canal short, somewhat recurved; aperture defective in the specimens. Altitude of figured specimen, 90 mm.; maximum diameter, 50 mm.

Figured specimen from beds believed to be of similar age to the Empire formation, on Bogachiel River, Clallam County, Wash., 1 mile above its mouth, collected by Ralph Arnold; U. S. Nat. Mus. 107781.

The figured specimen has had part of the spire completely decorticated and the shell has been more or less crushed, but preserves the characters sufficiently for description. A fragment from the same locality shows better-developed alternated sculpture. A curious feature is that the inner layers of the shell, where exposed, show zigzag structure recalling that of wave lines as often seen in sand rock built up by wave action. The lines of growth in the outer layer show only normal curves.

CHRYSODOMUS BAIRDII Dall, n. sp.

Pl. II, fig. 4.

Shell of moderate size, with about 5 tabulate whorls; apex defective in the specimens; suture narrowly channeled, with a single spiral cord in front of the channel, the tabulation slightly excavated and bordered in front by a similar spiral ridge which forms the summit of the shoulder of the whorl; below the shoulder the whorl is moderately convex and spirally sculptured by slightly elevated, alternating revolving ridges, of which one at the periphery is slightly more conspicuous than the others; these ridges, alternately larger and smaller, are separated by linear interspaces, and the larger spirals become more conspicuous anteriorly; aperture wide, angulated by the carina at the shoulder; canal defective in all the specimens; pillar callous, smooth. Altitude of figured specimen, 46 mm.; maximum diameter, 28 mm.

Miocene of Coos Bay, Empire formation, collected by B. II. Camman; U. S. Nat. Mus. 153905. Also from the upper Purisima formation of California, Ralph Arnold.

The specimen figured is partly an internal cast upon which, from a less perfect one, the sculpture has been restored. The species is evidently a precursor of the recent *Chrysodomus tabulatus* Baird, from which it differs by its shorter and rounder whorls, by the details of its sculpture, and by its greater constriction at the suture. It is named in honor of that author.

Genus LIOMESUS Stimpson.

Liomesus Stimpson, Can. Nat., n. s., II, p. 364, 1865.
Buccinopsis Jeffreys, not of Conrad.

It is interesting to find this genus, which is especially notable in the northwest-coast fauna, fossil and characteristic as long ago as the time of the Oregon Miocene. The British Crag affords *L. dalei* Sowerby, and *L. eburnea* Sars is a member of the Norwegian fauna coming as far south as the Doggerbank in the North Sea, but the three or four living American species are not reported from any locality south of the Aleutians.

LIOMESUS SULCULATUS Dall, n. sp.

Pl. V, figs. 2. 3.

Shell of moderate size, with about five well-rounded whorls; suture distinct, not channeled; sculpture of (on the last whorl about 15) clear-cut, uniform, flat-topped spiral ridges with equal or wider, not channeled, interspaces; the whole surface marked with very fine, almost microscopic spiral striation, which in the event of wear may disappear; the posterior ridge may be near the suture (giving a channeled aspect) or at some little distance from it; in general the interspaces become narrow anteriorly; aperture ovate, the pillar rather callous, the body with more or less callus, both smooth; the canal short, deep. Altitude of figured specimen, the apex being defective, 33 mm.; maximum diameter, 22.5 mm.

Miocene of Coos Bay Empire beds, collected by B. II. Camman; U. S. Nat. Mus. 153904. Also from the upper Miocene beds at Fossil Point, Coos Bay, by W. II. Dall.

Five specimens of this species were obtained, none of which retained the apex and only one the outer coat of the shell. It is nearest to *Liomesus canaliculatus* Dall, from the recent fauna of Bering Sea, a species in which the spire is proportionately much shorter and the sculpture quite different. Another species was obtained from the Miocene of Clallam Bay, Washington, by Arnold, characterized by a very different sculpture, having subnodulous sparse spiral cords with fine close-set spiral threads occupying the wide interspaces. The horizon of this species is earlier than that of the sandstones of Coos Bay above referred to, in which *L. sulculatus* occurs, but the the Miocene faunas of this region are, as yet, insufficiently known to afford a basis for exact correlation.

Family NASSIDÆ.

Genus MOLOPOPHORUS Gabb.

Molopophorus Gabb, Pal. California, II, p. 156, 1868; type, *Bullia (Molopophorus) striata* Gabb, op. cit., pl. 26, fig. 36; Tejon (Eocene) of California.

MOLOPOPHORUS GABBI Dall, n. sp.

Pl. III, fig. 8.

Shell small, stout, solid, of four and a half strongly sculptured whorls; apex smooth, of about two whorls, the nucleus normal, rather large for the size of the shell; subsequent whorls with a rounded cord in front of the suture, which at first is rather closely beaded; the nodules, however, become less close set and more spinose with growth, and on the last whorl, in some specimens, even sharply prominent and their number about a dozen; in front of this nodulous cord (which differs in prominence in different individuals) the whorl is more or less constricted; on the periphery are more or less prominent axial ribs, obsolete on the base, with wider interspaces, in number equal to the sutural nodulations, in strength variable with the individual; some specimens (like that figured) there may be on each rib two, or on others four, sharp subspinose nodulations, corresponding to spiral sculpture which is obsolete in the interspaces; both nodules and ribs may become obsolete near the aperture; base rounded with more or less obscure spiral threads; suture well marked, deep, but usually obscured by threadlike callosities which overrun it; canal very short, deeply excavated and recurved, producing a strong siphonal fasciole consisting of two sharp ridges and an intervening rather deep, smoothly excavated channel; aperture narrow behind, with a simple, sharp, outer lip; the body with a thin, widely extended callus, extending from the end of the canal nearly to the suture and over more than one-fourth of the last whorl. Altitude, 19 mm.; maximum diameter, 12 mm.

Eocene of Pittsburg, Columbia County, Oreg., collected by J. S. Diller at station 2714; U. S. Nat. Mus. 107377.

The three specimens collected show a wide range of variation in the strength of their sculpture. This and one or two other unpublished species of Oregonian fossils are included here, though not of the Coos Bay fauna, in order to put them on record.

Family MURICIDÆ.

Subfamily MURICINÆ.

Genus PURPURA Martyn.

Purpura Martyn, Univ. Conch., II, table and pl. 66, 1784; sole example, *Purpura foliata* Martyn, *loc. cit.;* not *Purpura* (Brug.) Lamarck, 1799.

Murex (sp.) Gmelin, Syst. Nat., VI, p. 3529, 1792.

Purpura Donovan, Nat. Rep., I, pl. 15, September, 1822.

Cerostoma Conrad, Jour. Acad. Nat. Sci. Philadelphia, VII, p. 263, 1837; not of Latreille, 1802.

Pterorhytis Conrad, Proc. Acad. Nat. Sci. Philadelphia for 1862, p. 560; Dall, Trans. Wagner Inst., III, pt. 1, p. 143, 1890.

Purpura Dall, Proc. Biol. Soc. Washington, XVIII, p. 189, 1905; Proc. U. S. Nat. Mus., XXIX, p. 427, 1905.

I have fully explained elsewhere in this paper (p. 47) why it is necessary to give up the Lamarckian use of the name *Purpura* and return to the usage of the ancients who applied the name to various purpuriferous Muricidæ. The shells long called *Purpura* in the Lamarckian sense will take the name of *Thais* Bolten, and the northern *Polytropa*, better known as *Purpura*, though not typical Lamarckian species, will be called *Nucella* Bolten.

PURPURA PERPONDEROSA Dall, n. sp.

Pl. II, figs. 2, 5.

Shell large, very heavy, with about four whorls exclusive of the nucleus; with three thick varices continuous up the spire, probably sharp edged when intact, but rounded by wear in the type specimen; spiral sculpture of (on the early whorls two, on the last whorl four or five) distant, moderately elevated, spiral cords; aperture large, the outer lip denticulate within, with a projecting spine or tooth anteriorly; body with a callous deposit, canal short, nearly closed, sutures obscure. Altitude, 73 mm.; maximum diameter, 41 mm.

Miocene of Coos Bay, Empire formation, collected by B. H. Camman; U. S. Nat. Mus. 107778.

The single specimen of this species obtained is much worn, as the figures indicate, but by a careful study of it the above data were secured.

It is, of course, the precursor of *Purpura foliata* Martyn, the common species of the Oregonian fauna of the present day, but it is larger, heavier, and more massive than any living species of its group.

Genus THAIS Bolten.

Purpura (ex parte) Bruguière, Encycl. Méth., I, p. xv, 1789 (not *Purpura* Martyn, 1784); no species cited.

Thais Bolten. Mus. Boltenianum, p. 54, 1798; first species, *Purpura neritoides* Lamarck (= *Murex fucus* Gmelin, 1792); Link, Beschr. Rostock Samml., p. 114, 1807; not *Thais* Fabricius, 1808.

Nucella Bolten (ex parte. *Cancellaria* olim). Mus. Boltenianum, p. 131, 1798; *Purpura filosa* Menke = *P. lapillus* L. var.

Nassa (sp.) Bolten. Mus. Boltenianum, p. 132, 1798; *Purpura lapillus* Linné; not *Nassa* Lamarck. 1799.

Purpura Lamarck (not Martyn), Prodrome, p. 71, 1799; sole example, *P. persica* (Linné).

Purpurarius Duméril, Zool. Anal., p. 166, 1806; nomenclature not Linnean; Froriep's German transl., p. 167 (*P. persica* cited), 1806.

Mancinella Link, Beschr. Rostock Samml., p. 115, 1807; first species, *Murex mancinella* Gmelin.

Stramonita Schumacher, Essai, p. 226, 1817; type. *Purpura hæmastoma* Lamarck.

Microtoma Swainson. Malac., pp. 72, 301, 1840; first species, *Purpura patula* Lam.; not *Microtoma* Laporte, 1833.

Purpura (sp.) Swainson, Malac., p. 301, 1840; *P. coronata* and *P. succincta* Lam.

Trochia Swainson, Malac., p. 302, 1840; sole example, *Purpura trochlea* Lam. (= *Purpura cingulata* Linné).

Polytropa Swainson, Malac., pp. 81, 305, 1840; type, *Purpura crispata* Chemn. (= *Purpura lamellosa* Gmelin).

Tribulus H. and A. Adams, Gen. Rec. Moll., I, p. 126, 1853; = *Thais* H. and A. Adams, op. cit., II. p. 655, 1858.

Thalessa H. and A. Adams, Gen. Rec. Moll., I, p. 127, 1853; = *Mancinella* Link.

Cronia H. and A. Adams, Gen. Rec. Moll., I, p. 128, 1853; sole example, *Purpura amygdala* Kiener.

Pinaxia A. Adams, Proc. Zool. Soc. London for 1853, p. 185, type. *Purpura coronata* A. Adams.

Adamsia Dunker, Proc. Zool. Soc. London for 1856, p. 357; type, *A. typica* Dunker; not of Forbes, 1840.

Canrena H. and A. Adams, Gen. Rec. Moll., II, p. 655, 1858; not of Link, 1807.

Purpurella Dall, Am. Jour. Conch., VII, p. 110, 1871; type, *Purpura columellaris* Lam.; not of Desvoidy, 1853, nor of Bellardi, 1882.

Agnewia Tenison-Wood, Proc. Roy. Soc. Tasmania for 1877, p. 29; new name for *Adamsia* Dunker, not Forbes.

Nacella (Bolten) Mörch, Cat. Yoldi, p. 101, 1852; err. typ. pro *Nucella* Bolten, not *Nacella* Schumacher, 1817.

Taurasia Bellardi, Moll. Terz. Piem. e Lig., III, p. 194, 1882; first species, *Purpura subfusiformis* Orb., op. cit., pl. 11, fig. 31.

Tribulus Tryon, Syst. Conch., II, p. 110, 1883; *Purpura planospira* Lam.

Purpurella Bellardi (not Dall or Desvoidy), Moll. Terz. Piem. e Lig., III, p. 193, 1882; sole example, *P. canaliculata* Bellardi, op. cit., pl. 11, fig. 35.

Lepsia Hutton, Trans. New Zealand Inst., XVI, p. 222, 1883; *Purpura haustrum* Martyn.

Planithais (Bayle, 1884) in Fischer, Man. de Conchyl., p. 645, 1884; *Purpura planospira* Lam.=*Tribulus* Adams.

Simplicotaurasia Sacco, Cat. Pal. Bac. Terz. Piem., No. 3081, 1890; Moll. Terz. Piem. e Lig., XXX, p. 74, 1904; new name for *Purpurella* Bellardi, not Dall.

Polytropalicus Rovereto, Atti Soc. Lig., X (p. 5 of extras), 1899; new name for *Polytropa* Swainson, not of Defrance.

Microstoma Cossmann, Essais Pal. Comp., V, p. 71, 1903; lapsus for *Microtoma* Swainson.

Plicopurpura Cossmann, Essais Pal. Comp., V, p. 69, 1903; new name for *Purpurella* Dall, not Desvoidy.

* * *

Nassa Bolten, Mus. Boltenianum, p. 132, 1798; type, *Purpura sertum* Lam.; not *Nassa* Lamarck, Prodrome, 1799.

Iopas H. and A. Adams, Gen. Rec. Moll., I, p. 128, 1853; first species and type. *P. sertum* Lam.

* * *

Cuma Swainson, Malac., pp. 87, 307, 1840; sole example. *C. sulcata* Sw.; not *Cuma* Milne-Edwards, 1828, nor of the Mus. Calonnianum, 1797.

Cymia Mörch, Malak. Blatt., VII, p. 98, 1861; new name for *Cuma* Swainson.

Tritonopsis Conrad, Am. Jour. Conch., I, p. 20, 1865; type and sole example. *Triton subalveatum* Conrad, Oligocene of Vicksburg.

Fasciolina Conrad, Am. Jour. Conch., III, p. 186, 1867; sole example. *Fasciolaria woodi* Gabb, Oligocene of New Jersey.

Cumopsis Rovereto, Atti Soc. Lig., X (p. 5 of extras), 1899; new name for *Cuma* Swainson (=*Cymia* Mörch).

Cymia Dall, Trans. Wagner Inst., III, p. 154, 1890; Cossmann, Essais Pal. Comp., V, p. 74, 1903.

The discussion of the genus generally known as *Purpura* Bruguière involves two phases—that of the actual characters of the animals themselves and the history of the systematic names which have been applied to them. For the former a careful study was made of about 50 species in the collection of the National Museum, and the several characters of each were tabulated, thus showing the constancy of each character in the group and the way in which certain characters intergrade among the species. Of the second phase the preceding synonymy is a summary which may be dismissed with a few explanatory remarks.

The genus *Thais* of Bolten is well constituted, containing a very uniform assembly of species which, with the single exception of a closely related *Acanthina*, will remain in the genus as at present understood. The name *Purpura*, as elsewhere explained, is preoccupied for a group of Murices, in conformity with the usage of the ancients as well as the early conchologists. It can not in any event be used for the present group with regard to the accepted rules for nomenclature. Bolten's genus included the large low-spired tropical forms, while the smaller and more fusiform northern species, called by Swainson *Polytropa*, were relegated to another group, *Nucella* Bolten, or to a third group, *Nassa* Bolten. *Nucella* is the prior name in the book, and by eliminating the earlier-named generic forms first, and thus fixing the name *Nucella* on the well-known *Purpura lapillus*, we are enabled to preserve the Lamarckian genus *Cancellaria*, which by the "first species" rule would have to take the name of *Nucella*.

Nucella thus takes the place of *Polytropa* Swainson and leaves the first and only remaining identifiable species of the Boltenian *Nassa* to bear that name. This species is the *Purpura sertum* of Lamarck, which had been separated by the brothers Adams under the name of *Iopas*. Lamarck's Nassas will carry a different name.

The remainder of the synonymy is self-explanatory, but it may be remarked that Swainson's reference of his genus *Cuma* to the authorship of Humphrey is erroneous. *Cuma* of the Museum Calonnianum (which was not written by Humphrey) is a compound of *Fasciolaria*, *Mitra*, and *Latirus*, and does not contain the species to which Swainson gave the name of *Cuma*. The anonymous author of the Museum Calonnianum, a few years later, in a reprint of part of the work for commercial purposes (issued without date or name of author or publisher) rejected his name *Cuma* and substituted *Unda* (reprint, p. 12), but neither have any just claim to be cited in anything except a purely historical synonymy.

The genus *Thais* will comprise even more than was supposed by its author. Many of the characters which have been relied on to separate the Lamarckian Purpuras into sections, subgenera, and even genera are of little physiologic or systematic importance, and are interchanged with remarkable freedom and almost numberless combinations among the several species. The small lirations or tubercles on the pillar near its anterior end are often present or absent indifferently in specimens of the same species, or even in the same individual at different ages, and are of vastly different value from the permanent plaits on the pillar, which are present at all ages of the individual. The sculpture is also, as is well known, liable to vary from smooth to imbricate or nodulous within the limits of the species. Certain forms, however, seem to have a constant and permanent type of sculpture, like *T. patula* and its close allies. Some of the species which live between tides have become modified in the direction of the limpet-like form best suited for such situations, the spire becoming short, the last whorl domelike, the pillar excavated, and the siphonal canal and fasciole almost obsolete. These changes are obviously adaptations to a relatively sedentary condition.

The prevalent sculpture in the group is spiral, modified into ridges, scales, nodes, or even spines. In only one group, *Cronia*, is regular axial ribbing a permanent feature of the shell. With the exception of the *Nucella* group, all the species have a subsutural groove, usually accompanied by a parietal elevated ridge parallel to the suture; in this groove the rectal tube lies and ejects effete matter, so it may save trouble to call the ridge the anal ridge, as it must be frequently mentioned. In many species, at the end of the groove, there is a sharp sulcus or notch in the edge of the outer lip close to the suture, by which, as in *Turris*, the feces may be ejected without fouling the water retained between the mantle and the rock on which the creature is seated, while the tide is out. In more active forms the groove may be merely prolonged without a sulcus and even without a developed anal ridge, while in *Nucella* there is neither sulcus, ridge, nor groove. The latter is also without liration inside the outer lip, having at most a few obscure tubercles at the adult stage within the margin. In the tropical forms it is not uncommon to find a few weak liræ on the anterior part of the pillar. In a very few species the smooth pillar has developed a keel on the edge bordering on the canal, and in *Nassa* (*Iopas*) a deposit of callus at this point and at the end of the anal ridge is supplemented by a similar deposit on the lip opposite, thus contracting the aperture and giving a peculiar aspect to the shell without in reality introducing any new feature of importance.

The genus *Purpurella* Bellardi (not Dall) was founded on a fossil possessing a subsutural groove and anal ridge with a smooth pillar; Bellardi's *Taurasia* was proposed for a species adding to these characters feeble lirations on the anterior part of the pillar. Both these characters occur indiscriminately among the species of *Cronia* as well as of other groups into which *Thais* is subdivided, so they can not be regarded as sufficient basis for a genus, to say nothing of the subfamily which a later writer has proposed for them.

The typical *Thais* has a broad pillar which is flattened or even concave; in the section *Tribulus*, as restricted by Chenu, the concavity is enlarged into an excavation, and strong dark-colored lirations are spread over the anterior surface of the pillar. There are, however, no true plications in this case.

In *Patellipurpura* the concavely arcuate smooth pillar is flattened and a thin callus with a sharply crenate edge is spread over its anterior portion and to the left of it, the siphonal canal is obsolete, and there is a small but sharply cut notch in the lip at the suture.

Closely allied in habit and in surface characters is *Plicopurpura* (*columellaris*), which has no notch and in which the aperture is contracted, dentate, and coarsely lirate, while a shallow subsutural groove is present. On the middle of the pillar a somewhat amorphous duplex thickened ridge winds into the spire, but there are no anterior lirations on the inner edge of the pillar. In *T. neritoidea* Lamarck, the type of *Thais*, there are no lirations, while the closely related *T. aperta* develops them distinctly.

These instances show the inadvisability of basing systematic divisions on minor characters without extensive comparisons. Several species which have been commonly associated with *Cymia* differ from *Stramonita* chiefly by the imbricated suture, a character of little importance, while they are entirely destitute of the chief characteristic feature of *Cymia*, the sharp, strong keel on the middle of the pillar. *Pinaxia* appears to be simply a diminutive *Thais* with a pillar lirate like that of *aperta* but, relatively to the size of the shell, more sharply. The operculum is exactly that of *Thais*. I have been tempted to propose a section for *T. melones* Duclos, *T. deltoidea* Lamarck, and one or two other short, heavy species with feeble sculpture, smooth pillar keeled at the canal, and low spire; but the fact that some allied species tend toward without attaining a pillar keel, has led me to omit it.

The operculum and soft parts of *Vexilla* are insufficiently known for its final classification.

The arrangement of the group adopted is as follows:

Genus CYMIA Mörch, 1861.

Type *C. tectum* Wood.

Genus THAIS Bolten, 1798.

Subgenus THAIS Bolten.

    Section *Thais s. s.* *T. neritoides* (Lamarck).
    Section *Tribulus* (Adams, 1853) Chenu. *T. planispira* (Lamarck).
    Section *Pinaxia.* A. Adams, 1853. *T. coronata* A. Adams.[a]
    Section *Mancinella* Link, 1807. *T. mancinella* (Gmelin).
    Section *Stramonita* Swainson, 1840. *T. hæmastoma* (Lamarck).
    Section *Lepsia* Hutton, 1883. *T. haustrum* (Martyn).
    Section *Patellipurpura* Dall (nov.). *T. patula* (Lamarck).
    Section *Plicopurpura* Cossmann, 1903. *T. columellaris* (Lam.)

Subgenus NASSA Bolten, 1798 (not Lamarck, 1799).

Type *T. sertum* (Lamarck)

Subgenus CRONIA Adams, 1853.

Type *T. amygdala* (Kiener).

Subgenus NUCELLA Bolten, 1798.

    Section *Nucella s. s.* *T. lapillus* (Linné).
    Section *Trochia* Swainson, 1840. *T. cingulata* (Linné).

In the north temperate region only species belonging to the subgenus *Nucella* are found living, and in America so far, north of Florida Strait, only *Cymia* and *Nucella* have been found fossil.

The following species is one of the most characteristic among those found living in the Oregonian fauna of the northwest coast of America:

THAIS (NUCELLA) LAMELLOSA Gmelin.

Buccinum plicatum Martyn, Univ. Conch., II, pl. 44, 1786; not of Linné, 1758.

Buccinum lamellosum Gmelin, Syst. Nat., VI, p. 3498, 1792; Schreibers, Vers. ein vollst. Conch., I, p. 166, 1793; Bolten, Mus. Boltenianum, p. 113, 1798; 2d ed., p. 80. pl. 1. fig. 1435. 1819; Dillwyn, Descr. Cat. Rec. Sh., II, p. 662, 1817.

Buccinum compositum Chemnitz, Conch. Cab., X, p. 179. vign. 21. figs. A, B, 1788; nomenclature not Linnean.

Buccinum crispatum Chemnitz, Conch. Cab., XI, pp. 70, 84, pl. 187. figs. 1802-1803. 1795.

Murex crispatus Lamarck, Anim. s. Vert., VII. p. 174. 1822; Encycl. Méth., pl. 419. fig. 2. 1816; Deshayes's Lam., Anim. s. Vert., IX, p. 576,1845.

Murex lactuca Eschscholtz, Zool. Atlas, II, p. 11, pl. 9, figs. 3a, 3b, 1829.

Murex ferrugineus Eschscholtz, Zool. Atlas, II, p. 10, figs. 2a, 2b, 1829.

Polytropa crispata Swainson, Malac., p. 305, 1840.

Purpura septentrionalis Reeve, Conch. Icon., III, *Purpura.* pl. 10, fig. 50. 1846.

Murex lactuca Middendorff, Beitr. Mal. Ross., II, p. 120, pl. 7, figs. 1-2. 1849; Fischer in Pinart. Voy. N. W. côte Am., p. 38, pl. E, figs. 4, 4a, 1875.

Purpura crispata Carpenter, Rept. Brit. Assoc. for 1863, p. 622, 1864; Keep, West Coast Shells, p. 32, fig. 13, 1887; Arnold, Pal. and Strat. San Pedro, p. 261. 1903.

Purpura plicata Martens, Mal. Blatt., XIX, p. 86, 1872.

Purpura lapillus var. *crispata* Tryon, Man. Conch., II, pp. 171-229. pl. 54. figs. 163-166. 1880.

Pliocene of San Diego and San Mateo counties, Cal.: Arnold. Pleistocene of California from San Diego to Santa Barbara, Cooper; and of Coos Bay, Oregon, Dall. Living from Santa Barbara, Cal., northward to the Aleutian Islands, Dall; most abundantly in the Vancouver region.

[a] *T. adamsi* Dall; not *Purpura coronata* Lamarck, 1822.

THAIS (NUCELLA) PRECURSOR Dall, n. sp.

Pl. IV, fig. 4.

Shell solid, subglobose, with four rapidly enlarging whorls; nucleus small, rather blunt; suture distinct, whorls evenly rounded; sculpture more or less variable but usually of simple, little-elevated spiral cords with narrower interspaces crossed by more or less evident lines of growth; aperture ovate, outer lip thickened but slightly reflected; body smooth; pillar short, concavely arcuate, moderately callous, and slightly flattened; behind the callus a narrow closed umbilical chink, and a strong, prominent, rounded siphonal fasciole; canal short, deeply indented. Altitude, 32 mm.; maximum diameter, 25 mm.

Fossil Rock, Coos Bay, in the Pleistocene conglomerate overlying the Miocene sandstone, collected by W. H. Dall; U. S. Nat. Mus. 153995 and 153924.

This species is doubtless a precursor of the variable form from the recent fauna commonly known by the name *Purpura emarginata* Deshayes. Yet a careful comparison with a large series of recent specimens from the adjacent region failed to disclose any which might reasonably be considered identical. Indeed, there are varieties of the Atlantic *T. lapillus* which more nearly approach it than any of the Pacific forms. Tryon indiscriminately "lumped" all the Northwest American Nucellas with *T. lapillus*, but there is only one species, *T. lamellosa*, which is closely related to *lapillus*. It alone among the forms of this region shows obscure denticulation within the aperture, as does *T. lapillus;* the other species uniformly have the aperture unarmed.

Genus STREPSIDURA Swainson.

STREPSIDURA OREGONENSIS Dall, n. sp.

Pl. III, fig. 6.

Shell small, short, stout, rather heavy for its size, with five and a half whorls; last whorl much the largest, with one small and two large revolving ridges, the posterior of which tends to tabulate the whorl; edges of the whorl in front of the appressed suture slightly swollen, the space between it and the shoulder of the whorl somewhat concave; the space between the shoulder and the next anterior revolving ridge also moderately excavated, and similarly between the anterior ridge and the canal; axial sculpture of about 17 longitudinal ridges, flexuous behind the shoulder, obsolete between the spiral ridges and on the base, more or less nodulous on the spiral ridges as figured; apical whorls nearly smooth; subsequent whorls spirally sculptured with fine, more or less alternated, sometimes paired threads; canal short, flexuous, with a strong siphonal fasciole; pillar and body conspicuously callous; outer lip defective in the specimen; callosity smooth, with no trace of an umbilical chink. Altitude, 30 mm.; maximum diameter, 21 mm.

Eocene of Pittsburg, Columbia County, Oreg., collected by J. S. Diller at station 2714; U. S. Nat. Mus. 107395.

Owing to the fact that the aperture is completely filled with a flinty matrix, it is impossible to say whether this species has the plications, usual to the type of *Strepsidura*, on the edge of the pillar. The general aspect of the shell is so like that of *S. turgidus*, however, that the reference is made provisionally, and subject to correction with further material.

Superfamily PTENOGLOSSA.

Family SCALIDÆ.

Genus EPITONIUM Bolten.

Scala (anonymous), Mus. Calonnianum, p. 23, 1797; type, *Turbo scalaris* Linné.
Epitonium (first section) Bolten, Mus. Boltenianum, p. 91, 1798; first species, *Turbo scalaris* Gmelin.
Cyclostoma Lamarck. Prodrome. p. 74, 1799; type and sole example, *Turbo scalaris* Linné.
Scala Dall, Bull. Mus. Comp. Zool., XVIII, p. 299. 1889.

Eighteen years ago I discussed the synonymy of these shells and showed that if the rules of the British Association, as originally promulgated, were followed we should have to call the wentletraps by the name *Cyclostoma* Lamarck. If we overlook the absence of a diagnosis, as is now generally accepted as allowable, Bolten's name *Epitonium* is available. The anonymous *Scala* appeared in a sale catalogue which indicated no publisher, and if we continue to use it we can do so only by disregarding the rules. This is probably inadvisable, as the break with the irregular nomenclature would have to come sooner or later, and it is probably best to have it over and done with. If we do not do so, the evil day is only postponed.

Subgenus OPALIA H. and A. Adams.

Opalia H. and A. Adams, Gen. Rec. Moll., I, p. 222, 1853, first species, *Scalaria australis* Lamarck.

Shell with the whorls united, the varices strong and riblike; no umbilical perforation or spiral sculpture; a basal disk present; the shell structure massive, and the coloration usually pure white.

Clathrus Oken, 1815, sometimes cited as a synonym of *Opalia*, is an exact synonym of *Epitonium* Bolten, 1798, and *Cyclostoma* Lamarck, 1799.

EPITONIUM (OPALIA) RUGIFERUM Dall, n. sp.

Pl. III, fig. 10.

Shell large, strong, stout, with seven or eight well-rounded whorls, crossed by (on each) about 13 stout, axially rugose varices, which are continuous up the spire, being appressed at the suture; the only spiral sculpture consists of a stout thread circumscribing the base and becoming embedded under the well-marked suture with the growth of the whorls; apex lost; spire rather acute, rapidly enlarging; aperture oval; varices less than half as wide as the interspaces, somewhat excavated on the posterior side. Length of seven whorls 60 mm.; diameter at truncate apex 4 mm.; maximum diameter of last whorl, 24 mm.

Pliocene of Rock Creek, Columbia County, Oreg.; J. S. Diller; U. S. Nat. Mus. 135121.

This fine species is nearly related to the ribbed form of *Opalia varicostata* Stearns, from the Pliocene of San Diego. Cal., but is more evenly ribbed, while the size of the whorls increases much more rapidly so as to make the shell less slender and the spire angle wider for the same length of shell.

Subgenus ARCTOSCALA Dall, nov.

Shell ashy, unpolished, not umbilicate, with numerous low reflected varices, a marked basal disk, and strong spiral sculpture, the varices appressed at the suture. Type, *Scalaria greenlandica* Perry, Conch., expl. pl. 28, No. 8, 1811.

This group differs from the polished white species of the Tropics, which have a somewhat similar sculpture, sufficiently to deserve a distinct name.

EPITONIUM (ARCTOSCALA) CONDONI Dall, n. sp..

Pl. III, figs. 1, 12.

Shell large, strong, elongated, with about 15 varices to the whorl, crossed by 10 or more little-elevated sharp narrow spirals, with wider interspaces occupied by faint spiral striæ; whorls eight or more, rather inflated, closely adherent, with their greatest diameter somewhat in front of the middle of the whorl; no umbilicus; varices similar, usually equidistant, striate or rugose axially and continuous with those of the preceding whorl; the angle at the front of the junction with the preceding whorl filled with a callous deposit; the interspaces are about twice as wide as the varices, the spiral sculpture sharp but not conspicuous, being more crowded toward the suture, especially in front of it; in well-preserved specimens they seem to crenulate the edges of the varices; aperture somewhat higher than wide; base (so far as observed) without any disk or bounding keel. Length of eight whorls, 73 mm.; maximum diameter, 22 mm.; diameter at truncated apex, 4 mm. Altitude of figured specimens, 32 and 70 mm.

Miocene of Eugene, Oreg.; also of Rock Creek, Columbia County, Oreg., W. H. Dall; U. S. Nat. Mus. 135122 and 107398. Fragments perhaps of this species were noticed in the Miocene sandstone of Coos Bay.

The species is named in honor of the late Prof. Thomas Condon, of the State University at Eugene, Oreg., well known for his paleontological researches and the generous manner in which he extended to students the use of his fine collection.

E. condoni recalls *E. greenlandicum* Perry, except that the spirals are very small keels rather than broad elevated bands. It attains a much larger size than any specimens of *E. greenlandicum* recorded. A form much nearer the latter was found by Madden in the Miocene beds of Controller Bay, Alaska, having about 11 varices to the whorl, which are slightly crenulated by the spiral sculpture. This species is more broadly conical than the recent *E. greenlandicum*.

Subgenus CATENOSCALA Dall, nov.

Shell resembling *Arctoscala*, but with a broad band of enamel laid over the anterior half of the whorl, covering both the spiral sculpture and the varices.

Type, *Catenoscala oregonensis* Dall; Miocene of Oregon.

The presence of this band of enamel is a feature quite new to the family and probably of generic significance, but the specimens in my possession are not sufficiently perfect to show the whole shell and, until the complete characters can be stated, it is probably best to regard it as a subgenus.

EPITONIUM (CATENOSCALA) OREGONENSE Dall, n. sp.

Pl. III, fig. 3.

Shell resembling *E. condoni*, but differing by its nearly flat *Terebra*-like whorls with two more varices to the whorl, and by a band of callus extending from the suture over the preceding whorl and its varices to the periphery of the whorl, covering about half the exposed portion of the whorl and on the earlier whorls even more than half; the younger whorls show little or no spiral sculpture and it is quite faint on the later whorls of the adult, where the edges of the varices seem to exhibit little or no crenation.   Length of two whorls, 20 mm.; least diameter of the upper whorl (of the two), 12 mm.; greatest diameter of the second whorl, 15.5 mm.   Altitude of figured specimen, 32 mm.

Miocene of Eugene, Oreg., W. H. Dall, U. S. Nat. Mus. 135123; and of the east side of Scow Bay, southeast of Port Townsend, Wash., near the west side of Oak Bay, Puget Sound, J. C. Merriam.

This species is quite peculiar in its callosity, no recent or fossil species known to me showing anything similar.   It might perhaps be regarded as an extension of the deposit mentioned in connection with the varices of *E. condoni*, but even so it is practically unique.   The presence of these very large forms of *Epitonium* is one of the characteristics of the Oregonian Miocene.

Superfamily TÆNIOGLOSSA.

Family SEPTIDÆ.

Genus GYRINEUM Link.

Gyrineum Link, Beschr. Rostock Samml., p. 123, 1807.   Type. *Murex gyrinus* Linné; Dall. Smithsonian Misc. Coll. (quarterly issue). XLVII, No. 1475. p. 131, 1904.

This genus includes the Tritons with continuous lateral varices.

GYRINEUM MEDIOCRE Dall, n. sp.

Pl. VII, fig. 6.

Shell large, solid, with five or more whorls and heavy prominent, rounded, continuous lateral varices; suture distinct with a narrow tabulation just in front of it; whorls rotund, canal short with no marked fasciole or sulcus behind it; axial sculpture of small rounded riblets (about 15 between the varices on the penultimate whorl), which on the upper whorls extend from suture to suture, on the later whorls become obsolete soon after passing the angle of the tabulation which they usually nodulate, and are more or less obsolescent on the last half of the last whorl in some specimens, while in the variety (see Pl. VII, fig. 9) they are more or less persistent; spiral sculpture of (on the penultimate whorl about 17) sulci alternately feeble and strong, as usual stronger on the canal; the interspaces are broad, flat, and finely spirally striate, except on the canal, where they become rounded and rugose or even beaded; canal short with a deep indentation, recurved, but without a marked sulcus behind it; varices heavy behind, with no sutural canal, more slender in front, denticulate within; a rather pronounced callus on the body and pillar; details of the aperture obscured by matrix. Altitude of figured specimen, 44 mm.; of a larger one, about 60 mm.; maximum diameter, respectively 30 and 43 mm.

Miocene of Coos Bay, Oregon, purchased from B. H. Camman; U. S. Nat. Mus. 153900. Also upper Miocene of Bogachiel River, Washington, Arnold.

GYRINEUM (MEDIOCRE var. ?) CORBICULATUM Dall, nov.

Pl. VII, fig. 9.

This has the general form of the preceding and differs from it chiefly in being less compressed and with less prominent varices, the riblets continuous over the last whorl, the spiral bands more numerous and narrower, separated by excavated channels instead of narrow sulci. The specimen is rather poorly preserved. Altitude, 70 mm.; maximum diameter, 42 mm.

Locality the same as the preceding; U. S. Nat. Mus. 153870

Genus ARGOBUCCINUM Mörch.

Subgenus FUSITRITON Cossmann.

ARGOBUCCINUM (FUSITRITON) CAMMANI Dall, n. sp.

Pl. IV, fig. 11.

Shell thin, rather slender, strongly constricted at the sutures; apex and canal defective in the specimens; varices resembling the ribs but larger, irregularly distributed, about two to a whorl; suture appressed; whorls subtabulate, sculptured with about 16 rounded ribs with much wider interspaces, slightly arcuate and obscurely nodulose where crossed by the stronger spirals; the ribs become obsolete on the base of the whorl; spiral sculpture in front of the shoulder of the whorl, of about nine more or less elevated straplike bands, faintly, finely spirally striate, with subequal or wider interspaces also more or less striated, the spirals grow stronger and the interspaces deeper toward the base; pillar smooth, more or less callous. Altitude of figured fragment, 36.5 mm.; maximum diameter, 30 mm.

Miocene of Coos Bay, Oregon, purchased from B. H. Camman; U. S. Nat. Mus. 153907.

Though very imperfect, the sculpture of the two specimens obtained is sufficiently characteristic to enable the systematic place and species to be determined. It differs from all the hitherto known species by the constriction of the coil at the sutures.

Cryotritonium Von Martens (*Valdivia* expedition) is synonymous with *Austrotriton* Cossmann, and, I am informed, was published about a month later.

ARGOBUCCINUM (FUSITRITON) COOSENSE Dall, n. sp.

Pl. VII, fig. 4.

Shell slender, elongate, with four or more whorls, the type with the apex and anterior end of the canal defective; varices rounded, prominent, about two to a whorl, in the figure the profile includes a varix at each edge of the last whorl, giving the shell a wider aspect than it presents if viewed from another angle; suture appressed, the shell not constricted in the sutural region; sculpture of 19 or 20 slightly arcuate ribs extending from the suture well over the periphery and then becoming gradually obsolete; the whorl is crossed by 28 to 30 flat, little-elevated straplike subequal spirals, slightly swollen where they cross the ribs, separated by subequal or narrower interspaces, which, as well as the spirals, are faintly, finely spirally striate; canal elongate, more or less arcuate and recurved, pillar smooth.   Altitude of figured specimen, 54 mm.; diameter at varices, 28 mm.; between the varices, 24 mm.

Miocene of Coos Bay, Oregon, purchased from B. H. Camman; U. S. Nat. Mus. 153903.

This specimen is easily discriminated from the Pliocene *F. angelensis* Arnold and the recent *F. oregonensis*, which occurs in the Fossil Rock conglomerate near by, on comparison of the minor sculpture.   The latter species is also more robust, with more inflated whorls and fewer ribs.

ARGOBUCCINUM (FUSITRITON) OREGONENSE Redfield.

Triton oregonense Redfield, Ann. Lyc. Nat. Hist. New York, IV, p. 165. pl. 11, fig. 2. 1846.
Fusus oregonensis Forbes, Proc. Zool. Soc. London for 1850, p. 274.
Tritonium cancellatum Middendorff, Beitr. Mal. Ross., III, p. 164. pl. 3, figs. 1–3, 1849; not of Lamarck.
Priene oregonensis Cooper, Seventh Ann. Rept. California State Mining Bureau, p. 261, 1868.
Tritonium (Priene) oregonensis Arnold, Pal. and Strat. San Pedro, p. 286, pl. 6, fig. 1, 1903.
Fusitriton oregonensis Dall, Smithsonian Misc. Coll. (quarterly issue), XLVII. No. 1475, p. 129, 1904.

Pliocene of San Pedro, Cal., Arnold; Pleistocene of San Pedro and Santa Barbara, Cooper; and of Fossil Rock, Coos Bay, Oregon, W. H. Dall.   Living from the Pribilof Islands southward to Japan on the west, and to Monterey, Cal., on the east, in moderate depths of water; dredged from deep water off San Diego, Cal., Raymond.

This well-known species is apparently represented by fragments in the Coos conglomerate at Fossil Rock.   It has been at various times confounded with the South American species called by Lamarck *Triton cancellatus*, but the two shells are certainly distinct.

Subgenus PRIENE H. and A. Adams.

Priene H. and A. Adams. Gen Rec. Moll., II, p. 654, 1858; Dall, Smithsonian Misc. Coll. (quarterly issue). XLVII. No. 1475, p. 132, 1904; type *Triton scaber* King.

PRIENE PACIFICA Dall, n. sp.

Pl. V, fig. 9; Pl. VI, fig. 2.

Shell large, stout, with about one inconspicuous varix to a whorl, the only prominent varix being the terminal one of the adult; whorls four or more, inflated, rotund; apex and anterior end of canal defective in the specimen; suture very distinct but not channeled; sculpture of (on the penultimate whorl) about 20 subequal rounded ribs, extending from the suture over the periphery of the whorl and becoming obsolete on the base, about one on each whorl slightly varicose; incremental lines hardly noticeable; spiral sculpture of (on the last whorl about 20) subequal, flattish ridges with nearly equal interspaces, growing coarser toward the canal, not swollen or perceptibly nodulose where they cross the ribs, nor spirally striated; canal short without marked fasciole, anteriorly defective in the specimen, deeply indented; outer lip more or less flaring, especially in front; aperture obstructed by matrix but the outer lip probably denticulate within. Altitude, 60 mm.; maximum diameter of last whorl, 50 mm.

Miocene of Coos Bay, Oregon, purchased from B. H. Camman; U. S. Nat. Mus. 153902. Also in the Purisima formation, Santa Cruz County, Cal., according to Arnold.

This is somewhat larger than the South American *P. scaber*, the recent type of the subgenus, but appears to be its nearest relative. The Purisima specimen has the spire less defective than that from Coos Bay, and shows four and a half whorls. Exclusive of the nucleus, which is usually lost, the shell probably had at least five whorls, and possibly six.

Genus CYMATIUM Bolten.

Subgenus LINATELLA Gray.

Linatella Gray, Guide Moll. Brit. Mus., p. 37, 1857; sole example, *Triton cingulatum* Lamarck; not
   Linatella H. and A. Adams, Gen. Rec. Moll., II, p. 655, 1858, in synonymy.
Linatella Dall, Smithsonian Misc. Coll. (quarterly issue). XLVII. No. 1475. p. 134. 1904.

CYMATIUM (LINATELLA) PACIFICUM Dall, n. sp.

Pl. VI, fig. 10.

Shell large, thin, except for the parietal callus, with five or more convex whorls which are subtabulate near the suture; sculpture of (on the upper whorls 4, and on the last whorl about 10) squarish revolving ridges with decidedly wider interspaces, smooth or with sparse obsolete spiral striation; axial sculpture only of lines of growth and a moderate terminal varix in the adult, which is defective in the specimen; nucleus lost; aperture with a short, rather straight canal, with a feeble siphonal fasciole; a broad sheet of callus over the body and pillar, the outer lip slightly expanded and varicose; body behind the pillar destitute of marked spiral sculpture. Altitude of shell, 106 mm.; of last whorl, 82 mm.; maximum diameter, 60 mm.

Miocene of Coos Bay, Oregon, purchased from B. II. Camman; U. S. Nat. Mus. 153899.

This species is shaped very much like a *Chrysodomus*, but is recognizable as belonging to *Cymatium* by its texture, its thin shell, and the broad parietal callus.

Family CASSIDIDÆ.

PRELINNEAN OR POLYNOMIAL REFERENCES.

Cassis Rumphius, Amboinische Rariteit Kammer. 1st ed. (p. 80?), 1705; first species. *Cassis cornuta*
   Rumphius (later of Linné); ed. 2. p. 80, 1741. This appears to be the first scientific use of the name,
   which is a Latin rendering of a Malayan word meaning "helmet shell" (= *Cassis* Scopoli).
Cassis Klein, Tent. Meth. Ostrac., p. 91, 1753; first species, *Buccinum glaucum* Linné (*Cassis lævis
   cinerea* Kl.); figured example *Buccinum areola* Linné (*Cassis lævis areola* c. Kl.). Klein figures
   none of the true helmet shells; his group is identical with *Bezoardica* Schumacher. It is not *Cassis*
   Klein. 1734 (Echin.).

Cassis Browne, Hist. Jamaica, p. 407, 1756; first species, Lister fig. 1008. = *Buccinum cornutum* β. Gmelin, p. 3473, 1792.

Semicassis Klein, Tent. Meth. Ostrac., p. 94, 1753; first species (also figured) *Cassis pila* Reeve (sec. von Martens; *Semicassis lævis* venter, major, etc., Klein). The group is *Semicassis* Mörch.

Galea Klein, Tent. Meth. Ostrac., p. 56, 1753; first species, *Buccinum perdix* Linné (*Galea striata pennata* Kl.); figured example *Buccinum echinophorum* Linné (*Galea striata echinophora* Kl.). Equals *Dolium* + *Cassidaria* Lam. + *Ampullaria* Lam. + *Purpura, Mitra, Melongena*, etc., auct., a characteristic Kleinian mixture. Klein's "genus" *Cassis bicornis* comprises incidentally *Bursa spinosa, Murex trunculus*, and *Cassidaria echinophora*, which should satisfy all tastes.

Cassis Martini, Syst. Conch. Cab., II. p. 2, 1771, ex parte. *Cassides volutatæ veræ*, p. 15, includes *Buccinum rufum, cornutum, tuberosum, testiculum*, etc., of Linné.

Cassis Da Costa, Elem. Conch., pp. 195, 290, 1775; figured example, *C. saburon*; the group = *Cassis* Rumphius.

Galeodes seu *Semicassides* Martini, Syst. Conch. Cab., II. p. 2, 1771. = *Melongena* sp., not *Semicassis* of Klein; = *Cassidulus* (anonymous), in Mus. Calonnianum.

Cassides Meuschen, Mus. Gevers, pp. 386–394, 1787; assembly similar to that of Klein.

Globosa Da Costa, Elem. Conch., pp. 193, 306, 1775; figured species, *G. echinophora*, which is included with *Dolium*, the *Cochlea globosæ* of Rumphius.

So far as nomenclature is concerned, the above citations are purely historical. They help us to understand how the use of the name grew, and bring us to the point where we may consider the genus as it appears in modern nomenclature.

The name *Cassis* was first introduced into scientific terminology by Rumphius who latinized the local name "helmet shell" in his "Treasury of Amboyna," as above indicated. His grouping was excellent; more than a century elapsed before the genus was recognized with so little admixture of other forms; in fact, his group is our modern genus *Cassis*, senso lato.. Cossmann has rejected the name *Cassis* because Klein used the word to denominate an echinoderm in 1734 as well as our mollusks in 1753. If we allow the polynomial literature to influence our acceptance of zoological names on the ground of priority (which I do not for a moment admit), we can not consistently omit to apply the rule of priority to the polynomial writers also; hence in the present instance *Cassis* is by many years the prior name, and should be adopted.

Notwithstanding the relatively small number of species contained in this family and the *Doliidæ*, much confusion has reigned in the nomenclature and even the latest reviews of it are more or less defective. I have therefore undertaken to review it from the beginning, hoping to arrive at a permanent result in accordance with the modern rules governing zoological nomenclature. It will be noted that with the beginning of formally binomial nomenclature in 1758, even in his heterogeneous genus *Buccinum*, the "father of natural history," recognized the group, though he did not formally christen it.

The family is composed mainly of globular or subtriangular shells, with a horny operculum and short spire, the whorls having at least a terminal varix, and, in the typical group, a succession of varices. The rhachidian tooth is multidentate, as are the inner laterals; the intermediate laterals have a few denticles, but the outer laterals are simple. There are no basal denticles on the rhachidian tooth. The protoconch is minute.

Genus CASSIS Scopoli.

Cassidea caudata Linné, Syst. Nat., ed. 10, p. 735, 1758. Section *b* of *Buccinum* L., comprising nine species of *Cassis*, of which the first is *C. echinophora* L.

Cassida Brunnich, Zool. Fund., p. 248, 1772; not of Linné, 1758 (Coleoptera);=*Cassis* Scopoli.

Cassis Scopoli, Intr. ad Hist. Nat., p. 393, 1777; contains (*a*) *Buccinum flammea*, etc., of Linné, and (*b*) *B. rufum, cornutum*, etc., of Linné, a very similar assembly to that of Klein; also Scopoli, Del. Insubr., II, p. 76, 1786.

Cassis Modeer, K. Vetensk. Acad. nya handl., XIV, pp. 107, 111, 1793; contains as examples *C. plicatum* and *cornutum* (L.).

Cassida (anonymous), Mus. Calonnianum, pp. 19, 81, 1797; contains species of *Cassidaria, Malea, Nassa*, and *Cassis* senso lato; not *Cassida* L., 1758 (Insecta). *Cassidula* of the same work is equivalent to *Melongena* auct.

Cassis Bolten, Mus. Boltenianum, p. 28, 1798, ex parte; divided as by Klein into veræ and spuriæ; first species of veræ is *Buccinum cornutum* (L.) Gmelin.

Cassidea Cuvier, Tableau Élém., p. 406, 1798; includes *Buccinum ribex, testiculus, rufum, cornutum*, and *tuberosum* L., as examples of five unnamed subdivisions of the genus.

Cassis Lamarck, Prodrome, p. 72, 1799; sole example, *Buccinum cornutum* L. Syst. des Anim. s. Vert., p. 79, 1801; same type.

Cassidea Bosc, Hist. Nat. Coq., V. p. 1, 1802; includes all the Cassides as well as *Oniscia*, figures *C. echinophora* Brug.

Cassis Roissy, Hist. Nat. des Moll., VI, p. 98, 1806; first species, *C. cornuta* L.

Cassidea Link, Beschr. Rostock Samml., p. 111, 1807; same species as Cuvier, with *C. flammea* and *pennata* L. added, and *C. ribex* omitted.

Cassis Montfort, Conch. Syst., II, p. 599, 1810; sole example, *C. cornuta* L. sp.

Cassis Perry, Conch., expl. pl. 33, 1811; first species, *C. flammea* L.

Cassis Oken, Lehrb. d. Naturg. (3), I, pp. ix, 171, 1815; first species, *C. cornutum*.

Cassidea Schumacher, Essai, pp. 75, 247, 1817; section α, *C. rufa* L.; section β, *C. flammea* L.; section γ, *C. oniscus* L.;=*Cassis* Scopoli.

Cassis Sowerby, Gen. Shells, fasc. 22, 1824; examples cited, *C. glauca* and *flammea*.

Cassis Blainville, Man. Mal., I, p. 410, 1825; section A. *C. tuberosa;* section B, *C. flammea.*

Cassis Stutchbury, Mag. Nat. Hist., n. s., I, p. 472, 1837; first species, *C. madagascariensis* Lam.; the list includes *C. cornuta.*

Cassis Swainson, Malac., p. 298, 1840; type, *C. cornuta* L.

Cassis Sowerby, Conch. Man., ed. 2, p. 100, 1842; *C. tuberosa.*

Cassidea Gray, Proc. Zool. Soc. London for 1847, p. 137;=*Cassidea* Schumacher.

Cassis (Scopoli) Gray, Proc. Zool. Soc. London for 1847, p. 137; *Buccinum flammeum* L.

Cassis Mörch, Cat. Yoldi, I, p. 113, 1852; subgenus of *Cassis;* first species, *Buccinum cornutum* L.

Cassis H. and A. Adams, Gen. Rec. Moll., I, p. 214, 1853; *C. cornuta* L. sp.;=*Cassis* Lamarck.

Cassis Philippi, Handb. Conch., p. 153, 1853;=*Cassis* Scopoli.

Cassis Gray, Guide Moll., p. 37, 1857; *C. cornutum* Quoy.

Goniogalea Mörch, Svensen Cat., p. 21, 1857; Mal. Blätt., XXIV, p. 37, 1877; first species, *Cassis madagascariensis* Lam.

Cassis Fischer, Man. de Conchyl., p. 659, 1884; *C. cornuta* (L.).

Cassis (Klein) Sacco, Moll. Terz. Piem. e Lig., VII, p. 11, 1890;=*Cassis* Lamarck, 1799.

Galeodocassis Sacco, Moll. Terz. Piem. e Lig., VII, p. 18, 1890; *G. anceps* Sacco; subgenus of *Cassis.*

Semicassis Sacco, Moll. Terz. Piem. e Lig., VII, p. 26, 1890; subgenus of *Cassis;* first species, *C. miolævigata* Sacco.

Cassidea Sacco, Moll. Terz. Piem. e Lig., VII, p. 19, 1890; subgenus; first species, *C. cypræiformis* Borson sp.

Cassisoma Rovereto, Atti Soc. Lig., X (p. 7 of extras), 1899; new name for *Cassis* Klein, 1753, non Klein, 1734;=*Cassis* (Rumphius, 1704) Lamarck, 1799.

Cassidea Cossmann, Essais de Pal. Comp., V, p. 123, 1903; type, *Buccinum cornutum* L.,=*Cassis* Scopoli.

Subgenus CYPRÆCASSIS Stutchbury.

Cypræcassis Stutchbury, Loudon's Mag. Nat. Hist., n. s., I, p. 214, 1837; type, *Cassis rufa* L.
Cypræcassis Sowerby, Conch. Man., ed. 2, p. 133, 1842; *C. testiculus.*
Cypræcassis Gray, Proc. Zool. Soc. London for 1847, p. 137. *C. testiculum.*
Cypræcassis Mörch, Cat. Yoldi, I, p. 113, 1852; first species, *C. rufa* L.; subgenus of *Cassis.*
Cassidea (Link) Herrmannsen, Ind. Gen. Mal., suppl., p. 25, December, 1852, selects *C. rufa* and *testiculus* as types.
Cassidea H. and A. Adams, Gen. Rec. Moll., I, p. 217, 1853; *C. testiculus* L. sp.
Cypræcassis Gray, Guide Moll., p. 37, 1857; *C. rufum.*
Cypræcassis Fischer, Man. de Conchyl., p. 659, 1884; *C. rufa* L. sp.; subgenus of *Cassis.*
Cypræicassis Cossmann, Essais de Pal. Comp., V, p. 129, 1903; type, *Buccinum rufum* L.; subgenus of *Bezoardica* Cossmann; = *Cypræcassis* Stutchbury.

Section LEVENIA Gray.

Levenia Gray, Proc. Zool. Soc. London for 1847, p. 137; type, *Cassis coarctata* Sowerby.
Levenia H. and A. Adams, Gen. Rec. Moll., I, p. 217, 1853; *L. coarctata* Sowerby.
Levenia Gray, Guide Moll., p. 37, 1857; *L. coarctata* Gray.
Levenia Fischer, Man. de Conchyl., p. 659, 1884; *C. coarctata* Sowerby (section of *Cassis*).
Levenia Cossmann, Essais de Pal. Comp., V, p. 121, 1903; section of *Cassidea* Cossmann, = *Levenia* Gray.

Large, heavy subtriangular shells, with a narrow aperture and conspicuous body callus, the spire low and inconspicuous.

The genus *Cassis* is divided into several subordinate groups, as follows:

Subgenus *Cassis* s. s. Shell subtriangular, heavy, varicose, the last whorl much the largest; with a short spire, the terminal callus spread over the body, with the edges more or less free, dentate on each side of a narrow aperture which is not canaliculate behind; canal short, strongly recurved, deeply indented, and with a strong siphonal fasciole in front of a rather deep sulcus; operculum ovoid, concentric, the nucleus near the middle of the outer edge. Type, *C. cornuta* L.

Section *Levenia* Gray. Shell thinner than typical *Cassis*, the callus thinner and less expanded, its margin adherent except near the canal; outer lip not reflected, inflected toward the posterior end; the aperture not channeled behind, operculum narrow and thin. Type, *C. coarctata* Sowerby.

Section *Morionella* Dall, nov. Shell thinner than typical *Cassis*, with the aperture having a wide and shallow channel behind; the aperture wide, lirate or denticulate on each lip; shell strongly axially sculptured; the canal wider, less deeply incised and much less reflected than in *Cassis* s. s. Type, *C. chevallieri* Cossmann, Parisian Eocene.

Subgenus *Cypræcassis* Stutchbury. Shell ovoid, the callus thick and closely adherent; the aperture narrow, canaliculate behind; the operculum said to be absent in the adult; varices, except the terminal one, few and inconspicuous or none. Type, *C. rufa* L.

The earliest American member of this family is the Claibornian *C. sowerbyi* Lea, which belongs to the next genus. The earliest true *Cassis* I have found recorded from European strata is the *C. mammillaris* Grateloup, from the Tongrian (and up to the Miocene), a form of which is queried by Sacco as perhaps Bartonian, corresponding respectively to our Jacksonian and middle Oligocene. This agrees fairly well with our American data, where the only true *Cassis* in the restricted sense, earlier than the Pleistocene, is *C. sulcifera* Sowerby, from the Oligocene of

Santo Domingo, Haiti, and Jamaica, and a closely related, if not identical, form from the Chattahoochee formation of Georgia, which has so far been obtained only in fragments. The *Cassis harpæformis* and *C. cancellata* Lamarck from the Parisian Eocene, with their wide apertures, relatively thin shells, and strong axial sculpture, have a very different aspect from modern species of *Cassis* of the type of *C. cornuta*. The other Parisian species, *C. chevallieri* Cossmann, shows these features even more emphatically and might serve as the type of a section to contain these early representatives of the family. In some respects they recall *Cypræcassis* more than *Cassis* s. s. *C. calantica* of the same region is a *Phalium*, not unlike our *P. globosum* Dall, from the Jacksonian of Mississippi and the lower Oligocene of Florida.

While it is true that the *Galeodocassis* of Sacco has a distinctive facies, and there is nothing quite like it among the more modern forms, I am obliged to agree with Cossmann that, when analyzed, the distinctive characters become so few and uncharacteristic that the group can hardly be maintained.

In the modern fauna *Cassis* is well represented in the Antilles, both by the typical forms and by species of *Cypræcassis*, but curiously enough only the latter is represented, with *Levenia*, on the tropical Pacific coast of America. Typical *Cassis* is also found in the Indo-Pacific province, Japan, and Australia, as is *Cypræcassis* but *Levenia* is restricted to western America.

Genus PHALIUM Link.

Phalium Link, Beschr. Rostock Samml., p. 112, 1807; first species, *Cassis glauca* Linné.

Cassidea Perry, Conch., expl. pl. 34, 1811; first species, *Cassis labiata* Perry (+*C. achatina* Lam., 1822).

Bezoardica α Schumacher, Essai, p. 248, 1817; type, *Buccinum glaucum* L.

Cassis Bowdich, Elem. Conch., I, p. 41, pl. 11, fig. 11, 1822; *C. glauca.*

Cassidea Sowerby, Conch. Man., ed. 2, p. 99, 1842; *C. glauca* or *erinaceus,* fig. 411.

Phalium Herrmannsen, Index Gen. Mal., suppl., p. 104 (as of Link), selects *Cassis glauca* L. as type, December, 1852.

Bezoardica Gray, Proc. Zool. Soc. London for 1847, p. 137; = *Bezoardica* α Schumacher; *Cassis glauca.*

Phalium Mörch, Cat. Yoldi, I, p. 113, 1852; subgenus of *Cassis;* first species, *Buccinum glaucum* L.

Semicassis H. and A. Adams, Gen. Rec. Moll., I, p. 215, 1853; *S. glauca* L. sp.

Phalium H. and A. Adams, Gen. Rec. Moll., I, p. 216, 1853; subgenus of *Semicassis;* first species, *S. areola* L. sp.

Bezoardica Gray, Guide Moll., p. 38, 1857; first species, *P. glauca.*

Casmaria Fischer, Man. de Conchyl., p. 659, 1884; section of *Semicassis; Cassis pyrum* Lam.

Bezoardica Fischer, Man. de Conchyl., p. 659, 1884; section of *Semicassis; Cassis glauca* L. sp.

Casmaria Sacco, Moll. Terz. Piem. e Lig., VII, p. 26, 1890; subgenus of *Cassis; Cassis tongriana* Sacco.

Casmaria Cossmann, Essais de Pal. Comp., V, p. 127, 1903; type, *Cassis pyrum* Lam.; section of *Semicassis* Cossmann;= *Casmaria* H. and A. Adams.

Bezoardica Cossmann, Essais de Pal. Comp., V, p. 128, 1903; type, *Buccinum glaucum* L.; = *Bezoardica* α Schumacher, 1817.

Subgenus CASSIDEA (Bruguière) Swainson.

Cassidea unguiculata Linné, Syst. Nat., ed. 10, p. 736, 1758; section *c* of *Buccinum* L.; contains *Cassis erinacea, glauca,* and *vibex* L., with two species of *Nassa,* in the order named.

Cassidea Bruguière, Encycl. Meth., I, pp. xv (1789), 414 (1792); new name for *Cassis* Klein (cf. p. 416, col. 1); first species, *Buccinum vibex* L.

Cassidea Swainson, Malac., p. 299, 1840; type, *Cassis vibex* L.

Cassidea Mörch, Cat. Yoldi, I, p. 112, 1852; subgenus of *Cassis;* first species, *Cassis vibex.*

Casmaria (pars) H. and A. Adams, Gen. Rec. Moll., I, p. 216, 1853; subgenus of *Semicassis; Cassis vibex* L.

Subgenus BEZOARDICA Schumacher.

Bezoardica β Schumacher, Essai, pp. 75, 248, 1817; Gray, Proc. Zool. Soc. London, for 1847, p. 137, No. 43; *B. areola* Gmelin.

Semicassis Mörch, Cat. Yoldi, I, p. 112, 1852: subgenus of *Cassis;* first species, *S. japonica* Reeve.

Semicassis Fischer, Man. de Conchyl., p. 659, 1884; subgenus of *Cassis; Cassis saburon.*

Semicassis Cossmann, Essais de Pal. Comp., V, p. 125, 1903; type, *Buccinum saburon* L., subgenus of *Cassidea* Cossmann; = *Semicassis* Mörch.

Section ECHINOPHORIA Sacco.

Echinophoria Sacco, Moll. Terz. Piem. e Lig., VII, p. 39, 1890; subgenus of *Cassis;* first species, *C. isselii* Sacco: type, *Buccinum intermedium* Brocchi.

Moderate-sized, thin, globose, or ovate shells with an ample aperture, thin and adherent body callus, the spire moderately elevated.

The genus *Phalium* is divided as follows:

Subgenus *Phalium* s. s. Shell smooth and polished, frequently coronated at the shoulder or with longitudinal riblets; outer lip dentate, reflected, subspinose in front; varices several; body callus thin, smooth and adherent behind, partly free in front, more or lest plicate over the pillar; the aperture usually channeled behind; operculum narrow, lunate, the nucleus in the middle of the outer side. Type, *C. glauca* Linné.

Subgenus *Cassidea* (Bruguière) Swainson. Shell ovate, smooth, polished, with only a terminal varix; body callus smooth and adherent throughout; otherwise as in *Phalium* s. s. Type, *C. vibex* Linné.

Subgenus *Bezoardica* Schumacher. Shell globose; spirally markedly sulcate over the whole surface, sometimes granose or coronate at the shoulder; body callus adherent behind, more or less free anteriorly, plicate or granose opposite the outer lip; the latter not spinose in front, more or less denticulate, reflected and heavy; a single terminal varix. Type, *Buccinum areola* Gmelin.

Section *Echinophoria* Sacco. Like *Bezoardica* but having the body callus nearly smooth and the spiral sculpture supplemented by nodosities more or less completely covering the whorl. Type, *Cassis intermedia* Brocchi (sp.), Oligocene of Italy.

Subgenus *Doliocassis* Dall, nov. Shell small, solid, ovate, protoconch large, smooth, polished, as in *Dolium;* surface with uniform spiral sulcation; no external varices; outer lip thickened internally, denticulate, not reflected; body callus thin, wholly adherent, plicate on the pillar and near the suture; canal short, obliquely truncate, with a distinct fasciole, behind which is a shallow sulcus, but the canal is not reflected as in *Phalium* or *Cassis.* Type, *Buccinum sowerbyi* Lea,[a] "Claiborne sands" of Alabama.

Phalium in America antedates typical *Cassis* and includes all the Eocene and Oligocene species except *Sconsia lintea, Galeodea petersoni, G. ? tuberculatus* Gabb, and *Cassis sulcifera.* There are several ill-defined and unfigured species of Conrad in the Eocene, but I believe they may all be included in *Phalium.* The new subdivision, *Doliocassis,* has the external appearance of a miniature *Dolium perdix,* together with a relatively much larger protoconch than is possessed by a *Cassis* one hundred times

---

[a] This fossil has been identified by some authors with *Cassis nupera* Conrad, an unfigured and insufficiently described species, about which Conrad himself was in doubt.

its size. The strictly internal varices are a characteristic feature. Most of the specimens obtained do not show the body callus, its sculpture, or the denticulations of the outer lip, but they are all present in fully mature specimens. A few specimens of *Bezoardica* show a second varix, but this is so unusual as to be abnormal, as much so as would be a specimen of *Phalium* s. s. which should show only a terminal varix.

In the matter of names for the divisions of *Phalium* it may be noted that the *Cassidea* of Bruguière was proposed as a substitute for *Cassis* Klein, 1753, not 1734, and *Cassis* Klein contained none of the typical genus *Cassis*, so *Cassidea* Bruguière can not be used for the latter. *Cassidea* was a heterogeneous group until Swainson fixed on *C. vibex* to typify it, in 1840. As the first section of *Bezoardica* Schumacher was already a synonym of *Phalium*, the name can be retained for the second section, for which the much later name of *Semicassis* Mörch has been frequently used.

PHALIUM (BEZOARDICA) TURRICULA Dall, n. sp.

Pl. IV, fig. 6.

Shell large, moderately thick, with an unusually elevated spire, with five sculptured whorls and a smooth nucleus of about two and a half whorls; axial sculpture of (on the penultimate whorl about 20) faint, obscure, somewhat flexuous ridges, chiefly noticeable from the nodulations which occur when the raised spirals cross them; the ridges are almost wholly absent from the last half of the last whorl; faint incremental lines also occur; spiral sculpture of (between the sutures 4, on the last whorl 15) narrow raised revolving ridges with much wider interspaces but no intercalary small threads; where the ridges cross the axial ridges they are more or less undulated and swollen, the peripheral ridge on the spire has these projections particularly marked; there is no spiral striation; the suture is wound on the fourth spiral and, when the latter is nodulous, is undulated more or less; the type specimen has two varices, which is exceptional in this group and may be an individual aberration; aperture longer than wide, the outer lip thickened and reflected, internally denticulate; body with a callus which is raised at its anterior margin; canal short, deep, strongly reflected, with a deep wide sulcus behind it; the outer lip is constricted just before forming the varix. Altitude, 80 mm.; maximum diameter, 50 mm.

Miocene of Coos Bay, Oregon, purchased from B. H. Camman; U. S. Nat. Mus. 153898.

The aperture of this fine shell is obstructed by a tough matrix, but enough is visible to deduce all the essential characters except whether the body callus is smooth or sculptured.

PHALIUM (BEZOARDICA) ÆQUISULCATUM Dall, n. sp.

Pl. V, figs. 1, 4.

Shell of moderate size, solid, heavy, ovate, with about five whorls beside the (decollate) nucleus; suture distinct, not channeled; sculpture of (on the last whorl 19) even, flat, straplike, raised, subequal spirals, separated by channeled, narrower, equal sulci or interspaces most of which carry a single minute intercalary thread, which on the base is as a rule slightly nearer the posterior side of the channel in which .

it lies; there are faint traces of fine spiral striation, and the posterior four or five of the major spirals are somewhat beaded or granulated by axial sulci which do not appear in the channels: the varices except the terminal one are inconspicuous and irregular; two specimens, including the largest, show none; the figured specimen, which is smaller though better preserved, has indications of two besides the terminal varix; aperture longer than wide, subovate; outer lip reflected and thickened, internally dentate; body with a thin smooth callus (not in the figured specimen); canal deep, short, twisted, recurved, with a deep smooth sulcus behind it. Altitude of figured specimen, 45 mm.; of a larger but still immature individual (decollate), 60 mm.; maximum diameter, respectively, 30 and 39 mm.

Miocene of Coos Bay, Oregon, purchased from B. H. Camman; U. S. Nat. Mus. 153896.

This is a very well-defined and uniformly sculptured species, which recalls "*Cassis*" *inflata* Shaw, of the recent West Indian fauna, but has not the granose body callus of that species. No species of this group now lives on the Pacific coast of North America as far as known.

Genus GALEODEA Link.

Galeodea Link, Beschr. Rostock Samml., p. 113, 1807; sole example, *G. echinophora* L.; not = *Galeodes* Bolten.

Morio Montfort, Conch. Syst., II, p. 479, 1810; type, *Buccinum echinophorum* L.; not *Morion* of Latreille, 1810 (Coleoptera).

Cassidaire, Lamarck, Extr. d'un Cours, p. 119, 1812; nude vernacular list name, cited by Cuvier, Règne Anim., II, p. 437, 1817, as a synonym of *Morio* Montfort, 1810.

Echinora Schumacher, Essai, pp. 75, 249, 1817; *Buccinum echinophorum* Linné.

Cassidaria Lamarck, Anim. s. Vert., VII, p. 214, 1822; first species, *Buccinum echinophorum* Linné; = *Morio* Montfort.

Cassidaria Bowdich, Elem. Conch., I, p. 40, pl. 11, fig. 5, 1882; *C. echinophora* Lam.

Cassidaria Sowerby, Gen. Shells, fasc. 23, 1824; type. *Buccinum echinophorum* L. Also Risso, Hist., IV, p. 183, 1826.

Cassidaria Blainville, Man. Mal., I, p. 409, 1825; *C. echinophora* L.

Cassidarea Swainson, Malac., p. 299, 1840; *C. echinophora* L.

Cassidaria Sowerby, Conch. Man., 2d ed., pp. 99, 307, 1842; *C. echinophora* L.

Galeodea Mörch, Cat. Yoldi, I, p. 3, 1852, as of Link; = *G. echinophora* L.

Galeodea H. and A. Adams, Gen. Rec. Moll., I, p. 218, 1853; *G. echinophora* L. sp.

Morio Philippi, Handb. Conch., p. 154, 1853; *Buccinum echinophorum* L.

Morio Gray, Guide Moll., p. 39, 1857; *M. echinophora*.

Galeoda Chenu, Man. de Conchyl., I, p. 209, 1859; *G. tyrrhena* and *echinophora*, = *Galeodea* H. and A. Adams.

Galeodia Conrad (as of Link), Jour. Acad. Nat. Sci. Philadelphia, n. s., IV, p. 293, 1860; *G. tricarinata* Conrad, Vicksburgian Oligocene.

Morio Fischer, Man. de Conchyl., p. 659, 1884: *M. echinophora* L. sp.; full genus.

Morio Sacco. Moll. Terz. Piem. e Lig., p. 53, 1890; = *Morio* Montfort.

Morio Cossmann. Cat. Illustré Bas. Paris, IV, p. 112, 1889; *M. echinophora* (L.).

Galeodea Sacco, Moll. Terz. Piem. e Lig., VII, p. 53, 1890: subgenus of *Morio*; type, *G. echinophora* L. sp.

Cassidaria Rovereto. Atti Soc. Lig., X (p. 7 of extras), 1899. = *Cassidaire* Lam., 1812. + *Galeodea* Link, 1807 (not *Galeodes* Olivier, 1791). + *Morio* Montfort, 1810 (not *Morion* Latreille, 1810).

Cassidaria Cossmann. Essais de Pal. Comp., V, p. 129, 1903; type, *Buccinum echinophorum* L., = *Cassidaire* Lam., 1812.

Section GALEODARIA Conrad.

Galeodaria Conrad, Am. Jour. Conch., I, p. 26, 1865; sole example, *G. petersoni* Conrad (1855); subgenus of *Galeodea* (Link) Conrad, Jacksonian Eocene.

Doliopsis Conrad, Am. Jour. Conch., I, pp. 26, 141 (not p. 150), 1865; type, *D. tricarinatum* Conrad.

Doliopsis Conrad (olim), Misc. Coll. Smithsonian Inst., Eocene Checklist of Invt. Foss., p. 37, No. 755; genus withdrawn and species referred to *Galeodaria* Conrad; not *Doliopsis* Monterosato. 1872.

Galeodaria Fischer, Man. de Conchyl., p. 660, 1884; subgenus of *Morio*; *G. petersoni* Conrad, Eocene.

The name *Galeodea* has by some been rejected on account of the existence of *Galeodes* Bolten, but the best opinion is opposed to such action. The next name is *Morio* Montfort, which has been supposed to be preoccupied by *Morio* Latreille, published in the same year. But an inspection of Latreille shows that he named his beetle *Morion* (a brown gem), not *Morio* (a fool), and the two names can perfectly well exist in nomenclature. The name *Morio* does not exist in Latreille's work and the substitution, or blunder, was made by a later author who has been copied without verification. The next name in order is *Echinora* Schumacher, 1817, as the vernacular *Cassidaire* of Lamarck, 1812, is a perfectly nude name rightly rejected in favor of *Morio* Montfort, by Cuvier, the Latin name *Cassidaria* not being proposed or defined until 1822.

Conrad's *Galeodaria* will form at most a section of the genus, being a precursor in the Eocene of the typical *Galeodea*. *Doliopsis* Conrad was founded on an immature specimen of *Galeodaria*.

The characters of *Galeodea* are as follows:

Shell thin, with a moderately elevated spire, appressed suture, and uniformly spiral sculpture; sometimes more or less nodulous on the more prominent spiral keels; with a conspicuous periostracum; the outer lip reflected and more or less transversely lirate, with a tendency to a more prominent denticle near the posterior angle and at the proximal end of the canal; inner lip with a broad callus, smooth or obsoletely lirate, with its margin more or less free in the adult; the canal elongate and recurved, with hardly a trace of a siphonal fasciole; operculum subovate with the nucleus midlateral on the outer side. Type, *G. echinophora* L.

The section *Galeodaria* hardly differs from the typical *Galeodea*, except in its small size and exaggerated callosities, and the series of regular, distant, not nodular keels separating the finer spiral sculpture into bands, which give it a peculiar aspect. The sole species is *G. petersoni* Conrad.

From *Sconsia*, *Galeodea* differs by its lighter shell, more conspicuous periostracum, more reflected outer lip, and less appressed body callus; and especially by its elongated, narrow, and deflected canal without any marked fasciole. The soft parts of *Sconsia* being yet unknown, the comparison can not be made complete. *Galeodea* is among the earliest representatives of its family, if not the very first, a recognizable species having been described by Müller from the Cretaceous of Aachen, while Gabb has named another from beds of Cretaceous age at Martinez, Cal. The *Sconsia alabamensis* from the upper Cretaceous of Alabama was described by Gabb from an imperfect internal cast, and therefore remains somewhat doubtful, but the subgenus is definitely established as early as the Claibornian. The *Morio tuberculatus* Gabb, from the Eocene of Martinez, Cal., is also found in that of Nehalem River, Oregon, and much resembles *Galeodaria petersoni* except that the sculpture is nodulous instead of carinate.

Subgenus SCONSIA Gray.

Oniscia Risso (as of Sowerby), Hist. Nat. Eur. Mér., IV, p. 185, 1826; sole example, *Cassidaria striata* Lamarck; not *Oniscia* Sby., 1824.

Sconsia Gray, Guide Moll., p. 39, 1857; *S. striata*.

Sconsia H. and A. Adams, Gen. Rec. Moll., I, p. 218, 1853; *Cassidaria striata* Lamarck.

Sconsia Fischer, Man. de Conchyl., p. 660, 1884; *S. striata* Lamarck, subgenus of *Morio*.

Sconsia Sacco, Moll. Terz. Piem. e Lig., VII, p. 71, 1890; =*Sconsia* Gray; subgenus of *Morio*.

Morionassa Sacco, Moll. Terz. Piem. e Lig., VII, p. 74, 1890; type, *M. amplectens* Sacco (abnormal?).

Galeodosconsia Sacco, Moll. Terz. Piem. e Lig., VII, p. 69, 1890; type, *Cassidaria striatula* Bonelli, 1825. Subgenus of *Morio*.

Sconsia Cossmann, Essais de Pal. Comp., V, p. 132, 1903; type, *Cassidaria striata* Lamarck. =*Sconsia* Gray

This group, well defined by its shell characters if we take only the recent forms into consideration, is gradually merged in the fossils into *Galeodea* on the one hand, *Morum* or *Bezoardica* on the other, through the medium of the precursory series. Some of the earlier forms, such as *S. lintea* Conrad, of the Vicksburgian, or *S. striatula* Sowerby, of the Londinian, have the canal more deeply incised, with the result that a well-defined siphonal fasciole appears with a parallel trough behind it, and it is to these forms that Sacco has given the name of *Galeodosconsia*. His *Morionassa* I believe to be an abnormal individual, having the spire acutely drawn out as sometimes happens in various gasteropod genera. The number of varices in this group is variable; usually not more than two occur.

The definition of the subgenus *Sconsia* is as follows:

Shell solid, ovoid, with a moderately prominent subacute spire; sculpture delicate and almost exclusively spiral; outer lip not reflected, thickened internally and transversely lirate without a posterior sinus; inner lip thin, hardly separated from the surface except near the anterior extreme, feebly transversely lirate when fully adult, in the young lirate only over the canal; canal straight, and not deeply incised, especially in the later forms; from the straightness and shallowness of the canal it follows that the siphonal fasciole is obsolete or nonexistent; suture usually more or less appressed; protoconch minute, polished, spirally feebly striate; system of coloration white with faint yellowish maculæ. The soft parts and operculum are unknown.

The earliest American species yet recorded is *S. lintea* Conrad, from the Vicksburgian, which exhibits all the characters of the subgenus, though it is a small species. There follow *S. lævigata* Sowerby, from the Oligocene of Haiti and Santo Domingo, with the variety *sublævigata* Guppy, from Bowden, Jamaica, and a very closely related if not identical form from the Chipola beds of Florida. These are succeeded by a larger species, which reverts somewhat toward *Galeodea* in having a perceptible fasciole, but on the whole may find a place here, the *S. hodgei* from the Duplin Miocene of the Carolinas and the "Alum Bluff" Miocene of Florida. The Pliocene has not afforded any *Cassididæ*, but the typical species of *Sconsia* appears in the recent fauna of the Gulf of Mexico and the Antilles with one or two mutations which have by Arthur Adams and Marrat been treated as species, but of which more abundant material is needed to confirm their status.

Genus OÖCORYS Fischer.

Oöcorys Fischer, Journ. de Conchyl. XXXI, p. 392. October, 1883; *O. sulcata* Fischer, op. cit., abyssal; Man. de Conchyl., p. 769, February, 1884.

Benthodolium Verrill and Smith, Trans. Connecticut Acad., VI. p. 177, May, 1884; *B. abyssorum* V. and S., abyssal.

Oöcorys Dall, Bull. Mus. Comp. Zool.. XVIII, No. 29, p. 228, March, 1889; section *Oöcorys* s. s., type *O. sulcata* Fischer; section *Benthodolium* (p. 229). type *B. abyssorum* Verrill and Smith.

This group was at first separated by Fischer as a distinct family, and in 1889 I accepted this view in the absence of testimony to the contrary. But the increase in the amount of material and resulting fuller study has obliged me to alter my opinion and refer the genus to the *Cassididæ*, in the vicinity of *Galeodea*. The difference in time between the publications of Verrill and Fischer is much less than would be supposed, because the number of the Journal de Conchyliologie for October, 1883, in which the description appeared, was not published earlier than February, 1884, antedating Verrill's paper only about two months. An examination of the material collected by the *Blake* and *Albatross* leaves one in a puzzled state of mind concerning specific limits as indicated by the shell, for no two specimens are alike. If we allow as wide a range for the species of *Oöcorys* as is allowed in Kobelt's Iconography of European Shell-bearing Mollusks to *Cassidaria echinophora*, we may easily come to the conclusion that there are but two species of *Oöcorys* in the North Atlantic, or even possibly but one. However, the majority of the Amèrican specimens are narrowly but deeply umbilicate with a distinct siphonal fasciole and elevated spire. The minority, like those of the eastern North Atlantic, have an excavated simple columella obliquely truncate without trace of any umbilicus or fasciole. In my final *Blake* report I suggested, pending further information, that the two forms be retained as sections representing respectively *Oöcorys* s. s. and *Benthodolium*, the nonumbilicate form being that of which Fischer first gave a description. Neither Watson's nor Locard's diagnosis is sufficient to make it clear whether any of the eastern Atlantic specimens show the umbilicus. If not, the *O. watsoni* of Locard may be the tall variety of *O. sulcata*, while the analogous mutation of *Benthodolium* is present in the *Albatross* material.

The radula of *Benthodolium* or *Oöcorys* is *Cassis*-like. The most essential distinction between the shells of *Galeodea* or *Sconsia* and *Oöcorys* is the smooth outer lip and adherent thin callus of the latter; the only other marked distinction lies in the operculum. I can not regard this as a family distinction, and in some specimens of *Benthodolium* I find unmistakable indications of teeth or ridges on the outer lip, also noted by Watson. The minute protoconch in *Galeodea* agrees with that of *Benthodolium*. In short, there seems little reason to doubt that *Oöcorys* belongs in the family *Cassididæ* near *Galeodea*, and is distinguished as a genus chiefly by its paucispiral operculum.

Genus MORUM Bolten.

Morum Bolten, Mus. Boltenianum, p. 53, 1798; sole example *M. purpureum* Bolten. =*Strombus oniscus* Gmelin 1792.

Lambidium Link, Beschr. Rostock Samml., p. 112, 1807; sole example. *Strombus oniscus* L.: = *Morum* Bolten.

Oniscia Sowerby, Gen. Shells, fasc. 24, 1824; type, *Strombus oniscus* L. Not of Risso, 1826.

Theliostoma Sowerby. Gen. Shells, fasc. 24, 1824, olim, =*Oniscia.*
Cassidara Sowerby. Conch. Man.. ed. 2, p. 307, 1842; a synonym of *Oniscia (oniscus)*, fide Sowerby.
Ersina Gray, Syn. Brit. Mus., 1840, fide Gray, Proc. Zool. Soc. London for 1847. p. 137; type, *Strombus oniscus* L.
Morum Mörch, Cat. Yoldi, I. p. 111. 1852; *Strombus oniscus* L.
Morum H. and A. Adams. Gen. Rec. Moll., I. p. 219. 1853; *M. oniscus* L. sp.
Oniscia Philippi, Handb. Conch., p. 154, 1853; =*Oniscia* Sowerby.
Morum Gray, Guide Moll., p. 40. 1857; *M. oniscus.*
Morum Mörch. Mal. Blatt.. XXIV, p. 39, 1877; *M. oniscus* L. sp.
Oniscia Fischer, Man. de Conchyl., p. 660, 1884; *O. oniscus* L. sp.
Plesioniscia Fischer, Man. de Conchyl., p. 660, 1884; section of *Oniscia; O. tuberculosa* Sowerby.
Oniscia Sacco. Moll. Terz. Piem. e Lig., VII, p. 76, 1890; =*Oniscia* Sowerby.
Lambidium Rovereto, Atti Soc. Lig., X (p. 7 of extras), 1899; =*Lambidium* Link, 1807.
Oniscia Cossmann. Essais de Pal. Comp.. V, p. 134, 1903; type. *Strombus oniscus* L.; =*Oniscia* Sowerby.

Section ONISCIDIA Mörch.

Oniscidia Swainson. Malac.. p. 299, 1840; cites *O. oniscus* L. and *O. cancellata* Sowerby, figuring the former. Evidently a typographical error for the name *Oniscia*, which is correctly spelled elsewhere in the text and index.
Oniscidia (Sw.) Mörch. Cat. Yoldi, I, p. 111, 1852; *O. cancellata* Sowerby.
Oniscidia H. and A. Adams, Gen. Rec. Moll., I. p. 220. 1853; subgenus of *Morum;* first species. *M. cancellatum* Sby.
Oniscia Gray, Guide Moll.. p. 40. 1857; *O. cancellata.*
Oniscidia Fischer, Man. de Conchyl.. p. 660. 1884; section of *Oniscia; O. cancellata* Sowerby.
Oniscidia Sacco. Moll. Terz. Piem. e Lig., VII, p. 76, 1890; subgenus of *Oniscia:* =*Oniscidia* auct.
Oniscidia Cossmann, Essais de Pal. Comp., V, p. 134. 1903; type, *O. cancellata* Sby.; section of *Oniscia.*

Section HERCULEA Hanley.

Herculea Hanley, in H. and A. Adams, Gen. Rec. Moll., II, p. 621. November, 1858; type, *Morum ponderosum* Hanley; subgenus of *Morum;* not *Herculia* Walker (Insecta), 1859.

The genus *Morum* was first recognized by Bolten, who gave it the very appropriate name it now bears, the most common species having a marked resemblance to a mulberry, so that, as noted by Argenville in 1757, its colloquial name was "la mure." Gmelin had referred it to *Strombus* and his specific name for the type species antedates that of Bolten by six years and must therefore be retained. Link, with his usual fondness for altering the names of his predecessors, though citing Bolten's name, proposed to replace it by *Lambidium.* Sowerby, ignorant of either apparently, proposed *Oniscia* still later. Swainson seems to have intended to adopt Sowerby's name, but it somehow got printed *Oniscidia,* though elsewhere in the text, and also in the index, it has Sowerby's spelling. This misprint was used by Mörch as a name for the forms of *Morum* like *M. cancellatum,* which have sharp reticulate sculpture, and as such it has been generally accepted. A further subdivision of this group was proposed by Hanley for species like his *M. ponderosum,* which have a deep posterior sulcus; and still later Fischer proposed for *M. tuberculosum* Sowerby the name of *Plesioniscia.* He gave no characters and there do not appear to be any of importance, so this section has not been accepted.

The genus *Morum* then stands as follows:

Section *Morum* s. s.; type, *M. oniscus* Gmelin; sculpture spiral, tubercular.
Section *Oniscidia* (Sw.) Mörch: type. *M cancellatum* Sby.; sculpture sharp. reticular, posterior end of the aperture without a sulcus.

Section *Herculea* Hanley; type, *M. ponderosum* Hanley; sculpture approaching *Oniscidia* but with a deep recurved sulcus at the posterior end of the aperture. *M. dennisoni* Reeve, of the West Indies, and *M. exquisitum* Adams and Reeve, of the Sulu Sea, belong in this section.

According to Sacco, *M. antiquum* Bayan from the Eocene of Monte Ilario is referable to this genus, and subsequent horizons of the Italian Tertiary contain representatives of the group as far as the Pliocene, though the recent and Pleistocene faunas do not include the genus in the region of Italy.

In America the first recorded appearance of the group is in the lower Oligocene of Vicksburg, Miss., from which *M. (Oniscidia) harpulum* has been described by Conrad, and a very similar if not identical species occurs in the middle Oligocene of the Chipola beds of northwestern Florida. The *M. (Herculea) domingense* of Sowerby appears in the Oligocene of Santo Domingo. The lower temperature of the Miocene seems to have been unfavorable to the genus, which disappears from all the faunas above the Oligocene and reappears only in the recent fauna of both coasts of middle America, the Gulf of California, and the West Indies, including the Bahamas. The typical section, *Morum*, is not known in the fossil state in America, and the earlier members of the group, as might be expected, are more generalized in their characters than those of the recent fauna. The earliest known species, *M. costellatum* Stoliczka, from the uppermost Cretaceous of southern India, is small and has a more elevated spire than any of its later representatives. The species of the Vienna basin Miocene approaches more nearly to *Oniscidia*, but we have so far found nothing corresponding to it in the American Miocene.

Family DOLIIDÆ.

This family is distinguished from the *Cassididæ* by the following characters: Protoconch large and heliciform; radula with two basal spines on the rhachidian tooth, the cusps of that and the laterals simple or minutely serrate rather than divided into a number of subequal denticles; shell with only a terminal varix and usually an inconspicuous body callus; aperture ample, the canal not markedly reflected; operculum wanting.

It is not improbable that the origin of both families was from a form which has much the aspect of *Pyrula* and of which several are known in the Cretaceous and basal Eocene. Conchologically the young of *Galeodaria* could not, in default of a knowledge of the adult, be separated from some of the Eocene Pyrulæ. From this prototype evolution seems to have been probable in several lines, as the existing *Pyrula* line, the *Galeodea* line, the *Malea* line, and the *Eudolium* line. True *Dolium* is perhaps the most modern type and hardly known as a fossil. The species from the Chalk described by Sowerby is a very defective internal cast of a large gasteropod referred to *Strombus* by D'Orbigny and Hoernes, and, with more probability, to *Pterocera* by Pictet and Martin. In considering the present genus, therefore, it may be disregarded.

The singular type described as *Ficulopsis* by Stoliczka, from the Cretaceous of India, has a remarkable external similarity to *Pyrula*, but the characters of the axis show it to belong to the *Volutidæ*, as elsewhere indicated, close to the forms from the same rocks which he has referred to *Fulguraria*. It seems to be, in fact, a volutoid in which the spire has become dwindled and domelike, while the body of the animal was contained chiefly in the last whorl and a half. The resemblances to *Pyrula* are therefore merely an instance of the convergence of dissimilar phyla due to external conditions. In searching the literature for records of *Dolium* s. s. in the fossil state I have found nearly all the references to the genus erroneous, if it be taken in the modern sense. The fossils mainly belong to the genera *Eudolium* or *Malea*. I have found nothing older than the Pleistocene, except the *Dolium galea* reported from the Miocene of Goose Creek, South Carolina, by Tuomey and Holmes. This fossil as figured is an internal cast, the figure of which has no marked resemblance to a *Dolium*, and does not appear to have the rotundity of *D. galea;* moreover, there seems to be evidence of an internal varix about the middle of the last whorl. I am inclined to believe, therefore, that the identification is erroneous, as the original specimen seems not to have been preserved. It is impossible to speak with certainty, but I suspect the cast to have belonged to one of the large thinshelled species of *Phalium* like *P. coronadoi* Crosse. At any rate, until more decisive information is received we may be permitted to doubt the existence of true *Dolium* before the end of the Pliocene. It may be added that *Dolium octocostatum* Emmons is undoubtedly an *Isapis*: the Doliums of the northwest coast seem to be all *Eudolium*, and those of the Panama and Antillean region belong to *Malea* as far as noted.

Genus EUDOLIUM Dall.

Dolium (sp.) Verrill and Smith, Am. Jour. Sci., 3d ser., XXII. p. 296, October. 1881; Trans. Connecticut Acad. Sci., V, p. 515, 1882; VI, p. 253, pl. 29, figs. 2a–c, 1884.

Doliopsis Monterosato. Notiz. Conch. Foss. M. Pellegrino e Ficarazzi, Palermo, 1872. pp. 8–9; type, *Dolium crosseanum* Mts.; not *Doliopsis* Conrad. 1865.

Doliopsis Fischer. Man. de Conchyl., p. 661, 1884; section of *Dolium*. type, *D. crosseanum* Monterosato: not *Doliopsis* Conrad. 1865 (=*Eudolium* Dall).

Eudolium Dall, Bull. Mus. Comp. Zool., XVIII, p. 232, March, 1889; new name for *Doliopsis* Monterosato, 1872, not Conrad, 1865; also Bull. 37, U. S. Nat. Mus., p. 134, June. 1889.

Eudolium Sacco, Boll. Mus. Zool. di Torino, V, No. 86, 1890; Moll. Terz. Piem. e Lig., VIII. 1891, p. 2; =*Eudolium* Dall. 1889.

Galeodolium Sacco. Boll. Mus. Zool. di Torino, V, No. 86, 1890; Moll. Terz. Piem. e Lig., VIII, p. 4. 1891; section of *Eudolium;* type. *D. muticum* Michelotti.

Tuberculodolium Sacco, Boll. Mus. Zool. di Torino, V, No. 86, 1890; Moll. Terz. Piem. e Lig., VIII. pp. 4. 9, 1891; section of *Eudolium;* type, *E. antiquum* Sacco.

Simplicodolium Sacco, Boll. Mus. Zool. di Torino, V. No. 86. 1890; Moll. Terz. Piem. e Lig., VIII. pp. 4, 13, 1891; section of *Eudolium;* type. *Pyrula fasciata* Borson.

Eudolium differs from *Dolium* s. s. (=*Tonna* Brunnich) by its smaller size appressed suture, straight nonreflexed canal, with inconspicuous siphonal fasciole and absence of an umbilicus, and the thin but evident body callus which, in the fully mature shell, is granulate or lirate, though not dentate as in *Malea*.

In Italy, according to Sacco, it makes its appearance in the Tongrian (lower Oligocene) and it is found continuously to the existing fauna. In America it is fully developed and forms a conspicuous fossil of the Astoria and Coos Bay Miocene, of the Pacific coast, while on the Atlantic coast it is represented only by recent species in deep water. Although Conrad referred his Astoria species to *Doliopsis*, in ignorance of their characters, they are not congeneric with his original *Doliopsis* (*quinquecosta*) from the Jacksonian of Mississippi.

EUDOLIUM PETROSUM Conrad.

Pl. XIV, fig. 6.

Dolium petrosum Conrad, Geol. U. S. Expl. Exp., appendix I. p. 727. pl. 19. figs. 3a, 3b, 4a, 4b, 1849.
Doliopsis petrosus Conrad, Am. Jour. Conch., I, p. 150, 1865.
Doliopsis biliratum Conrad, Am. Jour. Conch., I, p. 150, 1865; young shell of *D. petrosus* Conrad.

Shell large, thin, globose, with a nucleus of three smooth and four subsequent sculptured whorls; nucleus subacute; subsequent whorls with a single row of small sharp nodules forming a shoulder to the whorl, about 15 on the penultimate whorl, and a second series on the apical whorls, which are much less prominent, are usually covered by the suture, and are practically obsolete on the last whorl; from these nodules extend axially faint obsolete ridges which in the main wholly disappear before reaching the suture behind or the periphery of the whorl in front; other spiral sculpture consisting of (between the shoulder and the preceding suture about six) major flattish revolving ridges separated by subequal or narrower channeled interspaces often containing a much smaller intercalary thread, and in front of the shoulder two small and three large similar ridges followed by another bearing the secondary series of nodulations, in front of which ten major ridges, the first five with intercalaries, the remainder without, extend to the canal; the whole surface is obsoletely, minutely spirally striate; aperture longer than wide; outer lip thin, sharp, slightly reflected, pillar and body with a thin wash of callus, pillar elongated, twisted, with a shallow anterior sulcus; canal deeply sulcate, recurved with a strong fasciole and wide sulcus behind it. Altitude, 80 mm.; maximum diameter, 52 mm.

Miocene of Freshwater Bay, Clallam County, Wash., Ralph Arnold; U. S. Nat. Mus. 110425. Original types of Conrad, U. S. Nat. Mus. 3536; Miocene of Astoria, Oreg., J. D. Dana, U. S. Expl. Exp.

The original types of *Dolium petrosum* Conrad, are internal casts, which give only an imperfect idea of the external sculpture. One specimen, however, retains enough of the shell to enable us to identify it with the more perfect shell collected by Arnold, from which the above revised description has been drawn up. It is a handsome shell and differs from any of the recent species in possessing subspinose nodulations as well as spiral sculpture.

EUDOLIUM OREGONENSE Dall, n. sp.

Pl. VII, fig. 7.

Shell thin, globose, strongly spirally sculptured, with about five whorls exclusive of the nucleus; earlier whorls with three or four, last whorl with about 11 major spiral ridges, squarish, often irregularly squarely nodulous, with wider channeled interspaces, smooth, or containing one or more smaller intercalary ridges; the posterior major spiral runs close to the suture, giving it a channeled effect; the spirals on the apical whorls are often reticulated by obscure axial riblets subnodulous at the intersections, but these disappear on the later whorls, though the major spirals often continue to show irregular nodulation; last whorl much the largest, terminating in the adult in a slightly reflected and thickened outer lip with obscure denticulations on its inner edge; canal short, deeply excavated, with a deep sulcus behind it, twisted and more or less plicate; a thin wash of callus on the body.   Altitude of shell, 69 mm.; of last whorl, 60 mm.; maximum diameter, 51 mm.   Another specimen measures, respectively, 75, 64, and 53 mm.

Miocene of Coos Bay, Oregon, purchased from B. H. Camman; U. S. Nat. Mus. 153895.

It is quite evident from the specimens studied that this species varies in the strength and number of its intercalary spirals, and it is possible that these may sometimes approach the major spirals in size, so that the total number of subequal spirals on the body whorl might be nearly double the number mentioned in the above diagnosis.

Genus MALEA Valenciennes.

Cadium (sp.) Link, Beschr. Rostock Samml., p. 113, 1807 (= new name for *Cadus* Bolten, fide Link); first species *C. pomum* L.; other species typical *Dolium.*
Malea Valenciennes, Humb. Voy., Zool.. II. b. 324, 1833; type, *Malea latilabris* Val. = *Cassis ringens* Swainson.
Malea Mörch, Cat. Yoldi, I, p. 111. 1852; = *Malea* Valenciennes.
Cadium H. and A. Adams, Gen. Rec. Moll., I, p. 196, 1853; *C. pomum* L. sp.
Malea Gray, Guide Moll., p. 41, 1857; *M. pomum.*
Malea Fischer. Man. de Conchyl., p. 661, 1884; subgenus of *Dolium; D. ringens* Swainson.
Malea Sacco, Moll. Terz. Piem. e Lig., VIII, p. 18, 1891; = *Malea* Valenciennes.
Malea Cossmann, Essais de Pal. Comp., V. p. 139, 1893; type, *Buccinum pomum* Linné.

The name *Cadium* Link, sometimes used for this genus, was originally merely a substitute for *Cadus* Bolten, of which it was an exact synonym.   There seems to be no reason why it should take the place of the later but properly proposed *Malea*, which has become familiar.

Malea recalls *Cassis* in its size, weight, and conspicuous callosities.   These last are set on a comparatively thin coating of callus, and project into the lumen of the whorl from the body and pillar, while the aperture is still further contracted by an unusually heavy and callous outer lip.   The canal, too, is deeply incised and has no umbilical perforation.   In the recent species some anatomical differences also are noted between the animal of *Malea* and *Dolium*.   *Malea camura* Guppy, frequently confounded in the literature with *M. ringens*, the recent Panama species, occurs rather commonly in the Oligocene of the Antilles, Haiti, Santo Domingo, Jamaica, and on the Isthmus of Panama.   It is interesting to find the type, once widely spread in the Antillean region, now entirely extinct there, though surviving with slight modifications in the recent fauna of the Pacific coast.   In this it agrees with a fairly numerous group of mollusks which are not genetically akin to it, but which have endured similar vicissitudes.

Genus TONNA Brünnich.

Dolium Browne. Hist. Jamaica, p. 406, 1756; first species, *D. perdix;* nomenclature not binomial.
Ampullacea inflata Linné, Syst. Nat., ed. 10, p. 734, 1758; section *a* of *Buccinum* L., containing *Dolium olearium, galea, perdix, pomum,* and *dolium* (= *maculatum*) of Linné in the order cited; = *Dolium* Lamarck.   This group derives from the *Buccina ampullacea* of Lister, lib. IV, sect. 11, 1688.
Tonna Brünnich, Fundamenta Zool., p. 248, 1772; no species cited, but diagnosis given; = *Dolium* Lamarck.
Dolium (anonymous), Mus. Calonnianum, p. 19, 1797; contains five species of *Dolium; = Dolium* Lamarck.
Cadus Bolten, Mus. Boltenianum, p. 150. 1798; first species, *Buccinum perdix* Gmelin; *Dolium* auct.

Dolium Lamarck, Syst. des Anim. s. Vert., p. 79, 1801; sole example, *D. galea* L. sp.
Dolium Bosc, Hist. Nat. Coq., IV, p. 260, 1802; type, *Buccinum galea* L.
Dolium Roissy, Hist. Nat. des Moll., VI, p. 37, 1806; first species, *D. galea* L. (includes also *D. pomum*).
Cadium Link, Beschr. Rostock Samml., p. 113, 1887; new name for *Cadus* Bolten.
Dolium Montfort, Conch. Syst.. II, p. 451, 1810; type, *Buccinum galea* L.
Perdix Montfort, Conch. Syst., II, p. 447, 1810; type, *Buccinum perdix* L.; not *Perdix* Brisson (Aves), 1760.
Nassa sect. α, Oken, Lehrb. d. Naturg. (3), I, p. 276, 1815; first species, *Buccinum galea* L.; = *Dolium* Lamarck.
Dolium Schumacher, Essai, pp. 63, 209, 1817; sole example, *Buccinum perdix* Linné.
Dolium Cuvier, Règne Anim., II, p. 435, 1817; first species, *D. olearium*.
Dolites Krüger, Gesch. Urwelt, II. p. 418, 1823; = *Dolium*. fossil sp.
Dolium Blainville, Man. Mal., I. p. 409, 1825; *D. galea*.
Dolium Sowerby, Gen. Shells, fasc. 29, 1827; *D. olearium* and *fimbriatum*.
Dolium Swainson, Malac., p. 299, 1840; figures *D. galea* and cites *D. olearium* and *fimbriatum*; = *Dolium* Sby., 1827.
Dolium Sowerby, Conch. Man., ed. 2, p. 140, 1842; *D. maculatum*.
Dolium Mörch, Cat. Yoldi, I, p. 110, 1852.
Dolium Philippi, Handb. Conch., p. 154. 1853; = *Dolium* Lamarck.
Dolium H. and A. Adams, Gen. Rec. Moll., I, p. 196, 1853; *D. olearium* L. sp.
Dolium Gray, Guide Moll., p. 40, 1857; *D. perdix* figured.
Perdix Fischer, Man. de Conchyl., p. 661. 1884; section of *Dolium; Buccinum perdix* L.
Dolium Fischer, Man. de Conchyl., p. 661, 1884; *Buccinum galea* L.
Dolium Rovereto. Atti Soc. Lig., X (p. 7 of extras), 1899; = *Dolium* Lamarck.
Foratidolium Rovereto, Atti Soc. Lig., X (p. 7 of extras), 1899; new name for *Perdix* Montfort, non Brisson.
Dolium Cossmann, Essais de Pal. Comp., V. p. 137, 1903; type, *Buccinum galea* L.; with subgenera *Malea* and *Eudolium*.

We now proceed to the consideration of the group which has given its name to the family. For these the enormously capacious rounded shells with hooplike sculpture had long suggested the vernacular names of tuns, casks, or barrels, in Latin *Tonna*, *Dolium*, or *Cadus*. The first mentioned is a barbarous coinage, but had been in use since the time of Argenville, and the others were colloquially familiar in the latter part of the eighteenth century.

The first binomial appellation given to this group was *Tonna* of Brünnich, in his Fundamenta Zoologica. He defined the genus and put it in its natural place in the system, but, as in some other cases, mentioned none of the species of which the genus is made up.

The next person to treat the group as a genus was one of the anonymous authors of the Museum Calonnianum. This person adopted *Dolium* from Browne, a polynomial and pre-Linnean author, who had written on the natural history of Jamaica. A year later Bolten's system was published, and in it he adopted the name *Cadus* for these shells. It was not until three years later that Lamarck put the name *Dolium* on a scientific footing. Among subsequent authors no one seems to have noticed Brünnich's name except Herrmannsen, from whose Index others have cited it as a synonym of *Dolium*. According to the latest international code, *Tonna* fills all the requirements for a legitimate generic name, and under the circumstances there seems to be no escape from the necessity of adopting it, though *Dolium* has been in use for more than a century. As anonymous privately issued pamphlets have no standing in nomenclature, the Museum Calonnianum, without ostensible author or publisher, does not count. Therefore if we reject Brünnich's name we shall be obliged to adopt the next formally proposed binomial generic name, which is not *Dolium*, but *Cadus* Bolten, afterwards arbitrarily modified by Link to *Cadium*. This does not give us much comfort, for, of the two, *Tonna* is more euphonious and hardly more unfamiliar than *Cadus;* and since it is best, if reform must come, to make it radical, I have adopted *Tonna*, as it is clearly unjustifiable, under the rules, to retain *Dolium*.

This group is characterized by large, thin shells with spiral sculpture, an almost channeled suture, a slightly thickened and reflected outer lip, an absence of callosities on the body, and only a thin, smooth coat of enamel on the labium, which arches over the gutter in front of a very prominent siphonal fasciole, forming a small umbilical perforation. The canal is short, but deeply incised, and behind closely obliquely truncate. The periostracum is usually conspicuous, but extremely caducous, and is very rarely retained on cabinet shells. Most of the species have a low, blunt spire, but *T. perdix* L., in which the spire is produced and the profile of the shell thus rendered more oval, was made the type of a genus *Perdix* by Montfort. The name was preoccupied in ornithology, and is quite unnecessary. The species is reported from the elevated Pleistocene reefs of Barbados, and is the oldest undoubted fossil of its genus, so far as I have been able to discover.

The larval stage of *Tonna* has a free-swimming animal with a light horny shell resembling a small *Helix*, and was once described as a land shell by C. B. Adams. This enables it to survive transportation by currents to considerable distances, and the species are widely distributed in the Tropics. The animal is notable for secreting, in connection with its digestive apparatus, sulphuric acid of a strength sufficient to make polished marble effervesce.

Genus FICUS Bolten.

Bulla (sp.) Linné, Syst. Nat., ed. 12. p. 1184, 1767.
Ficus (sp.) (anonymous), Mus. Calonnianum, p. 32, 1797; *Bulla ficus* Linné.
Ficus Bolten, Mus. Boltenianum. p. 148, 1798; sole example, *Bulla ficus* Gmelin.
Pyrula Lamarck, Prodrome. p. 73, 1799; sole example, *Bulla ficus* Linné: Syst. des Anim. s. Vert., p. 82, 1801, same type.
Pirula Montfort, Conch. Syst., II, p. 486, 1810; same type.
Ficula Swainson, Malac., pp. 85, 307, 1840; same type.
Sycotypus Mörch, Cat. Yoldi, p. 110, 1852.
Sycotyphus Conrad, Am. Jour. Conch.. I, p. 151, 1865.

The name *Ficus* Bolten, based on the same type, and derived from early eighteenth century authors before Linné, has a year's priority over *Pyrula* Lamarck, and must be adopted.

FICUS MODESTUS Conrad.

Pyrula modesta Conrad, Am. Jour. Sci., 2d ser., V, p. 433, fig. 12, 1848.
Sycotyphus modestus Conrad, Am. Jour. Conch., I, p. 151, 1865.

Tertiary of Astoria, Oreg., collected by J. K. Townsend and W. Q. Brown.

This small species belongs to the typical *Ficus*. Conrad's original description and figure are reproduced in Appendix I of the present work (pp. 150–151). The present location of his type is unknown, but the species was collected at Astoria by W. Q. Brown, U. S. Nat. Mus. 110457. This specimen has a length of 47 mm. and a width of 29 mm.

Subgenus TROPHOSYCON Cooper.

Trophosycon Cooper, Bull. California State Mining Bureau, No. 4, p. 53, 1894.

Figshells with axial ribs or nodules, simple suture, and strongly curved canal. This group seems more nearly related to the Figshells than to the *Agasoma* with which Cooper associated it. The type is *T. kernianum* Cooper, op. cit., pl. 3, fig. 52.

FICUS (TROPHOSYCON) OREGONENSIS Conrad.

Fusus oregonensis Conrad, Am. Jour. Sci., 2d ser., V, p. 433, fig. 13, 1848.
Sycotyphus oregonensis Conrad, Am. Jour. Conch., I, p. 151, 1865.

Tertiary of Astoria, Oreg., collected by J. K. Townsend; Conrad.

I have not seen the type specimen, a figure of which, reproduced from Conrad, will be found in Appendix I of the present work (pp. 150–151).

According to Cooper, Conrad's *Sycotyphus ocoyanus* may have been based on the internal cast of a specimen belonging to this group. The type of the subgenus is in the collection of the California State Mining Bureau, if not destroyed in the San Francisco fire which followed the earthquake of 1906.

Family CERITHIOPSIDÆ.

Genus CERITHIOPSIS Forbes and Hanley.

Cerithiopsis Forbes and Hanley, British Moll., II. p. 367. 1853; type, *C. tubercularis* (Montagu).

CERITHIOPSIS EXCELSUS Dall, n. sp.

Pl. III, fig. 9.

Shell large for the genus, slender, with about 14 whorls; apex defective; later whorls with a closely appressed suture and moderately rounded; sculpture of numerous, slightly concavely arcuate, little-elevated, axial ribs with subequal or wider interspaces, crossed by numerous fine rounded threads with wider interspaces; the spiral threads overrun the ribs and (especially three or four which are stronger than the rest) are minutely nodulous in most cases at the intersections; here and there the whorls are crossed by a swollen varix, indicating a previous resting stage; base rather rounded, with about six prominent spiral threads, with wider interspaces which sometimes carry a much finer intercalary thread; canal short, recurved; aperture obstructed by matrix, the outer lip at resting stages slightly expanded and thickened. Altitude, 20.5 mm., maximum diameter, 6.5 mm.

Oregonian Eocene of North Fork of Umpqua River, at Schrum's ranch, station 2798, collected by J. S. Diller; U. S. Nat. Mus. 107400.

Family CERITHIIDÆ.

Genus BITTIUM Leach.

Bittium Leach,[a] in Gray, Proc. Zool. Soc. London for 1847, p. 154; type, *Murex reticulatus* Montagu.
    Section *Bittium* s. s. Type, *B. reticulatum* Mont. Sculpture nodosely reticulate.
    Section *Stylidium* Dall. Type, *Turritella eschrichtii* Middendorff. Sculpture of spiral grooves
    with flattish interspaces.

BITTIUM (STYLIDIUM) ESCHRICHTII Middendorff.

Pl. XIV, fig. 2.

Cerithium filosum Gould, Proc. Boston Soc. Nat. Hist., III. p. 120, 1849; not of Philippi, Zeitschr. für
    Mal., 1848, p. 143.
Turritella eschrichtii Middendorff, Beitr. Mal. Ross., II, p. 68, pl. 11, fig. 1, 1849.
Bittium filosum Carpenter, Rept. Brit. Assoc. for 1863, p. 655, 1864; Arnold, Pal. and Strat. San Pedro,
    p. 292, 1903.
Bittium (Stylidium) Eschrichtii Dall, Proc. U. S. Nat. Mus., XXXIII, No. 1564, p. 178, Oct., 1907.

Shell large for the genus, moderately thick, solid, with about ten whorls, including the nucleus; the latter is dextral, smooth, slender, and rather blunt at the apex; on the subsequent whorls sculpture of (on the spire four; on the last whorl, including the base, about ten) flat, wide, straplike revolving ridges, separated by much narrower channeled interspaces; the ridges are rarely made duplex by an incised line, and are crossed by evident incremental lines also visible in the channels, and on the last whorl there is sometimes a fine intercalary thread in some of the channels; the whole surface bears more or less obsolete, extremely fine striation; the recent shell is livid or whitish, with irregular brownish streaks and patches on the posterior half of the whorls; base rounded; canal extremely short, not recurved; aperture roughly semilunate, outer lip thin, simple; a thin wash of callus on the body, the pillar smooth, shorter than the aperture, a little twisted anteriorly. Altitude, 15 mm.; maximum diameter, 5 mm.

Pleistocene of Fossil Rock, Coos Bay, Oregon, collected by W. H. Dall at station 2950; U. S. Nat. Mus. 153992. Upper San Pedro formation, southern California. Living from the Aleutian Islands southward to Monterey, Cal., between tides.

Family TRICHOTROPIDÆ.

Genus TRICHOTROPIS Sowerby.

Trichotropis Sowerby, Zool. Jour., IV, p. 373, 1829; type, *T. bicarinata* Sowerby.
Tricophore Deshayes, Encycl. Méth., III, tabl., 1830.
Trichotropus Lesson, Ill. Zool., tabl. 41, 1832.
Trichopodus Swainson, Malac., p. 210, 1840; not of Lacépède, 1800.
Tropiphora Lovèn, fide Tryon, not *Tropiphorus* Schönherr (Coleoptera), 1842.
Iphinoë H. and A. Adams, Gen. Rec. Moll., I, p. 280, 1854; type, *T. unicarinata* Sowerby.
Verena Gray, Guide Moll. Brit. Mus., p. 44, 1857; type, *Trichotropis borealis* Sowerby; not *Verena* H.
    and A. Adams, 1854.
? *Valvatella* Gray, Guide, p. 157, 1857; type a nomen nudum.
Cerithioderma Conrad, Jour. Acad. Nat. Sci. Philadelphia, 2d ser., IV, p. 295, March, 1860; sole example,
    C. prima Conrad, op. cit., pl. 47, fig. 30, Eocene, Alabama.

---

[a] *Cerithiolum* Tiberi, 1869; a name given under the (mistaken?) supposition that *Bittium* had been used for a crustacean before 1847.

Mesostoma Deshayes, Anim. s. Vert. Bas. Paris, II, p. 416, 1861; first species, *M. pulchra* Desh., Eocene; = *Cerithioderma* Conrad.

Alora H. Adams, Proc. Zool. Soc. London for 1861, p. 27; type, *A. gouldii* Adams.

Ariadna Fischer, Jour. de Conchyl., XII, p. 255, 1864; type, *T. borealis* Sowerby.

Torellia Loven, in Jeffreys, Brit. Conch., IV, p. 244, 1867; type, *T. vestita* Jeffreys.

Crepitacella Guppy, Geol. Mag., IV, p. 500, 1867; type, *Melanopsis cepula* Guppy.

Trachysma Jeffreys MS., in Seguenza, Form. Terz. di Reggio, p. 269, 1879; type, *Cyclostoma delicatum* Philippi.

Dolophanes Gabb, Proc. Acad. Nat. Sci. Philadelphia for 1872. p. 273; type, *D. melanoides* Gabb, Oligocene (= *Crepitacella* Guppy); Dall, Blake Rept., Gastr., p. 270. 1889.

Trachyoma Tryon, Man. Conch., IX, p. 41, 1887 (err. typ. for *Trachysma* Jeffreys).

?*Separatista* Gray, Proc. Zool. Soc. London for 1847, p. 136; type, *Turbo helicina* Gmelin.

?*Turbinopsis* Conrad, Jour. Acad. Nat. Sci. Philadelphia, 2d ser., IV, p. 259, 1860; type, *T. hilgardi* Conrad, op. cit., pl. 46, fig. 29; Cretaceous.

?*Gyrotropis* Gabb, Proc. Acad. Nat. Sci. Philadelphia for 1876, p. 300; type, *G. squamosa* Gabb, op. cit., pl. 17, fig. 5; Cretaceous.

?*Haloceras* Dall, Bull. Mus. Comp. Zool., XVIII, p. 277, 1889: type, *Cithna cingulata* Verrill.

A considerable number of names have been used in connection with the subdivisions of this family, but studied in mass the characteristics shade very gradually into one another. *Iphinoë* looks very distinct from the typical forms, but, on analysis, its peculiar characters consist chiefly in the channeled suture, more naticoid form, and more emphatic siphonal angle. *Torellia* is more turbinate, with the siphonal angle obsolete, but the subtruncate pillar remains. The description of *Valvatella* (founded on an unpublished and unfigured species), except for the operculum, agrees fairly with *Torellia*.

Cerithioderma and the typical species (if not all the species) of *Mesostoma* Deshayes, are identical, and the dredging of a well-marked recent species in deep water of the West Indies by the *Blake* confirms its relations to *Trichotropis* rather than to the Cerithiidæ. *Alora* is unfigured and I have not seen a specimen. *Crepitacella* has a trichotropoid aspect, but the recent specimens found did not contain the animal and its place is still doubtful. *Separatista* and *Haloceras* are very probably loosely coiled trichotropids. *Turbinopsis* and *Gyrotropis* are more doubtful; the former may belong near *Modulus* and the latter near *Rapana*, but both have characters in common with *Trichotropis*.

I may note that, in Tryon's Manual, two of Jeffreys's species are figured, which I believe to be larval shells of some species like *Fusitriton* or *Cymatium*. These are "*Trichotropis*" *fimbriata* and *densistriata* Jeffreys.

Members of this family are rather rare as fossils, yet the characteristics of the following species, so far as they are visible, recall *Trichotropis* more than any other form known to me.

TRICHOTROPIS OREGONENSIS Conrad.

Cancellaria? oregonensis Conrad, Geol. U. S. Expl. Exp. (no name), pl. 20, fig. 8 (reversed), 1849; Am. Jour. Conch., I. p. 151, 1865.

Oligocene or Miocene concretions from the Astoria group, Astoria, Oreg., J. D. Dana; U. S. Nat. Mus. 3554 (figured type), 3549, and 3531.

The specimens are internal casts and external molds with the shelly matter disintegrated. A gutta-percha cast, however, reveals the sculpture fairly well.

The shell has about five whorls, subtabulate with a high angular shoulder, the whorls rapidly increasing; the pillar is smooth, without plaits, and the aperture rounded except at the anterior end, where there is an angle, but no canal or sulcus; the pillar is thin, simple, and oblique; the sculpture consists, above the shoulder and on the base, of fine threads with about equal interspaces; over the middle of the whorl there are six or eight stronger cords with much wider interspaces; the axial sculpture on the last whorl consists of 10 or 12 narrow, sharpish ribs, stronger and more rounded on the shoulder, which extend clear across the whorl; there are also very fine, close lines, like emphasized incremental lines, over most of the surface. Length of shell, about 25 mm.; of last whorl, 19 mm.; maximum diameter, 17 mm.

It seemed worth while to describe, as far as the material would permit, this species, which was only poorly figured by Conrad, who, sixteen years later, named his figure, even then without taking the trouble to describe the fossil. The characters all harmonize with *Trichotropis*, and while the siphonal angle is rather produced, it is hardly more so than in some recent species.

Family TURRITELLIDÆ.

Genus TURRITELLA Lamarck.

Tympanotonus Rumphius, Amboinische Rariteit Kammer, p. 101. pl. 20, fig. M., 1705; = *Turritella terebra* Lamarck. Not binomial.
Turbo (sp.) Linné, Syst. Nat.. ed. 10, p. 766, 1758.
Terebra (anonymous), Mus. Calonnianum, p. 23, 1797; sole identifiable species, *Turbo duplicatus* Linné.
Epitonium 2, Bolten, Mus. Boltenianum, p. 92, 1798; first species, *Turbo duplicatus* Gmelin.
Turritella Lamarck, Prodrome, p. 74, 1799: type, *Turbo terebra* Linné.
Epitonium Link, Beschr. Rostock Samml., p. 131, 1807; first species, *Turritella acutangula* (Link) Menke.
Haustator Montfort, Conch. Syst., II, p. 183, 1810; type, *Turritella imbricataria* Lamarck.
Turritellus Montfort, Conch. Syst., II, p. 211, 1810; type, *T. terebra* Linné.
Aculea Perry, Conch., expl. pl. 16, figs. 1–3, 1811.
Torcula Gray, Proc. Zool. Soc. London for 1847, p. 155; type, *Turritella exoleta* Lamarck.
Zaria Gray, Proc. Zool. Soc. London for 1847, p. 155: type, *Turritella duplicata* (Linné).
Terebellum Browne, 1756, not Rumphius 1705; both nonbinomial.

TURRITELLA OREGONENSIS Conrad.

Cerithiopsis? oregonensis Conrad, Am. Jour. Conch.. I. p. 151, 1865; name for figs. 13, 14, pl. 20, Geol. U. S. Expl. Exp.. atlas, 1849.

Oligocene or Miocene concretions from the Tertiary beds at Astoria, Oreg., J. D. Dana, No. 63; U. S. Nat. Mus. 110446.

A small, slender *Turritella* with about eight whorls; suture obscure; in front of it the whorl is flattish with two to five small, close-set spiral threads, in front of which are two (on the last whorl three) much stronger elevated spirals, with a deep groove between them, the anterior marginating the base, which is flattish, with a few weaker spirals; there is no axial sculpture except lines of growth; apex decollate, length of remainder 22.5 mm.; diameter at decollation, 3.0 mm.; maximum diameter of last whorl, 7.0 mm.

Conrad gave no description of this species.

Genus LITTORINA Ferussac.

Turbo (sp.) Linné, Syst. Nat., ed. 10, p. 761, 1758; ed. 12, p. 1233, sect. *Neritoidei*, 1767.

Lunella (sp.) Bolten, Mus. Boltenianum, p. 104, 1798.

Littorina Ferussac, Tabl. Syst., pp. xi, xxxiv, 1822; first species, *Turbo obtusatus* Linné, = *T. littoralis* (Lin.?) of Blainville, 1825; Rang, 1829; Pennant, Montagu, Donovan, etc. Rang, Man. Moll., p. 185, 1829; type cited, *L. littoralis* = *L. obtusata* (auct. contemp.).

Neritoides Brown, Ill. Conch. Gt. Brit., expl. pl. 43, figs. 14, 15, 21, 22, 1827; sole example, *Nerita littoralis* Montagu; Brown, Zool. Textb., I, p. 407, 1833, same type.

Turbo sp. Brown, Ill. Conch. Gt. Brit., expl. pl. 46, fig. 1, 1827; *T. littoreus* Linné.

Littorine Blainville, Man. Mal., I, p. 429, sole example, *T. littoralis*. Refers to Conch. Cab., V, pl. 185, fig. 1852, an error for 1854.

Bacalia Gray, Syn. Brit. Mus. 1840 and 1842, p. 90; a nomen nudum quoted in synonymy of *Littorina* by H. and A. Adams, Gen. Rec. Moll., I, p. 312, 1854.

Neritrema Recluz, Actes Soc. Linn. de Bordeaux, 3d ser., VII, p. 46, 1869; type, *Littorina obtusata* Linné.

In proposing his genus *Littorina*, Ferussac announces that he intends it to include the "marine Paludinas" (called *Trochus* by Adanson), and in speaking of the necessity of breaking up the genus *Turbo* he gives a list of species taken from Gmelin, indicating the groups into which he would transfer these species. This list begins with four "marine Paludinas" and contains one other later on. The first species is *Turbo obtusatus* Linné, which is followed by *neritoides, littoreus, muricatus,* and *afer.*

The next succeeding author is Blainville, who cites the genus by its French name but gives as example *Turbo littoralis*, which is cited as the type by Rang four years later. *Turbo littoralis* does not occur in Ferussac's list by name, because Gmelin followed Linné in placing it in *Nerita*, but the naturalists of that day, almost without exception, agreed in regarding *T. obtusatus* Linné as synonymous with his *Nerita littoralis*. Hanley has shown that *littoralis* is probably the same as *palliata* Say, but they were long confounded by authors, are very closely related, and must be placed in the same section of the genus. Unfortunately, in referring to Chemnitz for a figure of *littoralis* illustrated under the citation of *Turbo obtusatus Linnæi* (Conch. Cab., V, p. 234, fig. 1854) Blainville cited the wrong figure, 1852, which represents not *littoralis* but *littoreus* Linné. The result of this slip is that *littoreus* has been generally regarded as the type of *Littorina*, in defiance of Rang's plain statement that the type is *littoralis*, which was also Ferussac's first species.

The differences of form in the boreal group of *Littorina* (excluding the genus *Melarhaphe* Mühlfeldt in Menke, 1828, and the antarctic relatives of the genus) lead to a division of the group into sections as follows:

A. Shell small, low, turbinate, short spired, with obtuse apex, the sculpture feeble, the columella thick and excavated; viviparous. *L. littoralis* Linné.

B. Shell larger, finely spirally striate, the spire moderately acute and elevated; oviparous. *L. littorea* Linné.

C. Shell small, suture constricted, sculpture coarse and variable; viviparous. *L. rudis* Donovan.

The spelling *Littorina* was amended to *Litorina* by Menke as more classical, but, as Jeffreys remarks, *Littus* and *Litus* were used indifferently by the best Latin authors, and there is no authority, under the rules, for changing on such grounds a name once given.

LITTORINA PETRICOLA Dall, n. sp.

Pl. IV, fig. 9.

Shells of moderate size, thick, solid, turbinate, with five gradually increasing whorls; suture distinct, not channeled; upper surface of whorls lightly flattened, periphery and base rounded, axis imperforate; surface sculptured with inconspicuous incremental lines and numerous subequal close-set spiral threads, about two to a millimeter; aperture subovate; outer lip thick, sharp edged, not reflected; pillar thick, arcuate; base slightly subangular, throat obscurely spirally lirate or grooved. Altitude, 17 mm.; maximum diameter, 15.5 mm.

Pleistocene of Fossil Rock, Coos Bay, Oregon, Dall and Camman; U. S. Nat. Mus. 153991.

This species occurs in some abundance in the conglomerate of Fossil Rock, with which, unlike the *Crepidula princeps* and some other included rehandled Miocene species, it appears to be a contemporary. Its nearest relative in the recent fauna is without doubt the subarctic *L. grandis* Middendorff, which is a much larger and somewhat differently shaped species.

Family SOLARIIDÆ.

Genus ARCHITECTONICA Bolten.

Physeter (anonymous, not of Linné, 1758), Mus. Calonnianum. p. 25, 1797; *P. perspectivus* of the anonymous author.

Architectonica Bolten, Mus. Boltenianum, p. 78, 1798; first species, *Trochus perspectivus* Gmelin.

Solarium Lamarck, Prodrome, p. 74, 1799; type, *Trochus perspectivus* Linné.

Architectoma Gray, Proc. Zool. Soc. London for 1847, p. 151; err. typ. pro *Architectonica*.

Solarium Dall, Trans. Wagner Inst., III, p. 323, 1892; with sections *Solarium* s. s., *Stellaxis*, *Patulaxis*, and *Solariaxis*.

The following species belonging without doubt to the genus has the umbilicus completely filled with a tough matrix which resists exploration, so that it is impracticable definitely to assign the species to its section.

ARCHITECTONICA BLANDA Dall, n. sp.

Pl. III, figs. 4, 5.

Shell of moderate size, with a very narrow, deep suture, and about five whorls; surface nearly smooth, with (on the upper side of the whorl) about six spiral sulci, spaced as figured, the posterior four of which are sharply incised, the next anterior slightly and the last more widely channeled; the periphery is formed by (in front of the above-mentioned anterior channel) a broad, rounded spiral, followed by a much narrower one, and that by a wider one, the three rather close set and the last marginating the base; base flattish, with (near the periphery three, and nearer the umbilical region a group of four or five) sharp narrow sulci, the interspaces flat and marked only by obscure incremental lines; umbilicus rather narrow, obscured by hard matrix, as is the aperture. Altitude, 10 mm.; maximum diameter, 19 mm.

Eocene of Fall Creek, Oregon, collected by J. S. Diller at station 2697; U. S. Nat. Mus. 107414.

The single specimen, though rather imperfect, shows enough of the surface sculpture to render the species recognizable at any time.

Family CALYPTRÆIDÆ.

Genus CALYPTRÆA Lamarck.

Patella (sp.) Linné, Syst. Nat., ed. 10, p. 781, 1758.

Ancilia (sp.) Meuschen, Mus. Gevers, p. 245, 1787; nomenclature not Linnean.

Cheilea (sp.) Modeer, K. Vetensk. Acad., nya handl., XIV, p. 110, 1793.

Galerus (anonymous), Mus. Calonnianum, p. 5, 1797; *Patella chinensis* L.

Calyptræa Lamarck, Prodrome, p. 78. 1799; *Patella chinensis* L. (not *Calyptræa* Lam., Syst. Anim. s. Vert., p. 70, 1801; = *Cheilea* Modeer).

Trochita Schumacher, Essai, pp. 57, 184, 1817; *Patella chinensis* L., type of section α; *Trochita spiralis* Schum., type of section β; = *Trochus radians* Lam.

Mitrula Gray, Lond. Med. Rep., XV, p. 232, 1821; *Patella chinensis* Linné; not *Mitrula* Menke, 1830.

Trochatella Lesson, Voy. Coquille, II, p. 389, 1830; sole example, *T. araucana* Lesson, loc. cit., = *T. radians* Lam.

Infundibulum J. Sowerby, Min. Conch., I, pl. 97, 1815; type, *Trochus apertus* Sol.; not *Infundibulum* Montfort, 1810.

Sigapatella Lesson, Voy. Coquille, II, p. 389, 1830; type, *Trochus calyptræiformis* Lam.

Clypeola Gray, Proc. Zool. Soc. London for 1867, p. 735; first species, *Trochita clypeolum* Reeve· not *Clypeolum* Recluz, 1850.

Trochella Gray, Proc. Zool. Soc. London for 1867, p. 735; = *Sigapatella* Lesson.

Trochilla Swainson, Mal., p. 355, 1840; *T. auriculata* Sowerby; = *Calyptræa* Lam., 1799, not 1801.

Haliotidea Swainson, Mal., p. 354, 1840; *H. sigaretoides* Swainson (not of Anton, 1839); = *Sigapatella* Lesson.

Mitella Leach, Moll. Gt. Brit., p. 218, 1852; *Patella chinensis* Linné (+ *Mitrella* Gray, 1867, not Risso, 1826).

Galeropsis Conrad, Checkl. Eoc. Fos. N. Am., pp. 11, 34, 1866; not of Hupé, Rev. Mag. Zool., X, p. 125, 1858.

Haliotoideus Gray, Proc. Zool. Soc. London for 1867, p. 736; lapsus pro *Haliotidea* Swainson; not *Haliotoidea* Menke, 1839.

Mitrella Gray, Proc. Zool. Soc. London for 1867, p. 740; first species, *Patella chinensis* Montagu; = *Calyptræa* Lam., 1799.

Trochilina Gray, Proc. Zool. Soc. London for 1867, p. 741; first species, *Calyptræa conica* Broderip.

Poculina Gray, Proc. Zool. Soc. London for 1867, p. 742; first species, *Calyptræa unguis* Broderip; Chenu, Man. Conchyl., fig. 2340.

Galerus Gray, Proc. Zool. Soc. London for 1867, p. 742; first species, *Calyptræa extinctoria* Lamarck.

The genus *Calyptræa*, based on Lamarck's type of 1799, like most sedentary limpets, depends largely on its situs for its superficial characters. Originally individual, they have to some extent become habitual, perhaps owing to the direct action of the environment. From among the numerous names which have been proposed may be accepted a few which indicate sections convenient for subdividing the group, but which do not exclude the recognition of some more or less intermediate species.

Section *Calyptræa* Lamarck s. s. Type, *C. chinensis* (Linné). Paucispiral, thin, with feeble sculpture, the sutures obscure, colors usually pale, whorls more or less flattened.

Section *Trochita* Schumacher. Type *T. radians* Lamarck. Multispiral, heavy, with conspicuous periostracum, and frequently with prominent sculpture and marked coloration, the summit central and the axis imperforate.

Section *Sigapatella* Lesson. Type *Trochus calyptræiformis* Lamarck. Few, gradually increasing whorls with the suture distinctly impressed, the apex sublateral, the axis of the internal septum submarginal. with its free margin concave.

Galerus excentricus Gabb, from the Eocene of California, the type of Conrad's *Galeropsis*, appears, from its external characters, to belong to this section.

CALYPTRÆA (TROCHITA) INORNATA Gabb.

Pl. V, figs. 6, 11; Pl. VI, fig. 4.

Trochita inornata Gabb, Pal. California, II, p. 51, pl. 14, figs. 8, 8a, 1866.

Shell large, rather elevated, having about three whorls, the last of which is much the largest; form in general as figured, apex defective in all the specimens; shell thin, smooth except for lines of growth, but with irregularities due to its individual situs in each case; internal plate smooth, concave, its reflection forming a narrow umbilical chink; convexity of the whorls varying in different individuals, in some marked, in others the slope from the apex to the margin is nearly flat. Altitude of largest specimen, about 14 mm. (decapitate); latitude, 40 mm. Another specimen with more convex whorls has an altitude of 16 mm. and a maximum latitude of 32 mm.

Miocene of Coos Bay, Oregon, purchased from B. H. Camman; U. S. Nat. Mus. 153920, 153921, and 154016. Also collected by W. H. Dall from float rock, on the beach northeast of Rocky Point, near the entrance to Coos Bay. Upper Miocene near Halfmoon Bay, California, Gabb.

The fossil has the usual irregularities of the species of this genus, unlike most of which it is devoid of spines, pustules, or incised external sculpture, though it has not the regularity in coil of the species of *Calyptræa* proper.

This species, while normally smooth, depends on its substratum or situs for the character of its surface, and may be more or less undulated if seated on an irregular surface. It is also reported from the Purisima formation in the Santa Cruz quadrangle, California, by Arnold, but I have not examined specimens from this locality.

Genus CREPIDULA Lamarck.

Ancilia (sp.) Meuschen, Mus. Gevers, p. 246, 1787; nomenclature not Linnean.

Crypta (anonymous), Mus. Calonnianum, p. 4, 1797; *Patella fornicata* Linné.

Crepidula Lamarck, Syst. des Anim. s. Vert., p. 70, 1801; type, *Crepidula porcellana* Lamarck; Link, Beschr. Rostock Samml.. p. 143, 1807.

Crepdulus Montfort, Conch. Syst., II, p. 87, 1810; *C. fornicatus* Lam.

Proscenula Perry. Conch., expl. pl. 53, 1811; first species, *P. viridis* Perry.

Sandalium Schumacher, Essai, pp. 57, 183, 1817; type, *Patella porcellana* Linné.

Crepipatella Lesson. Voy. Coquille, Zool., II, p. 389, 1830; subgenus of *Crepidula* with *Crepidula adolphei* Lesson as type; = *Crepidula dilatata* Lam.

Syphopatella Lesson, Voy. Coquille, Zool., II, p. 390, 1830; subgenus of *Crepidula* (+*Ergæa* H. and A. Adams).

Crypta H. and A. Adams, Gen. Rec. Moll., I, p. 368, 1854; *Crepidula fornicata* Linné.

Prorenula "Perry" Adams, Gen. Rec. Moll., I, in synonymy, p. 368, 1854; lapsus, = *Proscenula* Perry.

Ianachus Mörch, Cat. Yoldi, I, p. 146, 1852; first species. *Crepidula plana* Say; H. and A. Adams, Gen. Rec. Moll., I, p. 369, 1854.

? Ergæa H. and A. Adams, Gen. Rec. Moll., I, p. 370, 1854: first species, *C. plana* Adams and Reeve, not Say.

Spirocrypta Gabb, Pal. California, I, p. 137, 1864; type, *S. pileus* Gabb, Cretaceous of California.
Inachus Gray, Proc. Zool. Soc. London for 1867, p. 737; lapsus, = *Ianachus* Mörch.
Garnotia Gray, Proc. Zool. Soc. London for 1867, p. 739; type, *Crepidula adunca* Sowerby.
? Ergæa Gray, Proc. Zool. Soc. London for 1867, p. 740; *C. walshi* Herrmannsen (+ *plana* Adams and Reeve) selected as type.
Noicia Gray, Proc. Zool. Soc. London for 1867, p. 740; type, *N. chinensis* Gray; not *Patella chinensis* Linné.
Tylacus "Conrad" Tryon, Man., VIII, pp. 104, 154, 1886; lapsus, = *Thylacus* Conrad (? *Capulidæ*), 1860.
Lyroscapha "Conrad" Tryon, Man., VIII, pp. 104, 147, 1886, in synonymy of *Crepidula*, no date; probably = *Liroscapha* Conrad, Am. Jour. Conch., V, p. 100, 1869; type, *L. squamosa* Conrad, op. cit., pl. 9, fig. 23 (*Acmæidæ ?*).

This genus is abundantly supplied with synonyms, which, so far as they are not due to ignorance, are based chiefly on minor modifications of the septum or the form of the shell. The latter being almost wholly dependent on the situs occupied by the animal affords no sound foundation for generic or subgeneric distinctions. I have not been able to examine specimens of *Ergæa*, which is stated to offer distinctive characters.

Our fossil species belong to the typical section.

CREPIDULA PRÆRUPTA Conrad.

Pl. VII, fig. 8.

Crepidula prærupta Conrad, Geol. U. S. Expl. Exp., p. 727, pl. 19, figs, 9, 9a, 10a, 10b, 1849.
Crypta prærupta Conrad, Am. Jour. Conch., I, p. 151, 1865.

Shell of moderate size, solid, ovate, of about one whorl; surface smooth except for irregular lines of growth; apex low, blunt, adherent, with no sutural sulcus, the extreme point of the shell elevated above the plane of the aperture, in the specimen figured, to an extent equal to about half the total height of the shell; margin simple, interior obstructed by matrix. Longitude, 30 mm.; maximum latitude, 20 mm.; altitude, 12 mm.

Coos Bay Miocene, purchased from B. H. Camman; U. S. Nat. Mus. 153925. Astoria beds, Astoria, Oreg., J. D. Dana, U. S. Nat. Mus. 3496, 3564.

While it is always difficult to discriminate species of this genus without an examination of the form of the septum, the present specimen differs sufficiently from the usual form of *C. princeps* to be provisionally regarded as distinct. The appressed apex and the absence of the sutural sulcus are characters by which it may be identified.

CREPIDULA ROSTRALIS Conrad.

Crepidula sp. ? Conrad, Geol. U. S. Expl. Exp., pl. 19, figs. 11a, 11b, 1849.
Crypta rostralis Conrad, Am. Jour. Conch., I. p. 151, 1865.

Astoria group, Astoria, Oreg., J. D. Dana, No. 22; U. S. Nat. Mus. 110447.

This species is represented by an internal cast of a *Crepidula* which, by its depressed form and straight beak, seems probably different from either of the preceding. It is hardly flat enough to belong to the section *Ianachus* and measures 20 mm. in length, 14 mm. in width, and about 6 mm. in height, the septum extending forward from the apex of the cast about 10 mm.

CREPIDULA PRINCEPS Conrad.

Pl. VIII; Pl. IX, fig. 5; Pl. X, fig. 2.

Crepidula princeps Conrad, Pacific R. R. Repts., V. p. 326, pl. 6, figs. 52, 52a, 1856.
Crypta grandis Gabb, Pal. California, II, p. 82, 1868; not of Middendorff.

Shell large, pretty uniform in character, of about one and a half whorls; nucleus wanting, the apex curved sharply in and up; between the first and second whorls a wide deep sulcus; surface marked by more or less conspicuous incremental lines; upper surface of the last whorl flattish, periphery evenly rounded, a wide, very shallow, inconspicuous sulcus in front of the suture near the aperture, opposite the right-hand end of the internal septum; this sulcus is more or less conspicuous according to the individual, but traces may almost invariably be noted; aperture entire, the margin simple, anteriorly sharp, posteriorly merging into a sort of broad pillar lip, especially in senile specimens; aperture ovate, short, nearly circular; septum wide, smooth, concave, occupying nearly half the area of the aperture, its ends produced, especially on the left, its edge widely emarginate as figured. Length of adult specimen, 82 mm.; of aperture, 56 mm.; maximum width of specimen, 54 mm.; of aperture, 44 mm.; altitude, 32 mm.

This is, so far as known, the largest species of the genus, and occurs normally in both Miocene and Pliocene beds, and adventitiously at Fossil Rock, Coos Bay (and probably elsewhere), in the Pleistocene. Its habits were much the same as those of recent species, including that of perching on the back of another specimen of the same species. Carried to an extreme, as in the group figured on Pls. IX and X, the result is a whorl almost closed. The specimen referred to has lost one individual from its series which if supplied would make an almost perfect rosette. I have seen similar whorls, dredged up from oyster beds in New Jersey, formed by the recent *Crepidula fornicata*, but of course not approaching the present species in actual size.

Miocene of the Empire formation, Coos Bay, Oregon, B. H. Camman; U. S. Nat. Mus. 153925. Lower Miocene of La Panza, San Luis Obispo County; of the head of Stevens Creek, Santa Clara County; and of Searsville road, 3 miles southwest of Stanford University, San Mateo County, Cal., Ralph Arnold. San Pablo formation, Kirkers Pass, California, J. C. Merriam. Pliocene of numerous localities in California, Watts, Eldridge, Arnold, Hamlin, and Hemphill, according to Arnold. Pleistocene of Fossil Rock, Coos Bay, Oregon, Dall; and Dead Man Island, San Pedro, Cal.; probably in both places derived from the adjacent older formation.

By its size this species is easily distinguished when adult from any other known form, and even when immature it is recognizable by the peculiar twist of the spire, the separation of the apical from the concluding whorl, and the remarkable pointed apex, which is, however, very frequently broken off or eroded. The obscure flattening of the upper portion of the last whorl also seems to be characteristic.

The confusion of this species with *C. grandis* Middendorff, which was initiated by Carpenter and continued by Gabb and others, would be quite inexcusable if those authors had had specimens for comparison. The two species are perfectly distinct and not even especially similar.

I must add that it is with much doubt that I regard the statements that this species is found (not rémanié) in beds ranging from the Miocene to the Pleistocene. The well-known mutability of species of this genus, and the immense changes which have taken place on the coast from a geological point of view during this period, render the continuance, unmodified, of so large a species as the present one extremely improbable from a biological standpoint. I commend the problem to the Californian students of paleontology.

It would seem to me much more likely that the species, if found outside the Miocene, occurs as a pebble might occur, or as *Exogyra costata* occurs in the Pliocene of North Carolina, and not as a normal member of the fauna. There is room for suspicion also that upper Miocene beds may have been regarded as Pliocene in some places where the defective state of the fossils, so general on the Pacific coast, has prevented a really critical comparison of closely allied species.

Family NATICIDÆ.

Genus NATICA Scopoli.

Natica Adanson, Senegal, p. 172, 1757; nomenclature not Linnean.
Natica Scopoli, Intr. Hist. Nat., p. 392, 1777; no type selected, *N. vitellus* L. included. Bruguière, Encycl. Méth., I, p. XVI, 1789. Lamarck, Prodrome, p. 77, 1799; sole example, *N. canrena* Linné.
Nerita (sp.) Linné, Syst. Nat., ed. 10, 1758; Martyn, Univ. Conch., II, 1784.
Lunatus (anonymous), Mus. Calonnianum, p. 21, 1797.
Cochlis Bolten, Mus. Boltenianum, p. 146, 1798; first species, *Nerita spadicea* Gmelin (list includes *Nerita vittata* Gmel.).
Natica Lamarck, Syst. des Anim. s. Vert., p. 95, 1801; Bosc, Hist. Nat. des Coq., III, p. 283, 1802; Roissy, Hist. Nat. Moll. V, p. 261, 1805; Link, Beschr. Rostock Samml., p. 140, 1807.
Naticus Montfort, Conch. Syst., II, p. 219, 1810; *N. canrenus* Linné.
Nacca Risso, Hist. Nat. Eur. Mérid., IV, p. 148, 1826; first species, *N. maxima* Risso = *N. fulminea*, fide Gray.
Stigmaulax Mörch, Cat. Yoldi, I, p. 133, 1852; first species, *N. sulcata* Born; subgenus of *Natica* with reticulate sculpture.
Cochlis Mörch, Cat. Yoldi, I, p. 133, 1852; first species, *N. vittata* Gmelin.
Cryptonatica Dall, Trans. Wagner Inst., III, pp. 362, 366, 1892; type, *N. clausa* Broderip and Sowerby.

The genus *Natica*, like most of the old genera, was at first somewhat heterogeneous, the list of species cited containing both *Natica* s. s. and others with a horny operculum. Since Lamarck fixed the genus on the forms with calcareous operculum, and the type must be selected from the original list, it follows that *Natica vitellus* Linné must be regarded as the type of the genus. A full revision of the group is not attempted here; the subdivisions have been indicated in my Wagner Institute memoir, and only that part which relates to the forms of the Oregon Tertiary is elaborated in the present paper. To *Natica* s. s. are referred species having the operculum spirally multisulcate; *Cochlis* includes those with a single marginal sulcus; and *Cryptonatica* Dall those with a smooth operculum and closed umbilicus. The latter is characteristic of temperate or boreal seas, as *Natica* s. s. is of warmer waters, though there are exceptions in cases where the species lives in sufficiently deep water to bring it into a temperature not normal to the latitude at the surface of the sea.

Subgenus NATICA s. s.

NATICA OREGONENSIS Conrad.

Pl. IV. fig. 7.

Sigaretus scopulosus (pro parte) Conrad, Geol. U. S. Expl. Exp , pl. 19, figs. 6b, 6c, 1849.
Lunatia oregonensis Conrad, Am. Jour. Conch., I, p. 151, 1865.

Shell ovate, solid, with four or five whorls, the spire rather elevated, and the general form not unlike that of *Lunatia pallida* Broderip and Sowerby, of the recent fauna; surface nearly smooth, with moderately conspicuous incremental lines; base somewhat produced: body with a polished callus which seems to have been dark colored, and which extends to and over the upper part of the pillar, filling the umbilicus with a nearly circular prominent callus, separated by a sulcus from the base on the left and with a sharply cut semicircular sulcus above it between the body callus and the umbilical callus; outer lip thin, simple. Altitude of type figured, 32 mm.; maximum diameter, 27.5 mm.

Miocene of the Empire formation at Coos Bay, Oregon, purchased from B. H. Camman; U. S. Nat. Mus. 153914. Also from the Miocene of Astoria, collected by J. D. Dana, of the United States Expl. Exp.; U. S. Nat. Mus. 3494, 3542, and 3555.

The small cast figured in 1849 as part of Conrad's *Sigaretus* he afterwards separated under the name above cited. Though very young and imperfect, it appears to be a young specimen of the species here figured and described. I therefore adopt Conrad's name, though not accompanied by any description, and the more willingly since adult specimens of the same species were collected by the Exploring Expedition at the same locality.

Subgenus CRYPTONATICA Dall.

NATICA (CRYPTONATICA) CONSORS Dall, n. sp.

Pl. V, fig. 10; Pl. VI, fig. 9.

Shell small, solid, rather thick, with four whorls; spire rather low, sutures appressed, general profile domelike; whorls evenly rounded, smooth except for lines of growth, the specimens show no spiral striation; aperture subovate, the body with a moderate callus, which extends to the upper part of the pillar and evenly fills the umbilicus, but is rather abrupt on the side away from the pillar, so that a sort of sulcus bounds the umbilical callosity on that side, though there is no perforation; outer lip thin, entire. Altitude, 29 mm.; maximum diameter, 26.5 mm.

Empire formation of Coos Bay, Oregon, purchased from B. H. Camman; U. S. Nat. Mus. 153917. Also 153988, 153915, from the same locality, and 153989, from the Miocene beds underlying the Coos conglomerate at Fossil Point, by W. H. Dall. Also by J. D. Dana, of the United States Exploring Expedition, from the Astoria group at Astoria; U. S. Nat. Mus. 3557 and 3580.

This is a not uncommon species and is distinguished from the preceding by its more depressed profile and the differences noted in the umbilical region.

The specimen numbered 153915 contains the operculum, which is externally smooth, with a slightly elevated ridge near the suture, as in the *Natica russa* Gould, one of the recent species on which the subgenus was founded. *N. russa* is a more depressed species with a differently formed umbilical callus, more like that of *N. clausa* Broderip.

Genus POLINICES Montfort.

Natica (sp.) Scopoli, Intr. Hist. Nat., p. 392, 1777.
Uber (anonymous), Mus. Calonnianum. p. 21, 1797.
Albula Bolten, Mus. Boltenianum, p. 20, 1798; not *Albula* Gronovius, 1763.
Polinices Montfort, Conch. Syst., II, p. 223, 1810; type, *Nerita mammilla* Linné.
Natica Risso, Hist. Nat. Eur. Mérid., IV, p. 147, 1826; not of Lamarck, 1799; Leach, Syn. Moll. Gt. Brit., p. 177, 1852.
Neverita Risso, Hist. Nat. Eur. Mérid., IV, p. 149, pl. 4, fig. 43, 1826; type, *N. josephinia* Risso = *N. olla* de Serres; Mörch, Cat. Yoldi, I, p. 132, 1852; Dall, Trans. Wagner Inst., III, p. 367, 1892.
Euspira Agassiz, ex parte, Sowerby, Min. Conch., German Ed., I, p. 14, 1842; first species, *Natica glaucinoides* Sowerby = *Natica labellata* Lam., 1804.
Lunatia Gray, Proc. Zool. Soc. London for 1847, p. 149; type, *Natica ampullaria* Lamarck; Dall, Trans. Wagner Inst., III, p. 369, 1892.
Cepatia Gray, Syn. Brit. Mus., 1840; idem, 1844, p. 60; Proc. Zool. Soc. London for 1847, p. 149; *Natica cepacea* Lam.; Eocene.
Velainia Munier-Chalmas, Annal. de Malac,. I, p. 335, 1884 = *Cepatia* Gray.
Naticina Fischer, Man. de Conchyl., p. 766, 1885; not of Guilding, 1834.
Sigaretopsis Cossmann, Cat. Illustr., III, p. 172, 1888; type, *Natica infundibulum* Wat.; Eocene, section of *Cepatia*.
Polynices (Montfort) Dall, Trans. Wagner Inst., III, p. 367, 1892.

Polinices in the wide sense includes the naticoids with a horny operculum, except those referred to *Ampullina*, of which the other characters seem to authorize its generic separation. The subordinate groups of *Polinices* in which we are at present interested are chiefly the following:

Polinices s. s. Type *Natica mammilla* Linné.
Neverita Risso. Type *Neverita josephinia* Risso.
Euspira Agassiz. Type *Natica labellata* Lamarck.
? *Cepatia* Gray. Type *Natica cepacea* Lamarck.

It seems that we shall have to give up *Lunatia* Gray in favor of *Euspira*, which has five years priority, and of which both the species mentioned when the name was first proposed appear to be Lunatias; though species belonging to *Ampullina* seem to have been included later.

Subgenus NEVERITA Risso.

POLINICES (NEVERITA) INEZANA Conrad.

Natica inezana Conrad, Pacific R. R. Repts., VII, p. 195, pl. 10, figs. 5, 6, 1857.
? *Natica ocoyana* Conrad, Pacific R. R. Repts., V. p. 328, pl. 7, fig. 57, 57a (in text; 51, 51a, on plate), 1855.
? *Natica saxea* Conrad, Geol. U. S. Expl. Exp., p. 727, pl. 19, fig. 7, 1849.
? *Neverita saxea* Conrad, Am. Jour. Conch., I, p. 151, 1865.
Neverita recluziana Gabb, Pal. California, II, p. 77, 1868; not of Deshayes, 1841.

Santa Ynez Mountains, California, Doctor Antisell, from Miocene beds, U. S. Nat. Mus. 12539; also from the Miocene of Posé or Ocoya Creek, California; Astoria group, at Astoria, Oreg., J. D. Dana, U. S. Nat. Mus. 3510 and 3540; Miocene of the Empire formation, Coos Bay, Oregon, purchased from B. H. Camman, U. S. Nat. Mus. 153988.

A specimen partly defective was figured by Conrad in the geologic report of the United States Exploring Expedition as *Natica saxea*, and was in 1865 referred by him to *Neverita*. This specimen seems to be lost; the specimens with contemporary labels marked *Natica saxea* in the collection are *Euspira* (*Lunatia*) and not the type figured. The figure looks as if it might have been taken from a *Neverita*, though it is rather poor. A *Neverita* does occur at Astoria, and a defective shell which was figured as one of the illustrations of *Sigaretus scopulosus* Conrad in the Exploring Expedition report (pl. 19, fig. 6d) is a specimen of it. We have another specimen of about the same size collected by Dana at Astoria; and another, better preserved, from the Miocene of Coos Bay. These three agree exactly among themselves, but not with the figure of *saxea*, which must have been taken from a very much larger specimen. The small ones are probably young shells, but without connecting material can not be regarded as representing *saxea*. They do, however, rather closely resemble Conrad's *Neverita inezana* from California.

Natica inezana was described from a handful of rather poor specimens which belong to two species, one a *Neverita* and the other an *Ampullinopsis*. The characters are mixed in the diagnosis, the tabulated suture belonging to the latter species and the open umbilicus to the former. The figured specimen which is marked as the type in the collection is a *Neverita*, and seems, as Gabb supposed, to be identical with the species later described by Conrad from the Miocene of Ocoya Creek, California. The same *Ampullinopsis* occurs at Astoria, probably in the Oligocene or lower Miocene, being rather variable in the elevation of its spire. It would seem not unlikely, therefore, that the *Neverita* may occur there too, and when better specimens are available it may prove to be identical with *N. saxea*. For the present, however, I prefer to utilize the name *inezana*, the small specimens of *Neverita* from Astoria and Coos Bay having many characters in common with that species. It is highly improbable that the species is identical with the recent *N. recluziana* Deshayes. In *recluziana* the umbilical callus fills the upper posterior part of the umbilicus, is continuous with the parietal callus, and, in the typical form, has the anterior third of the umbilical callus set off by a sharp sulcus, while a portion of the umbilical funnel in front of the latter remains permanently open. There is a variety *alta* Dall, with small narrow shell and exceptionally elevated spire. In the variety *imperforata* Stearns—found living in the vicinity of San Diego and in the Pleistocene of the upper San Pedro at Deadman Island—there is an additional thin deposit of callus filling the open part of the umbilicus and overflowing on the adjacent portion of the base.

The shell from the Miocene of Coos Bay, which I have referred to *N. inezana*, however, has the open part of the umbilicus behind the umbilical and to the left of it, with no dividing sulcus, and by these characters can be recognized at a glance.

Subgenus EUSPIRA Agassiz.

POLINICES (EUSPIRA) GALIANOI Dall, n. sp.

Pl. V, figs. 12, 13.

Shell of moderate size, solid, rather thick, moderately elevated, smooth except for the incremental lines and occasional faint spiral striæ; external coat usually wanting, in which case the whorl in front of the suture seems narrowly tabulate or even channeled, while the spiral striation is much stronger and the incremental lines coarser and often elevated; normally there are about six whorls and the spire is somewhat dome shaped, the whorl appressed at an inconspicuous suture; umbilicus moderate, open, its upper angle near the pillar lip filled with a small subtriangular callus; aperture ovate, narrower above, a thin callus on the body, the outer lip thin, simple. Altitude of figured specimens (fig. 12), 54 mm., (fig. 13), 43 mm.; maximum diameter of the first, 48 mm.

Empire formation of Coos Bay, Oregon, purchased from B. H. Camman; U. S. Nat. Mus. 153916 (figs. 12, 13), 153987; also at station 2952, northeast of Rocky Point, Coos Bay, W. H. Dall; and in the upper part of the Miocene, under the Coos conglomerate at Fossil Point, Coos Bay, by W. H. Dall, 153990, 154020, and 154012; Astoria group, Astoria, Oreg., J. D. Dana, 3540; also Bogachiel River, Washington, in the upper Miocene, Arnold.

The two figures given show the difference of the profile at the suture between a specimen which has lost its outer coat (fig. 12) and one in which it is intact (fig. 13). In the shell depicted in the first figure the mass occupying the umbilicus is matrix; the callus was situated in the small triangular space to the right of it. In some specimens the callus is proportionately larger, and part may have been broken off in the shell shown in fig. 12.

This is the common *Lunatia* or *Euspira* of the northwest coast Miocene, for which, after much search, I have been able to find no name in the literature, and so have given it the name of the distinguished Spanish explorer. It more nearly resembles *E. draconis* Dall, of the recent fauna, than the better-known *E. lewisii* Gould, for which it has doubtless often been mistaken, but is sufficiently distinct from both.

Genus AMPULLINA (Lamarck) Bowdich.

Ampullina Bowdich (as of Lam.), Elem. Conch., I, p. 31. 1822; type, pl. 9, fig. 2 (? = *Ampullaria depressa* Lam., not Sow.).

Ampullinopsis Conrad, Am. Jour. Conch., I, p. 27. 1865; sole example. *A. mississippiensis* Conrad, Vicksburgian.

Megatylotus Fischer, Man. de Conchyl., p. 766, 1885; type, *Natica crassatina* Lam., lower Miocene.

Amauropsis Mörch, App. Rink's Greenland, p. 79, 1857; type, *Natica helicoides* Johnston; Arctic Man., p. 127, No. 66, 1875.

?*Lupia* Conrad, Am. Jour. Conch., I, p. 27, 1865; type, *Ampullaria perovata* Conrad, Claibornian.

Globulus J. de C. Sowerby, in Index, Min. Conch., VI, p. 246, 1835; not *Globulus* Schumacher, 1817.

Euspira (sp.) Desor and Agassiz, Min. Conch., German ed., p. 320, 1842; type, *N. labellata* Lamarck.

Globularia Swainson, Malac., p. 345, 1840; first and only figured species, *Ampullaria sigaretina* Lam., Eocene; new name for *Globulus* Sowerby, not Schumacher.

Crommium Cossmann, Cat. Illustr., III, p. 177, 1888; type, *Ampullina willemeti* Deshayes, Eocene; section of *Ampullina*.

Amauropsella (Bayle MS.) Chelot, Bull. Soc. Géol. de France, 3d ser., XIII, p. 202, 1885; type, *Natica spirata* Lam.

Amaurellina Fischer, Man. de Conchyl., p. 766, 1885; = *Amauropsella* Chelot.

?*Amauropsina* (Bayle MS.) Chelot, Bull. Soc. Géol. de France, 3d ser., XIII, p. 203, 1885; type, *Natica canaliculata* Lam., Eocene.

The genus *Ampullina* was indicated by Lamarck as early as 1804, and mentioned in the vernacular by him in lectures, and by other authors, but, so far as I have been able to discover, the first publication of the name in Latin is by Lamarck's pupil, Bowdich, in 1822. The type is figured but not specifically named; it is probably *A. depressa* and certainly not *A. sigaretina*, which is usually cited as the type. Both, however, belong to the genus.

Conrad's *Ampullinopsis* was proposed for the American analogue or variety of *Natica crassatina* Lamarck, thus long preceding Fischer's *Megatylotus*, based on the European form of the same type.

Lupia Conrad differs from *Amauropsis* Mörch (which has nothing to do with *Amaura* of the Pyramidellidæ) by having the suture not channeled; otherwise they are extremely similar. *Amauropsella* and *Amaurellina* are based on a fossil which, by Deshayes's figures, is merely a heavy, thick-shelled *Amauropsis*.

While Agassiz later included some Ampullinas in his *Euspira*, his original two species appear to belong to *Lunatia*, but none of them agrees with his diagnosis, in which he says all the species known to him are "links gewunden." *Globularia* Swainson seems to be a synonym of *Ampullina*, or separated only by slight characters.

AMPULLINA (AMPULLINOPSIS) MISSISSIPPIENSIS Conrad.

Ampullinopsis mississippiensis Conrad, Am. Jour. Conch., I, p. 27, 1865; Vicksburgian.
Natica mississippiensis Conrad, Jour. Acad. Nat. Sci. Philadelphia, 2d ser., I, p. 114, pl. 11, fig. 10, 1848.
Ampullina crassatina var. *mississippiensis* Dall., Trans. Wagner Inst., III, p. 375, 1892; Harriman Alaska Exped., IV, p. 110, 1904.
Natica inezana (ex parte) Conrad, Pacific R. R. Repts., VII, p. 195, 1857.

Oligocene of Astoria, Oreg.; George Gibbs, U. S. Nat. Mus. 3575; Miocene (?) of the Santa Ynez Mountains, California, Antisell, 12359a; also from the Oligocene of Port Blakely, opposite Seattle, on Puget Sound, Washington, collected by Landis; and on Alaska Peninsula, at Chichagof Bay, Palache.

The specimens are too poorly preserved to enable a close comparison to be made, and exhibit more or less variation, especially in the height of the spire, but they are referred with much confidence to the American analogue or variety of the European *A. crassatina* Lamarck, of which in the Wagner Institute memoir I have already given a discussion.

For the benefit of students and to supplement Conrad's very short original description, I have prepared a new diagnosis from the above specimens.

Shell moderately large, thick and heavy, with about seven whorls; spire elevated for the genus, the whorls rounded, except for a narrow tabulation in front of the suture, which is more or less carinated at the anterior border, and in the young, is often gently rounded into the normal curve of the whorl; surface smooth, except for more or less conspicuous incremental lines and nearly microscopic spiral striulations which may or may not be distributed over the whole whorl; base rounded; umbilicus large, more or less filled with a solid callus, defective in all the specimens; aperture ovate, the outer lip thick, more or less attenuated to a thin simple edge leaving a flaring impression on internal casts as if the lip had been slightly reflected; inner lip more or less coated with a smooth callus. Altitude, 51 to 64 mm.; maximum diameter, 42 to 46 mm.; altitude of spire exclusive of last whorl, 13 to 22 mm. A young specimen has an altitude of 13 mm. and a maximum diameter of about 10 mm.

Subgenus AMAUROPSIS Mörch.

AMPULLINA (AMAUROPSIS) OREGONENSIS Dall, n. sp.

Pl. III, fig. 7.

Shell elevated, thin, with a narrowly channeled suture and about five whorls; apex rather blunt, whorls evenly rounded, recalling some of the species of *Campeloma;* surface smooth, almost polished, with one or two resting stages, indicated by slight axial ridges, on the last whorl; base rounded, with apparently no umbilical chink; aperture rounded, margin slightly oblique and somewhat thickened. Altitude, 19.5 mm.; maximum diameter, 14.5 mm.

Miocene of Coos Bay, Oregon, purchased from B. H. Camman; U. S. Nat. Mus. 107780.

The single specimen is almost decorticated, but enough of the outer layer remains to indicate the character of the surface and the channel in front of the suture. On the decorticated surface there are traces of spiral striæ in the basal region, but they may not have been visible on the uneroded surface. The specimen has been bored by a carnivorous gasteropod, probably a *Natica*, showing that it can not have been a fresh-water shell. It somewhat recalls the recent Greenlandic species of *Amauropsis*, but is a larger shell, and is proportionately much more elevated than *A. purpurea* Dall, the only recent species of the northwest coast.

Genus SINUM Bolten.

Catinus lactis Klein, Ostrac, p. 19, 1753; not binomial.
Auris veneris (anonymous), Mus. Calonnianum, p. 20, 1797: sole example, *Helix haliotidea* Linné; Hanley, Shells of Lin., p. 390, pl. 4, fig. 7, 1855.
Sinum Bolten, Mus. Boltenianum, p. 14, 1798; first species, *Helix haliotoidea* (Lin.); Gmelin, Syst. Nat., 3663, 1792, ex parte.
Sigaretus Lamarck, Prodrome. p. 77, 1799; *Helix haliotoidea* (Linné); not of H. and A. Adams, 1853.
Cryptostoma Blainville, Suppl. Edinb. Encycl., 1817; Malac., I, p. 467, 1825; type, *C. leachii* Blv., op. cit., 11, pl. 42, fig. 3,= *Sigaretus* Lamarck.
Cryptostomus Blainville, Bull. Soc. Philom., p. 120, 1818: = *Sigaretus* Lamarck.
Catinus H. and A. Adams, Gen. Rec. Moll., I. p. 212, 1853; not of Oken, 1815, *C. leachii* Blainville cited.
Raynevallia Ponzi (ubi ?), fide Tryon, Struct. Syst. Conch., 1883.
Sigaretus Dall, Trans. Wagner Inst., III, p. 378, 1892.

There is no question that Bolten's name is prior and must supplant the later but more familiar name of Lamarck based on the same type.

The genus is fully developed by the middle Eocene and is represented by characteristic species in the Clairbornian and subsequent Tertiary horizons, as well as the existing fauna.

SINUM SCOPULOSUM Conrad.

Pl. IV, fig. 10; Pl. V, fig. 8.

Sigaretus scopulosus Conrad, Geol. U. S. Expl. Exp., appendix, p. 727, pl. 19, figs. 6, 6a, only, 1849.
Catinus scopulosus Conrad, Am. Jour. Conch., I. p. 151, 1865.
Sinum scopulosum Meek, Smithsonian Checkl. Miocene Fos. N. Am., p. 32, 1864; Gabb, Pal. California, II. p. 114, 1868.
? *Sinum planicostum* Gabb, Pal. California, II, pp. 49, 78, pl. 14, fig. 6, 1868.

Shell of moderate size, obconic, solid, of three or more rapidly enlarging whorls; last whorl much the largest; nucleus minute, of one whorl, smooth; aperture ample, oblique, at angle of 45° to the vertical of the axis; suture distinct, appressed; surface sculptured with narrow straplike spirals (about three to 1 mm.) separated by narrow channeled sulci, and crossed by more or less evident incremental lines; base and periphery rounded: base excavated behind the gyrate pillar lip, but not showing any umbilical chink, so far as can be determined; outer lip simple; body with no marked callosity.   Altitude, about 24 mm.; maximum diameter, 25 mm.

. Miocene of Coos Bay, Oregon, purchased from B. H. Camman; U. S. Nat. Mus. 153913.   Also from the United States Exploring Expedition, Conrad's type, collected from the Miocene of Astoria by J. D. Dana, U. S. Nat. Mus. 3553.   Also (?) not rare in the Pliocene of San Fernando, Cal., according to Gabb (*S. planicostum*).

There is sufficient variation in the specimens examined to suggest the identity of Gabb's *planicostum* with Conrad's species, from which it seems to differ only by a somewhat more elevated spire.

Superfamily RHIPIDOGLOSSA.

Family TURBINIDÆ.

Genus ASTRÆA Bolten.

Turbo Linné, ex parte, Syst. Nat., ed. 10, 1758.
Sol (anonymous), Mus. Calonnianum, p. 27. 1797; first identifiable species, *Trochus tuber* Linné.
Astræa Bolten, Mus. Boltenianum, p. 79, 1798; first species, *Trochus imperialis* Gmelin: not *Astræa* of Lamarck, 1801.
Astralium Link, Beschr. Rostock Samml., p. 135, 1807; sole identifiable species, *Turbo calcar* (L.) Gmelin; Chemnitz, Conch. Cab., V, pl. 174, figs. 1718–1720.
Imperator Montfort, Conch. Syst., II, p. 198, 1810; type. *Trochus imperialis* Gmelin: Gray, Fig. Moll. An., IV, p. 88, 1850.
Calcar Montfort. Conch. Syst., II, p. 134, 1810: type, *Turbo calcar* Linné.
Calcar Schumacher, Essai, p. 193, 1817; sect. α, type, *Trochus longispina* Lamarck: sect. β, type, *Turbo calcar* Gmelin; Gray, Fig. Moll. An., IV, p. 87, 1850.
Bolma Risso, Hist. Nat. Eur. Mérid., IV, p. 117, 1826: *Turbo rugosus* Gmelin.
Cyclocantha Swainson, Malac., p. 348, 1840; type. *Trochus stellaris* Gmelin.
Canthorbis Swainson, Malac., p. 349, 1840; *Trochus imperialis* Gmelin.
Tubicanthus Swainson. Malac., p. 349, 1840; first species. *Turbo rugosus* Gmelin, but Gray, in 1847, selects the fourth, *Trochus cookii* Lam.,= *sulcatus* Mart.
Uvanilla Gray, Fig. Moll. An., IV, p. 87, 1850; first species, *U. oliraceus* Gray.
Pomaulax Gray, Fig. Moll. An., IV, p. 87, 1850; *Trochus undosus* Gray.
Guildfordia Gray, Fig. Moll. An., IV, p. 87, 1850; *Trochus guildfordiæ* Gray.
Pachypoma Gray, Fig. Moll. An., IV, p. 88, 1850; *Trochus inæqualis* Martyn.
Lithopoma Gray. Fig. Moll. An., IV, p. 88, 1850; *Trochus tuber* Linné.

The large group of Turbinidæ which has been designated of late as *Astralium* had an earlier name in *Astræa* Bolten.   Link, who had no scruples in regard to altering other people's names, gives as a synonym of his *Astralium* the designation *Astræa* Bolten, from which a little later Fischer eliminated *Xenophora*.   Without attempting to marshal the subgenera of *Astræa* on this occasion, we may take up the only one of them which is, so far known to be represented in the Tertiary of Oregon.

Subgenus PACHYPOMA Gray.

ASTRÆA (PACHYPOMA) PRECURSOR Dall, n. sp.

Pl. VI, figs. 5, 6.

Shell small for the group, solid, depressed, with about four or five whorls; apex decollated in the types; upper surface of the whorls flattish, with a deep sulcus near the periphery which is formed by a stout, rounded, slightly undulated cord having a wide, shallow sulcus on the basal side also; the suture is laid directly under this cord; upper surface of the whorls sculptured with about 30 stout oblique rounded ribs with subequal shallow interspaces, the ribs crossed close behind the suture by three or four obscure sulci, faintly nodulating them, the outermost sulcus is the deepest, and nearly cuts off the distal end of the ribs; the surface is also marked by well-defined incremental lines; base flattish, with five strong conspicuously nodulous cords with deep narrower interspaces; umbilical region callous, smooth, concave, with a peripheral ridge; columella arcuate, callous, pearly, with a thin layer of callus on the body, outer lip simple. Altitude, 25 mm.; maximum diameter, 35 mm.

Miocene of Coos Bay, Oregon, purchased from B. H. Camman; U. S. Nat. Mus. 153919.

This species recalls *P. inæquale* Martyn, of the Pleistocene and recent fauna in the same region, but is smaller and proportionately less elevated, with a more impressed umbilical region, which the aspect of the fossil indicates may have been in life of a dark or reddish color, instead of white as in the later species.

ASTRÆA (PACHYPOMA) INÆQUALE Martyn.

Trochus inæqualis Martyn, Univ. Conch., I, pl. 31, table, 1784; not of Gmelin, 1793.
Sol deradiatus (anonymous), Mus. Calonnianum, p. 27, No. 485, 1797; nude name.
Trochus gibberosus Pfeiffer, Krit. Regist. Mart. Chemn. Conch. Cab., p. 102, 1840; after Chemnitz, X, p. 286, vignette 23, A, B.
? *Trochus diadematus* Valenciennes, Voy. Venus, Zool., pl. 3, fig. 2, 1846 (probably *Pomaular undosus*, fide Carpenter).
Trochus ochraceus Philippi, Zeitschr. f. Mal., III, p. 101, No. 16, 1846.
Pachypoma gibberosum Carpenter, Rept. Brit. Assoc. for 1863, pp. 627, 651, 1864.
Astralium (Pachypoma) inæquale Pilsbry, in Tryon, Man. Conch., X, p. 244, pl. 57, figs. 51, 52, 1888.
Pachypoma inæquale Dall, Proc. U. S. Nat. Mus., XV, p. 199, pl. 19, figs. 4, 5; pl. 23, figs. 1, 5, 1892; var. *depressum* Dall, pl. 23, fig. 3; Arnold, Pal. and Strat. San Pedro, p. 231, 1903.

Pleistocene of Santa Barbara and San Pedro, California, Williamson, Arnold; fragments in the Pleistocene conglomerate of Fossil Rock, Coos Bay, Oregon, Dall.

From *Pachypoma precursor* the variety *depressum* Dall is distinguished by its larger size and the spiral sulci on the middle of the whorl which cut the obliquei ribs but leave unsulcate the ends of the ribs near either suture.

The recent shell occurs from Catalina Island northward to British Columbia, where it is abundant in the vicinity of Vancouver Island. The smooth white opercula are transported to many parts of the coast, where they are inlaid in wooden articles by the Indians as a favorite ornament. It also occurs semifossil in the prehistoric shell heaps.

Family TROCHIDÆ.

Genus TEGULA Lesson.

Tegula Lesson, Illustr. de Zoologie, livr. 17, pl. 51, no pagination on text, 1834; type, *T. pellis-serpentis* Mawe (+ *elegans* Lesson, loc. cit.).
Tegula H. and A. Adams, Gen. Rec. Moll., I, p. 426, 1854.

Tegula (*elegans*) was described in the unpaginated text of livraison 17, of Lesson's Illustrations, which appeared in 1834, though the series began in the winter of 1831–32. As it is the older name, if *Tegula* and *Chlorostoma* are related subgenerically, as seems to be the case, the rule is that the older name shall be borne by the genus and the newer by the subgenus concerned. Hence *Chlorostoma* must take subgeneric rank under *Tegula* as the genus.

Subgenus CHLOROSTOMA Swainson.

Chlorostoma Swainson, Malac., p. 350, 1840; first species, *Trochus argyrostomus* Gmelin.
Omphalius Philippi, Zeitschr. f. Malac., IV, p. 21, 1847; type, *Trochus nigerrimus* Gmelin.
Phorcus A. Adams, Proc. Zool. Soc. London for 1851, p. 156; not of Risso, 1826.
Neomphalius Fischer, Man. de Conchyl., p. 821, 1885; new name for *Omphalius* Philippi, not *Omphalia* De Haan, 1825.

According to Pilsbry, in his painstaking monograph of the Trochidæ, the passage from *Chlorostoma* into the forms called *Omphalius* is so gradual, and the characters overlap in so many instances, that no strict line of demarcation can be drawn between them. The typical *Chlorostoma* is characteristic at the present day of the faunas of Japan, the west coast of America, and the Antillean region. It is not, therefore, remarkable that we should find it represented among the faunas of the West American Tertiary.

Gray[a] notes that the animal of *Tegula* is deprived of frontal lappets between the tentacles, and probably they are rudimentary. In *Chlorostoma* (*funebrale*) they are reduced to small smooth-edged quadrate appendages to the inner bases of the tentacles. In the shell commonly known as *Phorcus pulligo* Martyn they are, however, of good size, though hardly meeting in the median line. This form has also no circumscribing rib or keel in the umbilical region, and a peculiar large funnel-shaped umbilicus. These differences seem to mark the species off from the other members of the genus and to be at least of sectional value. *Phorcus* was proposed for a very different trochoid shell by Risso and hence is not available for this section, which requires a new name. *Promartynia* is suggested as appropriate. *P. pulligo* is known as a fossil from the Pleistocene of San Pedro and San Diego, and abounds in the living state from San Pedro to Alaska, being particularly numerous in British Columbia, but so far it has not been detected in the Oregonian Pleistocene. It has the upper part of the pillar peculiarly excavated by a wide sulcus and passing almost imperceptibly into the basal margin of the aperture, the usual tooth or truncation of the pillar being reduced to a mere trace, or in some individuals wholly absent.

---

a Proc. Zool. Soc. London, 1856, p. 44.

Tegula (Chlorostoma) stantoni Dall, n. sp.

Pl. II, figs. 10, 11.

Shell thin, elevated, internally nacreous, with five or more whorls; nucleus decollate in the type specimen; surface of whorls finely axially striated by incremental lines; upper surface with three about equidistant spiral cords, the middle one a little more prominent than the others, the suture being laid just below the outer cord, which shows above the junction of the whorls like a narrow thread; base smooth for the most part, roundly convex, with a faint sulcus near the peripheral thread, and two or three flat spirals around the umbilical region; umbilicus imperforate, hardly depressed; pillar thin, arcuate, outer lip and base thin and simple, aperture obstructed by a hard matrix; upper surface of whorls slanting evenly from the suture. Altitude of decollate type, about 25 mm.; maximum diameter of base, 35 mm.

Miocene of Coos Bay, Oregon, purchased from B. H. Camman, U. S. Nat. Mus. 107777. Also in the lower Purisima formation, Santa Cruz County, Cal., Arnold.

This species has a marked superficial resemblance to the *Monodonta constricta* Lamarck, from the recent fauna of Australia, but is a larger, more depressed and thinner shell. The sculpture has much similarity to that of *Calliostoma cammani* from the same beds, but is less strong, while the shell is thinner, more elevated and the base more inflated. The base is that of *Chlorostoma* rather than of *Monodonta*, but the aperture, unfortunately, is filled by a refractory matrix. A species almost identical with *M. constricta* was obtained living at Scammons Lagoon, Lower California, and presented to the National Museum by Captain Scammon more than forty years ago (U. S. Nat. Mus. 182588), so it would not be entirely incredible if the type existed in the Tertiary of the Pacific coast.

The species is named in honor of Dr. T. W. Stanton, paleontologist to the United States Geological Survey, whose work on the Mesozoic faunas of America is well known.

Genus CALLIOSTOMA Swainson.

Trochus (sp.) Linné, Syst. Nat., ed. 10, p. 756, 1758; Martyn, Univ. Conch., table, vol. I, pl. 32, 33, 34, etc., 1784.
Trochulus (sp.) (anonymous), Mus. Calonnianum, p. 27, 1797.
Trochus (sp.) (anonymous), Mus. Calonnianum, p. 27, 1797; Bolten, Mus. Boltenianum, p. 83, 1798; Link, Beschr. Rostock Samml., p. 135, 1807.
Conulus Nardo, Atti II^da Riunione degli Sci. Ital., 1841, not of Fitzinger, 1833.
Calliostoma Swainson, Malac., pp. 218, 219, 351, 1840; type, *Trochus zizyphinus* var. *conuloides* Lamarck.
Ziziphinus Gray, Synopsis Brit. Mus., 1840; *Trochus zizyphinus.*
?*Lischkeia* Fischer, Icon. Coq. Viv., *Trochus*, p. 419, 1880; type, *Trochus moniliferus* Lamarck.
Eutrochus Pilsbry, Man. Conch., XI, p. 402, 1889; not of A. Adams, 1863 = *Astele* Swainson, Trans. Roy. Soc. Van Diemens Land, III, p. 38, 1855.
Leiotrochus (Conrad) Dall, Trans. Wagner Inst., III, pp. 399, 402, 1892, and p. 1653, 1903; type, *L. distans* Conrad, 1862.

The genus *Calliostoma* may for the purposes of this paper be divided into two sections—*Calliostoma* s. s., with an impervious axis, and *Leiotrochus*, with an umbilicus.

Turcica, which, in the absence of full data, was regarded as probably a subdivision of *Calliostoma*, proves to be more closely related to *Margarites* than to any other genus at present discriminated. *Eutrochus* Adams was based on a small Australasian shell which had already formed the foundation of Swainson's genus *Astele*, and for the umbilicate Calliostomas I proposed to revive Conrad's name *Leiotrochus*, based on a small umbilicate fossil species of the Maryland Miocene.

CALLIOSTOMA CAMMANI Dall, n. sp.

Pl. II, figs. 8, 9.

Shell thin, depressed-conic, of about four whorls; upper surface of the whorls with three strong, rounded revolving cords with wider interspaces, the channel between the posterior and the next anterior cord wider than the others; the third cord somewhat more prominent than the others, so that it forms the periphery of the whorl; below it, separated by a pronounced sulcus, is a similar but less prominent cord which forms the margin of the basal surface and on which the suture is laid; base flattish with several hardly raised flattened spiral bands, a stronger, more or less nodulous one surrounding the umbilical area, which is white with a depressed callous surface bounded by a rounded ridge; the pillar smooth, arcuate, ending in a blunt point beyond which the basal lip is thin and simple; upper surface with faint oblique incremental lines hardly interrupting the general smoothness; outer lip thin, sharp, produced at its upper termination along the whorl and crenulated by the spiral sculpture; aperture wider than high, pearly within, a thin wash of callus on the body; nucleus decollate in the type; there is a faint depression behind the pillar, but the shell is imperforate. Altitude of decollate type, 15 mm.; maximum diameter, 25 mm.

Miocene of Coos Bay, Oregon, purchased from B. H. Camman; U. S. Nat. Mus. 107776.

This strongly spirally sculptured species recalls the more acute and elevated *C. virginicum* of Conrad, from the Virginia Miocene. In its sculpture it resembles *Chlorostoma stantoni* Dall, of the Empire formation of Coos Bay, but can readily be discriminated.

Genus TURCICA A. Adams.

Turcica A. Adams, Proc. Zool. Soc. London, for 1854. p. 37; type, *T. monilifera* A. Adams, op. cit., pl. 27, fig. 1.

Ptychostylis Gabb, Proc. California Acad. Sci., III, p. 187, 1865; type, *P. caffea* Gabb; figured in Pal. California, II, pl. 3, fig. 27, 1866.

?Perrinia H. and A. Adams, Gen. Rec. Moll., I, p. 419, 1858; type. *P. angulifera* Adams

Thalotia Cooper, 1867, not *Thalotia* Gray, 1847.

The typical species of *Turcica* has not been accessible, but an examination of *T. imperialis* A. Adams, a closely related species, shows that it has a jaw; a radular formula $\dfrac{1}{\infty + 7 + 7 + \infty}$, the teeth not unlike those of *Margarites;* the epipodial appendages laterally wide, flouncelike, with finely papillose edge but no elongated cirrhi anywhere; the lappets between the tentacles with nearly entire margins not quite meeting in the mesial line; the tentacles long, with the eyes on separate peduncles outside of them; the operculum multispiral. These characteristics, taken with those of the shell, seem sufficient to establish the group as a genus.

The *Perrinia* of Adams has an internally lirate aperture and probably belongs elsewhere, the pseudolirations seen in thin species of *Turcica* being mere reflections of the external sculpture.

T. monilifera A. Adams is a very different shell from *Trochus moniliferus* of Lamarck, the type of the section or subgenus *Lischkeia* of Fischer.

T. caffea Gabb is not uncommon in the Pleistocene of southern California. It was referred to *Thalotia* by Cooper, but the type of *Thalotia* belongs to a perfectly distinct group.

TURCICA GABBI Dall, n. sp.

Pl. IV, fig. 5; Pl. VI, fig. 11.

Shell thin, pearly, elevated, conic, with more than four ample whorls; apex decollate; whorls sculptured with (on the upper whorls five) subequal, low, rounded cords with wider smooth interspaces, the peripheral cord and the one in front of it somewhat stronger than the others; suture slightly constricted; base with similar but more closely set and smaller revolving cords, with subequal interspaces; umbilical region imperforate, callous, smooth; pillar with two strong rounded knobs; basal and outer lip thin, simple; a thin wash of callus on the body. Altitude, 30 mm.; maximum diameter, 25 mm.

Miocene of Coos Bay, Oregon, purchased from B. H. Camman; U. S. Nat. Mus. 153968. Also noted in the upper Miocene at station 4073, south of Fossil Point, by W. H. Dall.

This species is the precursor of *T. caffea* Gabb, a species both Pliocene and recent on the coast of California. It is more elevated and the sculpture of the Oregon fossil is much simpler than that of its successor. Though the type specimen is very badly preserved, its main characters are fortunately quite evident and unmistakable.

Genus MARGARITES Leach.

Margarita Leach, Thompson's Ann. Phil., XIV, p. 202, 1819 (not of Leach, Zool. Misc., I, p. 107, 1815); Ross's Voy. App., p. 59, 1819; Broderip and Sowerby, Zool. Jour., IV, p. 363, 1828; Sowerby, Mal. Mag., I, p, 23, 1838; Dall, Blake Report, Gastr., p. 274, 1889; Pilsbry, Man. Conch., XI, p. 285, 1889; type, *M. helicina* Fabr.

Margarites (Leach, MS.) Gray, Ann. Mag. Nat. Hist., XX, p. 268, 1847; Moll. Gt. Brit., pp. 147, 197, 1852, *Helix margarita* Montagu, pl. 9, fig. 7; Dall. Trans. Wagner Inst., III, p. 406, 1892.

Eumargarita Fischer, Man. de Conchyl., p. 825, 1885.

Margaritopsis Thiele, Nachrbl. d. d. Mal. Ges., 1906, p. 15, footnote; type, *Margarita frielei* Krause.

Valvatella Smith, Proc. Mal. Soc. London, III, p. 206, 1899; not *Valvatella* Gray, 1857.

If we disregard the antarctic forms, the North Pacific species of the group commonly known as *Margarita* are divisible on the shell characters into four perfectly recognizable groups, besides which it is probable that anatomical examination will develop characters permitting still further division. *Margarita* being preoccupied by its own sponsor, we must accept his amended form of *Margarites*, which is the earliest subsequent name, and divide the genus as follows:

Subgenus *Margarites* s. s. Type, *M. helicina* Fabricius. Shell polished, depressed, smooth, few-whorled. Chiefly boreal.

Subgenus *Pupillaria* Dall, nov. Type, *M. pupilla* Gould. Shell dull, trochiform, unicolor, strongly spirally striated, sometimes radiately ribbed, and with more numerous whorls. Chiefly temperate seas.

Section *Lirularia* Dall, nov. Type. *M. lirulata* Cpr. Shell small, dull-surfaced, with variable color patterns, spirally strongly, and axially delicately sculptured. Tropical and warm temperate waters.

Section *Cidarina* Dall, nov. Type, *M. cidaris* A. Ads. Shell large, whitish, unicolor, with strong spiral sculpture sharply nodose, the umbilicus closed by a reflexed layer of callus, the suture channeled. Deep waters of the west coast of North America.

Eumargarita is an exact synonym of *Margarites; Margaritopsis* is based on minor differences of the radula, perhaps of sectional value; *Valvatella* was proposed by Gray for an undescribed and unfigured species from Greenland, having an imperforate axis and lamellose periostracum, perhaps a *Torellia*, but seemingly not identifiable. At any rate *Margarites* has ten years priority.

I regard *Solariella, Machæroplax*, and their near allies as constituting a distinct genus.

MARGARITES (LIRULARIA) CONDONI Dall, n. sp.

Pl. VI, figs. 7, 8.

Shell small, turbinate, with about five whorls; nucleus small, defective in the specimens; subsequent whorls narrowly subtabulate near the suture, rounded above and below; axial sculpture of fine, not crowded threads, which cover most of the surface, being most conspicuous in the sulci, but to a greater or less extent modifying or nodulating the raised spiral sculpture also; on the last whorl between the suture and umbilicus the surface is sculptured with about ten strong spiral threads, of which the previous whorls show four or five; the thread in front of the suture is small and nodulous; the next one, forming the boundary of the tabulation, is stronger than any of those succeeding, except at the umbilicus, where the cords increase in size and are conspicuously nodulous; the umbilicus is little or not at all perforate, the specimens not being decisive on that point; aperture subcircular, outer lip simple, inner lip arcuate, thin; body with a marked callus which extends over the umbilical region and may, in a perfectly adult specimen, almost or entirely close the umbilical chink; base roundly convex. Altitude of larger specimen, 13.5 mm.; maximum diameter, 13 mm.

Miocene of Coos Bay, Oregon, purchased from B. H. Camman; U. S. Nat. Mus. 153922.

This species is about the size of *M. pupilla* Gould, of the recent fauna, but by the characteristics of sculpture, etc., it seems more nearly related to the group of *M. lirulata* Carpenter. The latter is composed of rather small species, so, if the present one may be regarded as ancestral, the recent forms have sadly degenerated in the matter of size.

The species is named in honor of the late Thomas Condon, professor in the university at Eugene, Oreg., who was the first to point out the evolutionary succession in our fossil horses, and whose material formed the basis of much research by others, owing to his unselfish liberality to his coworkers in the same line of investigation.

Genus TURCICULA Dall.

Turcicula Dall, Bull Mus. Comp. Zool., IX, p. 42, 1881; type, *Margarita (Turcicula) imperialis* Dall; op. cit., XVIII, p. 376, pl. 22, figs. 1, 1a, June, 1889; Pilsbry, Man. Conch., XI, p. 330, 1889; Dall, Bull. 37, U. S. Nat. Mus., p. 162, pl. 22, figs. 1, 1a, 1889.

Bembix Watson, Jour. Lin. Soc. London, XIV, p. 603, 1879; type, *B. æola* Watson, op. cit,, p. 603; Chall.
    Rept., Gastr.. p. 95, pl. 7, fig. 13, 1886, Japan. Not *Bembix* De Koninck.
Bathybembix Crosse, Jour. de Conchyl., XL., p. 288, 1893 (March, antedated July, 1892): new name for
    Bembix Watson, not De Koninck.

This group, regarded at first as a subgenus of *Margarites*, I now consider to be of
generic rank. With the extension of the dredgings of the U. S. S. *Albatross* to the
Pacific, several species were found which were referred to this group, though all are
of considerably larger size, and have some characters not shown by the typical species
of *Turcicula*, which is known only from two dead shells, both decollate, and from the
archibenthal region of the Antilles. The impression had been growing that the large
Pacific shells now found to be represented from the Eocene to the present fauna of the
Pacific coast, notwithstanding a marked similarity of structure, might perhaps be
distinct from the Antillean type referred to; but this surmise was found illusory on
the receipt of a small species from Japan, *T. crumpii* Pilsbry, having precisely the
imbricate sculpture of *T. imperialis* and but slightly larger. There still remains, of
course, the possibility that the typical species of *Bembix* might prove distinct from
Turcicula, as it is evidently an immature shell, but the close resemblance of form and
sculpture to the *Turcicula* already known lends so little probability to this suggestion
that it may reasonably be disregarded. Schepman[a] has described and figured as the
adult of *B. æola* a shell which is without doubt a typical *Turcicula*. If this identification be correct[b] there can be no reason as to the true position of *Bathybembix*. The
apparent channeling of the suture in such species as *T. crumpii* and *bairdii* is due to
the proximity of elevated sculpture to the suture and not to the existence of an actual
channel.

The group is represented on the Atlantic side only by *T. imperialis[c]* and *T.
miranda* Dautzenberg, but in the Pacific the species range from Ecuador to Bering
Sea, in depths varying from 400 fathoms in the south to 25 fathoms in Bering Sea,
and always forming part of the off-shore fauna.

The fossil species so far known are from the Eocene and Oligocene. The Miocene
fauna appears to have been laid down close to the shore line, where as yet *Turcicula*
has not been discovered.

TURCICULA WASHINGTONIANA Dall, n. sp.

Pl. XVII, figs. 1, 2; Pl. XVIII, fig. 4.

Shell large, depressed-conic, pearly, of five or more whorls; nucleus defective;
later whorls with two more or less nodose spiral ridges, next to the anterior one
of which the suture is laid; these are separated by nearly smooth, much wider interspaces; periphery vertically compressed, distally bluntly rounded; base with four or
five obscure spirals, about equally spaced; umbilical region imperforate, with a thin
wash of callus; aperture inaccessible; axial sculpture chiefly incremental, with some
obsolete traces of narrow riblets near the posterior keel. Altitude of shell (decollate),
35 mm.; maximum diameter, 55 mm.; minor diameter, 46 mm.

---

[a] Leyden Mus. Notes, XXV, No. 4, 1905, p. 100, pl. 8, figs. 4, 5.

[b] The correctness of Schepman's view has been confirmed by the kindness of E. A. Smith, assistant in the British
Museum of Natural History, who compared specimens for me with the types of *æola* and finds them to "agree admirably"
in all essentials.

[c] *T. nevillei* Smith has been described from the Indian Ocean.

Oligocene of Restoration Point, Puget Sound, Washington, opposite Seattle, at station 4071, Arnold; U. S. Nat. Mus. 110448.

Differs from the next species in proportions, in its simpler and less nodose sculpture, and in its compressed periphery.

TURCICULA COLUMBIANA n. sp.

Pl. III, figs. 2, 11.

Shell large, thin, depressed, pearly, of about five whorls; nucleus defective in the type; subsequent whorls with a rounded carinal ridge at the periphery which more or less overhangs the subsequent suture; surface between the suture and periphery with (on the penultimate whorl 15) oblique, axial ribs, which a little more than halfway from the suture rise into rather sharp nodules more or less distinctly connected by an obscure spiral ridge; beyond the nodules the ribs become faint and the whorl is somewhat constricted between them and the carinal ridge; other axial sculpture of rather prominent incremental lines; base with about six obscure spiral ridges with much wider interspaces, the inner three less prominent and closer together, leaving a smooth space in the umbilical region; here there is a smooth callus with the center depressed and the periphery thickened and slightly raised; pillar smooth, arcuate; outer and basal lips, in the type, thin, sharp, simple; a thin wash of callus on the body. Altitude of shell, 37 mm.; maximum diameter, 50 mm.

Eocene of Rock Creek, Columbia County, Oregon, J. S. Diller; U. S. Nat. Mus. 107397.

This fine species carries the genus back to the Eocene. As might be expected, perhaps, the Oregonian fossil most nearly resembles the Californian *T. bairdii*, but is larger, stronger, more coarsely sculptured and less elevated. *T. santacruzana* Arnold (ms.), from the Oligocene San Lorenzo formation in the Santa Cruz district of California, is intermediate in form between *T. columbiana* and *T. bairdii*. It is still somewhat wider and more depressed in form than the recent shell, but resembles the latter in form and size much more nearly than it does the Eocene species.

Class PELECYPODA.

Order PRIONODESMACEA.

Suborder FOLIOBRANCHIATA.

Superfamily SOLENOMYACEA.

Family SOLENOMYACIDÆ.

Genus SOLEMYA a Lamarck.

Solemya Lamarck, Anim. s. Vert., V, p. 488, 1818: *S. australis* and *S. mediterranea* cited.
Solenimya Bowdich, Elem. Conch., II, pp. 8, 40, 1822; *S. australis*, pl. 2, fig. 17, selected as type.
Solemya Ferussac, Tableau Syst., p. xliv, 1822; Blainville, Man. Mal., I, p. 570, 1825; *S. australis* figured as type. Risso. Hist. Nat. Eur. Mérid., IV. p. 372, 1826.

---

a The vagaries of spelling into which we are plunged if we allow the right to reform any supposed barbarous spelling are well illustrated in the synonymy of this genus. I am firmly of the opinion that, with the exception of errors of the press, no alterations of any kind should be allowed unless the name involves a contradiction in terms, which is an extremely rare occurrence. The annoyance which may be caused to a competent Latinist by the recognition of a barbarism is of less importance than the fixity of names once given publication.

Solenomya Menke, Synopsis, ed. 2, p. 119, 1830; *S. mediterranea* Lam.
Stephanopus Scacchi, Osserv. Zool., p. 3, 1833; *S. mediterranea* Lam.
Solenymia Swainson, Malac., pp. 366, 317, 1840; *S. mediterranea* Lam.

SOLEMYA VENTRICOSA Conrad.

Solemya ventricosa Conrad, Geol. U. S. Expl. Exp., p. 723, pl. 17, figs. 7, 8. 1849.
Donax? protexta Conrad, Geol. U. S. Expl. Exp., p. 723, pl. 17, fig. 9. 1849.
Solena protexta Conrad, Am. Jour. Conch., I, p. 152, 1865.
Plectosolen protexta Meek, Checkl. Miocene Fos. N. Am., No. 242, p. 9, 1866.
Solen (Hypogella) protexta Gabb, Pal. California, II, p. 89, 1868.
Machæra patula Gabb, Pal. California, II, p. 89, 1868; not of Carpenter.

Miocene of Astoria, Oreg., J. D. Dana; U. S. Nat. Mus. 3486, 3567, and 3613. Types of the Exploring Expedition, figured as above stated.

Conrad's *Donax protexta* was based on an imperfect internal cast of a young specimen of *Solemya*, doubtless the same species as the larger and better-preserved specimens obtained simultaneously at the same locality. The original specimen (No. 3613) is still preserved.

The imperfect condition of the specimens prevents any very close comparisons with other species, but it is worthy of note that a species attaining nearly as large size as the fossil is a member of the recent fauna of the adjacent coast in deep water. It was described by me under the name *Solemya johnsoni*, and, so far as can be determined, is of somewhat different proportions from the Miocene fossil.

Superfamily NUCULACEA.

Family NUCULIDÆ.

Genus NUCULA Lamarck.

Nucula Lamarck, Prodrome. p. 87, 1799; type, *Arca nucleus* Linné.
Nuculana Link, Beschr. Rostock Samml., p. 155, 1807; new name for *Nucula* Lam.
Glycymeris (pars) Da Costa, Brit. Conch., p. 170, 1778; not *Glycymeris* Lamarck, 1799.
Nucula Dall, Trans. Wagner Inst., III, p. 571, 1898.

NUCULA TOWNSENDI Dall, n. nom.

Nucula cuneiformis Conrad, Am. Jour. Sci., 2d ser., V, p. 432, fig. 2, 1848; not of Sowerby, 1837.

Miocene of Astoria, Oreg., J. K. Townsend; U. S. Nat. Mus 3526a, J. D. Dana.

This species is represented in the National Museum by a single poorly preserved specimen, a good deal crushed, but with enough of the surface remaining to show that the shell had coarse and somewhat irregular concentric narrow ridges with subequal interspaces that are marked by fine radiating sulci, which in some places crenulate the crests of the ridges and appear to have existed over the whole surface, but especially in the depressions. The short end seems more abruptly truncate than in Conrad's figure, and he does not mention the radial striæ, but his figured specimen (now lost) seems to have been younger than the one here referred to. The shell much resembles *N. decussata* Sowerby. Longitude, 16.5 mm.; altitude, 15.0 mm.

Subgenus ACILA H. and A. Adams.

Acila H. and A. Adams. Gen. Rec. Moll., II, p. 545, 1858; first species, *Nucula castrensis* Hinds.

This group is represented in the rocks from the Cretaceous up, and in the recent fauna from both coasts of the northern and tropical Pacific.

NUCULA (ACILA) CONRADI Meek.

Pl. XII, figs. 4, 5.

Nucula divaricata Conrad, Am. Jour. Sci., V, p. 432, fig. 1, 1848; Geol. U. S. Expl. Exp., p. 723, pl. 18, figs. 6, 6a, 1849; not *N. divaricata* Hinds, 1843.
Nucula conradi Meek, Checkl. Miocene Fos. N. Am., p. 27, November, 1864; Am. Jour. Conch., I, p. 153, 1865.

Shell ovate, moderately convex, with rather inconspicuous beaks, the young proportionately more elongated than the adult specimens; beaks adjacent, slightly recurved; lunule and escutcheon not defined by any bounding line and at the best obscure, especially the former, which can hardly be said to exist; ends of the shell rounded, the margins in the middle of the slightly impressed space usually assigned to the escutcheon, pouting a little; base regularly arcuate, anterior dorsal slope with a flatter but still regular arch; surface sculptured with little-elevated radial threads somewhat variable in coarseness, separated by narrow sulci; these threads divaricate from a line near the middle of the valves and in old specimens a duplication of the divarication is frequent near the base; nearly all the specimens obtained are filled with a hard, tough matrix, so that the interior is inaccessible, but specimens from the upper layers of the Miocene of Fossil Point have 14 posterior and 24 anterior V-shaped hinge teeth; the inner margins of the valves are minutely crenate; the chondrophore is of moderate size and directed obliquely forward. Altitude of figured specimen, 14 mm.; longitude, 18 mm.; diameter, 8 mm. Fully adult specimens have a length of 20, a height of 16.5, and a diameter of 12 mm.

Rather common in the Oligocene and Miocene of the Empire beds, Coos Bay, Oregon, purchased from B. H. Camman (U. S. Nat. Mus. 153952) and also collected from the same locality by W. H. Dall (153980) in the upper beds of the Miocene at Fossil Point.

The species of *Acila*, being very similar, and one or more occurring in each horizon from the Cretaceous up, have been very puzzling and difficult to determine. The original *N. divaricata* Conrad (1848, not Hinds, 1843) was renamed *N. conradi* by Meek in 1864.

This is the Miocene type from Astoria, of which the original type specimen is in the National Museum, No. 3526. A few years later Conrad described from the Eocene (called by him Miocene) of San Diego Mission, California, a *Nucula decisa* which he figured (very badly) and afterwards united with his Miocene Astoria species. In this he was followed by Gabb and others. None of the figures or descriptions of this *decisa* are sufficient to identify the species. A fine large species from the Eocene of Pittsburg, Oreg., collected by Diller, was identified by me[a] with *decisa*. This identification was made because of the Eocene age of both, there being usually only one species of *Acila* in a single horizon. However, inasmuch as Conrad's original

---

[a] Trans. Wagner Inst., vol. 3, 1898, p. 573, pl. 40, figs. 1, 3.

type specimen seems lost, and his figure and description are worthless, it is probably best to apply a new name to the Oregonian Eocene species, which may be called *Nucula (Acila) shumardi* Dall.

Another species, *N. (A.) cordata* Dall, was described and figured [a] from the Miocene of Nehalem River, above Mist, Columbia County, Oreg., collected by Diller. This resembles *N. shumardi*, but is smaller and much more coarsely sculptured. It is more rostrate and elongate than *N. conradi*, which is an evenly ovate species. A species occurs in the Eocene of Alaska that may be identical with *N. shumardi*, but is known only from distorted casts. None of these has been recognized from the Coos Bay Miocene, except *N. conradi*, which more nearly resembles the recent *N. (A.) castrensis* Hinds, 1843, of which the *N. divaricata* Valenciennes, 1846, non Hinds, and *N. (A.) lyalli* Baird, are believed to be synonyms.

Family LEDIDÆ.

Genus LEDA Schumacher.

Leda Schumacher, Essai, p. 172, 1817; type, *Arca rostrata* Linné; Dall, Trans. Wagner Inst.. III, p. 579, 1898.

Subgenus LEMBULUS Risso.

Lembulus Risso, Hist. Nat. Eur. Mérid., IV, p. 319, 1825; type, *Leda pella* Linné (sp.)=*L. vossianus* Risso.

LEDA ACUTA Conrad.

Leda acuta Conrad, Am. Mar. Conch., p. 32, pl. 6, fig. 1, 1831; not of Sowerby. 1837; Dall. Trans. Wagner Inst., III, p. 592, 1898.

Miocene of uppermost beds at Fossil Point, Coos Bay, Oregon, collected by W. H. Dall; U. S. Nat. Mus. 154009. Miocene to recent on both coasts of America and in the Antilles.

This very characteristic and widespread species occurs in large numbers, though poorly preserved, in the uppermost Miocene sandstones at Fossil Point.

LEDA PENITA Conrad.

Nucula penita Conrad. Am. Jour. Sci., 2d ser., V, p. 433. fig. 10. 1848.
Neilo penita Conrad, Am. Jour. Conch., I, p. 153, 1865.

Miocene of the Astoria group, Astoria, Oreg., collected by J. K. Townsend. The type specimen appears to be lost.

Why Conrad should have referred this species to *Neilo* is inexplicable. It differs from *L. acuta* by the very anterior beaks, but is based on an internal cast of a specimen which appears to be lost, or at least of which the whereabouts is unknown. It is probable, however, that it might be recognized should other specimens turn up from the original locality.

LEDA WHITMANI Dall, n. sp.

Pl. XIV, fig. 4.

Shell large, solid, inequilateral, the posterior side longer, the valves rather convex; beaks full, slightly recurved, sculptured with fine, distant, slightly elevated,

---

[a] Op. cit., p. 573, pl. 40, fig. 4.

concentric threads; anterior dorsum arched, the anterior end defective; posterior dorsum markedly concave, with a striated, strongly impressed lanceolate escutcheon, the apposed margins prominently raised; posterior end rostrate, subtruncate, obliquely rounded; base arcuate; sculpture of concentric sulci obsolete on the dorsal half of the rostrum, feebler on the sides of the valve, and becoming deeper and stronger toward the basal margin; interior inaccessible. Length of remaining portion of valve, 23 mm.; length from beak to posterior end, 16 mm.; height, 17 mm.; double diameter of valve, 8 mm.

From Miocene matrix inclosed as a pebble in the Pleistocene Coos conglomerate, Fossil Point, Coos Bay, Oregon, collected by W. H. Dall; U. S. Nat. Mus. 153970.

Although an imperfect valve is all the material that has been obtained, the characters are so well marked that the species can readily be identified if found in more complete condition.

The species is dedicated to Marcus Whitman, the Oregon pioneer and missionary.

Two supposedly Miocene species were described in 1858, by Shumard, one from 5 miles north of Salem, in the Willamette Valley, under the name of *Leda willamettensis*. No measurements were given, the description is insufficient for recognition, and the types are lost and were never figured. The species must be considered unrecognizable. The other, *Leda oregona* Shumard, seems from the description to be a *Yoldia*, of which impressions were found a few miles south of Oregon City in Miocene sandstones.

Genus YOLDIA Mörch.

Section CNESTERIUM Dall, 1896.

YOLDIA (CNESTERIUM) STRIGATA Dall, n. sp.

Pl. XIV, figs. 9, 9a.

Shell thin, compressed, equivalve, inequilateral, polished; anterior end longer, equally arcuate above and below, anteriorly somewhat attenuated; posterior end a little shorter, subtruncate, slightly recurved, dorsal slope slightly concave, with the apposed margins compressed and projecting in the middle of the narrow escutcheon; lunule linear or nearly so; truncate end a little concavely flexuous; posterior basal margin evenly convexly arcuate; base a little prominent toward the middle; beaks inconspicuous, flattish, not raised above the general arch of the dorsum; surface smooth except for obscure incremental lines, and numerous sharp, slightly elevated, somewhat flexuous, oblique, distant ridges with the long slope extending basally and the short slope abrupt and almost undercut; these ridges vary slightly in individuals but in general cover the sides of the shell nearly to the beaks, and are usually obsolete on the anterior dorsal areas and on the rostrum; the shell gets proportionately broader, vertically, with age. Longitude of figured specimen, 37 mm.; altitude, 19.5 mm.; diameter, 5.5 mm. An older but less perfect individual measures, longitude, 43.5 mm.; altitude, 23.0 mm.; diameter, 7.5 mm.

Miocene of Coos Bay, Oregon, purchased from B. H. Camman; U. S. Nat. Mus. 153951.

The interior being filled with hard matrix, the characters can not be given, but a worn specimen indicates that there are at least 28 anterior and 22 posterior teeth on the hinge margin. The recent species of the Oregon coast, *Y. ensifera* Dall, is very similar but has the beaks much more anterior, is a narrower shell, and has the posterior extremity longer and less recurved. *Y. scissurata* Dall occurs in the lower Pleistocene of San Pedro, Cal.; it is a much smaller and proportionately more convex shell, with 20 anterior and about 14 posterior hinge teeth. It is found living in moderate depths from Sitka northward to the Arctic Ocean.

YOLDIA (CNESTERIUM) OREGONA Shumard.

Pl. XIX, fig. 4.

Leda oregona Shumard, Trans. St. Louis Acad. Sci., I, p. 121, 1858; Gabb, Pal. California, II, p. 121, 1868.
Neilo oregona (Shumard) Conrad, Am. Jour. Conch., I, p. 153, 1865.
Nuculana oregona Meek, Checkl. Miocene Fos. N. Am., pp. 5, 27, 1864.

Miocene of the Willamette Valley, south of Oregon City, Oreg., in soft yellow and white sandstone, casts coated with hydrated peroxide of iron, Evans and Shumard; similar rocks at Halls Ferry, 5½ miles southwest of Salem, Marion County, Oreg., and 6 miles southwest of Salem, A. J. Collier, U. S. Geol. Survey. U. S. Nat. Mus. 110449 and 110450.

Shumard's types seem to have been lost and the shell was never figured, but the specimens collected by Collier agree so well with Shumard's description and relative measurements that I have little doubt of their identity. It is also probable that it is the species referred to by Gabb when he stated that he had seen specimens of *Yoldia cooperi* from the Astoria Miocene.

The shell is indeed very similar to and perhaps the precursor of *Y. cooperi*, but it is quite distinct specifically. In *Y. cooperi* the beaks are much nearer the posterior end of the shell, which is also more narrowly attenuated. The pallial sinus of *Y. cooperi* is large and rounded in front, reaching a little in front of the middle of the shell; in *Y. oregona* it is shorter, not quite reaching the vertical of the beak; *oregona* has 17 posterior and 32 anterior hinge teeth, while in *cooperi* the number is 14 and 40, respectively; the external incised sculpture, so far as can be told from the casts, is quite similar. The specimens collected by Collier measure 51 mm. long and 26 mm. in greatest height, and were 7 or 8 mm. in diameter when the valves were closed.

Section PORTLANDIA Mörch.

YOLDIA (PORTLANDIA) IMPRESSA Conrad.

Nucula impressa Conrad, Geol. U. S. Expl. Exp., p. 723, pl. 18, fig. 7, 1849.
Yoldia impressa Conrad, Am. Jour. Conch., I, p. 154, 1865; Arnold, Pal. and Strat. San Pedro, p. 100, 1903.
Yoldia cooperi Gabb, Pal. California, II, pp. 59, 103, 1868, ex parte; not *Y. cooperi* Gabb, Proc. California Acad. Sci. for 1865, p. 189.

Upper Miocene of the Empire formation, Coos Bay, Oregon, W. H. Dall; U. S. Nat. Mus. 154013. Miocene of the Astoria group, Astoria, Oreg., J. D. Dana; U. S. Nat. Mus. 3490 (figured types), 3491.

Gabb was entirely wrong in supposing this species to be the young of his *Y. cooperi*, which does not belong even to the same section of the genus. Whether his statement that he had seen typical *Y. cooperi* from the Astoria Miocene is correct or not there is no means of determining at present. It does not occur among the collections made at that locality by the United States Geological Survey, at any rate.

Yoldia impressa is a thin, plump shell with a sharply pointed, strongly recurved posterior extremity. The surface is marked by incised lines in harmony with the lines of growth, regularly and somewhat widely spaced. Worn specimens show more than 22 anterior and 16 posterior hinge teeth, but none exhibit the entire series. The sharply recurved posterior tip is often broken off, giving a blunt look to the specimen, which might then be taken for a different species. The best-preserved specimen measures 19 mm. long; from the beaks to the end of the rostrum 10 mm.; height, 9 mm.; diameter, 6.5 mm. Other specimens reach 24 mm. in length. The lunule and escutcheon are sharply impressed and narrow, with their inner valve margins pouting a little. The concentric sulci do not extend over the umbonal and dorsal regions.

Genus MALLETIA Desmoulins.

MALLETIA ABRUPTA Conrad.

Nucula abrupta Conrad. Am. Jour. Sci., 2d ser., V, p. 423, fig. 3, 1848.
Neilo abrupta Conrad. Am. Jour. Conch., I, p. 153, 1865; Gabb, Pal. California, II, p. 122, 1868.

Miocene of Astoria, Oreg., J. K. Townsend.

I have not seen specimens of this species and the whereabouts of the type is unknown to me, but Conrad's figure looks like a *Malletia*, and his referring it later to *Neilo* shows that this was also his opinion. There are several recent species of *Malletia* in the Puget Sound region; the one most nearly resembling this fossil is *M. pacifica* Dall, a much larger species with less prominent beaks than are shown by Conrad's figure of *M. abrupta*.

Suborder FILIBRANCHIATA.

Superfamily ARCACEA.

Family LIMOPSIDÆ.

Genus LIMOPSIS Sasso.

LIMOPSIS NITENS Conrad.

Pectunculus nitens Conrad. Geol. U. S. Expl. Exp., p. 726, pl. 18, fig. 9, 1849.
Limopsis nitens Conrad. Am. Jour. Conch., I, p. 153, 1865; Gabb, Pal. California, II, p. 121, 1868.
?Pectunculus indet. Conrad. Geol. U. S. Expl. Exp., p. 726, pl. 18, fig. 11, 1849.
?Limopsis ?oregonensis Conrad. Am. Jour. Conch., I, p. 153, 1865; Gabb, Pal. California, II, p. 121, 1868.

Miocene of Astoria, Oreg., J. D. Dana; U. S. Nat. Mus. 3579, Conrad's type.

This species is a small, polished, nearly smooth shell which exhibits radial lines of minute punctures and in well-grown specimens has some small riblets near the basal angles. There are about five teeth on each side of the ligament, a short hinge line, and somewhat oblique valves. The valve margins appear to have been crenate, at least in the adult stage, and the valves show fine concentric sulci near the basal margin externally. The length is about 7 mm., the height 6.5 mm., and the diameter 3 mm.

The internal cast to which Conrad gave the name of *oregonensis* seems to have been lost; at all events, it is not with the other types, and the figure gives no indication of the genus to which it might belong. If to *Limopsis*, which Conrad himself doubted, it may be an internal cast of a full-grown specimen of *L. nitens*.

The best way to deal with such an unrecognizable name would be to drop it from the lists altogether, but if we are not permitted to do this it may find a refuge in the probable synonymy of *L. nitens*.

Family ARCIDÆ.

Genus GLYCYMERIS Da Costa.

Glycymeris (ex parte) Da Costa, Brit. Conch., p. 170, 1778; type, *Arca glycymeris* Linné.
Tuceta Bolten. Mus. Boltenianum, p. 172. 1798: type, *Arca pilosa* Linné.
Pectunculus Lamarck, Prodrome, p. 87, 1799; type, *Arca pectunculus* Linné.
Axinæa Oken, Lehrb. d. Naturg., pp. viii, 235, 1815; first species. *Arca pilosa* Linné.
Glycymeris Dall, Trans. Wagner Inst., III. p. 607, 1898; Jour. Conch (Leeds), XI. No. 5, p. 145. 1904.

This genus, so characteristic of the Atlantic Miocene, is also well represented on the Pacific coast.

GLYCYMERIS GREWINGKI Dall, n. sp.

Pl. II, fig. 13.

Shell solid, suborbicular, subequilateral, equivalve; beaks prominent, moderately convex, slightly separated by the area, which is narrow, in each valve forming a wide, very obtuse triangle with deeply incised angular sulci, radiating from the vertical of the beak; anterior slope slightly shorter and more rounded than the posterior, which is somewhat produced toward the lower portion; there is no distinct lunule or escutcheon; but a feebly differentiated anterior dorsal area is characterized by radial threads much finer than those on the anterior half of the disk; on the latter are about a dozen flat, little-elevated, radial ribs, separated by much narrower, channeled sulci, the whole with more or less obsolete fine radial striation; these radial ribs are distinct when the surface of the shell is intact; the anterior half of the disk, except when decorticated, nearly smooth except for close-set uniform numerous radial threads which cover the entire surface; when decorticated the internal structure shows ribs much like those normally exposed on the anterior half of the disk. Altitude of figured specimen, 38 mm.; longitude, 38 mm.; diameter 20 mm.

Miocene of Coos Bay, Oregon, purchased from B. H. Camman; U. S. Nat. Mus. 107784.

GLYCYMERIS CONRADI Dall, n. sp.

Pl. XI, fig. 2.

Shell solid, suborbicular, equilateral, with small, rather pointed umbones nearly touching, and an extremely narrow, short ligamental area between them; dorsal slopes nearly straight, subequal, base and ends equally evenly rounded; dorsal area on each side of the beaks smooth, disk with about 30 flat, wide radial ribs, widest in the center of the disk and becoming gradually narrower toward the ends of the shell, separated by much narrower channeled sulci, and radially finely obsoletely striate; concentric sculpture of well-marked incremental lines, and, toward the ends, with a certain number of low, irregular, feeble, concentric wrinkles. Altitude, 37 mm.; latitude, 39 mm.; diameter, 20 mm.

Miocene of Coos Bay, Oregon, purchased from B. H. Camman; U. S. Nat. Mus. 153949a. ?Astoria, Oreg., Miocene, J. D. Dana; U. S. Nat. Mus. 3541.

The specimen from Astoria is too imperfect to be certain of the species, but positively belongs to this genus.

GLYCYMERIS GABBI Dall, n. sp.

Pl. XI, fig. 5.

Shell large, rather thin, compressed, suborbicular, nearly equilateral; beaks defective, probably rather elevated, separated by a narrower ligamental area with about half a dozen angular sulci divaricating from the vertical of the umbones; dorsal slopes straight, nearly smooth, the posterior slope somewhat flattened; disk uniformly sculptured with about 34 narrow, flat radial ribs, separated by somewhat narrower channeled interspaces, the interspaces wider and the ribs narrower toward the ends of the shell; concentric sculpture of narrow, flat ridges, narrower and closer together toward the basal margin, but on the central part of the disk forming with the radial ribs nearly square reticulations; interior, as in other cases, filled with a refractory matrix. Altitude of shell, 51 mm.; latitude, 53 mm.; diameter, about 20 mm.

Miocene of Coos Bay, Oregon, purchased from B. H. Camman; U. S. Nat. Mus. 153949b.

A *Pectunculus patulus* was described and figured by Conrad in the report on the geology of the United States Exploring Expedition under Wilkes. The type is still preserved in the National Museum (No. 3605), but Conrad afterward recognized that the fossil was merely an imperfect internal cast of a specimen of his *Lucina acutilineata* of the same report. The species should therefore be expunged from the Astoria list. Further reference to it will be found under the head of *Phacoides acutilineatus*.

GLYCYMERIS BARBARENSIS Conrad.

Axinæa barbarensis Conrad, Pacific R. R. Repts., VI, p. 71. pl. 3, fig. 11, 1857; not *Axinæa barbarensis* Conrad, op. cit.. VII, p. 194. pl. 6, fig. 3. 1857 (Rancho Triunfo, Los Angeles,Cal.).
Axinæa patula Gabb. ex parte. Pal. California, II. p. 102, 1868.

Coast near Santa Barbara, Cal., Doctor Newberry, fide Conrad.

The two figures of *G. barbarensis* given by Conrad in the Pacific railroad reports (VI and VII) are of another type from either of the Oregon species, and both appear to be Eocene.

Conrad figured and described two distinct species of *Glycymeris* in these reports under one name. Both reports were written in 1856 and published in 1857. The date of transmittal of the reports printed in volume 7 is February 9, 1857, but there is no way known to me of determining the exact date of issue of either, as the volume number is inconclusive. The type of the species figured in volume 7 is preserved, and is a small valve (probably immature) not agreeing with the young of *G. veatchii*

Gabb, but having a strong likeness to the eastern *G. staminea* Conrad, of the Alabama Eocene. Curiously enough, there is attached to it a label in Doctor Antisell's handwriting, in which it is stated that the fossil is "*G. collinus* Conrad," a name which appears to be unpublished.

My own surmise is that Conrad described the shell under the latter name; but that Doctor Antisell, after receiving Conrad's manuscript, knowing that there was a species of the same genus in Conrad's report to Doctor Newberry of about the same date, in the volume preceding Antisell's report, too hastily concluded that they were the same and altered Conrad's manuscript, or the proofs, to correspond to this mistaken identification.

At any rate, the name *collinus* remains available for the second *G. barbarensis*, which will require a new name. Only an injudicious "lumping" would suffice to unite this species to either of those of the Miocene.

The *G. barbarensis* of Arnold's San Pedro monograph is not either of Conrad's species, but an undescribed form near *G. intermedia* Broderip, now living on the coast, which was too hastily united by Carpenter with Conrad's fossil. This misidentification had been accepted by most writers on West American shells until the present time, when a careful review of the material shows it to be an error.

A large species from the Miocene of Alaska was described by Grewingk under the name *Pectunculus kaschewarowi*. This species has high and pointed beaks and very numerous (50) flat radial ribs—more, in fact, than any other species known from the coast. It is probably distinct from any of the others. It is 45 mm. long and 47 mm. high, with a diameter of 25 mm. It is, according to Grewingk, widely distributed in the Tertiary of the Alaska Peninsula and the islands south of it from Kadiak to the Shumagins.

Genus ARCA (Linné) Lamarck.

Arca (L.) Lamarck, Prodrome, p. 87, 1799; type, *Arca noæ* Linné.

Subgenus SCAPHARCA Gray.

Scapharca Gray, Proc. Zool. Soc. London for 1847, p. 206; type *Arca inequivalvis* Bruguière.

ARCA (SCAPHARCA) DEVINCTA Conrad.

Arca devincta Conrad, Geol. U. S. Expl. Exp., p. 726, pl. 18, fig. 10, 1849.
Anomalocardia devincta Conrad, Am. Jour. Conch., I, p. 153, 1865.

Oligocene of Oregon, from the concretions at Astoria, J. D. Dana; U. S. Nat. Mus. 3499.

The original figure, being made from a specimen half buried in a tough concretion, gave little idea of the specific characters of the shell. I have taken the responsibility of breaking up the concretion of which the type specimen was composed and for the first time making it possible to get at the characters of the species. It proved to be allied to *A. staminata* Dall, of the Floridian upper Oligocene, a short trigonal species with very thick shell and elevated beaks; with about 30 flattish ribs with narrower channeled interspaces, the tops of the ribs above somewhat rippled by incremental concentric lines, and exhibiting distally four fine radial threads on the broad top of each rib. The interumbonal area is moderately developed, in the type

23 mm. long with a maximum width of 7 mm.; its sculpture is concealed by matrix; the type specimen is 32 mm. in length; if we allow 3 mm. for the decollate umbones it is 28 mm. high, with a maximum diameter of 28 mm. The muscular scars are small, the inner disk radially striate, the valve margins coarsely crenate, and the shell 3.5 mm. in thickness. The valves seem to have gaped a little behind.

The species is amply distinct from any of those noted from the coast Tertiary, and by means of the data above given can easily be recognized if found.

ARCA (SCAPHARCA) MICRODONTA Conrad.

Arca microdonta Conrad, App. Prel. Rept. W. P. Blake, House Doc. 129, p. 13, July, 1855; Pacific R. R. Repts., V, p. 323, pl. 3, fig. 29, 1857; not of Gabb, 1868, nor of Osmont, 1904.

Miocene of Tulare Valley?, California, W. P. Blake; U. S. Nat. Mus. 1844, Lower Miocene or Oligocene of southern California, Arnold. Miocene of the Astoria group, Astoria, Oreg., J. D. Dana; U. S. Nat. Mus. 3497.

This species is fairly well figured by Conrad and is remarkable for its straight hinge line and very anterior beaks. The type is a right valve with 26 simple rounded ribs and somewhat wider channeled interspaces. The dorsal area is nearly as long as the shell with six deeply cut ligamentary sulci on each valve; the beaks are markedly prosocœlous.

The shell is in remarkably good preservation for a Californian Miocene fossil, and even looks as if it might have come out of the San Pedro Pleistocene. The specimen from Astoria is an internal cast so inequilateral as to suggest no other west-coast species.

In Osmont's review of the Arcas of the Californian Neocene [a] he figures and discusses a species (which can not be identical with this) under the name of *A. microdonta.* If this proves to be undescribed it may take the name of *A. osmonti.*[b]

ARCA (SCAPHARCA) TRILINEATA Conrad.

Pl. XII, figs. 1, 2.

Arca trilineata Conrad, Pacific R. R. Repts., VI, p. 70, pl. 2, fig. 9, 1857; Proc. Acad. Nat. Sci. Philadelphia for 1856, p. 314, 1857; Osmont, Bull. Dept. Geol. Univ. California, IV, p. 91 (syn. excl.), pl. 4, figs. 4, 4a–c, 1904.

Shell large, solid, inequilateral, very slightly inequivalve; beaks small, rather high, incurved, and nearer the anterior end of the shell; separated by a long lozenge-shaped area with deeply incised ligamental furrows as figured; dorsal line on each side of the beaks nearly straight, from which anteriorly the margins are abruptly rounded away; base gently arcuate, posterior end more pointed, the dorsal margins oblique; sculpture of right valve of about 31 flat radial ribs, each mesially grooved, separated by narrower channeled interspaces and crossed by more or less conspicuous concentric threads which are less apparent in the interspaces; the left valve differs by having the ribs narrower and more rounded and the mesial sulci deeper and more channeled; toward the anterior end the concentric sculpture on the ribs is apparently

---

[a] Osmont, V. C., Bull. Dept. Geol. Univ. California, vol. 4, 1904.
[b] Osmont, op. cit., pp. 90, 91, pl. 8, figs. 2a–b.

more prominent and crowded; interior inaccessible. Longitude of figured specimen, 64 mm.; altitude (the beaks being defective), about 47 mm.; diameter, 36 mm.

Miocene of Coos Bay, Oregon, purchased of B. H. Camman; U. S. Nat. Mus. 153948. Upper Miocene of Washington and of southern California, Ralph Arnold. Pliocene of San Diego well (city park), H. Hemphill, U. S. Nat. Mus. 7934; also Homer Hamlin.

Arca schizotoma Dall (*sulcicosta* Gabb, 1866, not Nyst, 1836) is a lighter, more equilateral species, with fewer and broader ribs and narrower interspaces, according to Pliocene specimens from the San Diego well, received from H. Hamlin. Conrad's figure of *A. canalis* has the aspect of a *Cunearca*, and if so, it belongs to a different section from *schizotoma*, which also has an area differently sculptured from that of *trilineata*. *A. congesta* Conrad I have not seen, and the type is apparently lost.

Superfamily OSTRACEA.

Family OSTREIDÆ.

Genus OSTREA (Linné) Lamarck.

Subgenus CRASSOSTREA (Sacco).

Crassostrea Dall, Trans. Wagner Inst., III, p. 671, 1898; type, *Ostrea virginica* Gmelin.

OSTREA (CRASSOSTREA) TITAN Conrad.

Ostrea titan Conrad, Proc. Acad. Nat. Sci. Philadelphia,VI, p. 199, 1854; Pacific R. R. Repts., VI, p. 72, pl. 4, fig. 17a, pl. 5, fig. 17a, 1857.
Ostrea contracta Conrad, Rept. Mex. Boundary Survey, I, pt. 2, p. 160, pl. 18, fig. 1, 1857.
Ostrea tayloriana Gabb, Pal. California, II, p. 34, pl. 12, fig. 60, 1869; adolescent shell.
Ostrea georgiana Dall, ex parte, Trans. Wagner Inst., III, p. 684, 1898.

Miocene of Coos Bay, Oregon, purchased from B. H. Camman; U. S. Nat. Mus. 153955. Miocene of Texas, New Mexico, and California.

I have retained Conrad's name for the Pacific coast shell, instead of referring it to the prior *O. georgiana* as I did in the Wagner memoir, because, notwithstanding their probable identity, later collections from the typical locality of *O. georgiana* show that in the rare specimens of the latter that retain the thin outer coat of the shell it is marked with fine vermicular sculpture, which has not, so far, been detected on Pacific coast specimens. The latter are usually in a poor state of preservation and it can not yet be said that the two forms are specifically distinct, nevertheless, it seems best to keep them apart for the present until the question of external sculpture can be definitely settled.

Superfamily PECTINACEA.

Family PECTINIDÆ.

Genus PECTEN Müller.

Pecten (Klein, 1758) Müller, Prodr. Zool. Dan., p. 248, 1776; Lamarck, Prodrome, p. 88, 1799; type, *Ostrea maxima* Linné.
Pecten Dall, Trans. Wagner Inst., III, p. 689, 1898.

Subgenus CHLAMYS Bolten.

Section PATINOPECTEN Dall.

Patinopecten Dall, Trans. Wagner Inst.. III, p. 695, 1898; type, *Pecten caurinus* Gould.

This group is particularly characteristic of the Pacific coast faunas, from the Miocene to the present day.

PECTEN (PATINOPECTEN) COOSENSIS Shumard.

Pl. XVI, figs. 2, 2a; Pl. XVII, fig. 3.

Pecten coosensis Shumard, Trans. St. Louis Acad. Sci., I, pt. 2, p. 122, 1858; Gabb, Pal. California, II, p. 122, 1869.
Pecten coosaënsis Meek, Smithsonian Checkl. Miocene Foss., p. 3, 1868.
Pecten (Patinopecten) coosensis Dall, Trans. Wagner Inst., III, pt. 4, p. 700, pl. 26, fig. 2, 1898; Arnold, Tert. and Quat. Pect. California, Prof. Paper U. S. Geol. Survey No. 47, p. 61, pl. 6, fig. 2, pl. 7, figs. 2, 2a, 1906.

Shell equilateral, nearly equivalve, slightly longer than high, the valves well compressed and with smooth margins; right valve with 29 to 31 prominent T-rail-shaped ribs, flattened and sometimes feebly duplex above by reason of a median sulcus; interspaces about equal to the ribs at the margin, narrower above, deep, and more or less channeled; incremental lines close set, rather conspicuous, surface with a few obsolete radial striations; ears strongly concentrically striated, with two to four obsolete radial sulci; byssal notch wide, deep, with a well-marked fasciole; left valve with narrower, rounded, concave-sided ribs with wider roundly concave interspaces, crossed by numerous sharp, moderately elevated, concentric lines; ears subequal, obsoletely radially sulcate, and rather strongly concentrically striated. Altitude, 110 mm.; longitude, 115 mm.; longitude of hinge line, 54 mm.; diameter, 26 mm.

Miocene of Coos Bay, Oregon, purchased from B. H. Camman; U. S. Nat. Mus. 107791; also collected from the same locality by Shumard, Dall (153969), Diller, and others, and reported by Arnold from Benton County, Oreg., as collected by Diller.

PECTEN (PATINOPECTEN) PROPATULUS Conrad.

Pl. XV, figs. 1, 2; Pl. XVI, fig. 1.

Pecten propatulus Conrad, Geol. U. S. Expl. Exp., p. 726, pl. 18, figs. 13, 13a, 1849; Meek, Checkl. Mioc. Foss. N. Am., p. 26, 1864; Conrad, Am. Jour. Conch., I, p. 154, 1865; Gabb, Pal. California, II, p. 103, 1869.
Pecten (Patinopecten) propatulus Dall. Trans. Wagner Inst., III, p. 699. 1898; Arnold, Tert. and Quat. Pect. California, Prof. Paper U. S. Geol. Survey No. 47, p. 64, pl. 7, pl. 9, figs. 1, 1a, 2, 2a, 1906.

Miocene of the Astoria group, Astoria, Oreg., J. D. Dana; Clallam Bay, Fuca Strait, Washington, Arnold; Newport, Yaquina Bay, Oregon, Hill; Port Simpson, British Columbia, in California Acad. Sci., fide Arnold; Griswolds, San Benito County, Cal., Turner and Cooper.

This species has been confounded with the recent *P. caurinus* Gould, by Carpenter and others, but is sufficiently distinguished by its smaller size and more convex valves, and by having only 15 primary radial ribs.

Subgenus PSEUDAMUSIUM Adams.

PECTEN (PSEUDAMUSIUM) PECKHAMI Gabb.

Pecten peckhami Gabb, Pal. California, II, p. 59, pl. 16, figs. 19, 19a, 1868; Cooper, Seventh Ann. Rept. California State Min. Bureau, p. 258, 1888; Dall, Trans. Wagner Inst., III, p. 705, 1898.

Pecten (Pseudamusium) peckhami Arnold, Tert. and Quat. Pect. California. Prof. Paper, U. S. Geol. Survey, No. 47, p. 56, pl. 3, figs. 6, 7, 8, 1906.

Oligocene or Miocene of the Astoria group, Astoria, Oreg., J. D. Dana; U. S. Nat. Mus. 3575; also at various localities in Washington and California; Miocene of Ojai ranch, Ventura County, Cal., Peckham; and many other localities in California.

Superfamily MYTILACEA.

Family MYTILIDÆ.

Genus MYTILUS (Linné) Bolten.

Mytilus Bolten, Mus. Boltenianum, p. 157, 1798; Lamarck, Prodrome, p. 88, 1799; type, *M. edulis* Linné.

MYTILUS FICUS Dall, n. sp.

Pl. IX, figs. 1, 4.

Shell solid, thick, subpyriform, with rather blunt apical umbones; dorsal slope subarcuate, with a tendency to angulation somewhat behind the middle; posterior end ovately rounded; base somewhat swollen toward the middle, behind which it is nearly straight; apices slightly decurved; surface sculpture of incremental lines and coarse, wide, little-elevated, rounded wrinkles, without any radial furrows; interior filled with matrix. Longitude, 95 mm.; altitude, 47 mm.; diameter, 28 mm.

Miocene of Coos Bay, Oregon, purchased from B. H. Camman; U. S. Nat. Mus. 153950.

This species has many of the characteristics of the Pliocene and recent *M. californicus*, but is destitute of the radial sculpture found in that species and were not the variations of form so notorious in the Mytilidæ, the single specimen found might be said to differ in that respect also. The shell still retains the dark coloration characteristic of such species as *M. edulis* and *californicus*.

Genus MODIOLUS Lamarck.

Modiolus Lamarck, Prodrome, p. 87, 1799; type, *Mytilus modiolus* Linné; Dall, Trans. Wagner Inst., III, p. 790, 1898; Arnold, Pal. and Strat. San Pedro, p. 120, 1903.

Modiola Lamarck, Syst. des Anim. s. Vert., p. 113, 1801.

MODIOLUS DIRECTUS Dall, n. sp.

Pl. XII, figs. 11, 12.

Shell thin, elongate, covered with a brown periostracum of which the remaining portions show alternating zones of darker and lighter color; umbones low, inconspicuous, not very close to the posterior end of the valves, as figured; dorsal margin straight anteriorly, arcuate posteriorly, obliquely descending to the hinder end of the shell, which is bluntly rounded; umbonal ridge broad, prominent, extending from the beaks to the lower posterior end of the shell, the part of the disk immediately in front of it slightly excavated; basal margin slightly concave, arching anteriorly toward the subangulate anterior extremity, surface smooth or distally slightly concentrically wrinkled.   Longitude, 105 mm.; altitude, 40 mm.; diameter, 26 mm.

Upper Miocene of Coos Bay, Oregon, and also near Fossil Point, Dall, purchased of B. H. Camman; U. S. Nat. Mus. 154206 and 153947.   Miocene of the Astoria group, Astoria, Oreg., J. D. Dana; U. S. Nat. Mus. 110451.   Upper Miocene of Santa Cruz, Cal. ?, Arnold.

This species, without a careful comparison, would be taken for *M. rectus* Conrad, of which it is doubtless the precursor.   On comparison, however, it is evident that the anterior end of *M. directus* is proportionately much shorter than in *rectus*, and the posterior end still more so; the fossil is not alate above like the variety *flabellatus* Gould, and it is also more arcuate than *rectus*.

The Astoria specimen is very young.   Whether the specimens which have been reported from various other localities should be referred to *rectus* or *directus* depends on future scrutiny of the material, which unfortunately on this coast is rarely so perfectly preserved as to afford a basis for critical comparisons.

MODIOLUS INFLATUS Dall, n. sp.

Pl. XII, figs. 8, 9.

Shell short, stout, inflated, thin, externally smooth and polished, with traces of concentric zones of darker and lighter brownish coloration; umbones low, blunt, near the anterior end of the shell as figured; umbonal ridge inflated, distinct only on the anterior half of the shell; hinge line straight, about half as long as the shell, anterior dorsal margin arching into the wider, posterior, rounded end; base very slightly concave, anterior end narrower, rounded; sculpture only of more or less distinct incremental lines; interior brilliantly iridescent.   Longitude, 48 mm.; altitude, 27 mm.; diameter, about 22 mm.

Miocene of Coos Bay, Oregon, purchased from B. H. Camman; U. S. Nat. Mus. 153946.

On comparison with a large series of specimens of *M. capax* Conrad and *M. fornicatus* Carpenter, its nearest allies on the coast, this species appears less alate and angulate dorsally and more evenly convex anteriorly than the former.   *M. fornicatus* is a small species, averaging hardly more than an inch in length, and the present form is nearly twice that size.   The fossil is more bluntly rounded behind, and more inflated than *M. modiolus* of the same length.   With a general resemblance to several of the recent forms, it differs from each of them in some essential particulars.

It may be noted here that the *M. fornicatus* referred to in Arnold's San Pedro memoir was probably in part young specimens of *M. modiolus*, inasmuch as his measurements, 54 mm. long and 30 mm. in diameter, appear too large to have been taken from a typical specimen of *fornicatus*, which rarely exceeds half of those dimensions.

Order TELEODESMACEA.

Superfamily CYRENACEA.

Family CYRENIDÆ.

Genus CYRENA Lamarck.

Cyrena Lamarck, Anim. s. Vert., V, p. 551 bis, 1818; type, *C. zeylanica* Lamarck; Dall, Trans. Wagner Inst., III, p. 1441, 1903.

Subgenus LEPTESTHES Meek.

Leptesthes Meek, Prel. Rept. Geol. Survey Wyoming, p. 316, 1872; type, *Corbicula fracta* Meek.

?CYRENA FIBROSA Shumard.

Lucina fibrosa Shumard, Trans. Acad. Sci. St. Louis, I, p. 120, 1858.
Cyclas fibrosa Conrad, Am. Jour. Conch., I, p. 153, 1865.

Upper Eocene shales, found interbedded with the coal, at Coos Bay and Port Orford, Oregon, Shumard.

These shales contain a brackish-water fauna, including *Corbula*, *Cyrena*, *Goniobasis*, and fragments of plants, usually badly crushed. No lucinoid shell was found in them by the collectors of the United States Geological Survey. The *Cyrena* is very abundant, and there is nothing in the description of Shumard's unfigured species to invalidate the conclusion that it might have been based on *Cyrena*, as his *Cerithium klamathensis* is doubtless on a *Goniobasis*.

Superfamily CARDITACEA.

Family CARDITIDÆ.

Genus VENERICARDIA Lamarck.

Venericardia Lamarck, Syst. des Anim. s. Vert., p. 123, 1801; type, *V. imbricata* Lam.; Dall, Trans. Wagner Inst., III, p. 1416, 1903.

Section CYCLOCARDIA Conrad.

Cyclocardia Conrad, Am. Jour. Conch., III, p. 191, 1867; *C. borealis* Conrad; Dall, Trans. Wagner Inst., III, p. 1417, 1903.

VENERICARDIA SUBTENTA Conrad.

Cardita subtenta Conrad, Geol. U. S. Expl. Exp., p. 726, pl. 18, figs. 12, 12a, 1849.
Cardium subtentum Conrad, Am. Jour. Conch., I, p. 153, 1865.
Cardita ventricosa Gabb, Pal. California, II, p. 101, 1868; not of Gould, 1850; cf. Dall, Proc. Acad. Nat. Sci. Philadelphia, for 1902, p. 709; and Proc. U. S. Nat. Mus., XXVI, No. 1342, 1903.

Miocene of the Astoria group, Astoria, Oreg., J. D. Dana; U. S. Nat. Mus. 3502 (Conrad's types), 3515, and 3484. Variety *quadrata* Dall, 1 mile east of Clallam Bay, Washington, Arnold, and Coos Bay, Oregon, purchased of B. H. Camman; U. S. Nat. Mus. 153936 (part) and 110455.

The typical form is a small, ovate, delicately sculptured shell, with from 20 to 24 radial riblets more or less minutely nodulous. It is nearest to *V. ventricosa* (Gould)

Dall, but is shorter and with higher beaks. The variety *quadrata* is a larger, more quadrate shell with 25 to 26 low, rounded ribs.

The largest specimen of *subtenta* is 19 mm. high, 18 mm. wide, and 8 mm. in diameter; the largest specimen of the variety *quadrata* 28, 27.5, and 18 mm. in the respective dimensions.

The small but constant differences which separate the recent species of this group were also probably characteristic of the Tertiary species, but the condition of the fossils for the most part is so poor that it is difficult to recognize the discriminating factors. By most of the writers on Pacific coast paleontology the species have been indiscriminately lumped together, with each other and with some of the recent forms. A very careful comparison with the recent types indicates that none of the Miocene fossils can be prudently identified with either of the recent species of the coast.

VENERICARDIA CASTOR Dall, n. sp.

Pl. XI, figs. 1, 3.

Shell robust, solid, ventricose, thick, equivalve, inequilateral, with high, full, anteriorly recurved umbones; lunule short, cordate, defined by a deeply impressed line; escutcheon linear or none; ligament stout, seated on well-marked nymphs; sculpture of about 22 feebly defined flattish radial ribs, separated by much narrower, shallow, unchanneled interspaces, the whole crossed by rather rude, close-set, incremental lines; anterior dorsal slope shorter, excavated; posterior longer, convexly arcuate; base evenly rounded; interior smooth, muscular impressions somewhat impressed; margins with broad crenulations corresponding to the sculpture of the exterior. Altitude, 27 mm.; longitude, 25.5 mm.; maximum diameter, 17.0 mm.

Figured specimen collected by Arnold one-sixth mile east of East Twin River, Clallam County, Wash.; U. S. Nat. Mus. 153936.

This species has much of the oval form and elevated beaks of *V. subtenta*, but it is much larger and more coarsely sculptured, with the lunule more deeply impressed and the beaks more strongly prosocœlous. The characters of the interior of the valves, unfortunately, are inaccessible.

Superfamily LUCINACEA.

Family LUCINIDÆ.

Genus PHACOIDES Blainville.

Phacoides Blainville, Man. Mal., I. p. 450, 1825; type, *Lucina jamaicensis* Lamarck; Dall, Proc. U. S. Nat. Mus., XXIII, No. 1237, p. 805, 1901; Trans. Wagner Inst., III, p. 1359, 1903.

Section LUCINOMA Dall.

PHACOIDES ACUTILINEATUS Conrad.

Pl. XII, fig. 6.

Lucina acutilineata Conrad. Geol. U. S. Expl. Exp., p. 723, pl. 18, figs. 2, 2a–b, 1849.
Pectunculus patulus Conrad. Geol. U. S. Expl. Exp., p. 726, pl. 18, figs. 8, 8a, 1849.
Cyclas acutilineata Conrad. Am. Jour. Conch., I. p. 153, 1865.
Axinæa barbarensis Gabb, in syn., Pal California, II, p. 102, 1868; not of Conrad, 1857.
Axinæa patula Gabb, Pal. California, II, p. 102, 1868.
Phacoides (Lucinoma) acutilineata (Conrad) Dall, Proc. U. S. Nat. Mus., XXIII, No. 1237, p. 813, 1901.

Miocene of Astoria, Oreg., J. D. Dana; U. S. Nat. Mus. 3519 (types of *acutilineata*), 3605 (type of *patulus*). Miocene (upper) of Coos Bay, Oregon, at Fossil Point, W. H. Dall; U. S. Nat. Mus. 153976.

The *Lucina acutilineata* was well figured by Conrad, and the figure at present given is based on a younger specimen obtained at Coos Bay in the upper part of the Empire formation. It differs specifically from *Lucina borealis* of northern Europe and from *L. annulata* Reeve, the recent species of the California coast, with both of which it has often been hastily united.

I have thought it worth while to rewrite the diagnosis of the species from the Coos Bay specimen, as the original description is so brief and unsatisfactory.

Shell thin, flattish, suborbicular, equivalve, nearly equilateral; beaks low, inconspicuous, slightly behind the middle of the valve; valves little convex; lunule very small, narrow and short (in the figured specimen 2.5 mm. long), mostly situated on the right valve; sculpture, near the beaks, of fine, low, little-elevated, concentric lamellæ, the interspaces hardly wider; away from the beaks the interspaces become gradually wider and the lamellæ more elevated, between the latter the surface is sharply concentrically striated; ligament moderately long (in the figured specimen 8 mm.); dorsal slopes nearly straight, the remainder of the margins orbicularly rounded. Latitude of figured specimen, 23 mm.; altitude, 20.5 mm.; diameter, 7.5 mm. Fully adult specimens reach more than twice this size.

Family DIPLODONTIDÆ.

Genus DIPLODONTA Bronn.

Section FELANIELLA Dall.

DIPLODONTA (FELANIELLA) PARILIS Conrad.

Pl. XI, fig. 6.

Loripes parilis Conrad, Am. Jour. Sci., 2d ser., V. p. 432, fig. 7, 1848.
Mysia paralis Conrad, Am. Jour. Conch., I, p. 153, 1865 (not of Conrad, 1860 or 1866): Gabb, Pal. California, II, p. 100, 1868.
Diplodonta parilis Dall, Trans. Wagner Inst., III, p. 1182, 1900.

Shell large, smooth, moderately thick, slightly oblique, equivalve, inequilateral, with a thick brown periostracum which is sometimes preserved in the fossils; beaks low, inconspicuous, nearer the anterior end; dorsal slopes rounded, the anterior shorter, the remainder of the margin rounded, somewhat produced below and behind; surface smooth when not pitted by the pressure of sand grains in the matrix, with only the sculpture of faint incremental lines; valves somewhat inflated, their interior margins smooth, hinge as usual in the genus. Altitude of figured specimen, 24 mm.; latitude, 24 mm.; diameter, 10 mm.

Miocene of Coos Bay, Oregon, purchased from B. H. Camman; U. S. Nat. Mus. 153930. Also from northeast of Rock Point, near the entrance of Coos Bay, at station 2952, collected by W. H. Dall; U. S. Nat. Mus. 154018. Miocene of Astoria, Oreg., J. K. Townsend, and of Clallam Bay, Washington, Diller.

The similarity of this species to *Diplodonta acclinis* Conrad, of the Miocene of the Atlantic Coastal Plain, is very marked, though the species are distinguishable. The figure of *Diplodonta harfordi* Anderson[a] is not unlike this species, but has a longer and straighter hinge line, reminding one of a *Limopsis*.

[a] Proc. California Acad. Sci., 3d ser., Geol., II, No. 2, 1905, p. 197.

Family THYASIRIDÆ.

Genus THYASIRA Leach.

Thyasira Leach, in Lamarck, Anim. s. Vert., V, p. 492, 1818; type, *Tellina flexuosa* Montagu; Dall, Proc. U. S. Nat. Mus., XXIII, No. 1237, p. 784, 1901.

THYASIRA BISECTA Conrad.

Venus bisecta Conrad, Geol. U. S. Expl. Exp., p. 724, pl. 37, figs. 10, 10a, 1849.
Thyatira bisecta Meek, Checkl. Mioc. Fos. N. Am., p. 8, 1864.
Cyprina bisecta Conrad, Am. Jour. Conch., I, p. 153, 1865.
Conchocele disjuncta Gabb, Pal. California, II, p. 28, pl. 7, fig. 48, 1866.
Conchocele bisecta Gabb, Pal. California, II, p. 99, 1868.
Thyasira bisecta Dall, Proc. U. S. Nat. Mus., XVII, pl. 26, figs. 2, 5, 1895; Proc. U. S. Nat. Mus., XXIII, No. 1237, p. 789, 1901.

Miocene of Astoria, J. D. Dana; U. S. Nat. Mus. 3518 (Conrad's types) and 3500. Upper Miocene of Washington near Seattle, Arnold; Pliocene of San Pedro, Cal.; living in 69 fathoms, Puget Sound, near Seattle, Wash., Johnson.

This very remarkable shell is the largest of its family, far exceeding its congeners.

Superfamily CARDIACEA.

Family CARDIIDÆ.

Genus CARDIUM Linné.

Cardium (L.) Dall, Proc. U. S. Nat. Mus., XXIII, No. 1214, p. 383, 1900.

Subgenus CERASTODERMA Mörch.

CARDIUM (CERASTODERMA) COOSENSE Dall, n. sp.

Pl. XIII, figs. 3, 4.

Shell rounded, inflated, moderately thick, with prominent adjacent incurved umbones; anterior dorsal slope short, with a cordate smooth polished space (representing a lunule ?) in front of them; posterior slope longer, with an elongate, rather narrow lanceolate escutcheon inclosing the ligamental nymphs (in the figured specimen 11.5 mm. long); base and ends rounded; surface with a well-marked polished periostracum which is frequently preserved in the fossils; sculpture of about 45 (44 to 49) radial ribs separated by narrower, partly channeled interspaces; the ribs on the anterior third of the shell are subangular, and the interspaces narrower, those on the posterior and middle part are flatter with the interspaces wider and more distinctly channeled; all the ribs are crossed by more or less evident incremental lines, and these are emphasized at three or four resting stages on the disk; the margins are slightly crenulated by the sculpture. Altitude, 50 mm.; latitude, 48.5 mm.; diameter, 36.5 mm., in the figured specimen.

Miocene of Coos Bay, Oregon, purchased from B. II. Camman; U. S. Nat. Mus. 153933.

Although the specimens are far from perfect, the species can not be referred to any previously known from the coast. The ribs are more compact, more numerous, and less prominent than in *C. ciliatum* Fabricius or *C. corbis* Martyn; the shell is more ovate than in *C. californiense* or its variety *comoxense;* the ribs are much more numerous and the interspaces less channeled than in *C. decoratum; C. meekianum* is much more oblique and has the sculpture absent on the submargins; its ribs are also fewer.

The fossils still retain what seems to be a dark-brown remnant of the periostracum. Mr. Arnold informs me this species has been reported from the Miocene of Santa Cruz, Cal., under the name of *C. meekianum.*

CARDIUM (CERASTODERMA) DECORATUM Grewingk.

Cardium decoratum Grewingk, Beitr. zur Kenntn. N. W. Küste Amerikas; p. 274. pl. 4, fig. 3, a–g, 1850; Dall, Proc. U. S. Nat. Mus., XXIII, No. 1214, p. 390, 1900.

Miocene of Coos Bay, Oregon, W. H. Dall, U. S. Nat. Mus. 154004; also purchased from B. H. Camman. Also widely distributed in the lower Miocene of the Alaskan coast, and in the bowlder clays of the Pleistocene of Alaska and British Columbia.

The species seems to show a more abrupt transition from large and well-spaced to small and crowded ribs at the edge of the posterior submargin than is indicated by Grewingk's figures, but this may be a variable character.

CARDIUM (CERASTODERMA) CORBIS Martyn.

Cochlea corbis Martyn. Univ. Conch., tabl. fig. 80, 1784.
Cardium nuttallii Conrad, Jour. Acad. Nat. Sci. Philadelphia, VII, p. 229, pl. 17, fig. 3, 1837.
Cardium californianum Conrad, Jour. Acad. Nat. Sci. Philadelphia. VII. p. 229, pl. 17, fig. 4, 1837 (young shell).
Cardium nuttallianum Carpenter. Rept. Brit. Assoc. for 1856, p. 192, 1857.
Cardium corbis Carpenter. Rept. Brit. Assoc. for 1863. pp. 527, 642, 1864; Gabb, Pal. California. II, p. 98, 1868; Dall, Proc. U. S. Nat. Mus.. XXIII, No. 1214. p. 390. 1900.

? Miocene of Coos Bay, Oregon, W. H. Dall, U. S. Nat. Mus. 154004; Pliocene of California, Gabb; Pleistocene of Coos Bay, in Coos conglomerate at Fossil Point, W. H. Dall; and of Santa Barbara and San Pedro, Cal., Gabb and Arnold; living from Pribilof Islands, Bering Sea, southward to Morro Bay, Lower California.

The Miocene specimens appear to belong to this species, but are so poorly preserved that a positive identification is impracticable.

The *Cardium modestum* Conrad, 1856,[a] from the "Miocene" of San Diego, Cal., is probably an Eocene species; the type is still extant in the National Museum No. 1864. It is a small and quite distinct species, and may possibly be referable to *Trigoniocardia.* It is not the *Cardium modestum* Adams and Reeve,[b] and must therefore receive a new name. It may be called *C. blakeanum,* after Prof. W. P. Blake, who collected the specimen.

---

[a] Pacific R. R. Repts., V, 1856, p. 322. pl. 3, fig. 15.
[b] Voy. Samarang, Zool, 1850, p. 77. pl. 22. fig. 6.

Superfamily VENERACEA.

Family VENERIDÆ.[a]

Genus MACROCALLISTA Meek.

Section PARADIONE Dall, n. nom.

Chionella Cossmann, Cat. Illustr., I. p. 105. 1886; not *Chionella* Swainson. Mal., p. 335. note, 1840.
Paradione Dall, MS., 1901; type, *Cytherea ovalina* Desh.

? MACROCALLISTA VESPERTINA Conrad.

Cytherea vespertina Conrad, Am. Jour. Sci., 2d ser., V, p. 433, fig. 9. 1848.
Dione vespertina Meek, Checkl. Miocene Fos. N. Am., p. 10, No. 306, 1864; Conrad, Am. Jour. Conch.,
    I, p. 152, 1865.
Chione vespertina Gabb, Pal. California, II, p. 118, 1868.

Miocene of Astoria, Oreg., J. K. Townsend.

With the other types collected by Townsend, the present whereabouts of the specimen on which this species was found is unknown to me, and I have seen no specimens from the Miocene of Oregon which could safely be referred to it.

Genus CHIONE Megerle.

Section CHIONE s. s.

CHIONE SECURIS Shumard.

Pl. XI, fig. 8; Pl. XIII, figs. 2, 8, 9.

Venus securis Shumard, Trans. St. Louis Acad. Sci., I, No. 2, p. 122, 1858.
Chione succincta Gabb, Pal. California, II, p. 95, in syn., 1868; not of Valenciennes, 1840.

Shell large for the genus, heavy, equivalve, inequilateral, with elevated blunt beaks and a short cordate, slightly impressed lunule but no well-defined escutcheon; sculpture of numerous, low, narrow, flattish, subequal radiating ribs, with narrower, shallower interspaces, crossed by low, irregular, less conspicuous, concentric lamellæ; the radial sculpture becomes finer on the anterior portion of the shell near the margin, and is obsolete or absent on the posterior slope, though the concentric sculpture is more regular and close set on the posterior dorsal area; anterior slope of the valves short, the vertical of the beaks near the anterior fourth; posterior dorsal area markedly flattened, slightly arcuate; whole shell somewhat compressed; hinge as usual in the genus (see Pl. XI, fig. 8); muscular impressions not very large, moderately impressed; pedal retractor scars distinct, separated from the anterior adductors and rather deeply impressed; pallial line with a short triangular sinus as figured; inner margins of the valves finely crenulate. Longitude of adult, 77 mm; height, 70 mm.; diameter, 40 mm.

Upper Miocene sandstones below the Coos conglomerate at Fossil Point, Coos Bay, Oregon, Dall; U. S. Nat. Mus. 153942, 153971, 154007, 154022. Also abundantly, from the same rocks, purchased of B. II. Camman, and collected by Evans, according to Shumard. Miocene of Bogachiel River, Washington, Arnold.

One of the largest and finest species of the group, not intimately connected with any of the recent species of the present fauna.

---

[a] For a revision of the subdivisions of this family see Proc. U. S. Nat. Mus., XXVI, No. 1312, pp. 335-366.

Chione staleyi Gabb.

Pl. XIII, fig. 6.

? Dosinia staleyi Gabb, Pal. California, II. p. 24, pl. 7, fig. 42. 1866.
? Tapes staleyi Gabb, Pal. California. II, p. 57, pl. 16, figs. 17, 17a, 1868.

Shell rounded quadrate, somewhat compressed, solid, very inequilateral, equivalve; beaks low, small, anteriorly directed; lunule cordate, strongly concentrically striated, slightly projecting in the middle line, bounded by a deeply impressed line; escutcheon elongate, narrow, lanceolate, wider on the left than on the right valve; posterior dorsal slope convexly arcuate, posterior end rounded-truncate, anterior end rounded, base moderately, evenly arcuate; surface sculptured with low, close-set concentric lamellæ, crenate and reticulated by fine, close, subequal, rounded, radial ribs; the ribs have a tendency to associate in pairs and the sculpture is probably normally weaker on the beaks, where in the type specimen it is worn smooth; interior inaccessible, but the inner margins are probably crenate. Longitude, 53 mm.; altitude, 48 mm.; diameter, 25.5 mm.; altitude of lunule, 5.5 mm.

Miocene of Coos Bay, Oregon, purchased from B. H. Camman; U. S. Nat. Mus. 153943. Pliocene, Russian River, Sonoma County, Cal., Staley, fide Gabb.

I am somewhat in doubt as to the identity of this shell with Gabb's California fossil. The radiating riblets are coarser and laid down in pairs; the lunule instead of being depressed projects above its boundary; the shell is also considerably larger. Knowing the uncertainty of figures, I prefer to adopt Gabb's name instead of proposing a new one, at least for the present. The hinge is inaccessible, but the sculpture and external form are like *Chione*. Further material which will show the interior is needed to settle the question.

Chione bisculpta Dall, n. sp.

Pl. XI, figs. 10, 12.

Shell small, rounded, rathei thick, with rather small. full, and high beaks, inequilateral, equivalve; lunule cordate, striated, defined by a marked sulcus; escutcheon, if any, obscure; posterior dorsal slope rather straight, base and ends of the shell evenly rounded; sculpture of concentric ridges, a few of which in the middle of the disk are more prominent and wider than the others, which become obsolete toward the base; these ridges are crossed and more or less reticulated by small, rounded, radial, subequal, rather close-set ribs which are more conspicuous in the interspaces between the ridges; the beak in the type specimen is worn smooth, but was probably originally sculptured; hinge with three radiating cardinal teeth, the anterior smallest; there are no indications of lateral teeth; internal margins of the valve coarsely feebly crenulate; muscular scars strongly impressed; pallial line distinct, deeply impressed with a small triangular sinus not reaching the middle of the shell. Longitude, 45 mm.; altitude, 42 mm.; double diameter of the valve, 31 mm.

Miocene of Coos Bay, Oregon, purchased from B. II. Camman; U. S. Nat. Mus. 153941.

Of this species only a single right valve was obtained, but in very perfect condition nearly free from matrix. The peculiar combination of flattish ripples on the external disk, with a fine peripheral reticulation, is seldom seen.

Genus VENUS (L.) Lamarck.

Section VENUS s. s.

VENUS PARAPODEMA Dall. n. sp.

Pl. XI, fig. 11; Pl. XIII, fig. 1.

Shell small for the genus, subtriangular, equivalve, inequilateral, the anterior end shorter; beaks rather elevated, full, anteriorly directed over a deeply impressed, concentrically striated, cordate lunule; anterior slope short, excavated; posterior slope arcuate, slightly flattened, with no defined lunule; ligament strong, deep seated; base roundly arcuate; sculpture of numerous, flattish, crowded concentric low waves or ridges, slightly less prominent in the middle of the disk and becoming obsolete on the posterior slope; when eroded, riblike radial structure of the shell is often developed, but the surface, when intact, has no radial sculpture; interior inaccessible. Longitude, 59 mm.; altitude, 53 mm.; diameter, 33 mm.

Miocene of Coos Bay, Oregon, purchased of B. H. Camman, U. S. Nat. Mus. 143944; also as pebbles in the Coos conglomerate, W. H. Dall; U. S. Nat. Mus. 153979.

This species recalls *V. kennicottii* Dall, of the recent fauna, in size and form, but the concentric ripples of the fossil contrast strongly with the thin, sharp lamellæ of the recent shell. As in other Veneridæ, erosion of the shell substance reveals a radial internal structure which is invisible when the original surface is intact. It is decidedly more trigonal than *V. lamellifera* Conrad and could hardly be mistaken for it even when the latter has lost its lamellæ by wear. What appears to be a cast of *V. parapodema* was found on the west shore of Bering River, Controller Bay district, Alaska, a quarter of a mile below Green's cabin, in a hard Miocene shale, by Mr. Madden, of the United States Geological Survey; U. S. Nat. Mus. 4318.

The *Venus perlaminosa* Conrad, not rare in the Pleistocene of Santa Barbara, Cal., is a true *Venus*, and, like the rare recent *V. kennicottii* Dall, differs from all the eastern species of the genus in the obsolescence of the rough area of the hinge, which is the distinguishing character of the group. In *V. stimpsoni* Gould, of Japan, this feature seems to have wholly disappeared in the adult.

?VENUS ENSIFERA Dall, n. nom.

Venus lamellifera Conrad, Geol. U. S. Expl. Exp., p. 724, pl. 17, figs. 12, 12a, 1849; not *V. lamellifera* Conrad, Jour. Acad. Nat. Sci. Philadelphia, VII, p. 251, pl. 19, fig. 19, 1837.
Venus lamellifera Conrad, Am. Jour. Conch., I, p. 152, 1865.
Chione succincta (pars) Gabb, Pal. California, II, p. 95, 1868; not of Valenciennes, 1840.

Miocene of the Astoria beds, Astoria, Oreg., J. D. Dana; U. S. Nat. Mus. (type), 3611.

Conrad's specific name of 1849 had been previously used for another shell in 1837, so it is necessary to rename it.

The lamellæ were very profuse, and projected 2 or 3 mm. from the surface of the valve, which was finely closely radiately threaded between them. The hinge is inaccessible, but I should not be surprised if the shell proved to be a *Chione* when better specimens are available for study. It is however quite distinct from either of the Chiones described in this memoir from the Oregon Miocene.

Gabb's synonymy under *Chione succincta* is absurdly heterogeneous. His *Mercenaria* (= *Venus*) *perlaminosa* Conrad, originally described from the Pleistocene of Santa Barbara, according to Gabb a typical *Mercenaria*, still sometimes retaining a purple border to the interior of the valves, is also confounded with *Marcia kennerleyi* Reeve, an ashy-white shell of different form and hinge.

Genus MARCIA Adams.

MARCIA OREGONENSIS Conrad.

Pl. II, fig. 12; Pl. XI, fig. 9; Pl. XII, fig. 3.

Cytherea oregonensis Conrad, Am. Jour. Sci., 2d ser., V. p. 432, fig. 8, 1848.
Venus angustifrons Conrad, Geol. U. S. Expl. Exp., p. 724, pl. 17, fig. 11, pl. 18, fig. 1, 1a, 1849.
Venus brevilineata Conrad, Geol. U. S. Expl., Exp. p. 724, pl. 17, fig. 13, 1849.
Dione angustifrons Meek, Miocene Checkl., p. 9, 1864; Conrad, Am. Jour. Conch., I, p. 152, 1865.
Dione brevilineata Conrad, Am. Jour. Conch., I, p. 152, 1865.
Dione oregonensis Conrad, Am. Jour. Conch., I, p. 152, 1865.
Saxidomus gibbosus Gabb, Pal. California, II, p. 58, pl. 16, fig. 18a–b, 1866.
Chione oregona Gabb, Pal. California, II, p. 95, 1868.
Chione succincta (pars) Gabb, Pal. California, II, p. 94, in syn., 1868; not of Valenciennes, 1840.
Chione angustifrons Gabb, Pal. California, II, p. 118, 1868.

Shell thin, rather large, with moderately full, anteriorly twisted umbones situated at about the anterior fourth of the shell; equivalve, inequilateral, moderately convex; lunule cordate, bounded by an obsolete impressed line; escutcheon not defined; anterior slope rather straight, posterior arcuate; ends evenly rounded, the anterior slightly attenuated; base evenly arcuate; surface sculptured only with slightly elevated, close-set, concentric, incremental lines, a little stronger in front; ligament and hinge as usual in the genus; internal margins smooth, muscular impressions large, distinct; pallial line distinct with a short triangular sinus not reaching the middle of the shell. Longitude of large specimen, 60 mm.; altitude, 47.5 mm.; maximum diameter, 31.5 mm.

Miocene of Coos Bay, Oregon, purchased from B. H. Camman, U. S. Nat. Mus. 153945; 107786, figured from the same lot. Oligocene of Coos Bay, Oregon, at Miller's beach, station 2942, collected by W. H. Dall, No. 154085, internal cast, figured. Upper Miocene at Fossil Point, Coos Bay, Oregon, W. H. Dall, 153973. Miocene and Oligocene of Astoria, Oreg., J. D. Dana; type of *brevilineata*, U. S. Nat. Mus. 3606; types of *angustifrons*, 3492; cotypes, 3521, 3601, 3615. Pliocene of Eagle Prairie, Humboldt County, Cal., Gabb (as *S. gibbosus*).

This species is easily recognizable by its nearly smooth surface, not polished, but showing fine incremental lines like those of *Agriopoma*. It is very similar to and the probable progenitor of *Marcia subdiaphana* Carpenter, which is found living off the coast from Prince William Sound, Alaska, to the Santa Barbara Islands, California; and like that species it varies in profile from short to long ovate.

I have not seen the type of *C. oregonensis* and its whereabouts is unknown, but the description and figure leave little doubt that it was founded on a rather short specimen of this species. *V. brevilineata* and *angustifrons* were founded on types which are still in the National Museum and of whose identity there can be no doubt. *Saxidomus gibbosus* is merely a rather large specimen of this species, and, as the hinge was unknown to Gabb, was referred to *Saxidomus* at a venture.

Before taking leave of the Veneridæ it may be noted that the "*Tapes diversum* Sow.," from the Pleistocene of Santa Barbara, Cal., figured by Conrad in the Pacific railroad reports (V, pl. 4, figs. 31, 31a-b, 1856) is a typical specimen of *Paphia* (*Protothaca*) *staminea* Conrad, 1837. The type is No. 1847, U. S. Nat. Mus.

The Miocene "*Tapes montana*" Conrad (Pacific R. R. Repts., VII, p. 192, pl. 5, figs. 3–5, 1857) is apparently a typical *Paphia*, U. S. Nat. Mus. 13321.

Saxicava abrupta Conrad (Pacific R. R. Repts., V, p. 324, not figured), from the type (U. S. Nat. Mus. 1869), is a specimen of *Petricola carditoides* Conrad, 1837, which has grown in the boring of a pholad. The latter name of course takes precedence. The *S. abrupta* appears to be a Pleistocene shell.

Superfamily TELLINACEA.

Family TELLINIDÆ.

Genus TELLINA Linné.

Tellina Linné. Syst. Nat.. ed. 10, p. 674, 1758; Lamarck, Prodrome, p. 84., 1799, type *T. virgata* Linné; Dall, Proc. U. S. Nat. Mus. XXIII, No. 1210, p. 289, 1900.

TELLINA OREGONENSIS Conrad.

Tellina oregonensis Conrad, Am. Jour. Sci., 2d ser., V, p. 432, fig. 5, 1848; Am. Jour. Conch., I, p. 152, 1865.
Macoma nasuta Gabb, Pal. California. II, p, 95, in syn., 1868; not of Conrad, 1837.

Miocene of the Astoria group, Astoria, Oreg., J. K. Townsend; and of Clallam Bay, Washington, Diller; U. S. Nat. Mus. 110458.

Recalls in its general appearance and fine concentric striation *T. georgiana* Dall, of the recent Atlantic coast fauna.

TELLINA EUGENIA Dall, n. sp.

Pl. XIX, fig. 3.

Shell narrow, elongate, with an attenuate obliquely truncate rostrum, the surface finely concentrically striate near the margin and with the posterior dorsal area with more elevated concentric lamellæ; valves nearly equilateral, beaks low, dorsal slopes subequal, anterior end rounded, posterior attenuate and subtruncate; base nearly straight. Length, 55 mm.; height, 25 mm.; semidiameter of cast, 3 mm.

Miocene of Smith's quarry, Eugene, Oreg., C. A. White; U. S. Nat. Mus. 110459.

Much more narrowly rostrate than the following species and recalling *T. cumingi* Hanley, of the recent fauna, in its profile.

TELLINA ARAGONIA Dall, n. sp.

Pl. XIV, fig. 3.

Shell elongate, compressed, subequilateral, slightly inequivalve; beaks low, slightly behind the middle of the shell; right valve a little flatter than the other, with the rostrated posterior part of the shell somewhat bent to the right; dorsal slopes subequally oblique, the anterior slightly arcuate, the posterior slightly excavated; ligament strong on strong nymphs about (in the type) 15 mm. long; posterior end subrostrate, bluntly pointed below, with an obscure ridge from the beak forming on the right valve a narrow dorsal area; anterior end evenly rounded, base gently arcuate; surface smooth, finely concentrically grooved, with wider, flattish interspaces, the sculpture strongest in front. Interior inaccessible for the most part but with no indication of any internal umbonal rib. Longitude, 62 mm.; latitude, 32 mm.; diameter 12 mm.

Miocene of Coos Bay, Oregon, purchased of B. H. Camman, U. S. Nat. Mus. 153940.

This species recalls *T. oregonensis* Conrad, from the Astoria Miocene, but is more equilateral and larger, and shows no indications of the umbonal radial rib mentioned and figured by Conrad. The species is related to *T. bodegensis* Hinds, of the recent fauna, which has been also reported from the Pleistocene of California, and to *T. emacerata* Conrad, which is, however, much more inequilateral and more slender.

TELLINA EMACERATA Conrad.

Tellina emacerata Conrad, Geol. U. S. Expl. Exp., p. 725. pl. 18, fig.4. 1849: Am. Jour. Conch., I, p. 152, 1865.

Tellina bodegensis Gabb, Pal. California, II, p. 92, in syn., 1868; not of Hinds, Voy. Sulph., Zool., p. 67, 1845.

Miocene of Astoria, Oreg., J. D. Dana.

The type of this species is no longer among the specimens in the National Museum. The figure looks as if the species might be an *Angulus*, but, in an absence of any knowledge of the hinge, it seems best to leave it where Conrad placed it.

Subgenus MOERELLA Fischer.

TELLINA (MOERELLA) OBRUTA Conrad.

Tellina ? obruta Conrad, Am. Jour. Sci., 2d ser., V, p. 432. fig. 6. 1848; Am. Jour. Conch., I, p. 152. 1865.

Miocene of Astoria, Oreg., J. K. Townsend.

The type of this species is lost or at least its whereabouts is unknown, and the following species does not agree well enough with Conrad's figure to be identified with his species without further evidence.

TELLINA (MOERELLA) NUCULANA Dall, n. sp.

Pl. XVIII, fig. 2.

Shell small, subtrigonal, thin, compressed, very inequilateral, the beaks nearer the posterior end, which is obliquely truncate, dorsally compressed and very short; anterior end longer, rounded, base and dorsal slope subequally rounded; outer surface nearly smooth, with faint concentric sculpture in harmony with the incremental lines; internal surface polished, muscular impressions obscure. Length, 10.5 mm.; height, 8.0 mm.; diameter, 3.0 mm.

Miocene of Astoria, Oreg., J. D. Dana; U. S. Nat. Mus. 3529a.

The above species, which recalls the recent *T. salmonea* of the coast, was found in breaking up some of the extraneous rock attached to some of Dana's specimens. It is much more trigonal than Conrad's figure of *T. obruta*, and has much the same outline as *Psephidia ovalis* of the recent fauna.

Subgenus ANGULUS Megerle.

TELLINA (ANGULUS) ALBARIA Conrad.

Tellina albaria Conrad, Geol. U. S. Expl. Exp., p. 725, pl. 18, fig. 5, 1849; Am. Jour. Conch., I, p. 152, 1865; Gabb, Pal. California, II, p. 117, 1868; not *T. albaria* Conrad. Am. Jour. Conch., I, p. 138, pl. 11, fig. 7, 1865.

Miocene of Astoria, Oreg., J. D. Dana; U. S. Nat. Mus. 3614 (type), 3615, and 3529.

This species is abundant in the concretions, though the hinge is always inaccessible. It has much the aspect externally of *Angulus buttoni*, of the recent Californian fauna, but does not possess the thickened anterior rib which characterizes that species.

It is probable that there is more than one species of *Angulus* in this fauna, but the poor condition of the fossils and the impossibility of clearing the hinge from adherent rock make careful and exact comparisons impracticable.

There are two species described by Conrad, very briefly and without measurements, from the Astoria group, which have never been figured and of which the whereabouts of the type specimens is unknown. These are *Tellina bitruncata* and *T. nasuta* Conrad (1849, not *T. nasuta* Conrad, 1837), afterward renamed *T. subnasuta* (Conrad, 1865). These forms, under the circumstances, can not be identified; even the genus is and must remain uncertain. It is probable that they should be finally expunged from our catalogues.

Genus MACOMA Leach.

MACOMA ARCTATA Conrad.

Tellina arctata Conrad, Geol. U. S. Expl. Exp., p. 725, pl. 18, figs. 3, 3a, 1849; Am. Jour. Conch., I, p. 152, 1865.
Macoma arctata Gabb. Pal. California, II, p. 118, 1868.

Miocene of Astoria, Oreg., J. D. Dana; U. S. Nat. Mus. 3481, Conrad's types.

This species recalls *M. elongata* Hanley, from the recent Panamic fauna, but has the posterior extremity broader and less angulated. I have seen only Conrad's types. The species was not obtained at Coos Bay, and it is possible that it belongs in the Oligocene rather than the Miocene contingent of the Astoria concretions.

Conrad's *Tellina congesta* from the Monterey (Miocene) shale of California, though poorly preserved, also appears to be a *Macoma*, recalling *Macoma leptonoidea* Dall, from the recent fauna, but a smaller shell.

MACOMA CALCAREA Gmelin.

Pl. XIV, fig. 8.

Tellina calcarea Gmelin, Syst. Nat., VI, p. 3236, No. 38, 1792.
Macoma calcarea Dall. Proc. U. S. Nat. Mus., XXIII, p. 299, 1900.
Macoma tenera Leach, 1819, and *Tellina sabulosa* Spengler, 1798.

Shell thin, inequilateral, moderately inequivalve, with small, low, pointed beaks and the shorter posterior extremity bent to the right; length of posterior part of shell to that anterior to the vertical of the beaks as 11 to 28, or thereabouts; left valve the larger and more inflated; surface smooth except for more or less pronounced incremental lines and in each valve an obscure ridge bordering an ill-defined posterior dorsal area; form of the shell essentially as figured, but varying to some extent in different individuals; hinge normal, pallial impression inaccessible.. Longitude, 28.5 mm.; altitude, 18 mm.; diameter, 9 mm., of which 5 mm. belongs to the left valve.

Miocene of Coos Bay, Oregon, purchased from B. H. Camman; U. S. Nat. Mus. 153935 and 153938. Also collected by W. H. Dall from the upper Miocene sandstones of Fossil Point, Coos Bay, underneath the Coos conglomerate, 153982; in the lower Miocene, northeast of Rocky Point, Coos Bay, 154002; and dredged in Miocene gravel by the U. S. S. *Albatross* at station 3450, off Cape Flattery, in 75 fathoms.

This species seems to be the most common *Macoma* of the formation, and is usually very well preserved, with the valves united as in life. It is also found in the Pliocene of San Pedro (Arnold); the Pleistocene of California and most northern countries; and living in all Arctic and boreal seas, on the Pacific southward to the coast of Oregon. It attains, under favorable circumstances, a considerably larger size than the fossil above described, 43 mm. being a not uncommon length for the adult.

MACOMA NASUTA Conrad.

Tellina nasuta Conrad, Jour. Acad. Nat. Sci. Philadelphia, VII, p. 258. 1837; Hanley, Mon. Tellina in Thes. Conch., I, p. 314, pl. 64, fig. 224, 1846.
Macoma nasuta Dall, Proc. U. S. Nat. Mus., XXIII, No. 1210, p. 307, 1900; Arnold, Pal. and Strat. San Pedro, p. 163, pl. 16, fig. 3, 1903.

Shell thin, suboval, nearly equilateral, slightly inequivalve, the posterior end bent to the right; beaks small, low, adjacent, a little behind the middle of the shell; anterior dorsal slope passing evenly into the rounded anterior and arcuate basal curves; posterior dorsal slope straighter, more rapidly descending, the posterior end almost rostrate, bluntly pointed, with, in each valve, a rounded ridge descending from the beaks toward the lower posterior angle, the ridge in the right valve more prominent; surface smooth or even polished, sculptured only by incremental lines of which the stronger are more or less zonally arranged; hinge normal. Longitude of an average specimen, 37 mm.; altitude, 25 mm.; diameter, 11 mm.

Miocene of Coos Bay, Oregon, purchased of B. H. Camman; U. S. Nat. Mus. 153941. Collected from the upper Miocene sandstones at Fossil Point, Coos Bay, by W. H. Dall, 153981; from the shore northeast of Rocky Point, Coos Bay, by W. H. Dall, 154002 and 154003; from the Oligocene (?) sandstones at Millers Beach, Coos Bay, by W. H. Dall, 154087; Pliocene and Pleistocene of California, Arnold; living from Kadiak to Lower California, Dall.

Common, but rarely well preserved. Specimens reported from west of Kadiak Island, Alaska, have invariably proved, when I could examine them, to be the allied *M. inquinata* Deshayes. According to Conrad this is not the *Tellina nasuta* of the report on the fossils of the Wilkes Exploring Expedition,[a] which was left unfig-

[a] Geol. U. S. Expl. Exp., 1849, p. 725.

ured, and of which the type is lost; notwithstanding this, he named the latter *Tellina subnasuta* in 1865.   Neither is it the same as Conrad's *T. oregonensis*, as supposed by Gabb in 1868.

MACOMA ASTORI Dall, n. sp.

Pl. XIV, figs. 1, 11.

Shell suboval, nearly equilateral, slightly inequivalve, subrostrate, with the posterior extremity bent to the right; valves thin, moderately convex, the right valve slightly less so than the left; beaks low, adjacent, nearly medial; anterior dorsal slope arcuate, anterior end evenly rounded; posterior direct, posterior end bluntly pointed; base nearly evenly arcuate; surface smooth except for more or less impressed incremental lines somewhat zonally distributed; an obscure fold in each valve, near the margin, borders a posterior dorsal area; interior inaccessible.   Longitude, 50 mm.; altitude, 35 mm.; diameter, 14 mm.   The height of the original specimen of fig. 11 is 44 mm.

Miocene of Coos Bay, Oregon, purchased from B. H. Camman; U. S. Nat. Mus. 153937 and 153939.   Also from upper Miocene sandstones of Fossil Point, Coos Bay, W. H. Dall, 153978.

The larger specimen represented by fig. 11 was at first regarded as a variety or distinct species, but more careful study shows that the difference of outline on the posterior slope is due to erosion.

M. calcarea is a narrower species and proportionally more attenuated behind; *M. edentula* Broderip and Sowerby, which comes nearest to *M. astori*, is a more inflated and inequilateral species, the beaks being nearer the posterior end of the shell, while in *M. nasuta* they are farther away and the valves are more conspicuously flexuous.

MACOMA MOLINANA Dall, n. sp.

Pl. XIV, fig. 12.

Shell of moderate size, rather inflated, thin, nearly equivalve, not quite equilateral, the posterior end subrostrate and bent to the right; beaks small, low; anterior end longer, rounded in front, rather swollen; posterior end compressed, the dorsal margin rapidly descending to the narrow subtruncate termination; an obscure ridge, more evident on the right valve, bounds a narrow posterior dorsal area; ligament short; surface smooth or polished, sculptured only by irregularly distributed fine concentric striations in harmony with the incremental lines; hinge normal, the pallial sinus extending a little in front of the middle of the disk, rounded, not rising above the equator of the disk; muscular impressions large and distinct; a rather strong radial concave flexure behind the rostrum.   Longitude of internal cast, 40 mm.; altitude, 28.5 mm.; diameter, 14 mm.

Collected from the Oligocene(?) sandstones at Millers Beach, by W. H. Dall; U. S. Nat. Mus. 154088.

This species recalls *M. inflatula* Dall, from Alaska, but is a much larger shell; it is more flexuous and more wedge-shaped than *M. nasuta*, having the anterior part considerably inflated, while the pallial line is quite different from that of *nasuta*.

MACOMA sp. indet.

A small *Macoma* is represented by an impression collected by Dana at Astoria, which seems to be different from any above referred to; but the specimen does not afford data for a recognizable description, and I put it aside until further information can be had in regard to the species.

Superfamily SOLENACEA.

Family SOLENIDÆ.

Genus SOLEN (Linné) Scopoli.

Solen (L.) Scopoli, Dall, Trans. Wagner Inst., III, p. 949, 1900.

Section PLECTOSOLEN Conrad.

Plectosolen Conrad, Am. Jour. Conch., II, p. 103, 1866; Fischer, Man. Conchyl., p. 1111, 1887, selects *Solen angustus* Deshayes, from Conrad's list, as type.

Plectosolen protextus Conrad, from the Miocene of Astoria, proves from an examination of the type specimen to be the internal cast of a young *Solemya*.

SOLEN (PLECTOSOLEN) CURTUS Conrad.

Solen curtus Conrad, Am. Jour. Sci., 2d ser., V, p. 433, fig. 14, 1848.
Plectosolen curtus Conrad, Checkl. Eoc. Fos. N. Am., p. 8, No. 239, 1866.
Ensis curtus Meek, Checkl. Miocene Fos. N. Am., p. 12, No. 416, 1864; Conrad, Am. Jour. Conch., I, p. 152, 1865; Gabb, Pal. California. II, p. 116, 1868.

Miocene of Astoria, Oreg., J. K. Townsend.

The whereabouts of the type of this species is unknown to me, and I am obliged to rely entirely on Conrad's figure for comparisons.

SOLEN (PLECTOSOLEN CURTUS var. ?) CONRADI Dall, n. sp.

Pl. XII, figs. 7, 10.

Shell short, thin, wide, the extremities subequal in width; beaks terminal, ligament about one-fifth of the length; dorsal margin slightly arcuate, compressed and slightly pouting; posterior end truncate, gaping, with the angles rounded; base slightly arcuate; anterior end with the margins slightly thickened and expanded, obliquely truncate, the valve perceptibly constricted just behind the margin; surface smooth except for lines of growth, polished; hinge normal; pallial sinus rather shallow and irregular in form. Length of figured specimen, 56 mm. Length of full-grown individual, 70 mm.; width, 18 mm.; diameter, 11 mm.

Miocene of Coos Bay, Oregon, purchased from B. H. Camman, U. S. Nat. Mus. 153934. Also from Clallam Bay, Washington, in the Miocene shales, Arnold and Diller.

This form differs from Conrad's figure of *S. curtus* by being decidedly straighter, by the greater sharpness of the anterior basal angle, and by the presence of a distinctly marked dorsal area behind the hinge.

It is possible that these differences may be due to the draftsman, but the difference of locality being taken into account, it seems more prudent for the present to regard the shells as distinct. So much confusion has been caused hitherto in Pacific coast paleontology by confounding different things together that I am disposed to err, if at all, on the side of caution in this regard.

Superfamily MACTRACEA.

Family MACTRIDÆ.

Genus SCHIZOTHÆRUS Conrad.

Cryptodon Conrad, Jour. Acad. Nat. Sci. Philadelphia, VII, p. 235, 1837; sole example. *Lutraria nuttallii* Conrad, op. cit. Pl. XVIII, fig. 1; not *Cryptodon* Turton, 1822.
Tresus Gray, Ann. Mag. Nat. Hist., January, 1853, p. 42; not *Tresus* Walckenaer, Arachnida, 1833.
Schizothærus Conrad, Proc. Acad. Nat. Sci. Philadelphia, VI, 1852, p. 199. 1853.
Tresus Dall, Trans. Wagner Inst., III, p. 885, 1898.

Gray's generic name preceded that of Conrad by about four weeks, but was itself preoccupied in zoology.

SCHIZOTHÆRUS PAJAROANUS Conrad.

Venus pajaroana Conrad, Pacific R. R. Repts., VII, pt. 1, p. 192. Pl. IV, figs. 1. 2. 1857. Meek, Smithsonian checkl. Miocene fos. N. Am., p. 9, 1864.

Miocene of Pajaro River, Santa Cruz County, Cal., Conrad. Miocene of the Empire formation, Coos Bay, Oreg.; purchased from B. II. Camman, one specimen. U. S. Nat. Mus. 153929a.

The specimen from Coos Bay was mixed with a number of specimens of *Spisula albaria* and at first, since the hinge was inaccessible, was not discriminated from them. To Dr. Ralph Arnold is due the recognition of Conrad's poorly figured species, of which better specimens, showing the hinge characters, were obtained by him in Santa Cruz County. It has a general resemblance to *Spisula albaria*, but is more inequilateral, gapes slightly behind, and has the typical hinge of *Schizothærus*.

Genus SPISULA Gray.

Spisula (Gray) Dall, Trans. Wagner Inst., III, p. 878, 1898.

Subgenus HEMIMACTRA Swainson.

Section MACTROMERIS Conrad.

Although the details of the hinge are inaccessible in the following species, their similarity to recent species of the same region (which can be accurately determined) is so great that it is with much confidence I refer them to their probable subdivision of the genus.

SPISULA (HEMIMACTRA) ALBARIA Conrad.

Pl. X, fig. 1.

Mactra albaria Conrad, Am. Jour. Sci., 2d ser., V, p. 432, fig. 4, 1848; Am. Jour. Conch., I, p. 152, 1865; Meek, Checkl. Miocene Fos. N. Am., p. 11, No. 362, 1864.
Standella planulata Gabb, Pal. California, II, p. 91, in syn., 1868; not of Conrad, 1837.

Shell large, solid, ventricose, rounded-triangular, subequilateral, equivalve, with prominent, minutely pointed, slightly recurved beaks; surface smooth, except for more or less evident incremental lines; the lunule and escutcheon are not defined by any sulcus, but the dorsal slopes are wide and flattish; anterior end more attenuated, posterior end wider, more arcuate, and with the valves a little gaping on the distal part of the dorsal slope, both ends rounded and the base evenly arcuate; valves very convex, especially behind the vertical of the beaks, which is nearly in the exact middle of the valves; hinge as usual in the genus; pallial sinus moderate, angular; the inner margin of the valves entire. Altitude, 72 mm.; longitude, 90 mm.; diameter, 43 mm.

Miocene of Columbia River, near Astoria, J. K. Townsend, fide Conrad. Miocene of the Empire formation, Coos Bay, Oregon, purchased from B. H. Camman; U. S. Nat. Mus. 153929. Upper Miocene beds at Fossil Point, Coos Bay, W. H. Dall, 153972; and near base of Miocene at Rocky Point, Dall, 153999; also at Millers Beach and Goldwashers Cove, Coos Bay, Dall, 154092 and 154015. Also the sandstones near Eugene, Oreg., Dall.

The anterior end is often relatively longer in the young shells 25 or 30 mm. long. There is no recent species closely akin to this one in the fauna of the northwest coast.

This is one of the most common and characteristic of the Miocene fossils of Oregon. It varies more or less in the length of the posterior extremity as compared with the other, some specimens being very inequilateral, a variation which may also be noted in the recent species of the present fauna.

SPISULA (HEMIMACTRA) PRECURSOR Dall, n. sp.

Pl. XIV, fig. 10.

Shell small, compressed, subequilateral, equivalve; with rather prominent, incurved smooth beaks and no trace of lunule or escutcheon; anterior end somewhat attenuated, rounded; posterior end broader, more convex, obsoletely obliquely subtruncate above; base evenly arcuate; surface of the valves smooth except for incremental irregularities; slightly, irregularly, concentrically wrinkled toward the extremities, especially on the dorsal slopes; valves not gaping behind; interior inaccessible. Altitude, 30 mm.; longitude, 41 mm.; diameter, 14 mm.; vertical of the beaks about 19 mm. behind the anterior extremity.

Miocene of the Empire formation, Coos Bay, Oregon, purchased from B. H. Camman; U. S. Nat. Mus. 153928. Also upper Purisima formation, Santa Cruz district, California, according to Arnold.

This species, though on a smaller scale, recalls *Spisula alaskensis* Dall, of the recent fauna. It appears to be rare in the sandstones, as Mr. Camman obtained only a single specimen. It is readily separated from *S. albaria* by its more compressed form and protracted narrower anterior extremity, and the blunter posterior end.

Genus MULINIA Gray.

MULINIA OREGONENSIS Dall, n. sp.

Pl. IX, figs. 2, 3; Pl. XIII, fig. 5.

Shell solid, heavy, rude, elevated, much higher than long, with very prominent incurved beaks, equivalve, inequilateral; beaks full, rounded, anteriorly recurved, without any distinctly marked lunule or escutcheon; surface with heavy, rude, irregular, concentric waves or incremental thickenings; dorsal margins rapidly declining, basal margin nearly straight; surface in front of the beaks deeply concave; interior margins of the valve smooth, hinge heavy with a relatively large chondrophore or ligamental pit. Altitude, 45 mm.; latitude, 35 mm.; diameter, 50 mm.

Miocene of Coos Bay, Oregon, purchased from B. H. Camman; U. S. Nat. Mus. 153927 and 153977.

This remarkably coarse and elevated species seems to be not uncommon in the sandstones. One valve was found by me in the upper portion of the series under the Coos conglomerate at Fossil Point, Coos Bay. No species with similar characters is known to succeed it in the Pliocene or recent faunas.

Superfamily MYACEA.

Family MYACIDÆ.

Genus MYA (Linné) Lamarck.

Mya (L.) Lamarck, Prodrome, p. 83, 1799; type, *M. truncata* L.: Dall, Trans. Wagner Inst., III, p. 857, 1898; not *Mya* Modeer, 1793.
Chama Da Costa, ex parte, Brit. Conch., p. 232, 1778; not of Linné, 1758.

MYA TRUNCATA Linné.

Mya truncata Linné, Syst. Nat., ed. 10, p. 670, 1758; Dall, Trans. Wagner Inst., III, p. 857, 1898.
Mya praecisa Gould, Proc. Boston Soc. Nat. Hist., III, p. 215, 1850; Moll. U. S. Expl. Exp., p. 585, fig. 498, 1852.

Miocene of Coos Bay, Oregon, purchased of B. H. Camman; U. S. Nat. Mus. 153956. Miocene of Alaska on the Peninsula and the islands of Unga and Kadiak, and the Aleutians, Grewingk. Pleistocene of the boreal regions generally. Living from Puget Sound northward and westward to the Arctic seas and northern Japan.

Several well-preserved specimens were obtained from Mr. Camman, but the species does not appear to be common.

Genus CRYPTOMYA Conrad.

Sphænia Conrad, Jour. Acad. Nat. Sci. Philadelphia, VII, p. 234, 1837.
Cryptomya Conrad, Proc. Acad. Nat. Sci. Philadelphia, IV. p. 121, 1848; type, *S. californica* Conrad, Jour. Acad. Nat. Sci. Philadelphia, VII, pl. 17, fig. 11, 1837; Dall, Trans. Wagner Inst., III, p. 859, 1898.

CRYPTOMYA OREGONENSIS Dall, n. sp.

Pl. XI, fig. 4.

Shell small, thin, subequilateral, moderately inequivalve; beaks low, subcentral, adjacent; right valve slightly larger; dorsal slopes subequal, the posterior slightly compressed and subangular, the anterior evenly declining to the rounded anterior margin; posterior end bluntly rounded, base evenly arcuate; surface rude, the only sculpture being the irregular, more or less marked, concentric, incremental lines; interior mostly inaccessible, the hinge apparently typical, but very heavy and strong for the size of the shell. Longitude, 22 mm.; altitude, 15 mm.; diameter, 8 mm.

Miocene of Coos Bay, Oregon, purchased of B. H. Camman; U. S. Nat. Mus. 153931. Also from the upper part of Miocene sandstone, under the Coos conglomerate, at Fossil Point, collected by W. H. Dall, 153984.

This species appears to be not uncommon. Its most striking characteristic is its subrhombic shape, the recent *C. californica* being of nearly the shape in miniature of *Mya arenaria*, and the *C. ovalis* Conrad, from the Tertiary of Monterey County, Cal., having the beaks more posterior and the anterior half of the valves conspicuously expanded, vertically, compared with the part behind the beaks. I do not agree with Gabb's opinion that *C. ovalis* should be considered a synonym of *C. californica*, if any dependence is to be placed on Conrad's figure of 1856.

Family SAXICAVIDÆ.

Genus PANOPEA Ménard.

Panopea Ménard, Ann. du Muséum, Paris, IX, p. 135, 1807; Dall. Trans. Wagner Inst., III, p. 827, 1898.
Glycimeris Lamarck, 1799, H. and A. Adams, 1856, and Gray, 1857; not of Da Costa, 1778, Lamarck, 1801, nor Schumacher, 1817.

PANOPEA ESTRELLANA Conrad.

Mya abrupta Conrad, Geol. U. S. Expl. Exp., p. 723, pl. 17, fig. 5, 1849; not *Panopea abrupta* Deshayes, 1843.
Glycimeris estrellana Conrad, Pacific R. R. Repts., VII, p. 194, pl. 7, fig. 5, 1857.
Glycimeris abrupta Conrad, Am. Jour. Conch., I, p. 152, 1865.
Glycimeris generosa Gabb, Pal. California, II, p. 90, in syn., 1868; not of Gould, 1850.

Miocene of Astoria, Oreg., J. D. Dana; U. S. Nat. Mus. 3479, 3608 (type); also by J. K. Townsend. Miocene of the Estrella Valley, California, 13320, Conrad's type. A smaller, more equilateral, and more slender species than Gould's recent shell.

Genus PANOMYA Gray.

Panomya Gray, Fig. Moll. An., V, p. 29, 1857; type, *P. norvegica* Spengler; Dall, Trans. Wagner Inst., III, p. 832, 1898.

PANOMYA (AMPLA var. ?) CHRYSIS Dall, nov.

Pl. XI. fig. 7.

Shell of moderate size, rude, rather thin, inequilateral, equivalve, gaping in front and more widely behind; beaks slightly anterior, with two obscure ridges, one extending vertically, the other from the beak to the basal posterior angle, separated by a shallow, ill-defined constriction; dorsal slopes subequally oblique, the anterior shorter; the anterior end obliquely subtruncate and widely gaping; base nearly straight; valves convex, compressed a little near the base; hinge teeth obsolete; pallial impressions as usual in the genus, broken up irregularly as figured. Longitude of shell, 51 mm; width, 38 mm.; diameter, 23 mm.

Miocene beds of Goldwashers Gulley, Coos Bay, Oregon, collected by Dall; U. S. Nat. Mus. 154093.   Also in the upper Purisima formation, Santa Cruz district, California, fide Arnold.

This species recalls *P. norvegica* Spengler, of the recent fauna, but is less cylindrical and does not gape as widely.   The hinge does not appear to differ from that of *P. ampla* Dall, the recent Alaskan species, but is only partially visible.   The external surface is visible only in some small areas, but has all the characters of *P. ampla*, from which the valves differ in being thin, instead of enormously thickened, and in wanting the conspicuous anterior oblique truncation of the living species.

Superfamily ADESMACEA.

Family PHOLADIDÆ.

Genus PHOLADIDEA Goodall.

Section PENITELLA Valenciennes.

PHOLADIDEA PENITA Conrad.

Pholas penita Conrad, Jour. Acad. Nat. Sci. Philadelphia, VII, p. 237, pl. 18, fig. 7, 1837.
Pholas concamerata Deshayes, Mag. de Zool., Guérin, pl. 17 and text, 1840.
Penitella Conradi Valenciennes. Pl. Voy. Venus, pl. 24. fig. 1, 1846.
Pholadidea penita Carpenter, Rept. Brit. Assoc. for 1863, p. 637. 1864; Dall, Trans. Wagner Inst., III, p. 819. 1898; Arnold, Pal. and Strat. San Pedro. p. 184. 1903.
Penitella penita Gabb, Pal. California, II. p. 88, 1868.

Miocene of Coos Bay, Oregon, purchased of B. H. Camman; U. S. Nat. Mus. 153957.   Pleistocene of California at Santa Barbara, Gabb.   Living from Santa Barbara northward to the Aleutian Islands, Dall; Bering Island, Stejneger.

In following Gabb, who united *Penitella spelæa* Conrad, with *P. penita*, in the Wagner Institute Transactions,[a] I was misled.   On inspection of Conrad's type from the Pleistocene of San Pedro, it appears identical with *P. ovoidea* Gould, 1851, a name which has several years' precedence.

P. ovoidea can be distinguished from *P. penita* by being much shorter and more ovoid behind the lateral sulcus, and by the vacant space between the umbonal plate and the umbo, whereas in *P. penita* the plate is closely appressed to the umbo.

Family TEREDINIDÆ.

Genus XYLOTRYA Leach.

Xylotrya (Leach MS.) Gray, Proc. Zool. Soc. London for 1847, p. 188; type, *Teredo bipalmulata* Lamarck, 1801.   H. and A. Adams, Gen. Rec. Moll., II, p. 333, 1856; Gray. Fig. Moll. An., V, p. 28, 1857.
Bankia Gray, Syn. Brit. Mus., 1840; nude name?

?XYLOTRYA sp. indet.

Miocene of Astoria, Oreg., J. D. Dana; U. S. Nat. Mus. 3571, 3574.   Miocene of Coos Bay, Oregon, purchased of B. H. Camman; 153964 and 153965.

Fossil wood bored through and through by some species of shipworm is common in the Miocene beds of Oregon, but the borings so far as examined contain no remains

---

of the shell or pallets. As the genus *Xylotrya* is the characteristic form of this coast in the recent fauna, it is altogether more probable that these borers belonged to *Xylotrya* than to *Teredo*, properly so called. The borings are of various calibers, but I have seen none closely approaching in size the *Teredo pugetensis* of White, from the Puget group (Eocene) of Washington.

Some of these specimens passed through Conrad's hands in 1849 and doubtless influenced him in proposing the name of *Teredo substriata*, for which, however, his figures represent only *Dentalia*.

As it is impossible to determine the species, to say nothing of the genus, of shipworms from the borings alone, I refrain from applying any specific name to these specimens.

Order ANOMALODESMACEA.

Superfamily ANATINACEA.

Family THRACIIDÆ.

Genus THRACIA Blainville.

Thracia Blainville, Dict. Sci. Nat., XXXII, p. 347, 1824; Man. Mal., II. p. 660, 1827; type *T. corbuloidea* Blainville; Dall, Trans. Wagner Inst., III. p. 1522, 1903.

THRACIA TRAPEZOIDEA Conrad.

Pl. II, fig. 14; Pl. XIII, fig. 7.

Thracia trapezoides Conrad, Geol. U. S. Expl. Exp., p. 723, pl. 17. fig. 6, 1849; Am. Jour. Conch., I, p. 152, 1865.

Miocene of the Astoria group, J. D. Dana; U. S. Nat. Mus. 3604 (Conrad's types). Miocene of Coos Bay, Oregon, purchased from B. H. Camman; 107785 (figured) and 153953.

Shell thin, smooth, except for incremental lines which become sublamellose on the posterior dorsal area; valves slightly unequal, nearly equilateral, moderately convex, with an umbonal ridge bounding the lower side of the posterior dorsal area, in front of which the valves are slightly concave; dorsal slopes subequal, anterior end rounded, posterior squarely truncate; base arcuate, a little prominent in the middle; interior inaccessible. Longitude 53 mm.; altitude, 40 mm.; diameter, 19 mm.

The specimens from Astoria are smaller than those from Coos Bay, but appear to belong to the same species.

T. mactropsis Conrad, from the Tertiary of Monterey County, Cal., is a much more triangular shell, apparently without the compressed posterior dorsal area usually present in this genus. The Eocene *T. dilleri* Dall, from the adjacent Arago formation, is much more elongated in proportion to its height.

THRACIA CONDONI Dall, n. sp.

Pl. XIX, fig. 5.

Shell large, moderately convex, nearly equilateral, rounded in front, abruptly truncate behind, the base gently arcuate, the posterior dorsal slope slightly excavated, the anterior gently rounded; an obscure ridge extends from the beak toward the basal portion of the truncation, which is somewhat rounded; the beak in the right valve little elevated above the general hinge line; outer surface nearly smooth, more or less minutely granulose with variably prominent incremental lines; muscular impressions faint; pallial sinus wide, subquadrate, blunt in front, not reaching the vertical from the beak. Length, 60 mm.; height, 44 mm.; semidiameter, 8 mm.

Miocene of Smith's quarry, near Eugene, Oreg., Thomas Condon and C. A. White, two right valves in soft greenish sandstone, U. S. Nat. Mus. 110460.

This species somewhat resembles the recent *T. conradi* of the Atlantic coast, but has less prominent umbones and a generally more quadrate shape. It is considerably larger and less rostrate than *T. trapezoidea* Conrad. It has somewhat the shape of a *Saxidomus*, but a much thinner and less solid shell. The hinge is not accessible.

Class SCAPHOPODA.

Family DENTALIIDÆ.

Genus DENTALIUM Linné.

Dentalium Linné. Syst. Nat. ed. 10, p. 785. 1758; Pilsbry, Man. Conch.. XVII. p. xxix, 1898.

DENTALIUM CONRADI Dall, n. nom.

Teredo substriatum Conrad. Geol. U. S. Expl. Exp. p. 728, pl. 20, fig. 7a (only) 1849.
Dentalium substriatum Woodward, in Carpenter, Rept. Brit. Assoc. for 1856, p. 367, 1857; Conrad, Am. Jour. Conch., 1, p. 151, 1865; Gabb, Pal. California, II, p. 115. 1868; not *D. substriatum* Deshayes, Mem. Soc. Nat. Hist.. Paris, II, p. 366, pl. 18. figs. 1, 2, 1825.

Miocene of Astoria, Oreg., J. D. Dana; U. S. Nat. Mus. 3481 (part). Miocene of Coos Bay, Oregon, fragments observed by W. H. Dall; and of Clallam Bay, Washington, Diller.

This large, finely striated *Dentalium* seems to be rather frequent in the Miocene of Clallam Bay. The name used by Conrad being preoccupied, I have proposed a new one.

DENTALIUM PETRICOLA Dall, n. nom.

Teredo substriatum Conrad. ex parte. Geol. U. S. Expl. Exp., p. 728, pl. 20, figs. 7, 7b (only) 1849.

Miocene of Astoria, J. D. Dana, and Coos Bay, Dall; also in Miocene rocks of Clallam Bay, Washington, Diller. U. S. Nat. Mus. 3481 (part) and 3528.

This species is similar to the other in size and form, but perfectly smooth. It occurs less frequently than *D. conradi*, but is not very uncommon in the rocks of the Oregonian Miocene.

Subkingdom MOLLUSCOIDEA.

Class BRACHIOPODA.

Order TELOTREMATA.

Superfamily RHYNCHONELLACEA.

Family RHYNCHONELLIDÆ.

Genus HEMITHYRIS D'Orbigny.

HEMITHYRIS ASTORIANA Dall, n. nom.

Terebratula nitens Conrad, Geol. U. S. Expl. Exp., p. 726, pl. 19. figs. 1, 1a, 1849; not *T. nitens* Hisinger, Lethea Suecica, p. 77, 1836.
Rhynconella nitens Conrad, Am. Jour. Conch., I, p. 154, 1865.
Rhynchonella nitens Meek, Checkl. Miocene Fos. N. Am., p. 3. No. 45, 1864

Miocene shale of Astoria, Oreg., J. D. Dana; U. S. Nat. Mus. 3487 (types).

This is a very pretty *Hemithyris* with polished surface, having the form and profile of *Frieleia halli* Dall, from the recent fauna, but with the fold wider, deeper, and in the opposite direction. It has not the prominent beak or inflated body of *H. psittacea*, which also is much more strongly radially striated. The interior is inaccessible.

Order NEOTREMATA.

Superfamily DISCINACEA.

Family DISCINIDÆ.

Genus DISCINISCA Dall.

DISCINISCA OREGONENSIS Dall, n. sp.

Pl. II. fig. 6.

Shell large, depressed-conic, of a blackish-brown color, subcircular when normal; upper valve only known; apex defective; general surface marked with concentric, not very conspicuous incremental lines crossed by very fine, numerous, radiating striæ. Altitude of type specimen, about 8 or 9 mm.; maximum diameter, 35 mm.

Miocene of Coos Bay, Oregon, purchased from B. H. Camman; U. S. Nat. Mus. 107779.

This species recalls the Miocene species of the Atlantic Coastal Plain, *D. lugubris* Conrad, but seems larger, less elevated, and of less solid structure. The interior of the type being filled with matrix, the internal muscular and other markings are unfortunately inaccessible.

Subkingdom ARTHROPODA.

Class CRUSTACEA.

Superorder OSTRACODA.

Family CYPRIDÆ.

In breaking up the soft fine-grained shales, the product of the consolidation of fine marine silt, at Millers Beach, Coos Bay, impressions were noticed which appeared to be due to the former presence of a smooth species of *Cypris*. U. S. Nat. Mus. 154091.

Superorder CIRRIPEDIA.

Family BALANIDÆ.

Genus BALANUS Linné.

BALANUS TINTINNABULUM Linné, var. COOSENSIS Dall, nov.

Pl. XIX, figs. 1. 6.

?Balanus tintinnabulum (L.) Darwin. Mon. Cirripedia. I, p. 194, pl. 1. figs. a–l. 1854.

Miocene of Coos Bay, Oregon, purchased from B. H. Camman; U. S. Nat. Mus. 153960.

The fine *Balanus* which I have figured does not preserve the opercular valves in any of the four specimens obtained. As the specific characters are largely dependent on the sculpture and form of these appendages, I have referred the specimens to the recent species to which they seem most nearly allied, as a variety, pending the discovery of the opercular valves. The specimen figured is about 50 mm. in greatest diameter and 30 mm. in height.

Subkingdom VERMES.

Class ANNELIDA.

Order POLYCHÆTA.

Suborder TUBICOLA.

Genus SERPULA Linné.

?SERPULA OCTOFORIS Dall, n. sp.

Pl. XX, figs. 1. 2.

Miocene of Coos Bay, Oregon, purchased from B. H. Camman; U. S. Nat. Mus. 153963.

Among the fossils obtained from Mr. Camman, collected from the Empire formation at Coos Bay, was a mass of fan-shaped profile, about 100 mm. high, measured along the lateral edges; 140 mm. in greatest breadth; and about 35 mm. in average thickness. In general appearance this fossil resembles a mass of *Vermicularia* or *Serpula* tubes, more or less worn by weathering and the action of the waves on the beach.

A careful inspection of the fossil arouses doubts as to its true nature which I am unable to resolve definitely, and I have therefore placed it provisionally in the genus *Serpula*, with great doubt as to whether it will permanently remain there.

The mass consists, as will be seen by the figure, of agglutinated tubules, radiating roughly from a common center or root which has not been preserved. On close examination the tubes appear more as if they had been bored through a solid substance than as if they had formed a solid mass by agglutination. They impinge upon each other at various points so that apertures open from one tube into another, which is something the shipworms sedulously avoid. The interior of the tubes is nearly smooth, more or less transversely striated toward the aperture, which, when perfectly preserved, is of a "figure-of-eight" shape, but when, as usual, broken back by beach wear, is transversely oval. The contraction of the "figure-of-eight" is marked in some cases by a faint ridge extending longitudinally a few millimeters into the tube. So far I have observed these ridges only on one side of the tube, the other side in each case having been broken or worn away. Notwithstanding the fact that the tubes look as if they were borings into a solid substance, the material of which they are composed appears in general to have been deposited either in layers parallel with the tube itself or concentrically where interstices appear to have been filled with matter of the same sort. There are a number of cavities evidently secondary, due to the boring of *Pholas* or other boring mollusk into the mass, but this may have occurred after the original had been fossilized. The substance of the mass is not fossil wood as in the case of *Xylotrya* borings, but of the same appearance as the casing of the tubes themselves, and apparently of animal origin. But I have not found any recent *Serpula* which has apertures of the shape here described, nor which, in masses, has intercommunication between the tubes. Nor is there any sponge which closely approaches this enigmatical form in its tubulation. The borings of *Limnoria* are short, and occupy space in masses of wood, which these certainly did not, while the structure of tubular coral is entirely different. The explanation of the true relations of this fossil will be awaited with interest.

Class ECHINODERMATA.

Order HOLECTYPOIDA.

Impressions of indeterminable fragments of sea-urchin tests, recalling the surface of *Conoclypeus*, appear on parts of concretions from Astoria and Coos Bay, but nothing which can be definitely identified. U. S. Nat. Mus. 3509 shows some of the impressions collected by Dana at Astoria. Spines belonging to some form like *Toxopneustes* or *Strongylocentrotus* are also found in some of the specimens, as in No. 3522.

Order CLYPEASTROIDA.

Family SCUTELLIDÆ.

Genus SCUTELLA Lamarck.

Subgenus ECHINARACHNIUS Leske.

SCUTELLA (ECHINARACHNIUS) OREGONENSIS W. B. Clark.

Pl. VII. fig. 2.

Disk small, subcircular, depressed, margin not notched at the ambulacral extremities, the edge rounded and blunt in the young, somewhat flatter in the larger specimens; anal pore above and within the margin; star symmetrical, the two posterior petals shorter, the apex behind the center; petals not reaching the margin; ambulacral furrows of the base feeble, hardly traceable; whole surface when perfect covered with prominent pustules, rather crowded, and originally bearing small spines; dome of the upper surface rising evenly rounded from the margin to the apex. Diameter of figured specimen (transverse), 28 mm.; maximum vertical diameter, 3 mm.

Miocene of Coos Bay, Oregon, purchased of B. H. Camman; U. S. Nat. Mus. (figured) 153959. Upper Miocene sandstones at Fossil Point, W. H. Dall, 153962, 153997, and 153975.

The figure is enlarged one-half. A fuller description will be given by Professor Clark in his forthcoming monograph of our Tertiary echini.

This differs from *S. gabbi* Rémond, by its less symmetrical star and by the anal pore being more distant from the margin.

Order SPATANGOIDA.

Family ECHINONEIDÆ.

Genus GALERITES Lamarck.

?GALERITES OREGONENSIS Dana.

?*Galerites oregonensis* Dana. Geol. U. S. Expl. Exp., p. 729, pl. 21, figs. 5, 6, 6a, 1849.

Miocene of Astoria, Oreg., J. D. Dana; U. S. Nat. Mus. 3498.
Indeterminable small fragments of the test.

Subclass OPHIUROIDEA.

OPHIURITES sp. indet.

Fragments of arms of ophiuroid origin are found both at Astoria and Coos Bay, but not in a condition to permit the identification generically, to say nothing of the species to which they belong. Of these, U. S. Nat. Mus. 3683 was collected at Astoria by J. D. Dana, and 153958 at Coos Bay, by B. H. Camman.

Subclass ASTEROIDEA.

ASTERITES sp. indet.

Pl. XIX, fig. 2.

The central portion of a five-armed starfish—of which the arms are densely covered with slender, slightly curved, longitudinally striated spines, about 3 or 4 mm. in length—was obtained from B. H. Camman, who collected it from the Miocene sandstone of Coos Bay; U. S. Nat. Mus. 153961. It is unfortunate that this interesting specimen is not in a condition to exhibit its characters more distinctly, but it is figured so as to draw attention to the presence in these beds of a member of this group.

Subkingdom CŒLENTERATA.

Class ANTHOZOA.

Order MADREPORARIA.

Family TURBINOLIIDÆ.

Genus STEPHANOTROCHUS Mosely.

STEPHANOTROCHUS sp.

Miocene of Astoria, Oreg., J. D. Dana; U. S. Nat. Mus. 3575. Pliocene clays of Los Angeles, Cal., Hamlin?

Two imperfect specimens which T. W. Vaughan is disposed to refer to the genus *Stephanotrochus*, or to a closely related form, are among the collections of the Exploring Expedition under Wilkes.

Though the genus has been definitely recognized only in the recent state, it is probable that it not only occurs in the Miocene of Astoria, but also that some poorly preserved solitary corals obtained by Homer Hamlin [a] from the clays of the Los Angeles tunnel may be identical with the older and more northern form.

Subkingdom PROTOZOA.

Class RHIZOPODA.

Order FORAMINIFERA.

Numbers of small, calcareous Foraminifera occur scattered through the fine-grained shale near Millers Beach, Coos Bay, but owing to the toughness of the matrix they are almost impossible to extricate. The genera observed were *Cristellaria*, *Cyclammina*, *Pulvulina*, and *Polymorphina*, an assembly recalling that indicated by

---

[a] Cf. *Radiolites hamlini* Stearns (Science, n. s., XII, No. 294, August 17, 1900, pp. 247–250). Part of these specimens are regarded by T. W. Vaughan as undoubtedly solitary corals, probably of the genus *Stephanotrochus*.

Anderson in his study of the Eocene rocks of the Mount Diablo Range in California,[a] as occurring in the Kreyenhagen shale. It is notable, however, that in the Arago formation, of undoubted Eocene age, which underlies the supposed Oligocene of Millers Beach, no Foraminifera were observed, nor were there any in the distinctively Miocene or Pleistocene beds of the same vicinity. This may be due to the fact that the coarse-grained matrix of the Empire formation and Coos conglomerate is unfavorable to the preservation of these delicate organisms.

[a] Proc. California Acad. Sci., 3d ser., Geology, vol, 2, No. 2, 1905, pp. 192–193.

A FURTHER ACCOUNT OF THE FOSSIL SEA LION PONTOLIS MAGNUS, FROM THE MIOCENE OF OREGON.

By Frederick W. True,

Head Curator, Department of Biology, U. S. National Museum.

In 1905[a] I published a diagnosis of a new genus and species of fossil sea lion based on a skull from Oregon (Pls. XXI, XXII, XXIII). As this article is brief and contains a summary of the circumstances under which the skull was found, as well as measurements, it is reprinted here. The present addition to that account gives the information available from the specimen in more detail and with a more complete discussion. The original account is as follows:

At the suggestion of Mr. William H. Dall, the National Museum purchased from Mr. B. H. Camman, of Empire City. Coos County, Oreg., in 1898, a portion of a large fossil skull from the soft Miocene sandstone of that locality. The specimen, as I am informed by Mr. Dall, was found by Mr. Camman in the sandstone bluff on the east side of the lower part of Coos Bay, between Empire City and the "south slough," in the formation to which Mr. J. S. Diller has given the name of the "Empire beds."

Upon examination, the skull proves, as Mr. Camman had supposed, to be that of a sea lion. It represents a genus allied to *Eumetopias*, but much larger. The fragment consists of the brain case, or cranium proper, together with the pterygoids and the palatines as far forward as the posterior end of the hard palate. Both zygomatic processes of the squamosal are broken off near the root, and the right parietal bone has been lost, leaving a large opening through which the whole interior of the brain case can be examined. The tympanic bullæ are crushed and splintered off down to the level of the basioccipital and so mingled with the matrix that their form is lost. The surrounding foramina are also obliterated, and the base of the skull thus presents a broad, nearly flat surface, the appearance of which is at first sight very misleading. In other respects, however, the fragment is in an excellent state of preservation, and presents characters which plainly indicate its affinities. * * *

PONTOLEON new genus.

Similar to *Eumetopias*, but with the ventral surface of the basioccipital nearly plane, and the dorsal surface strongly concave. Postglenoid process of the squamosal strongly produced distally and directed somewhat posteriorly, so that the glenoid fossa is broader distally than proximally. Dorsal surface of squamosal, between the wall of the cranium and the zygomatic process, concave anteroposteriorly throughout its whole extent. Hard palate abbreviated, the posterior margin concave.

PONTOLEON MAGNUS, new species.

Size much larger than that of the largest of existing eared seals. Skull when complete probably about 50 cm. (or 20 inches) long. Distance from the occipital condyles to the posterior end of the hard palate nearly equal to the mastoid breadth of the skull. Occipitomastoid processes widely divergent, compressed laterally, nearly plane internally. External wall of the ascending plate of the palatines thickened, forming a strong rounded ridge. Posterior nares as broad as deep.

Type.—No. 3792, U. S. N. M. (Vert. Pal.). Empire beds (Miocene) of Empire City, Oreg. Collected by B. H. Camman.

---

[a] Diagnosis of a new genus and species of fossil sea lion from the Miocene of Oregon: Smithsonian Misc. Coll. (quarterly issue), vol. 48, pt. 1, No. 1577, May 13, 1905, pp. 47–49.

143

Dimensions of the type skull of Pontoleon magnus and of two adult skulls of Eumetopias jubata.

Measurements.	Pontoleon magnus, type (No. 3792).	Eumetopias jubata.	
		Bering Id., Kamchatka (No. 49729).	St. Paul Id., Alaska (No. 49730).
	cm.	*cm.*	*cm.*
Total length (basi-cranial)...............	....	40.1	36.5
Total height posteriorly (from line of occipitomastoid processes to top of occipital crest in a straight line).....................	19.1	17.0	15.2
Greatest breadth between occipitomastoid processes.............	a 24.8	23.2	21.6
Greatest breadth between outer margins of zygomatic processes of squamosal.......	b 25.0	23.9	23.1
Greatest breadth between outer margins of occipital condyles...................	11.0	9.0	8.6
Height of occiput from upper margin of foramen magnum to top of occipital crest.....	11.2	9.2	8.1
Height of foramen magnum...............	5.7	4.5	4.7
Breadth of foramen magnum..............	4.1	3.9	3.7
Length of an occipital condyle.............	8.1	6.2	6.4
Breadth of an occipital condyle............	3.7	3.4	3.1
Greatest transverse breadth of occipital crest......	15.4	15.8	13.8
Breadth between occipital condyles inferiorly...............	c 1.7	2.1	1.7
Greatest breadth of occipitomastoid process antero-posteriorly...........	7.1	5.9	5.2
Distance from inferior margin of foramen magnum to outer inferior angle of exoccipital.............	8.6	8.2	7.8
Distance from outer inferior angle of exoccipital to postglenoid process of squamosal..	10.2	7.8	7.2
Distance from inferior margin of foramen magnum to tip of hamular process of pterygoid.............	13.4	11.6	10.9
Distance from tip of hamular process of pterygoid to posterior end of hard palate.....	10.2	6.0	5.1
Distance from surface of occipital condyles to end of hard palate.................	24.1	19.1	17.2
Greatest breadth between outer walls of ascending plates of palatines at their posterior end.............	8.6	5.7	5.6
Greatest breadth of posterior nares.................	5.1	3.6	3.9
Length of glenoid fossa of squamosal (transverse).......	7.1	7.5	6.3
Length of glenoid fossa of squamosal (antero-posterior).................	4.1	3.9	3.2

a Actually 24.0 cm., but the left side is broken and 0.8 cm. has been added to agree with the right side.
b Actually 23.0 cm., but the right side is broken.
c The condyles are a little defective below.

DESCRIPTION OF THE TYPE SKULL.

Genus PONTOLIS True.

Pontoleon True, Smithsonian Misc. Coll. (quarterly issue), XLVIII, No. 1577, p. 47, May 13, 1905. (Preoccupied.)
Pontolis True, Proc. Biol. Soc. Washington, XVIII, p. 253, Dec. 9, 1905.

PONTOLIS MAGNUS True.

Pontoleon magnus True, Smithsonian Misc. Coll. (quarterly issue), XLVIII, No. 1577, p. 48, May 13, 1905.

Inferior aspect.—The basis of the skull presents a broad, rather feebly concave surface, bounded anteriorly and posteriorly by the posterior nares and occipital condyles, respectively, and laterally by the broad occipitomastoid processes. The concavity is deepest in the median line and grows gradually shallower to the mastoids. This even concavity is due in part to the almost complete obliteration of the tympanic bullæ and basal foramina and to the absence of the transverse rugosities for the insertion of the rectus anticus muscles, which were either little developed or have been obliterated. The median longitudinal ridge adjoining the foramen magnum, which is characteristic of all sea-lion skulls, is present, but feebly developed.

Anteriorly, the basal surface joins the roof of the posterior nares, which are rather deeply concave, and bounded by the thick pterygoid walls. The nares are not floored over by the posterior extension of the bony palate, as in *Otaria*, but are open far forward, as in *Eumetopias*, *Zalophus*, and other otarids. External to the pterygoid walls are the very broad glenoid fossæ of the squamosal, which resemble those of *Eumetopias*, but are somewhat directed backward.

Lateral aspect.—The lateral aspect of the cranium is characterized by the deep concavity of outline between the occipital condyles and occipital crest, which is only approximated in *Callotaria* and adult male skulls of *Eumetopias*. This concavity is due to the strong backward development of the occipital crest midway between the vertex and base, and to the retreating outline of the supraoccipital immediately above the condyles. The appearance is perhaps partially due to distortion of the skull. The lateral walls of the cranium are as strongly convex as in *Zalophus*, and from the appearance of the surfaces at the vertex, it seems probable that a high sagittal crest was originally present, as in adult *Zalophus* and *Eumetopias*. The thick and strongly projecting free margin of the glenoid fossa and the great anteroposterior breadth of the occipitomastoid process are also especially striking characteristics of this aspect of the skull of *Pontolis*.

Superior aspect.—The upper surfaces of the skull of *Pontolis* are so much broken as to render the interpretation of the contours difficult, but it may be noted that the margin of the occipital crest is evenly rounded, as in *Otaria*, but as thick as or thicker than in adult males of *Eumetopias*. The zygomatic processes appear to have been very thick at the base, leaving a proportionally narrower space between their inner face and the wall of the cranium than in other sea-lion skulls.

Occipital.—The supraoccipital is slightly convex immediately above the foramen magnum, as in all sea-lion skulls, but evenly concave over the general surface higher up, resembling the same part in *Eumetopias* (adult males) rather than in *Zalophus*, *Callotaria*, etc., but without a clear indication of the strong median ridge found in *Eumetopias*. The foramen magnum is round and the condyles are without the sharp internal border found in other genera, but this is doubtless due to the wearing away of the edges in the fossil. The paroccipital processes are broader and more transverse than in the recent genera, though approximating those of *Eumetopias* in this respect. They have not, however, more than a slight indication of the prominent rounded ridge which occupies their posterior and distal surface in *Eumetopias*, and in that respect more resemble those of *Otaria*.

It has already been remarked that the under surface of the basioccipital of *Pontolis* is broad and nearly flat, in contrast with that of the existing genera, owing in part to the feeble development of the median ridge immediately anterior to the foramen magnum, and in part to the obliteration of the foramen lacerum posterius. On the right side, the latter foramen can be traced, but is clogged by a piece of dense bone which must belong elsewhere. The upper surface of the basioccipital within the brain case, on this side, has been filled with plaster by the preparator, but on the left side the outlines of the foramen lacerum posterius are traceable. The median depression on the upper surface [a] is about as deep as in *Otaria;* more so than in *Eumetopias* and much less than in *Zalophus* and *Callotaria*.

Sphenoid.—The inferior surface of the body of the sphenoid is in the same general plane with the basioccipital. Depressions marking the position of the foramen lacerum medium are conspicuous a little posterior to the insertion of the pterygoids. On the upper surface of the basisphenoid the sella turcica is marked by a depression less deep than in *Eumetopias* and *Zalophus*. This is bounded posteriorly by the clinoid plate, which is broadly triangular in outline and rounded in front where the posterior

---

[a] Possibly a vascular recess, according to Murie.

clinoid processes were given off. These processes are lacking in the skull, and the extent of their development can not be determined. The lateral borders of the clinoid plate are not emarginate, as in existing genera, but convex; this appearance, however, may be due in part to the imperfection of these edges. More anteriorly is the elongated processus olivarius, and on each side very distinct grooves leading backward from the foramen lacerum anterius to the foramina ovale, lacerum medium, and lacerum posterius. These are disposed in a manner closely similar to that of the same channels in *Eumetopias*. The foramen ovale is obliterated, but a rather deep depression marks its location on the left side. On the same side a conspicuous depression indicates the position of the foramen lacerum medium, immediately behind which is a triangular rough mass, which is obviously the anterior end of the petrous portion of the temporal, similar in shape to the same bone in *Eumetopias*, but broader. This mass is followed, posteriorly, by a deep, irregular cavity, probably representing in part the foramen lacerum posterius and in part the vacuities left by the absence of the posterior part of the petrous portion of the temporal.

Anteriorly, the sphenoid is broken off at the suture between the presphenoid and orbitosphenoid, which remains open late in the Otariidæ.

Temporal.—The temporal is remarkable chiefly for the great anteroposterior breadth and strong distal development of the glenoid fossa. These characteristics are not shared by existing genera of Otariidæ, in all of which the fossa is narrowed distally, though least so in *Otaria*. In spite of the large development of the glenoid fossa just mentioned, the zygomatic process is so thick at the root that the space between its ramus and the wall of the cranium is much less relatively than in any of the existing Otariidæ, and considerably less absolutely than in *Eumetopias jubata*, though adult skulls of that species are a fourth smaller than that of *Pontolis*. As the zygomatic processes are broken off close to the root, nothing can be definitely determined as to the original form of their distal ends.

The tympanics, as already mentioned, are so much crushed and abraded that their original form can not be determined, though they were probably as flat as or flatter than in *Zalophus* and *Arctocephalus*. The paroccipital and mastoid elements of the occipitomastoid process can not be distinguished, but the inferior surface of the mastoid is much flatter and broader anteroposteriorly than in the existing sea lions.

Parietals and frontals.—The wall of the cranium on the left side is preserved to a point a little farther forward than the line of the anterior margin of the glenoid fossa. It therefore probably includes a portion of the posterior end of the frontal, though the suture is not traceable. As in *Eumetopias*, the general surface is somewhat concave superiorly and is narrowed anteriorly. In *Zalophus* and other existing genera, except *Eumetopias*, the brain case is more oblong or quadrate in form, owing to the stronger development of the anterior cranial fossæ, while in *Otaria* a distinct postfrontal process develops in this region. A strong sagittal crest probably existed in *Pontolis* as in *Eumetopias*, but it is wanting in the fossil skull.

Palatines.—The palatal region is remarkable for the abbreviation of the bony palate, the length from the hind margin of the palate to the posterior margin of the pterygoid immediately above the hamular process nearly equaling the length from the latter point to the occipital condyles. In existing genera the former length is about half the latter, except in *Otaria*, in which it is hardly more than a fourth.　The skull of *Pontolis* is broken opposite the posterior end of the bony palate, but a small portion of the posterior end remains on the left side.　The vertical plates of the palatines are remarkably bulbous externally, at the point marking the suture with the pterygoids and alisphenoids.　Below this swelling a rather deep groove runs parallel with the inferior free margin of the wall of the nares.　This groove is not present in *Otaria*, but is developed to a minor degree in *Zalophus*, *Arctocephalus*, and other existing genera.

Pterygoids.—The suture between the pterygoids and palatines is obliterated. The posterior free margin of the pterygoids is emarginate, but much more nearly vertical than in existing genera, except *Otaria*.　The hamular processes appear to have been well developed, but their original form is uncertain.　This is a point of little importance on account of the large individual variation in the form of the process in the several genera of Otariidæ.　In the skull of *Pontolis*, a fragment of bone has been placed at the end of the right pterygoid, but it is not certain that it belongs there.　The free margin of the right pterygoid has been too much chiseled out. The walls of the alisphenoid canal have been chiseled away, or were already broken off when the skull was found.

Fossæ of the cranial cavity.—Compared with that of *Eumetopias*, the anterior cranial fossa is remarkable inferiorly for its postero-external extension; also for the oblique posterior boundary, due to a thickening of the internal parietal ridge.　The middle fossa is restricted externally from the same cause.　The shape of the posterior fossa is not determinable exactly, on account of defects in the skull, but it appears to have extended outward less than in *Eumetopias*.

DESCRIBED SPECIES OF FOSSIL SEA LIONS.

Fossil remains of sea lions are extremely rare, and but few species have been established.　The family Otariidæ is dismissed with but a word or two by Zittel (Paleontologie, vol. 4, Vertebrata, Mammalia, 1891–1893) and no mention of fossil forms is made in such works as Beddard's Mammalia (1902).　The fossil species supposed to be referable to the family which were made known prior to 1880 were reviewed by J. A. Allen in his History of North American Pinnipeds, published in that year.　One or two later ones are included in Trouessart's Cataloque Mammalium, Supplement, 1904.　The names of these species and the material on which they were based is as follows:[a]

1. *Otaria? prisca* Gervais, Zool. et Paléont. franc., 1850–1855, p. 276, pl 8, fig. 8.
    Based on a tooth.　"Van Beneden has since determined it to be referable to *Squalodon*" (Allen).
2. *Otaria ondriana* Delfortrie, Actes Soc. Linn. Bordeaux, livr. 4, 1872, p. 28.
    Based on a last upper molar from the bone breccia of Saint-Médard-en-Jalle, near Bordeaux.
3. *Otaria leclercii* Delfortrie, Actes Soc. Linn. Bordeaux, livr. 4, 1872, p. 28.
    Based on an outer lower incisor from the same locality.　Van Beneden contended that these teeth belonged to his genus *Palæophoca*, a fossil phocid, allied to *Monachus*, and Allen concurred in the opinion that they were not otarine.
4. *Mesotaria ambigua* Van Beneden, Ann. Mus. roy hist. nat. Belg.. I. 1877, p. 56, pl. 1.
    Based on the bones of the greater part of the skeleton, and numerous teeth; skull wanting. Assigned by Allen to the Phocidæ, as probably allied to *Cystophora* and *Macrorhinus*.

a See Allen, J. A., History of North American Pinnipeds, 1880, p. 217.

5. *Otaria jubata* (foss.) Ameghino, Mam. fósil. Argentina, 1889, p. 343.

Remains frequently found, according to Ameghino, in the postpampean marine formations, assigned provisionally to the lower Quaternary.

"Alrededores de La Plata, Punta de Lara, Quilmes, etc." (Ameghino).

6. *Arctocephalus williamsi* MacCoy, Prodrome Palæontol. Victoria, decade 5, 1879, pls. 41–44.

Pliocene. Based on an "old male skull." Considered by Allen (Pinnipeds, p. 770) as not differing materially from females of *Zalophus lobatus* (Gray).

7. *Arctocephalus fischeri* Ameghino, Bol. Acad. Nac., Argentina, Cordoba, IX, 1886, p. 214; Act. Acad. Nac., Argentina, Cordoba, VI, 1889, 342 (=*Otaria fischeri* H. Gervais and Amegh., Mam. foss. de l'Amér. Sud, 1880. p. 223; nomen nudum).

Oligocene. Based on a fragment of the horizontal ramus of a mandible, with the alveoli of the last three molars, from "las barrancas del Paraná." Resembles *Arctophoca falklandica* (=*Arctocephalus australis* Zimm.), but is smaller. (*Arctophoca* Peters is considered by J. A. Allen a synonym of *Arctocephalus* F. Cuvier.)

8. *Arctocephalus forsteri* (foss.) Péron, Voyage dans terres australes, 1816, II. p. 37.

Pleistocene of New Zealand. Trouessart credits this fossil form to Péron (by error written " Lesson "), but there is no mention of it on the page cited.

It will readily be seen that whether any of the nominal species of fossil sea lions, with one exception, are valid, is a matter of little importance in the present connection, as they are not based on the skull, and could not, owing to this circumstance, be correlated with *Pontolis*. The exception relates to *Arctocephalus williamsi* MacCoy, which was founded on an "old male skull," according to the original describer, but which, as we have seen, is considered by Allen as not differing materially from a female skull of *Zalophus lobatus*, a recent species. After an examination of the original figures, I concur in this opinion.

It is an interesting fact, brought out in the foregoing diagnosis and description, that *Pontolis* is closely related to *Eumetopias jubata*, a living species of the region in which the fossil was found. That it was the progenitor of *Eumetopias* is probable, though such an opinion can not be asserted with much positiveness on the basis of the single fragment now available. The fossil skull proves, however, that sea lions existed in the North Pacific region in Miocene time. They either originated there, or if derived from some other region, must have entered the fauna of the North Pacific at a still earlier epoch.

APPENDICES.

The following rare and to many inaccessible brief papers on the paleontology of the Pacific coast Tertiary are reprinted with the intention of making them more easily available for students, especially of the Pacific States, where the originals would often prove difficult of access. The reprints are arranged in the order of their original publication, and are followed by a bibliography of the whole literature from the time of Carpenter's summary of it in his British Association Report of 1863 to and including the year 1905. A few earlier titles, omitted or insufficiently referred to by Carpenter, and a few later items of importance have been added.

149

FOSSIL SHELLS FROM TERTIARY DEPOSITS ON THE COLUMBIA RIVER, NEAR ASTORIA.[a]

By T. A. CONRAD.

[page 432] The following interesting Miocene species were collected by J. K. Townsend, and are described at his request:

Nucula divaricata (figs. 1a, 1b).—Subovate, convex, with divaricating striæ, extremities rounded; ligament margin very oblique, slightly curved; basal margin curved; beaks near the anterior extremity.

N. cuneiformis (fig. 2).—Ovate, ventricose in the middle, with strong lines of growth; anterior side short, margin rounded; posterior side cuneiform; subtruncated at the extremity; basal margin rounded.

N. abrupta (fig. 3).—Somewhat elliptical, convex; truncated anteriorly; ligament margin rectilinear, oblique; posterior margin obliquely truncated, contracted.

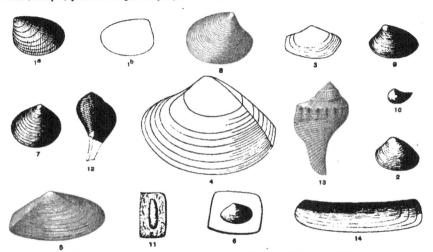

FIGS. 1–14.—Fossil shells from Tertiary deposits on Columbia River, near Astoria.

Mactra albaria (fig. 4).—Triangular, ventricose; beaks medial; umbonal slope angulated; anterior and posterior margins nearly equally oblique; posterior extremity truncated, direct; basal margin regularly curved.

Tellina oregonensis (fig. 5).—Elliptical, thin, much compressed; valves flattened, and having regular concentric fine lines; anterior submargin somewhat angulated, the margin nearly direct, truncated; beaks rather nearest to the anterior extremity; posterior end acutely rounded.

In the cast, an oblique shallow furrow meets the apex on the posterior side.

T. obruta (fig. 6).—Ovate, compressed, thin; very inequilateral; ligament margin elevated; basal margin rounded; anterior hinge margin straight and very oblique, extremity truncated.

[a] Am. Jour. Sci., 2d ser., vol. 5, 1848, pp. 432–433.

Loripes parilis (fig. 7).—Lentiform, inequilateral, not ventricose; length and height equal, summit slightly prominent; margins very regularly rounded.

Cytherea oregonensis (fig. 8).—Suborbicular, ventricose, inequilateral; summits prominent; surface with fine lines of growth; anterior extremity acutely rounded; basal margin rounded; posterior margin obtusely rounded. This species is remarkably similar in form to *C. ovata* Rogers, a fossil of the Virginia Miocene; but it wants the impressed concentric lines of that species.

[page 433] *C. vespertina* (fig. 9).—Acutely ovate, ventricose; very inequilateral; summits prominent; surface with concentric lines, which are not very smooth and regular; posterior side somewhat cuneiform; anterior extremity acutely rounded; basal margin rounded.

A number of specimens were together in a small fragment of rock, all of which were much smaller than the one selected to figure.

Nucula penita (fig. 10).—Ovate acute, ventricose; anterior side very short, obtuse; ligament margin concave; posterior side rostrated, acute; basal margin rounded.

Somewhat similar in outline to the Virginia Miocene *N. acuta*, but has a much shorter anterior side. It is a cast, and the character of the exterior is unknown.

Bullina petrosa (fig. 11).—Narrow-cylindrical; margin of labrum straight, extremity elevated above the apex; spire slightly raised above the shoulder, which is oblique and angulated.

Pyrula modesta (fig. 12).—Pyriform, thin, with approximate prominent alternated revolving lines reticulated with minute longitudinal lines; spire very short, conical; upper portion of body whorl regularly rounded.

Fusus oregonensis (fig. 13).—Fusiform, with unequal prominent revolving lines, a few of which are considerably larger than the others on the upper portion of the body whorl; they are also coarser toward the base, and alternated in size; shoulder with a series of tubercles, one of the larger on the body whorl somewhat tuberculated; a prominent line margins the suture; spire conical, the volutions reticulated and tuberculated.

Solen curtus (fig. 14).—Slightly curved, short, convex, equally wide at the extremities; anterior margin very obliquely truncated, reflected, rounded toward the base; posterior extremity truncated, slightly oblique.

APPENDIX II.

FOSSILS FROM NORTHWESTERN AMERICA.[a]

By J. D. DANA.[b]

1. CETACEAN.

[page 722] Vertebræ and fragments of other cetacean bones are occasionally found in the argillaceous sandstone of Astoria (south side of the Columbia, about 13 miles above its mouth), and may be picked up along the shores of the river.—Pl. 16, fig. 1, represents one of the vertebræ, of its natural size.

2. FISHES.

In the same region, just alluded to, we obtained the remains of four species of fossil fish.

Fig. 2, pl 16, represents a species allied to *Trigla*. It was found (as figured) in a concretion of limestone in the argillaceous rock. The surface of the mass having been worn on the river's banks, the skeleton is exposed to view in the manner here shown. A large part of the vertebral column remains, and portions of the bones of the head, with parts of the pectoral fin, and many of the scales. The bones and scales have the color, translucency, and hardness of tortoise shell. The scales have the surface strongly striated below the central line, and a pectinate lower margin; they are also concentrically and neatly marked with delicate lines of growth. The striated character is owing to thin trenchant ridges, which have a serrulate edge. The form is suborbicular, the larger approaching quadrate, and the smaller somewhat hexagonal; the lower margin is strongly arcuate. The vertebræ are longer than its breadth.

Fig. 3, pl. 16, is another species, of which we have only a cast in a fragment of argillaceous slate. The genus we have not made out.

Figs. 1, 2a, 2b, pl. 17, of natural size, represent large vertebræ from the same locality. Those of the latter two figures pertain, as we suppose, from the very open texture and fine calcareous plates, to a species of shark. The first is also very open in its texture, and owes its apparent solidity to the limestone with which it is mineralized. In the specimen, edges of vertical plates are seen occasionally on the sides (as on the left side of the figure, and also on the back top edge toward the right), and on the broken surface (front of figure) there are a few irregular oblique plates either side of the center, as represented; all indicating a very coarsely cellular structure.

3. CRUSTACEA.

Callianassa oregonensis (Dana).—Remains of a single species of Crustacea are found in the calcareous concretions of the argillaceous rock near Astoria. (See pl. 17, fig. 3.) It is related to *Callianassa*, a genus whose species live mostly in holes on muddy shores. The compressed form and nearly equal length and breadth of the hand and carpus are characteristic of this family of Crustacea.

[page 723] The joints of the leg figured have a smooth surface. The under margin of the hand and thumb is straight and denticulate. The inner margin of the thumb and finger is slightly crenulate. The finger is narrow, slightly arcuate. subacute, and shuts rather closely upon the thumb. The length of the hand is nearly three-fourths of an inch, and its breadth three-eighths of an inch; the carpus has the same length, and is little broader; its upper and lower margins are entire; the next joint preceding is but one-eighth of an inch broad, and apparently somewhat shorter than the carpus.

Balanus.—In the soft argillaceous shale remains of a barnacle are found, but in too imperfect a state to be characterized. A figure is given on pl. 17, fig. 4.

[a] Geol. U. S. Expl. Exp., 1849, Appendix 1, pp. 722-730.
[b] Descriptions of Mollusca, Radiata, and plants by T. A. Conrad, with notes by Dana.

4. MOLLUSCA.

The fossil shells of Astoria have been described for this place by Mr. T. A. Conrad, whose labors in conchology in general, and especially in the department of Tertiary species, are well known. We insert his descriptions in his own words, adding a few measurements from the specimens.

1. *Mya abrupta* (Conrad).—Subelliptical, slightly ventricose, widely gaping posteriorly. Surface marked with concentric undulations. Beaks separated, nearly medial, slightly prominent. Anterior margin acute, orbiculate; posterior margin abrupt, arcuate, somewhat reflexed; basal (inferior) margin arcuate; dorsal margin short, straight, nearly parallel with the base.—Pl. 17, figs. 5, 5a. .

Astoria, Oreg.

[Length 2¾ inches; height $\frac{47}{100}$ L.; thickness (and breadth of gaping behind) $\frac{42}{100}$ L., or $\frac{56}{100}$ H. Apical angle 162°.]

2. *Thracia trapezoides* (Conrad).—Trapezoidal; ventricose; flank flattened, carinate, side anteriorly compressed. Surface faintly concentric undulate, and neatly but unequally marked with concentric striæ. Beaks prominent, medial. Posterior margin truncated, basal margin tumid at middle.—Pl. 17, figs. 6a, 6b, natural size.

Astoria, Oreg.

[Length 1$\frac{1}{10}$ inches; height $\frac{73}{100}$ L.; thickness $\frac{45}{100}$ L., or $\frac{58}{100}$ H.; apical angle 140°. Cast having the surface faintly concentric undulate. Muscular impressions rather indistinct, the posterior quite small, palleal sinus large.]

Solemya ventricosa (Conrad).—Oblong; ventricose; dorsal and basal margins straight and parallel. Anterior side narrowed, the margin orbiculate. Posterior margin scalloped, the inferior half truncated obliquely inward. Beaks distant from the anterior extremity.—Pl. 17, figs. 7, 8, natural size.

Astoria, Oreg.

[Length 3¾ inches; breadth 1½ inches. Lateral surface smooth, radiated with narrow bands.]

Donax? protexta (Conrad).—Much elongate, ventricose; anterior margin orbiculate, posterior side produced; basal margin straight; ligament margin straight and oblique. Beaks little prominent. Sides somewhat flattened inferiorly, contracted slightly [page 724] from beak to base; cavity most capacious between the umbones.—Pl. 17, fig. 9, natural size.

Astoria, Oreg.

[Length about 1½ inches; height one-half inch; beak one-third inch back of the front; apical angle 140°.]

Venus bisecta (Conrad).—Oblique, subrhomboidal, ventricose, with robust lines of growth. Anterior side very short, truncate, angulate below, having a submarginal vertical furrow, and the inferior margin at its termination slightly excavate. Posterior surface strongly excavate from the upper side of the beak to the posterior margin, and subcarinate below the excavation; ligament and superoposterior margin forming together a regular curve. Basal margin arcuate, a little tumid behind the middle.—Pl. 17, figs. 10, 10a, natural size.

Astoria, Oreg.

[Length 2 inches; height $\frac{88}{100}$ L.; thickness $\frac{44}{100}$ L. or $\frac{49}{100}$ H.; distance anterior to beak one-third inch; apical angle 120°. Valves quite thin.]

Venus angustifrons (Conrad).—Obliquely cordate, ventricose. Anterior side narrow, rounded. Posterior extremity somewhat truncated, arcuate; ligament margin elevated, arcuate; basal margins arcuate. Exterior surface everywhere convex, marked with fine lines of growth.—Pl. 17, fig. 11, natural size.

Astoria, Oreg.

[Length 1¾ inches; height $\frac{70}{100}$ L., or 1¼ inches; part anterior to beak 5 lines; apical angle 134°; valves quite thin.]

Venus lamellifera (Conrad).—Subtrigonal, ventricose, ligament margin very oblique and slightly curved, long, posterior margin direct, truncate; basal arcuate. Lateral surface everywhere convex, and having thin concentric elevated lamellæ.—Pl. 17, figs. 12, 12a, natural size.

Astoria, Oreg.

[Length 2 inches; height $\frac{83}{100}$ L.; valve very stout; cast excavate just below palleal impression.]

Venus brevilineata (Conrad).—Subtrigonal, ventricose. Anterior extremity truncate; ligament margin elevated, curved; posterior margin subtruncate; basal margin strongly arcuate. The specimen is a cast, and it is remarkable for a series of irregular vertical impressed lines or sulci, toward the base, which must correspond with prominent lines on the interior of the valve.—Pl. 17, fig. 13.

[Length of cast 2 inches; height $\frac{40}{100}$ L.; thickness $\frac{3}{100}$ L. The irregular sulci on the lower half of the cast are nearly half an inch long, and extend upward from the palleal impression. The sinus in the palleal impression is acute triangular. The surface of the cast is faintly concentric undulate.]

[NOTE.—Figs. 1. 1a, pl. 18, represent still another *Venus*, with a very thick valve, and smooth cast, having the sides evenly convex. It resembles the *angustifrons*, but is hardly as ventricose, and the valve in that is very thin. Length of cast 2½ inches; height 1.6 inches; thickness 1 inch.]

[page 725] *Lucina acutilineata* (Conrad).—Suborbicular; ligament margin short, straight, and a little oblique; posterior margin somewhat truncate widely, nearly direct; supero-anterior margin truncate. Surface with concentric lamelliform striæ and intermediate fine lines; anteriorly with a slightly prominent fold. Basal margin orbiculate. This species is very nearly related to *L. contracta* (Say), a recent shell of the Atlantic coast, and fossil in the Miocene of Virginia. It differs from Say's species in being proportionally more elevated, and in having a much shorter ligament margin.—Pl. 18, figs. 2, 2a, b, natural size.

Astoria, Oreg.

[Length 1½ inches; height slightly less than length; thickness $\frac{11}{100}$ L.; the more prominent ridges of the surface nearly a line apart.]

Tellina arctata (Conrad).—Oblong subelliptical, compressed; front very obliquely truncate and a little sinuous, below reflected; basal margin arcuate; ligament margin declining, arcuate; posterior extremity rounded. Beak nearest the anterior extremity.—Pl. 18, figs. 3, 3a.

Astoria, Oreg.

[Length 2 inches; height $\frac{66}{100}$ L.; thickness $\frac{26}{100}$ L., or $\frac{40}{100}$ H.; apical angle 124°. Valves very thin.]

Tellina emacerata (Conrad).—Elliptical, much compressed; anterior extremity obliquely truncate, straight from the apex, front reflected; dorsal margin posteriorly declining; posterior margin rounded; inferior margin arcuate. Lateral surface marked with fine, regular, closely arranged, concentric, impressed lines.—Pl. 18, fig. 4, natural size.

Astoria, Oreg.

[Length 1½ lines; height half the length; apical angle about 140°.]

Tellina albaria (Conrad).—Thin smooth, subtriangular; beaks medial; anterior extremity obtuse; posterior margin regularly rounded; basal margin straight at middle.—Pl. 18, fig. 5.

Astoria, Oreg.

Tellina nasuta (Conrad).—Subtriangular, convex, anterior side with a slight prominent fold, angulated anteriorly; anterior margin curved above, truncated at the extremity; posterior margin rounded. Beaks medial. Anterior basal margin arcuated; basal margin tumid near the middle.

Astoria, Oreg.

Tellina bitruncata (Conrad).—Elliptical, compressed; anterior side reflected; extremity truncated; posterior margin obliquely truncated. Ligament margin short, straight, parallel with the anterior basal margin; basal margin slightly contracted in the middle; posterior extremity acutely rounded.

Astoria, Oreg.

Nucula divaricata (Conrad).—Subovate, convex, with divaricating striæ. Extremities [page 726] rounded; ligament margin very oblique, slightly arcuate; basal margin arcuate. Beaks near the anterior extremity.—Pl. 18, figs. 6, 6a.

Astoria, Oreg.

Nucula impressa (Conrad).—Oblong ovate, convex, with regular concentric impressed lines. Anterior extremity rostrate, slightly recurved, extremity truncated; ligament margin arcuate, slightly declining; rounded behind. Beaks submedial. Basal margin arcuate, slightly contracted near the anterior extremity.—Pl. 18, figs. 7a, b, c, d, e.

Astoria, Oreg.

[Length 1 inch; breadth very nearly half an inch. Apical angle 155° to 160°. The fine lines of the surface are neat, but closely crowded.]

Pectunculus patulus (Conrad).—Suborbicular, convex, with radiating lines. Hinge margin elongate. Extremities rounded; anterior margin curved inward; posterior margin, nearly direct.—Pl. 18, figs. 8, 8a, natural size.

Astoria, Oreg.

[Length 1½ inches; height about 1½ inches.]

Pectunculus nitens (Conrad).—Suborbicular, oblique, smooth and polished, with fine obsolete radiating lines, extremely neat. Hinge margin quite short, rectilinear; posterior margin slightly arcuate.—Pl. 18, figs. 9, *a*, *b*, natural size.

Astoria, Oreg.

[Length one-third inch; height $\frac{1\cdot6}{100}$ L.]

Arca devincta (Conrad).—Rhomboidal. Ribs narrow, flattened, and little prominent anteriorly; on the posterior side wider, slightly convex, and longitudinally striated. Beaks distant.—Pl. 18, figs. 10, 10*a*.

Astoria, Oreg.

Arca ———.—A cast having a rhomboidal outline, with prominent distant beaks.—Pl. 18, figs. 11*a*, *b*.

Cardita subtenta (Conrad).—Not longer than high, broad obovate, ventricose, with about 22 rounded, not very prominent radiate costæ, and with strong concentric wrinkled lines. Posterior extremity somewhat truncate.—Pl. 18, figs. 12, 12*a*.

Astoria, Oreg.

[Length and height three-fifths inch; thickness two-fifths inch; apical angle 105°.]

Pecten propatulus (Conrad).—Large, subequivalve, suborbicular, compressed; costæ about 17, rounded, narrow, interstices much wider than the ribs; ears unequal.—Pl. 18. figs. 13, 13*a*.

Astoria, Oreg.

[Length and height 4 inches.]

Terebratula nitens (Conrad).—Ovate, smooth and glossy. Superior valve convex; inferior valve flattened toward the base; basal margin sinuous; beak prominent, [page 727] curved. Valves very thin. This shell is remarkable for having the peculiar luster and consistence of many species of *Anomia*. The shell is partially removed, and the surface exhibits obsolete radiating lines.—Pl. 19, figs. 1, 1*a*.

——? .—A broken shell from the argillaceous shale below Astoria.—Pl. 19, fig. 2.

Dolium petrosum (Conrad).—Ovate globose with revolving ribs about on the body whorl; shoulder angulate, tuberculate, below the angle having a slightly concave space, with a revolving prominent line. Spire scalariform, and rather elevated; volutions 5.—Pl. 19, figs. 3*a*, *b*, 4*a*, *b*, 5*a*, *b*, natural size.

Astoria, Oreg.

There are three specimens of this species, all of which are casts. In the smallest the tubercles are very prominent, and less so in the others; and there is a row of small tubercles below the flattened space on the upper part of the body whorl.

Sigaretus scopulosus (Conrad).—Obliquely oval, somewhat ventricose, flattened on the upper half of the body whorl. Disks with numerous revolving lines.—Pl. 19, figs. 6, 6*a*, *b*, *c*, *d*, natural size.

Astoria, Oreg.

Natica saxea (Conrad).—Subglobose. Whorls five, convex, with distinct lines of growth; a broad brown band at base of the shell, and a lighter-colored brown band revolves on the upper part of the whorls, contiguous to the suture; a narrow darker band margins the suture. Umbilicus large, partially covered by a callus.—Pl. 19, figs. 7*a*, *b*. Natural size.

Astoria, Oreg.

This species closely resembles *N. heros* (Say) in contour and in the umbilicus; but the brown band at the base is, I believe, wanting in the *heros*.

Bulla petrosa (Conrad).—Cylindrical, narrow, sides gently curved.—Pl. 19, fig. 8, natural size.

Astoria, Oreg.

Crepidula prærupta (Conrad).—Oblique, oblong, somewhat elliptical and ventricose, with simple lines of growth. Sides flattened, beak narrowed and laterally curved; the side toward which the apex is directed, slightly contracted, and having a somewhat sinuous margin.—Pl. 19, figs. 9, 9*a*, natural size; 10*a*, *b*, views of a cast, probably of this species.

Astoria, Oreg.

Crepidula ———? .—This species, of which there is only a cast in the collection, is very much depressed, with the summit narrow and nearly straight, subacuminate, broadest across the beak, the sides there being somewhat dilated.—Pl. 19. figs. 11*a*, *b*, natural size.

Astoria, Oreg.

Rostellaria indurata (Conrad).—Subfusiform, with oblique, curved, rounded ribs [page 728], whorls contracted or narrow toward the suture. The specimens are fragments of casts. The lip does not appear to have been greatly expanded.—Pl. 19, fig. 12, natural size.

Astoria, Oreg.

Cerithium mediale (Conrad).—Turreted, with fine acute revolving lines; whorls angulated in the middle, and having a row of tubercles on the angle; suture impressed: whorls contracted beneath the suture.—Pl. 20, fig. 1, natural size; 1a, cast.

Astoria, Oreg.

Buccinum ? derinctum (Conrad).—Elevated, with numerous wrinkled revolving lines; whorls flattened and sloping above. Middle of revolutions of the spire nodulous. Margin of the labrum profoundly arcuate.—Pl. 20, figs. 2, 2a, natural size.

Astoria, Oreg.

Fusus geniculus (Conrad).—Fusiform, with closely arranged revolving lines, alternate in size. Whorls of the spire angulated below the middle, and with longitudinal ribs on the inferior half. Body whorl with short ribs on the angle, and beneath the revolving lines are larger and more prominent than above.—Pl. 20, fig. 3.

Fusus corpulentus (Conrad).—Fusiform. Body whorl ventricose, suddenly contracted at base, flattened and sloping toward the suture; whorls of the spire angulated and nodulous in the middle, flat and sloping above.—Pl. 20, fig. 4, cast, natural size.

Nautilus angustatus (Conrad).—Compressed. Septa sinuous and profoundly angulated toward the periphery; from the angle the outer margin of the septa is parallel with the periphery, and anteriorly suddenly becomes transverse across the margin or periphery.—Pl. 20, figs. 5. 6, natural size.

Astoria, Oreg.

[The largest specimen of this species in the collections is 9 inches in diameter.]

Teredo substriata.—Nearly straight and evenly cylindrical, very slightly tapering. Surface minutely and very neatly striate longitudinally.—Pl. 20, figs. 7, 7a, b, natural size.

Astoria, Oreg.

NOTE.—The figures from 8 to 13, inclusive, on pl. 20, representing species from Astoria, are given of natural size, without names.

Fig. 8 is an external cast; and fig. 8a an internal cast.

Fig. 9 is an external cast.

Figs. 10, 11 are external casts; 10a, 11a are internal casts.

Figs. 12, 13, species of *Turritella*, natural size.

Fig. 1, pl. 21, an imperfect cast

[page 729] *Foraminifera*.—Figs. 2 to 4, inclusive, pl. 21, represent three species of Foraminifera found rather abundantly, but poorly preserved, in the soft argillaceous shale on the shores below Astoria.

5. RADIATA.

Galerites oregonensis (Dana).—Figs. 5, 6, 6a represent a species of the Echinidæ, occurring only in broken fragments and scattered spines in the Astoria argillaceous shale. associated with minute Foraminifera. Specimens are so imperfect that we refer it with hesitation to the genus *Galerites*. The spines are half an inch long, very slender, delicately striate, with the striæ punctate or subcrenulate.

NOTE.—Fig. 7, pl. 21, represents what appears to be a fossil. but it shows no regular characters beyond what is observed in the figure. The texture is soft. with the color brownish black, differing decidedly from the rock in which it is embedded. The texture would suggest the idea of the ink bag of a sepia, but other characters do not seem to sustain this view.

Fig. 203 is another doubtful fossil. It appears at first sight to be a coral extending through the limestone in convoluted or intersecting plates, 1½ to 2 lines thick, consisting of hexagonal cells. But the cells are very unlike those of any coral within the knowledge of the writer. The interstices are extremely thin, and the cells are destitute of rays or septa of any kind. Their diameter is nearly half a line, and the length 1½ to 2 lines; and they are transverse in position, being oblong across the plates, like horizontal columns or cells of a honeycomb. They differ widely in form and position from the cells of the Bryozoa and Hydroidea, and seem rather to pertain to the spawn of some species of mollusk. This is only a suggestion, offered with much hesitation.

6. PLANTS.

Abies? robusta (Dana).—Only one species of fossil plant with distinct leaves was observed by the writer in the Astoria deposits. This, like most of the specimens, occurs in a limestone nodule. It is represented in fig. 9, pl. 21. It is one of the Coniferæ, and appears to be a species of *Abies*. The leaves are attached to a stem, and apparently were placed somewhat irregularly around it. They are very stiff and rigid, four-sided, with sharp angles and flat surfaces, the section being rhomboidal; the width is a line, and the transverse diameter about one-third the width.

Near the mouth of Frasers River a dark-blue slate was observed by a party from the *Vincennes*, and specimens obtained, one of which is represented in fig. 10. pl. 21. It is supposed to pertain to the Tertiary formation of the coast, and to he of the same age with that of Astoria. The leaves are all beautifully preserved, as shown in the figure.

No. 1 may be a *Lycopodium*, or possibly a *Juniperus*.

[page 730] Nos. 2, 3, 4, 5, 6, 7, 8, 9 are leaves of one or more species of *Taxodium*.

No. 10 appears to be a leaf of a *Smilar*.

Nos. 11, 12, 13, 14, 15 of uncertain species. 11 and 12 are opposite sides, probably, of similar leaves; and 13, 14, 15 are like No. 11.

The same specimen contains, at *a*, a round piece of fossil resin, probably from some of the coniferous plants whose leaves are here embedded.

Fig. 11, pl. 21, represents a very thin calcareous leaf-like expansion, occurring in the argillaceous shale near Astoria. It is too imperfect to be fully characterized. The specimen is apparently one of the calcareous algæ. The frond is very thin, and deeply lobed; the lobes longitudinally undulate: the surface very smooth, and without markings of any kind. It is extremely tender, and its thickness does not exceed that of common writing paper.

Appendix III.

NOTES ON SHELLS, WITH DESCRIPTIONS OF NEW SPECIES.[a]

By T. A. Conrad.

[page 199] **CRYPTODON, Con.**

The name of this genus, founded on *Mya cancellata.*[b] having been previously applied by Turton to another group of bivalves, and now adopted by some conchologists, it is necessary to change it, and I therefore propose *Schizotherus*, in allusion to the profound channel which indents the hinge on both sides of the cardinal teeth.

Schizotherus nuttallii.

Cryptodon nuttallii Con., Journ. A. N. S., vol. 7, p. 235, pl. 18, fig. 1, [1837].

UNIO.

Unio mortoni Con., December, 1835.

U. turgidus Lea, 1837.

Mr. Lea's description of this species was read at a meeting of the Philosophical Society in December, 1834, but not published before 1837.

MIOCENE SPECIES ?

OSTREA.

Ostrea titan.—Elliptical or oblong; extremely thick and ponderous, contracted toward the hinge; ligament cavity profound; upper valve slightly arched; surface coarsely laminated. Length 10½ inches. [page 200] Locality, San Luis Obispo, Cal.

This huge species is embedded in friable limestone which contains abundance of siliceous sand rounded by attrition. No other fossil can be detected in the portions of limestone which accompany the specimens.

CRETACEOUS SPECIES.

PHOLAS.

Pholas pectorosa.—Ovate-cuneate; anteriorly inflated, contracted in the middle; posterior side cuneiform; disk with radiating ribs, largest anteriorly, and interrupted by concentric furrows; anterior side very short, margin obtusely rounded or subtruncated; basal margin rounded anteriorly, contracted medially, straight posteriorly.

Locality, Tinton Falls, Monmouth County, N. J.

This rare species was found by the late Lardner Vanuxem. It is a cast, on the right valve of which an impressed line runs obliquely from the apex, while on the opposite valve there is a corresponding furrow, and the three ribs nearest the posterior end are more remote from each other than in the right valve.

INOCERAMUS Sow.

Inoceramus senseni.—Rounded; both valves profoundly curved; beaks involute, the volutions of the larger valve, 3, contiguous in both valves. Length 1½ inches; width 2¾ inches.

Locality, Missouri River, Nebraska; Mr. Senseny.

Inoceramus perovalis.—Oval, convex, slightly oblique; beaks medial, both dorsal margins equally declining; basal margin acutely rounded; surface with obsolete concentric undulations. Height about 1¼ inches; length less than the height.

Locality, Chesapeake and Delaware Canal; Mr. Vanuxem.

---

[a] Proc. Acad. Nat. Sci. Philadelphia, vol. 6, January 31, 1853, pp. 199–200.

[b] The genus was founded on *Lutraria nuttallii*, while *Mya cancellata* was the type of the simultaneously proposed genus *Platyodon* Conrad.—W. H. D

Appendix IV.

DESCRIPTIONS OF NEW FOSSIL SHELLS OF THE UNITED STATES.[a]

By T. A. Conrad.

[page 273]

GNATHODON Gray.

Gnathodon lecontei (pl. 24, figs. 1, 2).—Obliquely ovato-triangular, ventricose; anterior side short, the margin regularly rounded; posterior side cuneiform; umbonal slope oblique, carinated; carina not prominent, obtuse, except on the umbo, where it is rather acute; right valve with two cardinal teeth separated by a profound pit; left valve with one cardinal bifid tooth nearly direct; lateral teeth prominent and acute; posterior one elongated, slightly curved; anterior one about half the length of the posterior tooth, slightly curved.

Locality, southern district of Upper California; Doctor Le Conte.

This interesting species approaches the recent *G. cuncatum* nearer than the fossil *G. grayi*. It is much smaller than those, and the carinated umbonal slope is a character which prominently distinguishes it from either.

No recent species of *Gnathodon* is known to occur in California and this fossil may be of the Miocene period. If it is still existing, it will probably be found where the fresh water of the Gila mingles with the salt water of the Gulf of California.

Doctor Le Conte, to whom I have dedicated this interesting shell, found it north of Carisco Creek, in limestone beds formed almost entirely of the species, and farther in the desert it occurred in clay, lying almost horizontally. This is at a distance of 120 miles from the Gulf of California and 150 miles from the Pacific.

CRETACEOUS SPECIES.

EXOGYRA Say.

Exogyra caprina (pl. 24, figs. 3, 4).—Ventricose; larger valve having the umbo spiral, or shaped like a ram's horn; back with obtuse or obsolete angles and furrows, and undulated strong lines of growth; superior valve convex.

Locality, San Felipe Creek, near Rio Grande, western Texas; Doctor Woodhouse.

A single specimen of this curious species was obtained by Mr. Edward H. Kern in New Mexico, and Doctor Woodhouse found it abundantly in Texas. The strata in which they occur are probably synchronous with those of New Jersey. Doctor Woodhouse found, also, *Exogyra boussingaultii* D'Orbigny and *Gryphæa pitcheri* Morton in western Texas.

[page 274]

AVICULA.

A. abrupta (pl. 24, figs. 5, 6).—Suborbicular, convex; posterior margin nearly direct; extremity of hinge on a line with the posterior margin.

Locality, Nimrod Woodward's farm, New Jersey.

This small species is well preserved, but very thin and fragile. I found two right valves, one of them perfect.

A. petrosa (pl. 24, fig. 15).—Subquadrangular, very oblique, ventricose; anterior hinge extremity sharply angulated; anterior margin obliquely subtruncated inferiorly; posterior extremity subangulated.

Locality, Chesapeake and Delaware Canal.

A single cast of this species is in the collection of the Academy. On the apex are two tubercles, which must represent corresponding pits in the interior of the shell.

---

[a] Jour. Acad. Nat. Sci. Philadelphia, new ser., vol. 2, pt. 3, January, 1853, pp. 273–276.

159

SOLEMYA.

S. planulata (pl. 24, fig. 11).—Elliptical, compressed, sides flattened; end margins rounded; hinge and basal margins nearly parallel.

Localities, Monmouth County, N. J.; Alabama.

Casts of this species are not uncommon in the Cretaceous limestone of Alabama. They exhibit a flat groove, which margins the posterior side of the anterior cicatrix; this groove represents the interior rib, and rapidly widens from its inferior acute extremity toward the apex.

CRASSATELLA.

C. subplana (pl. 24, fig. 9).—Subtriangular, compressed or plano-convex; anterior margin obtusely rounded; posterior extremity subtruncated; posterior basal margin straight or slightly contracted; disk marked with numerous prominent acute concentric ridges and fine concentric lines.

Locality, Arneytown, N. J.

Allied to *C. regularis* D'Orbigny.

SPONDYLUS.

S. capax (pl. 24, fig. 8).—Ovato-triangular, profoundly ventricose; summit elevated; ribbed; larger ribs about seven in number, not elevated, remote and armed with irregular spines, arched or foliated, a few of them rather elongated, curved and pointing downward; intermediate ribs rounded, unequal, not very prominent and rough with numerous arched scales; submarginal areas profoundly impressed or excavated; inner margin thickened and profoundly crenate.

Locality, Nimrod Woodward's farm, New Jersey.

I have found fragments of this beautiful fossil, whenever I have visited the locality above named, for many years past, and more than fifteen years since obtained a whole specimen, which was presented to my friend, Dr. William Fleming, of Manchester, England. Yet it does not appear to have been described, and may have been regarded as a variety of Morton's *Plagiostoma dumosum*, an Eocene species.

[page 275]

PANOPÆA.

P. decisa (pl. 24, fig. 19).—Oblong, ventricose, concentrically waved or furrowed; slightly contracted posteriorly; posterior hinge line nearly parallel with the base; posterior margin truncated obliquely inward; basal margin nearly straight; beaks situated about one-third the shell's length from the anterior margin.

Locality, Burlington County, N. J., Mr. Budd; Chesapeake and Delaware Canal, Doctor Morton.

ARCA.

A. uniopsis (pl. 24, fig. 17).—Oblongo-rhomboidal, contracted in the middle; posterior hinge and basal margins parallel; beaks situated about one-fourth of the shell's length from anterior extremity; dorsal area narrow; umbonal slope rounded. (A cast.)

Locality, Burlington County, N. J.

TELLINA.

T. densata (pl. 24, fig. 14).—Ovato-triangular, compressed?, the right valve convex; the left nearly flat, or a little plano-convex anteriorly; posterior side reflected; anterior margin regularly rounded; posterior subtruncated, direct.

Locality, Burlington County, N. J.; Mr. Budd.

A cast of a large species, with the impression of the hinge representing large and prominent teeth.

LUCINA.

L. pinguis (pl. 24, fig. 18).—Suborbicular, ventricose; inequilateral; posterior margin truncated obliquely inwards; basal margin subangulated posterior to the middle.

Locality, New Jersey?

CARDIUM.

C. protextum (pl. 24, fig. 12).—Suboval or subtriangular, inequilateral, ventricose; ribs about 28 in number, narrow, rounded, obsolete on the posterior submargin; posterior extremity obliquely truncated, beaks prominent; basal margin rounded; umbonal slope undefined; posterior end gaping. (A cast.)

Locality, Burlington County, N. J.

This beautiful species has an analogue in the European chalk, and is somewhat similar in form to *C. hiantulum* Ag.

VENILIA? Morton.

V. rhomboidea (pl. 24, fig. 7).—Rhomboidal; cavity of valves profound; sides concave; anterior side very short; umbo very prominent and curved as in *Isocardia;* umbonal slope profoundly carinated; posterior slope concave, depressed; posterior margin rectilinear, oblique, biangulated; disk with two or three wide shallow concentric furrows. (A cast.)

Locality, Burlington County; Mr. Budd.

PECTEN.

P. quinquenaria (pl. 24, fig. 10).—Ovate, much compressed, with five distant ribs, broad and rounded on one valve, narrow and subangulated on the opposite valve. (A cast.)

Locality, Chesapeake and Delaware Canal: Doctor Morton.

[page 276]
ASTARTE.

A. parilis (pl. 24, fig. 16).—Small, triangular, equilateral, compressed; basal margin regularly rounded; angles of the end margins situated at about equal distances from apex and base; disk concentrically undulated.

Locality, Monmouth County, N. J.

DENTALIUM.

D. subarcuatum (pl. 24, fig. 13).—Slightly curved; tapering very gradually, flattened on the side of the outward curve, where a longitudinal raised line is margined by an impressed line on each side; on the inside curve is a longitudinal impressed line; another impressed line runs on one of the sides. (A cast and fragment.)

Locality, New Egypt, N. J.

37351—No. 59—09——11

APPENDIX V.

NOTES ON SHELLS, WITH DESCRIPTIONS OF THREE RECENT AND ONE FOSSIL SPECIES.[a]

By T. A. CONRAD.

[page 31] *Gnathodon flexuosum*, Con. Amer. Journal of Science and Arts, vol. 38, p. 93 (figured), 1840.

G. rostratum Petit. 1853. Rev. et Mag. de Zool., p. 552.

G. trigonum Petit is probably identical with *G. lecontei* Con., fossil in California (Journ. Acad. Nat. Sc., Jan., 1853). Petit's description was published July, 1853.

NOTE ON THE GENUS TRIGONELLA, Con.

This name being superseded, I propose to substitute that of *Pachyderma*.

DESCRIPTION OF A NEW DOLIUM.

D. album.—Oblong-suboval, with convex ribs, which are closely arranged, except on the shoulder; about 18 on the body whorl; spire conical, with rounded volutions, columella perforated at base; lip simple, margin acute.

This species most nearly resembles *D. perdix* in form, but is proportionally much narrower, with the ribs more distant and prominent on the shoulder, and with a channel round the suture which the other does not possess. The spire is less elevated, the species much smaller, and the color nearly white without spots.

DESCRIPTION OF A NEW CONULARIA.

C. indentata.—Elongated, quadrate, tapering very gradually, angles somewhat truncated and crossed by numerous indentations; surface minutely granulated by fine equal decussated lines.

Locality, Galena, Ill.; Mr. Germain.

This species has distant septa, and the middle of each side has an obsolete, slightly impressed, longitudinal line; on the cast there are two carinated approximate lines, with an impressed line on each side of them.

[page 32]

DESCRIPTION OF A NEW BULIMUS.

B. lineolatus.—Oblong-ovate, thin, slightly umbilicated; whorls six, smooth; columella reflected, very narrow; lip reflected, very thin and acute; color white and fulvous, variegated, with dark-brown stripes, aperture more than half the length of the shell; spire conical.

Inhabits volcano of Cartago, Costa Rica.

This species approximates *B. pazianus* of D'Orbigny, but is more ventricose, has a shorter spire, broader bands, narrower columella, and the lip is somewhat reflected, which is not a character of the allied species. That shell has the aperture less than half the length of the shell, whilst the other has it more than half its length.

DESCRIPTION OF A NEW ALASMODONTA.

Subovate, thin, slightly contracted medially; umbonal slope rounded, slightly ventricose; ligament margin elevated; posterior margin obliquely truncated, the extremity subangulated and much above the line of the base; epidermis olivaceous, with a few obscure rays; cardinal tooth single in the right valve, long, compressed, elevated, triangular; in the left valve widely trifid, the posterior lobe obsolete, and situated posterior to the apex; within bluish. Length 1⅜, nearly; height seven-eighths.

Locality, ———; J. G. Anthony.

Exteriorly this shell closely resembles *U. collinus* Con., when young and without spines.

[a] Proc. Acad. Nat. Sci. Philadelphia, vol. 7, March, 1854, pp. 31–32.

APPENDIX VI.

DESCRIPTIONS OF FOSSIL SHELLS FROM THE EOCENE AND MIOCENE FORMATIONS OF CALIFORNIA.[a]

By T. A. CONRAD.

[page 9]

I. EOCENE.

CARDIUM Lin.

1. *C. linteum* Conrad (pl. 1, fig. 1).—Cordate, ventricose subequilateral, with closely arranged radiating lines, umbonal slope subcarinated; posterior submargin with closely arranged smooth striæ, fine, but much larger than those of the disk.

Locality, Cañada de las Uvas. Allied to *C. nicolleti* Con., but very distinct.

DOSINIA Scopoli.

2. *D. alta* Con. (pl. 1, fig. 2).—Elevated equilateral?, posterior side short; disk with fine closely arranged concentric lines, becoming large toward the base; posterior extremity obtuse, direct.

Locality, Cañada de las Uvas, with the preceding.

MERETRIX, Lam. CYTHEREA, Lam.

3. *M. uvasana* Con. (pl. 1, fig. 3).—Suboval, convex, inequilateral, margins rounded; beaks distant from anterior margin; disk with concentric, rather distant ribs, which were probably laminiform when perfect.

Locality, Cañada de las Uvas.

There is but one broken valve of this species, in hard sandstone and with the ribs broken off.

4. *M. californiana* Con. (pl. 1, fig. 4).—Subcordate, ventricose, inequilateral; posterior extremity truncated somewhat obliquely inwards; basal margin nearly straight in the middle; lunule lanceolate; anterior extremity acutely rounded.

Locality, occurs at the Cañada de las Uvas, with the preceding species. Allied to *M. poulsoni* Con.

CRASSATELLA Lam.

5. *C. uvasana* Con. (pl. 1, fig. 5).—Subtriangular, compressed, concentrically sulcated above, and having a few slight concentric undulations inferiorly; ligament slope very oblique, rectilinear; anterior extremity regularly rounded.

Locality, Cañada de las Uvas, with the preceding species.

6. *C. alta* Conrad.—This species occurs in the same rock with the preceding, but only in small fragments. It appears to have been abundant, as it likewise is at Claiborne, Ala. The fracture has resulted from breaking the rock, as the shell appears to have been perfect and not waterworn.

---

[a] Report of Mr. T. A. Conrad on the fossil shells collected in California by Wm. P. Blake: House Doc. No. 129, July, 1855. pp. 9-20. This document, a thin octavo, was an appendix to Blake's preliminary geological report of the Pacific Railroad survey, Conrad's report forming Article I. It was printed without illustrations. The same descriptions were reprinted in the quarto final reports (vol. 5, 1856, pp. 320-329). The final report contained the illustrations, the numbers of which do not correspond exactly to those assigned in the octavo. The principal other discrepancies between the two prints are here indicated by brackets or footnotes. Some of them are obviously mere typographical errors.

163

[page 10]   **MYTILUS Lin.**

7. *M. humerus* Con. (pl. 1. fig. 10).—Ovate. ventricose, summit acute; anterior margin rectilinear; basal margin rounded; anterior extremity [obtusely rounded; posterior extremity[a]] less obtuse: disk with minute radiating lines.

Locality, Cañada de las Uvas, with the preceding fossils.

CARDITA Brug.

8. *C. planicosta* (pl. 1. fig. 6).—Obliquely cordate: ribs about 22, broad and flattened, separated by a narrow groove which becomes obsolete toward the base; ribs on the posterior slope narrow, indistinct, and crossed by numerous profound wrinkles. Lunule small, cordate, profoundly impressed; inner margin crenate.

Locality, Cañada de las Uvas, with the preceding fossils. *Venericardia planicosta* Lam., An. sans Vert. (Desh. ed.), Vol. VI. p. 381.

This common species occurs much larger, though less perfect, than the one represented. This shell occurs abundantly in the Eocene strata of Maryland, Virginia, and Alabama, and is quite as characteristic of the American as of the European Eocene period. I discovered it in Maryland in 1829, and at that time regarded it as the first indication of the occurrence of deposits in the United States synchronous with those of the London clay. Professor Rogers has since named this shell *Venericardia ascia*.

NATICA Adanson.[b]

9. *N. œtites?* Con. (pl. 1. fig. 7).

Locality, Cañada de las Uvas, with the preceding fossils.

N. œtites Conrad. Foss. Shells of Tert. Form., October, 1833.

10. *N. gibbosa* and *semilunata* Lea. Cont. to Geol., December, 1833. There is but one specimen of this shell, which I refer with doubt to a Claiborne species. The outline is similar to that of the latter, but the aperture is concealed in the rock, which prevents the necessary comparison to determine the identity or the difference.

2.[c] *N. alveata* Con. (pl. 1. figs. 8 and 8a).—Volutions five, flattened above, carinated on the angle. a few minute obsolete lines revolve on the upper side of the whorls; aperture inclining to an obovate form; umbilicus small.

Locality, Cañada de las Uvas.

This species is remarkable for its truncated whorls, which are channeled by the carina on the margin. There are no analogous species in the Eocene of the Atlantic slope.

TURRITELLA Lam.

11. *T. uvasana* Con. (pl. 1. fig. 12).—Subulate, whorls with the sides straight and oblique above. rounded below, and having large revolving striæ with intermediate minute lines; striæ near the suture on the upper part of the whorls finer than the prominent lines below.

Locality, occurs with the preceding, in Cañada de las Uvas.

[page 11] This species is allied to *T. obruta* Conrad (*T. lineata* Lea), but that Claiborne shell differs in having fewer revolving lines, and in being indented at the suture.

VOLUTATITHES[d] Swains.

12. *V. californiana* Con. (pl. 1. fig. 9).—Resembles *V. sayana* Con., but smaller, having numerous rounded tubercles instead of the comparatively few spiniform ones of the latter. The tubercles are somewhat oblique; base with rather distant impressed lines.

Locality. Cañada de las Uvas. with the preceding.

BUSYCON?

13. *B?. blakei* Con. (pl. 1, fig. 13).—Fusiform, body whorl bicarinated; shoulder profoundly tuberculated; tubercles acute, transversely compressed; lower angle distant, entire. Surface covered with

---

a Words in brackets omitted in quarto.
b Adamson in quarto.
c This is made No. 11 in the quarto, and all the remaining numbers are one higher.
d Misprint for Volutilithes. –W. II. D

rather fine unequal or alternated wrinkled lines; upper side of the whorls flattened and sloping: whorls of the spire angulated and tuberculated in the middle.

Locality, Cañada de las Uvas, with the preceding.

The beak of this shell being broken, its form and length are uncertain, and the aperture being concealed in the rock, the generic character can only be inferred from the contour of the shell. This corresponds with *Busycon*, except in the biangular form of the body whorl, in which respect it differs from any undoubted species that I have seen.

CLAVATULA? Swains.

14. *C.? californica* Con. (pl. 1, fig. 11).—Fusiform; spire conical, volutions rounded, somewhat flattened above; body whorl ventricose; beak short and narrow.

Locality, Cañada de las Uvas, with the preceding. Allied to *C. proruta* Con., of the Claiborne Eocene, but proportionably narrower.

II. FOSSILS OF THE MIOCENE AND RECENT FORMATIONS OF CALIFORNIA.

CARDIUM Lin.

15. *C. modestum* (n. s.) Con. (pl. 2, fig. 15).—Very small; ribs about 22, narrow: concentric wrinkled lines on the disk; posterior margin direct, truncated: umbonal slope angular; ligament margin parallel with the basal, and forming nearly a right angle with the posterior margin.

Locality, San Diego.[a]

NUCULA Lam.

16. *N. decisa* (n. s.) Con. (pl. 2, fig. 19).—Suboval or subrhomboidal, posterior margin obliquely truncated; disk with devaricating striæ.

Locality, San Diego, with the preceding.

[page 12] This species resembles, in its divaricating striæ, *N. divaricata* of the Oregon Miocene but the lines are proportionally larger, and the shell is smaller and different in outline.

CORBULA.

17. *C. diegoana* Con. (pl. 2, fig. 16).—Triangular, ventricose, inequilateral, extremities subangulated: anterior margin very oblique, rectilinear; posterior margin forming with the ligament margin a slightly curved line, about equal in obliquity to the anterior margin; basal margin profoundly and nearly equally or regularly rounded.

Locality, Mission of San Diego.

MERETRIX Lam.

18. *M. uniomeris* Con. (pl. ii, fig. 20).—Ovate, very inequilateral, convex; posterior side cuneiform; ligament margin very oblique, rectilinear; posterior extremity truncated, direct; beak distant from anterior margin.

Locality, Monterey County, 18 miles south of Tres Piños, in sandstone.

19. *M. decisa* Con. (pl. ii, fig. 27).—Subquadrate, convex, very inequilateral; ligament slope very oblique, nearly straight; posterior extremity truncated; cardinal and lateral teeth robust. (Cast.)

Locality, Ocoya Creek, in friable ferruginous coarse sandstone. (For the associate fossils, see pls. vi, vii, and viii.)

20. *M. tularana* Con. (pl. ii, figs. 22 and 22a).—Suboval or subtriangular, inequilateral, convex anteriorly; compressed and cuneiform posteriorly, anterior extremity acutely rounded and as nearly in a line with the beak as the base; basal margin tumid medially; posterior extremity subtruncated.

Locality, Tulare Valley.

(NOTE.—This specimen is a clay cast, and was found in a bowlder that had been washed down from the hills at the head of the Tulare Valley, about 20 miles west of the Cañada de las Uvas.—W. P. B.)

---

[a] "Mission" added in quarto.

TELLINA Lin.

21. *T. diegoana* Con. (pl. ii, fig. 28).—Ovate-elliptical, compressed, inequilateral, concentrically striated. Slope carinated; posterior extremity suddenly produced or rostrated, and below the posterior basal margin.

Locality, San Diego, in sandstone.

22. *T. congesta* Con. (pl. ii, figs. 14, 18, 21).—Subtriangular, ventricose, inequilateral; anterior margin obliquely truncated; anterior basal margin subrectilinear, oblique, extremity angulated, [page 13] much above the line of the base; posterior margin and posterior basal margin regularly rounded.

Localities, Monterey, Mission of San Diego, Carmelo.

This interesting species is very abundant at Monterey, in indurated drab-colored clay. There is merely a chalky trace of the shell remaining. It occurs in a somewhat similar rock at Carmelo, and in sandstone at San Diego. Fig. 21 is from San Diego, 22 from Monterey, and 23 from Carmelo.

23. *T. pedroana* (n. s.) Con. (pl. 2, fig. 17).—Subtriangular, inequilateral, compressed; anterior dorsal margin oblique, rectilinear; anterior extremity truncated, posterior margin regularly rounded, basal margin subrectilinear.

Locality, San Pedro; recent formation.

A thin smooth species, of which only one valve was obtained.

ARCA Lin.

24. *A. microdonta* Con. (pl. 2, fig. 29).—Rhomboidal, ventricose, thick in substance; anterior side very short; umbonal slope rounded. Ribs 25, prominent, narrow, wider posteriorly, except on the posterior slope, where they are small and not prominent, about five in number. Cardinal teeth small, numerous, closely arranged, larger toward the extremities. Inner margin profoundly dentate; dorsal area rather wide and marked with about six impressed lines; beaks distant.

Locality, Tulare Valley?: Miocene.

There is but one valve in the collection, and it has some resemblance to *A. arata* Say, of the Maryland Miocene. The locality is given by Mr. Blake with a mark of doubt.

TAPES.

25. *T. diversum* Sow. (pl. ii, figs. 24, 24a, and 26).—Obtusely oval or suborbiculary ventricose, inequilateral; disk with numerous radiating prominent striæ or ribs, and concentric wrinkled lines, which are profound anteriorly; posterior margin nearly direct, obtusely rounded or subtruncated; inner margin with small crenulations; ligament plate broad and profoundly indented.

Locality, San Pedro, in calcareous marl; recent formation.

SAXICAVA Fleur. de Bell.

26. *S. abrupta* Con. (pl. ii, figs. 25 and 25a).—Suboval, ventricose, inequilateral; concentrically wrinkled; anterior margin obtusely rounded obliquely inward; posterior extremity truncated, direct, dorsal and basal margin nearly parallel.

Locality, San Pedro; recent formation.

PETRICOLA Lam.

27. *P. pedroana* Con. (pl. ii, fig. 23).—Elliptical, profoundly inequilateral, compressed, undulated concentrically, and with very minute closely arranged radiating lines.

[page 14] Locality, occurs with the preceding shell; recent formation.

One broken valve of this species occurred in the same specimen of rock in which they had bored. Some specimens of the *Saxicava* are entire, and fill the cavities they have formed, when living.

SCHIZOTHŒRUS Conrad.

28. *S. nuttalli* Con. (pl. iii, figs. 33 and 33a).—Ovate, ventricose, gaping widely posteriorly; moderately thick in substance; anterior side short, abruptly rounded at the extremity; posterior side elongated extremely truncated; dorsal line slightly concave; umbo not prominent; basal margin profoundly

rounded; hinge plate broad, cartilage pit large, obliquely ovate, profound; cardinal teeth in the left valve two, one in the right valve; anterior cardinal plate broad, with an angular depression throughout its entire length, posterior one narrow, with a deep angular channel in which is a bifid plate in the right valve; cavity of shell and umbo profound.

Locality, San Pedro, in calcareous marl; recent formation.—W. P. Blake.

I have referred this shell to the same genus in which I placed *Lutraria nuttalli* of the California coast. The hinge is very similar to that of *Lutraria*, but the long deep channels of the hinge are similar to those of *L. nuttalli*, the animal of which differs from that of *Lutraria*. I do not know of any recent species of the latter genus in California.

LUTRARIA? Lam.

29. *L. traskei* Con. (pl. iii, fig. 30).—Suboval, ventricose, inequilateral, hinge and basal margin nearly parallel; posterior margin subtruncated and slightly oblique, or approaching a direct outline; posterior extremity rounded.

Locality, Carmelo; Miocene? (Received from John B. Trask, by whom it was collected.—W. P. B.)

MACTRA Lin.

30. *M. diegoana* Con. (pl. iv, fig. 35).—Triangular ventricose, inequilateral, anterior side oblique, rectilinear; umbonal slope carinated and nearly terminal; basal margin profoundly and regularly rounded.

Locality, San Diego; Miocene?

This species is nearly allied to *M. albaria* of the Oregon Miocene, which probably belongs to the same rock as the present species. The concentric ridges represented in the figure are caused by weathering, as the disk was originally smooth.

MODIOLA Lam.

31. *M. contracta* Con. (pl. iv, fig. 35).—Elongated, narrowed anteriorly, contracted submedially; basal margin widely contracted; disk with numerous minute radiating lines.

Locality, Monterey County, 18[a] miles south of Tres Pinos [Piños]; recent formation.

A portion of the shell remains, showing traces of fine radiating lines. Miocene?

[page 15] #### MYTILUS Lin.

32. *M. pedroanus* Con. (pl. —, fig. 40).—Oblong-subovate, ventricose, dorsal line ungulated medially, angle rounded; beak projecting slightly beyond the basal margin; posterior extremity rounded; basal margin rectilinear.

Locality, San Pedro; recent formation.

PECTEN Lin.

33. *P. deserti* Con. (pl. —, fig. 41).—Suborbicular, both valves convex; ribs about 23, rounded, somewhat flattened toward the base, about as wide as the interstices; [in the lower valve much wider than the interstices,[b]] and the valve more convex than the opposite one; ears equal in the upper valve; left ear of lower valve extended downward and very obliquely striated; cartilage pit profound; a submarginal channel parallel with the upper margin.

Locality, Carrizo Creek, Colorado Desert; Miocene.

ANOMIA Lin.

34. *A. subcostata* Con. (pl. —, fig 34).—Obtusely ovate, thick in substance, umbo of larger valve ventricose, hinge thickened, surface of this valve obtusely undulated concentrically and marked with waved, wrinkled, very irregular interrupted ribs, not much raised except toward the base, where they are larger and somewhat tuberculiform, upper valve entire, or with obsolete radii toward the base.

Locality, Carrizo Creek, Colorado Desert; Miocene.

Allied to *A. ruffini* of the Virginia Miocene, but thicker, less expanded, and with the radii more numerous and more riblike.

---

[a] 16 in quarto. [b] Words in brackets omitted in quarto.

OSTREA Lin.

35. *O. vespertina* Con. (pl. —, figs. 36, 37, 38).— Ovate, subfalcate, lower valve plicated or ribbed more or less profoundly; hinge long and wide, sharp and somewhat pointed; ligament cavity wide, profound, minutely wrinkled; margins abrupt: cavity not very deep; muscular impression large, impressed; upper valve flat, irregular, plicated on the margin; a submarginal furrow, slightly impressed, crenulated [nearly to its basal curve, profoundly crenulated *a*] toward the hinge.

Locality, Carrizo Creek; Miocene.

35. *O. vespertina* Con., Jour. Acad. Nat. Sc., new series, vol. 2, part 4, p. 300.—This species is very similar in form and plications to *O. subfalcata* Con., of the Virginia Miocene.

36. *O. heerman[n]i* Con., [Proc.] Acad. Nat. Sc. Philadelphia [VII, 1855, p. 267].*b*—Very irregular in form, thick,*c* ovate and often dilated: lower valve shallow; exterior very irregular, with large distant angular radiating ribs, and with pits,*d* irregular cavities; cartilage pit broad and oblique; upper valve flat or concave, with a profoundly irregular surface. Length 5¾ inches, height 6½ inches.*e*

Locality, Carrizo Creek, Colorado Desert. Dr. Heermann.

[page 16] This large oyster shell probably belongs to the same deposit which contains *O. vespertina* and *Anomia subcostata*. The surfaces of most specimens have a resemblance to worm-eaten wood, having been evidently sculptured by some marine animal.*f*

PENITELLA.

37. *P. spelœum* Con.*g* (pl. —, 43, 43a, 43b).— Ovate, ventricose, anteriorly inflated with fine radiating lines and transverse wrinkles, transverse furrow medial, angular, slightly oblique; posterior side cuneiform, truncated at the extremity, which is direct, and with prominent, acute, wrinkled concentric lines, front dorsal margin widely recurved, trisulcate; cardinal plate broad, sulcated process slender, direct.

Locality, San Pedro; recent formation.

No trace of the coriaceous cup, characteristic of this genus, remains in the collection. It is widely distinct from the recent species of the California coast, *P. penita* Conrad.

FISSURELLA Lam.

38. *F. crenulata* Sow. (pl. —, fig. 44).—Oblong subovate, slightly contracted laterally opposite the foramen. Shell with numerous radiating conspicuous compressed lines; foramen large, subovate, not nearly central, inner margin crenulated, thickened basal margin sinuous: inner margin of foramen broadly callous: cavity profound.

F. crenulata Sowerby, Zankerville [Tankerville] Catalogue.

Locality, San Pedro; recent formation. This is the largest fossil species I have seen.

CREPIDULA Lam.　CRYPTA Humph.

39. *C. princeps* Con. (pl. —, fig. 52).—Oblong ovate, thick and ponderous, contracted or compressed superiorly; upper side or portion of the shell sloping, back regularly rounded; beak prominent, rounded, laterally curved: apex distant from the margin of the aperture: diaphragm very large, with a very sinuous margin.

Locality, Santa Barbara; recent formation.

This is the largest species that has come under my observation, and is very distinct from any that has yet been described.

---

a Words in brackets omitted in quarto.

b This species is not figured in the Philadelphia Proceedings, nor in the quarto Pacific R. R. report, nor anywhere else, so far as known. It is believed to be identical with *O. haitensis* Sowerby. The imperfect reference of the original has been completed by the insertion of the words in brackets.—W. H. D.

c "Thick" omitted in quarto.

d "And" inserted in quarto.

e Footnote added in quarto: "The figures which are given in Pl. — are from a smaller and more characteristic specimen than that of which the dimensions are given by Mr. Conrad. The specimen which is figured is, however, much worn and broken on the edges." See note *b*, above.

f These specimens were picked up by Dr. Heermann in the bed of the creek, and were undoubtedly derived from a portion of the stratum of shells that I found in situ.—W. P. Blake.

g "*P. spelœa*" in quarto.

NARICA.

40. *N. diegoana* Con. (pl.—, fig. 39).—Subglobose, sides flattened; obtuse above.
Locality, San Diego; Miocene?
Partially imbedded in the rock and its form not accurately determined.

[page 17]

TROCHITA Schum.

41. *T. diegoana* Con. (pl. —, fig. 42.)—Conical; volutions three, rounded, smooth; body whorl ventricose.
Locality, occurs with the preceding; Miocene?

CRUCIBULUM Shum.

42. *C. spinosum* Con. (pl. —, fig. 46).—Moderately elevated, suboval, armed with numerous prominent spines in radiating series; spines smaller, and the series more closely arranged anteriorly; apex subcentral?, prominent, acute; shell with concentric wrinkles.
Calyptræa spinosa? Sowerby.
Locality, San Diego? Recent on the coast of Peru.

NASSA Lam.

43. *N. intastriata* [a] Con. (pl. —, fig. 49).—Ovate-acute; whorls 5½, rounded, cancellated; longitudinal striæ nodulous, except toward the base of body whorl; a deep sulcus behind the beak, two upper volutions entire; labrum striated within; spire conical, longer than the aperture.
Locality, San Pedro; recent formation.
The surface of this shell is roughened by a tubercle on the longitudinal, at each intersection of the revolving lines.
44. *N. pedroana* Con. (pl. —, fig. 48).—Subfusiform, smooth; volutions rounded, spire conical, longer than the aperture, which is elliptical; columella very regularly concave.
Locality, occurs with the preceding; recent formation.
This small species resembles *Nassa lunata* Say, as the preceding approximates *N. trivittata* Say. This is very remarkable, as the two latter are recent shells of the Atlantic coast, associated with each other, both in the sea and in the Miocene deposits of Virginia and Maryland.

STREPHONA Browne. OLIVA Lam.

45. *S. pedroana* Con. (pl. —, fig. 51).—Small, elliptical; spire conical, about equal in length to the aperture; base of columella with a prominent fold.
Locality, occurs with the preceding; recent formation.
A small abundant species, sometimes waterworn, without any prominent character except the fold at the base, which is more conspicuous, considering the size of the shell, than is usual in the genus.

LITTORINA Fér.

46. *L. pedroana* Con. (pl. —, fig. 50).—Suboval; spire very short; body whorl abruptly rounded above; aperture obliquely subovate.
Locality, occurs with the preceding; recent formation.

STRAMONITA Shum. PURPURA Lam.

47. *S. petrosa* Con. (pl. —, figs. 47 and 47a).—Subglobose; whorls four, subangulated; body whorl with three revolving rows of distant tubercles [page 18] and flattened at the summit. Spire conical; penultimate whorl with one series of tubercles.
Locality, Tulare Valley. (Found with *Meretrix tularana* Con. (pl. ii, figs. 22 and 32a. Both specimens are clay casts, but very perfect.—W. P. B.)

III. TERTIARY SHELLS OF THE ISTHMUS OF DARIEN.

MIOCENE?

Mr. Blake has forwarded me casts of three bivalves. They are forms which are new to me, and probably Miocene species. The *Gratelupia*, except in being truncated posteriorly, much resembles *G. hydeana* Conrad, an Eocene fossil.

---

[a] " *N. interstriata* " in quarto.

GRATELUPIA Desmoulins.

48. *G.? mactropsis* Con. (pl. —, fig. 54).—Triangular, inequilateral; dorsal margins equally oblique, straight; basal margin rounded anteriorly, slightly curved posteriorly, posterior extremity truncated, direct, considerably above the line of the base.

Locality, Isthmus of Darien.

MERETRIX.

49. *M. dariena* Con. (pl. —, fig. 55).—Obtusely and obliquely subovate; ventricose; inequilateral; anterior extremity angulated and situated much nearer the beak than the base; anterior dorsal line straight and oblique; beak not prominent; basal and posterior margins profoundly rounded.

Locality, occurs with the preceding.

TELLINA Lin.

50. *T. dariena* Con. (pl. —, fig. 53).—Subtriangular, compressed; anterior hinge margin rectilinear, very oblique, extremity truncated, direct; posterior extremity regularly rounded; base moderately curved.

Locality, occurs with the preceding.

IV. MIOCENE FOSSILS FROM OCOYA CREEK.

The following are descriptions of some of the fossils from Ocoya Creek (Pose Creek), which occur only as casts. The collection contains many of these casts, but the descriptions are principally based upon the drawings made at the locality by Mr. Blake.

NATICA.

51. *N. ocoyana* Con. (pl. vi, fig. 57).—Spire conical, volutions three or four, rounded on the sides, depressed above; body whorl very wide, depressed.

Locality, Ocoya Creek; W. P. Blake.

52. *N. geniculata* Con. (pl. vi, fig. 67).—Globose, volutions angulated above; spire short, conical; body whorl contracted near the summit.

Locality, Ocoya Creek; W. P. Blake.

[page 19] Resembles *N. alveata* Con., of the California Eocene. (See p. 10.)

BULLA.

53. *B. jugularis* Conrad (pl. vi, figs. 62, 62a, 62b).—Oblong elongated, much contracted toward the apex; acutely rounded at the base.

Locality, Ocoya Creek; W. P. Blake.

PLEUROTOMA.

54. *P. transmontana* Conrad (pl. vi, fig. 69).—Fusiform, with rugose revolving lines and distant short longitudinal undulations on the body whorl; volutions of the spire rounded; longitudinally undulated.

Locality, Ocoya Creek; W. P. Blake.

[55. *P. ocoyana* Conrad (pl. vi, fig. 71).—Short fusiform body, whorl ventricose, contracted near the suture, surface marked with revolving lines and numerous longitudinal furrows.

Locality, Ocoya Creek; W. P. Blake.] [a]

SYCOTOPUS.[b]

56. *S. ocoyanus* Conrad (pl. vi, fig. 72).—Spire depressed; whorls flattened above; shoulder subangulated, sides somewhat flattened, columella profoundly rounded above and concave below.

Locality, Ocoya Creek; W. P. Blake.

TURRITELLA.

57. *T. ocoyana* Conrad (pl. vii, figs. 73, 73a, 73b).—Volutions 13 or 14, straight at the sides, rounded at base, and having well-marked revolving lines, base broad; volutions suddenly tapering to the apex.

Locality, Ocoya Creek; W. P. Blake.

[a] The description of *P. ocoyana* does not appear in the quarto, but the numbers jump from 55 to 57 and the name is included in the catalogue that precedes the descriptions.

[b] "*Syctopus*" in quarto; =Sycotypus.—W. H. D.

COLUS.

58. *C. arctatus* Conrad (pl. vii, fig. 76).—Narrow fusiform; whorls rounded; beak very slender, somewhat sinuous.

Locality, Ocoya Creek, California; W. P. Blake.

TELLINA.

59. *T. ocoyana* Conrad (pl. vii, fig. 75).—Elliptical compressed inequilateral; posterior extremity acutely rounded, much above the line of the base; anterior end somewhat acutely rounded; cardinal teeth robust.

PECTEN.

C0. *P. nevadanus* Conrad (pl. viii, fig. 77).—Ovate. flat or slightly concave; ribs 17?, large, flattened on the back; interstices strongly wrinkled transversely.

This shell is so much nearly allied to *N. humphreysii* of Maryland that. taken in connection with *P. catillifornis*[c] (pl. viii). it may be regarded as a Miocene species. The strata in which they occur may safely be referred to that period.

Locality, Ocoya Creek: W. P. Blake.

[page 20] 61. *P. catillifornis*[a] Conrad (pl. viii, fig. 83).—Orbicular planoconvex, with radiating striæ and distinct rounded ribs; ears equal.

Locality, Ocoya Creek; W. P. Blake.

This large pecten has such a general resemblance to *P. madisonius* Say, of the Virginia Miocene, that I have no doubt that it existed at the same period, or at least after the Eocene. There is none such now living on the coast of California, and none in the Eocene, of this group of large pectens, which occur almost everywhere in the Miocene deposits of the Atlantic slope.

In addition to the above-described species, there are many specimens and drawings in which the specific characters are not preserved with sufficient distinctness for description. Among these are individuals of the genera [*Cardium?* or][b] *Arca. Solen. Dosinia.* and *Venus.*

---

[a] "P. catilliformis" in quarto.   [b] Words in brackets omitted in quarto.

APPENDIX VII.

NOTE ON THE MIOCENE AND POST-PLIOCENE DEPOSITS OF CALIFORNIA, WITH DESCRIPTIONS OF TWO NEW FOSSIL CORALS.[a]

By T. A. CONRAD.

MIOCENE.

Post-Pliocene deposits of shells occur at various places on the coast of California, as Santa Barbara, San Pedro, etc., but I have seen specimens of Miocene fossils from no other locality on the coast than near the former town, where they were obtained by Doctor Heermann, who informs me that they are very little elevated above the sea, and that the post-Pliocene fossils rest immediately upon them. This Miocene deposit consists chiefly of fine loose brown sand and small corals, the most of which are a species herein described as *Idmonea californica*. The shells have been described in the Proceedings for February, 1855, page 267, and consist of *Mercenaria perlaminosa, Pecten heermanni, Diadora crucibuliformis, Pandora bilirata,* and *Cardita occidentalis.*

The *Mercenaria* and *Pecten* are closely related to species of the Virginia Miocene, and indeed there is an extraordinary analogy in all the above-mentioned shells to species of the Atlantic Miocene deposits; and what is equally remarkable, they have no resemblance to the existing California species, many of which are embedded in sand above them; affording perhaps a stronger contrast between the two groups than occurs in any other part of the world. The Atlantic Miocene and post-Pliocene, on the contrary, contain a few species in common and others which are analogous.

IDMONEA Lamouroux.

Idmonea californica.—Branches compressed, slender, bifurcated; tubular openings projecting, irregularly grouped, but disposed to form in transverse series: longitudinal line between the openings or cells, microscopic or obsolete; reverse surface planoconvex, transversely wrinkled and slightly furrowed; section exhibiting 15 to 20 angular pores.

The branches of this species are about one-eighth of an inch wide. I have not seen any among them anastomosed. It belongs to the genus *Crisisina* D'Orbigny.

Among these corallines is a species of *Tubulipora,* a *Retepora,* and a *Lichenopora* which may be named—

Lichenopora californica.—Adhering; tubular openings numerous, arranged in irregular branching rays; central depression rather deep and with numerous unequal pores. Diameter about one-fourth of an inch.

POST-PLIOCENE.

Near Santa Barbara and San Pedro Doctor Heermann collected a number of fossil shells of the same species which inhabit the adjacent coast, among which are *Platyodon cancellatum* Conrad, *Schizotharus nuttallii* Con., *Venus nuttallii* Con., *Tellina nasuta,* and *Tapes diversa* Sowerby, among the bivalves, and a number of univalves.

[a] Proc. Acad. Nat. Sci. Philadelphia, vol. 7, December, 1855, p. 441.

Appendix VIII.

DESCRIPTIONS OF THREE NEW GENERA, TWENTY-THREE NEW SPECIES MIDDLE TERTIARY FOSSILS FROM CALIFORNIA, AND ONE FROM TEXAS.[a]

By T. A. Conrad.

[page 312]

JANIRA Schum.

Janira bella.—Subtriangular; inferior valve convex, ribs 14 or 15, square, about as wide as the intervening spaces, very prominent, some of them with [page 313] one or two longitudinal obsolete lines; disk finely wrinkled concentrically; upper valve flattened, deeply depressed toward the apex; ribs rather narrower than those of the opposite valve, obscurely bicarinated above, disk ornamented with close, fine, squamose, concentric wrinkles. Length 4 inches; height 3¾ inches.

Locality. Santa Barbara, Cal.; Doctor Newberry.

PALLIUM Klein.

1. *P. estrellanum.*—Suborbicular; lower valve ventricose, slightly undulated; ribs 17, broad, little prominent, convex, with an intermediate linear rib, from which the larger ribs are separated by an impressed line; upper valve convex, somewhat undulated, ribs flattened and the intermediate small ribs with a longitudinal impressed line on the lower part of the valve. Height 2½ inches.

Locality, Estrella Valley, California; Dr. Newberry.

2. *P. crassicardo.*—Obtusely ovate or suborbicular, thick; lower valve ventricose; ribs 15–16, elevated, back rounded, sides flattened, disks radiato-striate, 9 or 10 on the ribs, intervals of ribs concave, umbo or whole disk at wide intervals having a tendency to be humped and nodose; upper valve convex or slightly ventricose; ears large, equal; hinge thick, with prominent, acute, oblique teeth; fosset profound, muscular impression very large. Height 5 inches.

Locality, Monterey County, Cal.; A. S. Taylor.

PECTEN Lin.

1. *Pecten meekii.*—Suborbicular, compressed; ribs 19, not very prominent, convex-depressed on the back, angulated on the sides. Height 6½ inches.

Locality, San Rafael Hills; Mr. Antisell.

2. *P. altiplectus.*—Obtusely ovate; ribs squamose, slender, nine of them distant, profoundly elevated. Height 2½ inches

Locality, with the preceding; Mr. Antisell.

PACHYDESMA Conrad.

P. inezana.—Triangular, equilateral; anal side subcuneiform; teeth robust.

Locality, Santa Ynez Mountains; Mr. Antisell.

MULINIA Gray.

M. densata.—Subovate, ventricose, thick, very inequilateral; posterior side very short comparatively, contracted; extremity subtruncated, much above the line of the base; posterior basal margin very oblique and contracted; anterior end obliquely truncated; anterior basal margin rounded; summits prominent, distant; lateral teeth very robust and prominent; inner margin entire. Length 2¾ inches.

Locality, Santa Barbara, Cal.; Doctor Newberry.

---

[a] Proc. Acad. Nat. Sci. Philadelphia, vol. 8, December, 1856, pp. 312-316.

THRACIA Leach.

Thracia mactropsis.—Subtriangular, subequilateral, ventricose; anterior side cuneiform or subrostrated, posterior end regularly rounded; ligament margin very oblique: base regularly and profoundly rounded; umbonal slope abruptly rounded; summit prominent, posterior to the middle of the valve; anterior extremity angular.   Length 1 inch.

Locality, Monterey County, Cal.; Doctor Newberry.

MYA Lin.

Mya montereyana.—Suboval, slightly ventricose, thin, inequilateral; summit hardly prominent, anterior end subtruncated? posterior end acutely rounded, [page 314] the extremity situated more nearly on a line with the beak than the base; disk concentrically rugoso-striate.   Length 1½ inches.

Locality, Monterey, Cal.; Dr. Newberry.

ARCA Lin.

1. *Arca canalis.*— Subtrapezoidal, ventricose; ribs 24–26, flattened, scarcely prominent, divided by a longitudinal furrow; disk concentrically wrinkled; umbo ventricose; summits prominent, remote from the center.   Length 2½ inches; height 1¾ inches.

Locality, Santa Barbara, Cal.

2. *Arca trilineata.*—Trapezoidal, somewhat produced, inequilateral, ventricose; ribs 22–24, scarcely prominent, square, wider than the intervening spaces, ornamented with three impressed or four raised lines; disks concentrically wrinkled; summits prominent; beaks approximate.   Length 3 inches.

Locality, occurs with the preceding.

3. *Arca congesta.*—Rhomboidal, ventricose, inequilateral; ribs about 27, convex on the back, wider than the intervals which are transversely striate; anterior ribs crenate; ligament margin elevated; posterior end obtusely rounded; summits prominent.   Length five-eighths inch.

Locality, California; Doctor Newberry.

AXINÆA Poli.   PECTUNCULUS Lam.

Axinæa barbarensis.—Lentiform, subequilateral, concentrically wrinkled; ribs about 37, scarcely prominent, flat, defined by an impressed line, wanting on the submargins and obsolete toward the base; summits slightly prominent.   Length 1¾ inches; height rather more than 1¼ inches.

ARCOPAGIA.

Arcopagia medialis.—Oval, both valves slightly ventricose, anteriorly; upper valve much contracted or concave toward the umbonal slope, which is angulated; postumbonal slope slightly contracted in the middle, emarginate at base; the corresponding slope of the lower valve deeply folded, reflected toward the extremity; disks rugoso-striate concentrically.   It has an affinity to *A. biplicata* Conrad, but is proportionally longer.

Locality, Monterey County, Cal.; A. S. Taylor.

TAPES Sowerby.

Tapes linteatum.—Oblong-oval, ventricose; buccal side short, extremity obtusely rounded; anal side elongated, end regularly rounded; ligament margin long, oblique, straight; disks radiated with fine unequal lines, except on the postumbonal slope, which is entire.   Length 2 inches.

Locality, ——; Doctor Newberry.

CRYPTOMYA Conrad.

Cryptomya ovalis.—Oval, compressed, posterior end truncated: umbonal slope angulated on the umbo; beaks medial; basal margin medially truncated; disk medially flattened.

Locality, Monterey County, Cal.; Doctor Newberry.

CYCLAS Klein.   LUCINA Lam.

Cyclas tetrica.—Suboval, compressed? Very inequilateral, somewhat oblique; disks concentrically striate; larger striæ prominent, acute, distant, the intervals with four or five unequal, fine, wrinkled lines; beaks scarcely prominent above the dorsal line.   Length 1¾ inches.

Locality, Monterey County, Cal.; A. S. Taylor.

[page 315] *Spondylus estrallensis.*—Obtusely ovate; both valves ventricose; ribs 17, not very prominent, rounded, rugose; valves with radiating striæ.

Locality, Estrella Valley; Mr. Antisell.

DOSINIA Scopoli.

1. *Dosinia longula.*—Regularly ventricose, inequilateral, longitudinally oval; margins and base regularly rounded; summit prominent; buccal margin more obtusely rounded than the anal. Length 1½ inches.

Locality, Monterey, Cal.; Doctor Newberry.

2. *Dosinia alta.*—Obtusely subovate or suboval from beak to base; posterior margin curved, profoundly oblique; base regularly and rather acutely rounded; summits prominent, oblique; surface marked with numerous fine, concentric, impressed lines; beaks medial. Height 4 inches.

Locality, Monterey, Cal.; Doctor Newberry.

LUTRARIA.

Lutraria transmontana.—Longitudinally ovato-triangular, inequilateral. thin; anal side subcuneiform; surface concentrically indented, umbo irregularly plicated.

Locality, Rancho Triumpho, near Los Angeles; Mr. Antisell.

SCHIZOPYGA Conrad.

Bucciniform; columella concave, plicate; lower part of body volution deeply channeled, the channel emarginating the columella.

Schizopyga californiana.—Volutions rounded, having revolving ribs and longitudinal furrows, giving the ribs a nodulous character; basal excavation profound.

Locality, Santa Clara, Cal.; Doctor Newberry.

TAMIOSOMA Conrad.

An elongated tube, apparently entire, porous and cellular throughout its substance; interior filled with numerous irregularly-disposed vaulted cells connected by longitudinal slender tubes, funnel-shaped beneath; aperture resembling that of *Balanus.*

Tamiosoma gregaria.—Subquadrangular, elongated, longitudinally furrowed and striate, and having fine, undulated, transverse lines; mouth small, oblique; upper part of the tube oblique, deeply indented or balaniform, and coarsely striated longitudinally. Length, 8 inches.

Locality, Monterey County, Cal.; A. S. Taylor. Growing in clusters like *Balani.* No sutures, indicating separate valves; cells very thin plates, convex surface downward.

ECHINODERMS.

ASTRODAPSIS Conrad.

Suboval, depressed; ambulacral areas elevated or ridged; ambulacra nearly straight, widely open at the extremity; mouth central; anus submarginal, beneath; radiating grooves as in *Laganum.*

Astrodapsis antiselli.—Pentangular, suboval; ambulacral ridges rounded on the back, straight and oblique on the sides; interambulacral areas profoundly depressed, angulated in the middle; point of divergence of the ambulacra depressed below the level of the ridges, not quite central, but anterior to the middle; anus small, almost marginal. Length 1¾ inches.

Locality, Monterey County, Cal.; A. S. Taylor.

[page 316] ### MELLITA Klein.

Mellita texana.—Suborbicular; very wide anterior to the middle; ambulacra moderately curved, nearly closed; lunules five, moderately wide.

Locality, Texas; Dr. Francis Moore.

Form of *M. testinata* Klein, but the ambulacra are proportionally longer and narrower, and the middle lunule much shorter. (A Tertiary fossil.)

APPENDIX IX.

DESCRIPTION OF THE TERTIARY FOSSILS COLLECTED ON THE SURVEY.[a]

By T. A. CONRAD.

[page 69]

CALIFORNIA FOSSILS.

UNIVALVE.

SCHIZOPYGA Conrad.

Bucciniform; columella concave, plicate; lower part of body volution deeply channeled, the channel emarginating the columella.

Schizopyga californiana (Pl. II, fig. 1).—Volutions rounded, having revolving ribs and longitudinal furrows, giving the ribs a nodulous character; basal excavation profound.—Proceedings Acad. Nat. Sci., December, 1856, p. 315.

Locality, Santa Clara, Cal.; Doctor Newberry.

The above genus is probably related to *Cancellaria*.

BIVALVES.

CRYPTOMYA Conrad.

Cryptomya ovalis (Pl. II, fig. 2).—Oval, compressed, posterior end truncated; umbonal slope angulated on the umbo; beaks medial; basal margin medially truncated; disk medially flattened.—Proceedings Acad. Nat. Sci. for December, 1856, p. 314.

Locality, Monterey County, Cal.; Doctor Newberry.

Rather smaller than the recent *C. californica*, less regularly oval, inequilateral, etc.

THRACIA Leach.

Thracia mactropsis (Pl. II, fig. 3).—Subtriangular, subequilateral, ventricose; anterior side cuneiform or subrostrated, posterior end regularly rounded; ligament margin very oblique; base [page 70] regularly and profoundly rounded; umbonal slope abruptly rounded; summit prominent, posterior to the middle of the valve; anterior extremity angular. Length 1 inch.—Proceedings Acad. Nat. Sci., December, 1856, p. 313.

Locality, Monterey County, Cal.; Doctor Newberry.

MYA Lin.

Mya montereyana (Pl. II, fig. 4).—Suboval, slightly ventricose, thin, inequilateral; summit hardly prominent; anterior end subtruncated?, posterior end acutely rounded, the extremity situated more nearly on a line with the beak than the base; disk concentrically rugoso-striate. Length 1¼ inches.—Proceedings Acad. Nat. Sci., December, 1856, p. 313.

Locality, Monterey, Cal.; Doctor Newberry.

This and the preceding fossil belong to the same rock in which the *Schizopyga* occurs, the group having no resemblance to that of Estrella, or other localities referred to in this paper.

Mya? subsinuata (Pl. II, fig. 5).—Somewhat sinuous, ovate, slightly reflected at both ends; contracted medially or from beak to base.

Locality, Monterey County, Cal.

---

[a] Pacific R. R. Repts., vol. 6, pt. 2, No. 2, 1857, pp. 69-73.

176

ARCOPAGIA Leach.

Arcopagia medialis (Pl. II, fig. 6).—Oval, both valves slightly ventricose anteriorly; upper valve much contracted or concave toward the umbonal slope, which is angulated; postumbonal slope slightly contracted in the middle, emarginate at base; the corresponding slope of the lower valve deeply folded, reflected toward the extremity; disks rugoso-striate concentrically.—Proceedings Acad. Nat. Sci., December, 1856, p. 314.

Locality, Monterey County, Cal.; A. S. Taylor.

TAPES Sowerby.

Tapes linteatum (Pl. II, fig. 7).—Oblong-oval, ventricose; buccal side short, extremity obtusely rounded; anal side elongated, end regularly rounded; ligament margin long, oblique, straight, disks radiated with fine, unequal lines, except on the postumbonal slope, which is entire.—Proceedings Acad. Nat. Sci., December, 1856, p. 314.

Locality, California; Doctor Newberry.

ARCA Lin.

1. *Arca canalis* (Pl. II, fig. 8).—Subtrapezoidal, ventricose; ribs 24–26, flattened, scarcely prominent, divided by a longitudinal furrow; disk concentrically wrinkled; umbo ventricose; summits prominent, remote from the center.—Proceedings Acad. Nat. Sciences, December, 1856, p. 314.

Locality, Santa Barbara, Cal.; Doctor Newberry.

2. *Arca trilineata* (Pl. II. fig. 9).—Trapezoidal, somewhat produced, inequilateral, ventricose; ribs 22–24, scarcely prominent, square, wider than the intervening spaces, ornamented with three impressed or four raised lines; disks concentrically wrinkled; summits prominent; beaks approximate. Length 3 inches.—Proceedings Acad. Nat. Sciences, December, 1856, p. 314.

Locality, occurs with the preceding.

3. *Arca congesta* (Pl. II, fig. 10).—Rhomboidal, ventricose, inequilateral; ribs about 27, convex [page 71] on the back, wider than the intervals, which are transversely striate; anterior ribs crenate; ligament margin elevated; posterior end obtusely rounded; summits prominent. Length, five-eighths inch.—Proceedings Acad. Nat. Sciences, December, 1856, p. 314.

Locality, California; Doctor Newberry.

AXINÆA Poli. PECTUNCULUS Lam.

Axinæa barbarensis (Pl. III, fig. 11).—Lentiform, subequilateral, concentrically wrinkled; ribs about 37, scarcely prominent, flat, defined by an impressed line, wanting on the submargins and obsolete toward the base; summits slightly prominent.

MULINIA Gray.

M. densata (Pl. III, fig. 12).—Subovate, ventricose, thick, very inequilateral; posterior side very short comparatively, contracted; extremity subtruncated, much above the line of the base; posterior basal margin very oblique and contracted; anterior end obliquely truncated; anterior basal margin rounded; summits prominent, distant; lateral teeth very robust and prominent; inner margin entire.—Proceedings Acad. Nat. Sciences, December, 1856, p. 313.

Locality, Santa Barbara and shores of San Pablo Bay?, California; Doctor Newberry.

DOSINIA Scopoli.

1. *Dosinia longula*.—Regularly ventricose, inequilateral, longitudinally oval; margins and base regularly rounded; summits prominent; buccal margin more obtusely rounded than the anal.—Proceedings Acad. Nat. Sciences, December, 1856, p. 315.

Locality, Monterey, Cal.; Doctor Newberry.

2. *Dosinia alta* (Pl. III, figs. 13a and 13b).—Obtusely subovate or suboval from beak to base; posterior margin curved, profoundly oblique; base regularly and rather acutely rounded; summits prominent, oblique; surface marked with numerous fine, concentric, impressed lines; beaks medial. Height 4 inches.—Proceedings Acad. Nat. Sciences, December, 1856, p. 315.

Locality, Monterey, Cal.; Doctor Newberry.

PECTEN Lin.

Pecten pabloensis (Pl. III, fig. 14).—Orbicular, compressed, thin, concentrically wrinkled; ribs 18–20, slender; little prominent, with an intermediate radiating line.

Locality, San Pablo Bay, California; Doctor Newberry.

PALLIUM Klein.

P. estrellanum (Pl. III, fig. 15).—Suborbicular; lower valve ventricose, slightly undulated; ribs 17, broad, little prominent, convex, with an intermediate linear rib, from which the larger ribs are separated by an impressed line; upper valve convex, somewhat undulated, ribs flattened, and the intermediate small ribs with a longitudinal impressed line on the lower part of the valve.—Proceedings Acad. Nat. Sciences, December, 1856, p. 313.

Locality, Estrella Valley, California; Doctor Newberry.

JANIRA Schum.

Janira bella (Pl. III, fig. 16).—Subtriangular; inferior valve convex, ribs 14 or 15, square, about as wide as the intervening spaces, very prominent, some of them with one or two longitudinal obsolete lines; disk finely wrinkled concentrically; upper valve flattened, deeply [page 72] depressed toward the apex; ribs rather narrower than those of the opposite valve, obscurely bicarinated above, disk ornamented with close, fine, squamose, concentric wrinkles.   Length, 4 inches; height, 3¼ inches.—Proceedings Acad. Nat. Sciences, December, 1856, p. 312.

Locality, Santa Barbara, Cal.; Doctor Newberry.

OSTREA Linn.

Ostrea titan (Pl. IV, fig. 17; Pl. V, fig. 17a, profile).—Produced from beak to base, straight or slightly curved, substance very thick, coarsely laminated; upper valve flat, very thick, somewhat gibbous; lower valve profoundly ventricose, umbonated, the summit rising above the beak of the opposite valve. Length, ——.—Proceedings Acad. Nat. Sciences, 1855.

Locality, San Luis Obispo, Cal.

FOSSILS OF GATUN, ISTHMUS OF DARIEN.

MALEA Valenc.

Malea ringens (Pl. V, fig. 22).

Dolium ringens (Cassis) Swainson.

Locality, Gatun.   This shell inhabits the Pacific coast of South America, and the genus is unknown in the Atlantic.

TURRITELLA Lam.

1. *Turritella altilira* (Pl. V, fig. 19).—Subulate, carinated; volutions with two distant, elevated, revolving, crenulated ribs, interstices with revolving lines; body volutions bicarinated at the angle.

Locality, Gatun; Doctor Newberry.

2. *Turritella gatunensis* (Pl. V, fig. 20).—Subulate; volutions each with two slightly concave spaces; body volution ventricose, much larger than the penultimate, having about 20 revolving lines, seven or eight of which are on the base, which is flattened; three lines on the body volution larger than the others, the two lower ones remote.

Locality, occurs with the preceding.

TRITON Lam.

An imperfect cast of an unknown species occurs with the preceding.

I have compared the above three univalves with what recent species and figures I have access to, and can not identify them; but if they should be representatives of existing shells they will doubtless prove to be inhabitants of the Pacific coast, of the Isthmus, or of South America.

CYTHEREA? Lam.

Cytherea? (*Meretrix*) *dariena?* (pl. V, fig. 21).—*Meretrix dariena* Con., Desc. of Foss. and shells collected in California by William P. Blake, p. 18.   I have referred this shell to *Cytherea*, as it is probable that *Venus meretrix* may prove the type of a genus distinct from *Cytherea*.

TAMIOSOMA Conrad.

An elongated tube, apparently entire, porous and cellular throughout its substance; interior filled with numerous irregularly disposed vaulted cells connected by longitudinal slender tubes, funnel-shaped beneath; aperture resembling that of *Balanus.*

Tamiosoma gregaria (Pl. IV, fig. 18).—Subquadrangular, elongated, longitudinally furrowed [page 73] and striate, and having fine, undulated, transverse lines; mouth small, oblique; upper part of the tube oblique, deeply indented or balaniform, and coarsely striated longitudinally.   Length 8 inches.

Locality, Monterey County, Cal.; A. S. Taylor.

Growing in clusters like Balani.   No sutures, indicating separate valves; cells very thin plates, convex surface downward.

PANDORA Lam.

Pandora bilirata (Pl. V, fig. 25) Conrad, Proceed. Acad. Nat. Sciences for 1855, vol. vii, p. 267.
Locality, Santa Barbara, Cal.

CARDITA Brug.

Cardita occidentalis (Pl. V, fig. 24), Ib.
Locality, Santa Barbara, Cal.

DIADORA.

Diadora crucibuliformis (Pl. V, fig. 23), Ib.
Locality, Santa Barbara, Cal.

APPENDIX X.

REPORT ON THE PALEONTOLOGY OF THE SURVEY.[a]

By T. A. CONRAD.

[page 189] DEAR SIR: Accompanying this is the description of the fossils collected by you in south ern California.

In the Proceedings of the Academy of Natural Sciences for 1855, page 441, I have remarked that the Miocene of Santa Barbara contains a group of shells more analogous to the fossils of the Atlantic slope than to the existing shells of California; but it is evident, from the specimens in your collection, that there must be subdivisions in those Tertiary deposits of California which range between the Eocene and Pleiocene periods, for the group of the Estrella Valley and Santa Ynez (Barbara) Mountains does not appear to contain one species, even, analogous to any in the Santa Barbara beds, and, on the contrary, some of them remind us of the existing Pacific fauna. Thus *Dosinia alta* is closely allied to *D. simplex*, *Hinnites crassa* related to *Hinnites gigantea*. *Pachydesma* and *Crytomya* [*Cryptomya*] are existing California genera, represented in the Miocene, and which do not occur in the Atlantic. I think it probable that the Estrella group 'may prove to be of later origin than that of Santa Barbara. There is another at San Diego, of which I have seen but a few specimens, and can not yet determine its relation to the other groups. In referring these fossils to the Miocene group, it is not with the understanding that they are exactly parallel with European or even Virginian Miocene strata, but that they are unquestionably situated between the Eocene and newer Pliocene, containing no species analogous to the former, which is admirably characterized in California by its general forms, and even by a few well-known Claiborne species. Like the Miocene of Virginia, the *Estrella* group is characterized by large and even comparatively gigantic species of Pectinidæ, so unlike any living on the coasts of California or the Atlantic States. It would seem that this family then reached their maximum of development and the genus *Pallium* was first introduced, and of far larger size than any which now exist. It is worthy of remark that the generic character is developed on a far grander scale than appears in subsequent epochs, the prominent teeth and thick hinge reminding us of the genus *Spondylus*.

Every new collection of Miocene fossils shows more clearly the connection between some of the Tertiary strata of California and those of Virginia. The species in the present collection are far more interesting than any others of the same formation on the Pacific slope which I have yet seen. It does not appear that this group of fossils has any living representative in the present fauna of the Pacific coast, but several of them approximate to extinct Virginia species; and I am not sure that the large *Pecten magnolia*, herein described, is not identical with the Virginia species *P. jeffersonius*. I think it may safely be assumed that the San Rafael Hills, Santa Ynez Mountains, and Estrella Valley contain strata which are parallel to the Miocene sands and clays of the James and York rivers, in Virginia. No doubt there are groups of different geological age, as the species vary greatly in different localities; but in your collection I find not one Eocene species, and none more recent than the Miocene, except the few shells collected from the [page 190] coast deposits, consisting of recent species, among which I recognize *Pachydesma crassatelloides* Con., *Venus nuttali*, *Saxidomus nuttali*, and other species which live in the same latitude. This is most likely a recent, or post-Pliocene formation. It occurs in the valley of San Luis Obispo and at Santa Barbara.

[a] Pacific R. R. Repts., vol. 7, 1857, pp. 189-196. This report is addressed to Thomas Antisell, M. D., geologist of the expedition.

The large pectens, so like to Virginia species to which I have alluded, suggest the probability that large species of *Busycon* may yet be found in California. If so, it will be very interesting to compare them with the eastern forms.

I have no doubt but that the Atlantic and Pacific oceans were connected at the Eocene period; and the fossils herein described afford strong evidence that the connection existed during the Miocene period.

Of the Miocene shells collected by Mr. Blake in California, and described by me, I believe that no species, except *Pecten deserti*, and perhaps *Anomia subcostata*, is to be found in the present collection.

Yours, etc.,

T. A. CONRAD.

Doctor ANTISELL.

HINNITES Defrance.

Hinnites crassa (pl. 1,[a] figs. 1 and 2).—Ovate or subovate, thick, irregular, with large, rounded, unequal, radiating, irregular ribs, squamose, and with foliated spines on the lower part of the valves or near the base; intervals of the ribs with three or four squamose, prominent lines; hinge profoundly thickened; fosset profoundly excavated, angular; muscular impression very large.

Locality, Santa Margarita, Salinas Valley.

This species is remarkable for the thickness of the hinge and the upper part of the valves in old specimens. It resembles the recent California species *H. gigantea* Gray; and it probably attains a larger size than the latter.

PECTEN Lin.

Pecten meekii (pl. 1, fig. 1).—Suborbicular, compressed; ribs about 19; lower valve convex, with broad ribs, not very prominent, convex depressed on the back, angulated on the sides, about as wide as the intervening spaces, and scarcely prominent at the base; upper valve convex depressed, with narrower and less prominent ribs, ears equal, moderate in size.

Locality, San Rafael Hills, California.

Named in honor of F. B. Meek. A very large species, comparable to *P. jeffersonius* in size, but very distinct from all of the large pectens of the Atlantic States. The upper valve is nearly flat, and both are thin for so large a shell.

Pecten deserti Conrad (Blake's collection, desc. p. 15).—Suborbicular, both valves convex; ribs about 23, rounded, somewhat flattened toward the base, about as wide as the interstices, in the lower valve much wider than the interstices, and the valve more convex than the opposite one; ears equal in the upper valve; left ear of lower valve extended downward, and very obliquely striated; cartilage pit profound; a submarginal channel parallel with the upper margin.

Locality, Carrizo Creek, Colorado Desert; Carrizo Creek of Estrella River.

Pecten discus (pl. 3, fig. 1).—Suborbicular, slightly oblique, profoundly compressed or dis- [page 191[coidal, thin; ribs about 17, rather distant, not very prominent, narrow, subtriangular, slender, and more distant toward the lateral margins; ears very unequal, rather small.

Locality, between La Purisima and Santa Ynez.

This species is described from a cast beautifully preserved in indurated clay. The height is about 2 inches. The upper valve appears to have been nearly flat.

Pecten magnolia (pl. 1, fig. 2).—Suborbicular, ribs 11, very large, prominent, convex-depressed on the back, laterally angulated, longitudinally rugoso-striate.

Locality, Santa Ynez Mountains, Santa Barbara County, Cal.

This species will compare in size with *P. jeffersonius* Say, and is so remarkably similar to it that it may prove to be the same species when more perfect specimens are collected.

Pecten altiplicatus (pl. 3, fig. 2).—Obtusely ovate, thin; ribs squamose, slender, nine of them distant, profoundly elevated, an intermediate small rib and fine radiating striæ, ears ——.

Locality, San Rafael Hills, Santa Barbara County.

There is but one imperfect valve of this species in the present collection. It is remarkable for the great prominence of its larger ribs. Height 2½ inches.

---

[a] Err. typ. for Plate II.

PALLIUM Conrad.

Pallium estrellanum (pl. 3, figs. 3 and 4).—Suborbicular; lower valve ventricose; ribs about 17, broad, flattened, not very prominent, with an intermediate small rib, longitudinal, sulcated below the umbo or bilinear; ears rather small, equal, with five or six radiating prominent rugose lines. Height 4 inches.

Locality, Estrella, Cal.

The flat valve of this species does not accompany the specimen of the other valve. The shell attains a larger size than any fossil *Janira* (which it resembles) I have heretofore seen. The hinge is furnished with six distant diverging prominent teeth, and presents a marked contrast to that of the genus *Pecten*, more nearly resembling the hinge of *Spondylus*. The specimens are imperfect and worn, but there are indications on one or two that the ribs were carinated or subcarinated on the margins. One small specimen has the ribs inferiorly ornamented with fine, rugose, prominent transverse lines, and each rib with three longitudinal prominent striæ, and is also striated longitudinally.

This genus originated in the Miocene period, and there it attained its maximum in size and prominence of the generic character. *Hinnites* also and *Pecten* have similar gigantic proportions in the strata, which I have considered the equivalents of the English Miocene, and which certainly occupy a stratigraphical position immediately above the Eocene formation.

SPONDYLUS Bond. Lam

Spondylus estrellanus (pl. 1, fig. 3).—Obtusely ovate, both valves ventricose; ribs about 17, not very prominent, rounded, rugose, interstices convex-depressed; valves with radiating striæ, distinct about the base, obsolete above; posterior side subcuniform; cardinal area narrow.

Locality, Estrella Valley, California.

This species has thick valves, is about 4 inches in height, and has entire or unarmed ribs; the ears are broken, but they are apparently very unequal, and the beaks are not very distant. The lateral tubercles or teeth of the hinge are prominent, conical, and very robust. In some specimens the radiating striæ are very distinct near the posterior margin.

[page 192]   ### TAPES? Mühlf.

Tapes montana (pl. 5, figs. 3 and 5).—Suboval, ventricose, very inequilateral; posterior margin very oblique and rounded, end obtusely rounded; basal margin slightly contracted medially; disk with concentric impressed lines.

Locality, San Buenaventura.

Tapes inezensis (pl. 7, fig. 1).—Less ventricose than the preceding, with a rounded base, and prominent concentric lines.

Locality, Santa Ynez Mountains.

VENUS Lin.

Venus pajaroana (pl. 4, figs. 1 and 2).—Obliquely ovate-obtuse, ventricose, very inequilateral, anterior margin obtusely rounded, posterior side subcuniform; posterior end truncated obliquely inward.

Locality, Pajaro River, Santa Cruz.

ARCOPAGIA Brown.

Arcopagia unda (pl. 4, figs. 3 and 4).—Subtriangular; right valve profoundly ventricose anteriorly; profoundly sinuous posteriorly, or contracted from beak to beak; anterior end regularly and obtusely rounded; beaks nearly central; valves rugose-striate concentrically.

Locality, shore of Santa Barbara County, Cal.

This species is described from one imperfect valve, which resembles *A. biplicata* Con. It is somewhat larger than that species, has a much larger umbo, is less curved, being almost straight. In the same rock is a cast of a bivalve resembling a shell I have described under the name of *Carditamon [a] carinata*. There is in the collection another cast of this shell in limestone, from Estrella.

CYCLAS Klein.   LUCINA Lam.

Cyclas permacra (pl. 7, fig. 4).—Compressed, inequilateral, concentrically rugose-striate, striæ distinct and acute.

Locality, Sierra Monica.

[a] Err. typ. for *Carditamera*.

The specimen described is imperfect. It somewhat resembles *C. pandata* Con. (*Lucina compressa* Lea), but differs in having prominent lines.

Cyclas estrellana (pl. 6, fig. 6).—Suboval, inequilaterally ventricose; valves extremely thick; surface with concentric lines, probably mere lines of growth on the middle, but prominent and robust anteriorly. Locality, Estrella.

Length, 3¼ inches. A broken cast, with a large portion of the shell of the left valve crystallized, and exhibiting a remarkable thickness over the umbo.

ARCA Lin.

Arca obispoana (pl. 5, fig. 1).—Oblong, or trapezoidal; very inequilateral, ventricose; ribs about 26, little prominent, flattened; sides rectangular with the back; transversely rugose, or subcrenulated. Locality, San Luis Obispo Valley, California.

This species has been described from very perfect casts in an argillaceous gray marl.

[page 193]

PACHYDESMA Conrad.

Pachydesma inezana (pl. 5, figs. 2 and 4).—Triangular, equilateral, convex; anterior and posterior margins equally oblique; anterior extremity rounded; posterior extremity acutely rounded, posterior side subcuneiform; cardinal and lateral teeth robust. Locality, Santa Ynez Mountains, Santa Barbara County, Cal.

This species is smaller than *P. crassatelloides* Con.; proportionally shorter, with straighter lateral outlines, more robust teeth, and a broader cardinal plate. It is the first fossil species of the genus that I have seen. The only recent species inhabits the coast of California. Length, 3 inches.

CRASSATELLA Lam.

Crassatella collina (pl. 6, figs. 1 and 2).—Triangular, inequilateral, ventricose, thick; anterior and posterior margins very oblique, and nearly equal in slope—the anterior a little incurved, the posterior straight or a little sinous; umbo contracted or laterally compressed and triangular; summit prominent; posterior side cuneiform. Locality, Santa Ynez Mountains.

A fragment of one valve, the lower portion wanting. Length, 1¾ inches.

OSTREA Lin.

Ostrea subjecta (pl. 2, fig. 3).—Very irregular, valves sometimes subplicated; cardinal area broad and carinated laterally; cartilage pit but slightly impressed. Locality, between Santa Clara River and Los Angeles Valley, on the Sierra Monica.

Height, 2 inches. (In pl. 2 this fossil is improperly included under the *O. panzana*.)

Ostrea panzana (pl. 2, fig. 4).—Ovate, thick, lower valve with a few lateral distant radiating plicæ; upper valve thick, concentrically undulated and rugose; hinge area wide and carinated on the margins. Localities, Panza and Estrella valleys.

Height, 2¾ inches. The hinge of this shell resembles that of the preceding; and, possibly, it may be the old shell of that species, the specimens of which, in the collection, are evidently all young shells. At Gaviote Pass specimens of *O. panzana* occur twice the size of those from the above localities.

DOSINIA Scopoli. ARTHEMIS[a] Poli.

Dosinia alta (pl. —, fig. —).—Obtusely subovate or suboval, slightly ventricose; elevated; posterior margin curved, profoundly oblique; base irregularly and profoundly rounded; summits prominent, acute; surface marked with numerous fine concentric impressed lines?, beaks medial. Locality, Salinas River, Monterey County, Cal.

There is but only one cast in the collection; portions of the shell remaining appear to have concentric sulci. It is quite an elevated species, occurring 4 inches in height at Hill's ranch, Salinas River. (The illustration of this specimen has been accidentally omitted.)

Dosinia longula (pl. 7, fig. 2).—Shell regularly ventricose, inequilateral, longitudinally oval, margins and base regularly rounded; summit prominent, anterior margin more obtusely rounded than the posterior. Locality, occurs with the preceding.

[page 194] Height, 1¾ inches; length, 1⅜ inches. A cast with a thin chalky coating of the shell, without a trace of external lines.

---

[a] Err. typ. for *Arthemis*.

Dosinia montana (pl. 6, fig. 4).—Suboval, inequilateral; length greater than height; convex; anterior margin regularly and obtusely rounded; posterior margin and base regularly rounded; disk concentrically sulcated; beaks.

Locality, occurs with the preceding.

Dosinia subobliqua (pl. 6, fig. 5).—Obtusely subovate, slightly oblique, convex; height exceeding the length; concentrically sulcated.

Locality, occurs with the preceding.

With these species of *Dosinia* occur a small *Venus*, a *Natica*, and *Pecten*, in limestone.

MYTILUS Lin.

Mytilus inezensis (pl. 8, figs. 2 and 3).—Subovate-oblong? ventricose anteriorly; compressed posteriorly; ribs radiating, numerous, bifurcated, and trifurcated near the inferior margins.

Localities, Santa Ynez Mountains and Santa Ynez River.

A few fragments of this species present the character of the ribs well defined, but the outline of the shell is uncertain.

LUTRARIA Lam.

Lutraria transmontana (pl. 5, fig. 6).—Longitudinally ovate-triangular, inequilateral, thin; anterior end and base regularly rounded; posterior side cuneiform, extremity rounded; summits prominent; surface concentrically indented or subplicated, umbonal region concentrically plicated; plicæ irregular.

Locality, Rancho Triumpho, Los Angeles.

This shell is allied to *L. papyria* Con., and is well preserved in a hard, dark-colored limestone. There is another specimen from the shore between San Luis and Santa Barbara.

AXINEA Sow. PECTUNCULUS Lam.

Axinea barbarensis (pl. 6, fig. 3).—Subglobose; equilateral; ribs about 35, little prominent, convex-depressed, interstices narrow, square.

Locality, occurs with the preceding.

Height, 1¼ inches.

MACTRA?

Mactra? gabiotensis (pl. 7, fig. 4).—Triangular, equilateral; anterior extremity acutely rounded; posterior extremity subangulated; umbonal slope carinated, slightly curved.

Locality, Gaviote Pass.

A cast about 1 inch long, associated with a species of *Mytilus* and *Infundibulum gabiotensis*[a]. It may belong to the genus *Schizodesma* Gray.

GLYCIMERIS Lam. PANOPÆA Menard.

Glycimeris estrellanus (pl. 7, fig. 5).—Oblong or inclined to be trapezoidal, ventricose, very inequilateral, irregularly plicated concentrically, plicæ more approximate and profound on the umbo, valves profoundly gaping posteriorly, margin obliquely truncated; ligament margin incurved, elevated posteriorly.

Locality, Panza and Estrella valleys.

A cast allied to *Panopæa reflexa* Say; length, 3 inches.

[page 195] ### PERNA Lam.

Perna montana (pl. —, fig. —).—Elevated, anterior margin nearly straight; hinge line slightly incurved.

Locality, San Buenaventura, Santa Barbara County.

An imperfect cast, about 4½ inches in height, allied to *P. maxillata*, of Virginia, from which it differs in having a straighter front and incurved cardinal margin. (Not illustrated.)

---

[a] This shell is subsequently described and figured under the name *Trochita costellata*.

UNIVALVES.

TROCHITA.

Trochita costellata (pl. 7, fig. 3).—Convex or convex-depressed; volutions 3½; suture distinct; surface irregular and marked by radiating interrupted ribs, which are obsolete or wanting above, and distinct, though little prominent, toward the periphery; apex not central and slightly prominent.

Locality, Gaviote Pass.

A cast in sandstone. There are two very perfect casts, one more elevated than the other, with a less distinct suture and radii.

TURRITELLA Lam.

Turritella inezana (pl. 8, fig. 4).—Subulate, thick; sides of volutions straight, with an obtuse carina on each side of the suture, and contiguous to it.

Locality, Santa Ynez Mountains.

A large species with the last volution 1¾ inches wide. The specimen is an imperfect cast with portions of the crystallized shell remaining. There are traces of two or three revolving lines on one of the volutions.

Turritella variata (pl. 8, fig. 5).—Subulate, volutions with straight sides, each with four to six revolving prominent ribs, body whorl with a broad furrow revolving above the angle of the base.

Locality, Santa Ynez Mountains.

A variable species; one specimen of which shows two revolving lines on the upper part of each whorl distant from three equidistant ribs beneath, all nearly or quite equal in size. Others have six unequal equidistant ribs but I believe the species is always excavated at base.

NATICA.

Natica inezana (pl. 10, figs. 5 and 6).—Subglobose; whorls five; spire prominent; volutions depressed or slightly channeled above, scalariform; umbilicus of ovata-acute outline, patulous toward the base.

Locality, Santa Ynez.

A large species, abundant, but the specimens are imperfect. Portions of the shell remain on the cast, and are crystallized. Height, 2¾ inches.

MULTIVALVES.

Balanus estrellanus (pl. 8, fig. 1).—Very large, subconical, not elevated; valves sculptured with close, undulated, or very irregular radiating lines.

Locality, Estrella.

Height about 2 inches; width, 2½ inches. A single specimen is in the collection, with its external characters almost obliterated.

[page 196]

ECHINODERM.

ASTRODAPSIS Conrad.

Astrodapsis antiselli (pl. 10, figs. 1 and 2).—Pentangular, suboval; disk with five broad angular profound depressions; ambulacra not greatly curved, open at the marginal extremities; apex central or subcentral, beneath flat, or slightly depressed, with five distinct furrows; anus submarginal.

Locality, Estrella.

Masses of limestone appear to be composed chiefly of the fragments of this species, and contain many entire, but apparently waterworn specimens. In this respect it resembles a Miocene rock on the Patuxent River, Maryland. Length, 1¾ inches.

Appendix XI.

DESCRIPTIONS OF NEW FOSSILS FROM THE TERTIARY FORMATION OF OREGON AND WASHINGTON TERRITORIES AND THE CRETACEOUS OF VANCOUVER ISLAND, COLLECTED BY DR. JOHN EVANS, UNITED STATES GEOLOGIST, UNDER INSTRUCTIONS FROM THE DEPARTMENT OF THE INTERIOR.[a]

By B. F. Shumard, M. D.

[page 120] **TERTIARY SPECIES.**

Lucina fibrosa Shumard.

Shell compressed, convex, inequilateral, length greater than the height; buccal margin obtusely subangulate above, obliquely subtruncate below; basal margin very slightly arched, or straight in the middle and rounded at the extremities; anal margin rounded; ligament margin straight in young specimens and gently arched in the adult; ligament impression lanceolate, deeply excavated, wrinkled, margined by a slightly elevated carina; beaks obtusely rounded, slightly elevated; surface with inequidistant concentric lines of growth, and a broad transverse fold in advance of the beaks. With a magnifier we can perceive close, fibrous, longitudinal striæ in the spaces between the concentric lines; these are quite irregular and frequently bifurcate. In old age the shell assumes a subquadrate form, and the basal margin is quite straight or even slightly concave.

Length, about 26 lines; height, 20 lines; thickness, 9 lines. There are fragments in the collection which show that this species considerably exceeds these proportions.

Formation and locality. – Obtained by Doctor Evans in dark argillaceous shale at Port Orford, Oregon Territory and at Davis's coal mine. The specimens under observation are crushed and distorted from pressure.

Corbula evansana Shumard.

Shell subtrigonal, gibbous, slightly inequivalve, inequilateral, length greater than the height; buccal margin short, rounded; anal end oblique, prolonged, somewhat rostrate, obliquely truncated at the extremity; posterior slope forming nearly a right angle with the umbo. An elevated sharp carina extends from the beak of each valve to the posterior inferior extremity, and interior to this is a second carina, which is somewhat rounded and usually most distinct in the right valve; basal margin obtusely rounded, slightly produced near the middle, and in most specimens slightly contracted posteriorly; beaks flatten[page 121]ed near the anterior margin, convex, rather prominent, incurved; surface marked with fine, rather distinct, concentric striæ, and generally with several distinct folds. The cardinal tooth of the right valve is thick, trigonal, and placed under the beak nearest the buccal side, while the cavity for receiving the tooth of the opposite valve is triangular, deep, and situated directly under the beak. The substance of the shell is rather thick, and at the cardinal margin quite robust.

Length, 7½ lines; height, about 5 lines; thickness, 4½ lines. These proportions vary somewhat with the age of the shell.

Although the collection contains many specimens, not one of them retains its original form, all being more or less distorted from pressure.

[a] Trans. Acad. Sci. St. Louis, vol. 1, No. 2, 1858, pp. 120–123.

In a few specimens the posterior slope exhibits a double carina on only one of the valves and a single exterior one on the other, but generally there are two carinæ on each valve.

Our shell resembles *C. densata* (Conrad), from which it is distinguished by the double carina on the posterior side and its thinner valves.

Formation and locality.—This species is exceedingly abundant in the dark aluminous shale at Davis's coal mine, and at the coal mines of Port Orford, where it is associated with *Lucina fibrosa* and *Cerithium klamathensis*.

Leda willamettensis Shumard.

Shell small, oblong-ovate, convex, inequilateral; buccal margin gently arched, and forming with the cardinal margin nearly a right angle; anal side prolonged, rostrated, truncated at the extremity; basal margin slightly arched; cardinal border oblique in advance of the beak and slightly excavated behind; beaks submedial, not very prominent. The surface markings are entirely obliterated on the only specimen we have obtained of this species.

Formation and locality.—Occurs with *Lucina parilis* in dark-gray siliceous limestone, at Brooks's lime quarry, Willamette Valley, 5 miles north of Salem, Oregon Territory.

Leda oregona Shumard.

Compare *Leda (Nucula) impressa* (Conrad), in Geology of U. S. Exploring Expedition.

Shell rather large, ovate, compressed, convex; anterior extremity strongly arched; posterior extremity rostrate, slightly recurved, truncated; basal margin forming a broad curve, slightly contracted near the posterior extremity; ligament margin slightly concave; beaks situated a little in advance of the middle; surface neatly ornamented with regular, concentric, impressed lines, becoming more approximate above; [page 122] hinge with a line of closely set oblique teeth on each side of the beak.

Length, 20 lines; height, 10 lines.

The specimens in the collection were obtained by Doctor Evans and the writer, in the autumn of 1851, from the Willamette Valley, a few miles south of Oregon City, Oreg. They are all internal casts in fine-grained, soft, yellowish and white argillaceous sandstone of the Miocene epoch. Their surfaces are coated with a thin film of brown hydrated oxide of iron. One of the specimens, a mold of the exterior, shows the surface markings very plainly.

Pecten coosensis Shumard.

Shell large, suborbicular, much compressed; valves flattened convex, the superior one more depressed than the other; surface ornamented with from 27 to 31 coarse, radiating, prominent ribs, which are flattened, and marked with an obscure, median, longitudinal groove toward the palleal margin; on the inferior valve the ribs are about equal in width to the spaces, but on the superior one the spaces are much the widest; ribs and spaces crossed by numerous fine, subimbricating, concentric striæ of growth; ears nearly equal, those of superior valve marked with distinct striæ, and folds running parallel with their lateral borders; those on the anterior one are crossed by from six to eight indistinct, radiating ribs; anterior ear of lower valve deeply emarginate for the passage of the byssus, striated, and marked with three or four rather broad, radiating ribs; striæ of posterior ear nearly vertical; ligamentary pit triangular and rather deep.

Apicial angle, excluding the ears, 100°.

This species is subject to more or less variation. In some specimens we find the ribs of the middle of the shell bearing a longitudinal, slightly elevated, rounded carina, with a shallow groove on either side, while toward the lateral margins they are marked only with a single median groove. In other specimens the ribs exhibit merely a plain surface, without groove or carina.

Formation and locality.—This fine species Doctor Evans found in great profusion at the mouth of Coos Bay, in slightly coherent sandstone of the Miocene period.

Venus securis Shumard.

Shell large, ovate-subtrigonal, moderately convex, length a little greater than the height; basal margin and anterior extremity rounded; posterior extremity subangulated; buccal side very short, excavated under the beaks; posterior portion [page 123] long, angulated from beak to posterior inferior end;

corselet excavated superiorly, becoming nearly plane below, and forming almost a right angle with the umbonal region; ligament impression very deep and its edges strongly defined; lunule cordate, somewhat longer than wide, deeply impressed, and its edges strongly defined; beaks rounded, elevated incurved, situated nearest the anterior extremity; surface marked with subimbricating ribs and fine striæ, the ribs attenuated in front and posteriorly; on reaching the posterior angle they are suddenly directed obliquely upward over the corselet and reduced to fine imbricating striæ. The anterior muscular impression is rather large, broad ovate and distinct, the posterior one is shallow subovate, broadly rounded below, narrow and truncated above; palleal impression broad and distinctly impressed; sinus triangular, not deep.

When the exterior crust of the shell is removed, we find numerous radiating ribs extending from beak to base, crossed by very closely arranged concentric waved lines, and the whole surface presenting a remarkably elegant appearance.

The dimensions of a full-grown specimen are, for the length, $2\frac{2}{10}$ inches; height, $2\frac{3}{10}$ inches; thickness $1\frac{5}{10}$ inches.

Formation and locality.—Collected by Doctor Evans in gray, fine-grained sandstone of the Miocene age, at the mouth of Coos Bay, Cape Blanco, and on the shores of the Columbia a short distance above Astoria, Oreg. At all of these localities it is quite common.

Appendix XII.

ON THE PLEISTOCENE FOSSILS COLLECTED BY COL. E. JEWETT AT SANTA BARBARA, CAL., WITH DESCRIPTIONS OF NEW SPECIES.[a]

By Philip P. Carpenter, B. A., Ph. D.

The study of the recent and Tertiary mollusks of the west coast of America is peculiarly interesting and instructive, for the following reasons. It is the largest unbroken line of coast in the world, extending from 60° N. to 55° S., without any material salience except the promontory of Lower California. Being flanked by an almost continuous series of mountain ranges, the highest in the New World, it might reasonably be supposed that the coast line had been separated from the Atlantic from remote ages. The almost entire dissimilarity of its faunas from those of the Pacific Islands, from which it is separated by an immense breadth of deep ocean from north to south, marks it out as containing the most isolated of all existing groups of species, both in its tropical and its temperate regions. When we go back in time, we are struck by the entire absence of anything like the boreal drift, which has left its ice scratchings and arctic shells over so large a portion of the remaining temperate regions of the northern hemisphere, and also by the very limited remains of what can fairly be assigned to the Eocene age. The great bulk of the land on the Pacific slope of North America (so far as it is not of volcanic origin) appears to have been deposited during the Miocene epoch. Here and there only are found beds whose fossils agree in the main with those now living in the neighboring seas. To trace the correspondences and differences between these and their existing representatives may be expected to present results analogous to those now being worked out with such discerning accuracy from the various newer beds of modern Europe.

The first collection of Californian fossils seen in the east was made near Santa Barbara by Col. E. Jewett in 1849; but no account was published of them before the list in the British Association Report (1863), page 539. They consist of 46 species, of which 29 are known to be now living in the Californian seas, and others may yet be found there. The following 10 are Vancouver species, some of which may travel down to the northern part of California:

Margarita pupilla,
Galerus fastigiatus,
Bittium filosum,
Lacuna solidula,
Natica clausa,

Priene oregonensis,
Trophon orpheus,
Chrysodomus carinatus,
C. tabulatus, and
C. dirus.

Some of these are distinctly boreal shells, as are also *Crepidula grandis* (of which Colonel Jewett obtained a giant, 3½ inches long, and which now lives on a smaller scale in Kamtchatka) and *Trophon tenuisculptus* (whose relations will be presently pointed out). So far, then, we have a condition of things differing from that of the present seas, somewhat as the Red Crag differs from the Coralline. But in the very same bed (and the shells are in such beautiful condition that they all appear to have lived on the spot, which was perhaps suddenly caused to emerge by volcanic agency) are found not only tropical species which even yet struggle northward into the same latitudes (as *Chione succincta*), but also species now found only in southern regions, as *Cardium graniferum* and *Pecten floridus*. Besides these, the following, unknown except in this bed, are of a distinctly tropical type, viz:

Opalia var. insculpta.
Chrysallida sp.

Pisania fortis.

From a single collection made only at one spot, in a few weeks, and from the very fragmentary information to be derived from the collections of the Pacific railway surveys (described by Mr. Conrad,

[a] Ann. and Mag. Nat. Hist., 3d ser., vol. 17, April, 1866, pp. 274-278.

and tabulated in the Brit. Assoc. Report, 1863, pp. 589–596), it would be premature to draw inferences. We shall await with great interest the more complete account to be given by Mr. Gabb in the report of the California Geological Survey. With the greatest urbanity, that gentleman has sent his doubtful Pleistocene fossils to the writer, to be compared with the living fauna; but it would be unfair here to give any account of them, except that they confirm the foregoing statements in their general character.

The following are diagnoses of the new species in Colonel Jewett's collection.

TURRITELLA JEWETTII.

T. testa satis tereti, haud tenui, cinerea rufo-fusco tincta; anfr. subplanatis, suturis distinctis; lirulis distantibus (quarum t. jun. duæ extantiores) et striolis subobsoletis spiralibus cincta; basi parum angulata; apertura subquadrata; labro tenui, modice sinuato.

Hab.—Santa Barbara, Pleistocene formation (Jewett). San Diego, on beach (Cassidy).

This species comes nearest to *T. sanguinea* Rve., from the gulf, but differs in the faintness of the sculpture. Mr. Cassidy's specimens may be washed fossils, or very poor recent shells.

BITTIUM ?ASPERUM.

B. testa *B. quadrifilato* forma, magnitudine, et indole simili, sed sculptura intensiore; eodem vertice nucleoso abnormali; sed, vice filorum, costulis spiralibus costas spirales superantibus, subnodulosis; t. jun. costulis ii. anticis majoribus, alteris minimis; postea plerumque iv. subæqualibus, interdum iii. interdum aliis intercalantibus; sculptura basali intensiore; costis radiantibus subarcuatis.

?= *Turbonilla aspera* Gabb, in Proc. Acad. Nat. Sc. Philadelphia, 1861, p. 368.

Hab.—Santa Barbara, fossil in Pleistocene beds; abundant (Jewett). San Pedro, San Diego, Catalina Islands, 30–40 fms. (Cooper), State Col. No. 591 c.

Mr. Gabb informs me that his *Turbonilla aspera* is a *Bittium*. Unfortunately, the type is not accessible; and as the diagnosis would fit several closely allied species, it can not be said with precision to which it rightfully applies. As this is the commonest of the group, it is presumed that it is the "*Turbonilla*" intended. Should the type, however, be recovered, and prove distinct, this shell should take the name of *B. rugatum*, under which I wrote the diagnosis, and which was unfortunately printed in the Brit. Assoc. Report, p. 539. The fossil specimens are in much better condition than the recent shells as yet discovered.

BITTIUM ARMILLATUM.

B. testa *B. aspero* simili; anfr. nucl. ii. lævibus, tumentibus, vertice declivi, celato; dein anfr. ix. normalibus planatis, suturis impressis; t. adolescente seriebus nodulorum tribus spiralibus extantibus, supra costas instructis; costis radiantibus circ. xiii. fere parallelis, seriebus, a suturis separatis, spiram ascendentibus; t. adulta, costulis spiralibus, interdum iv., intercalantibus: costulis radiantibus creberrimis: costis suturalibus ii. validis, haud nodosis; basi effusa, liris circ. vi. ornata; apertura subquadrata; labro labioque tenuibus, columella vix torsa, effusa, vix emarginata.

Hab.—Santa Barbara, Pleistocene, 1 sp. (Jewett). San Pedro, San Diego (Cooper).

The sculpture resembles *Cerithiopsis*; but the columella is pinched, not notched.

OPALIA (?CRENATOIDES var.) INSCULPTA.

O. testa *O. crenatoidei* simili; sed costis radiantibus pluribus, xiii.–xvi., in spira validis; anfr. ult. obsoletis; sculptura spirali nulla: punctis suturalibus minus impressis, circa fasciam basalem lævem postice, non antice continuis.

Hab.—Santa Barbara, Pleistocene, 1 sp. (Jewett).

Very closely related to *O. crenatoides*, now living at Cape St. Lucas, and, with it, to the Portuguese *O. crenata*. It is quite possible that the three forms had a common origin.

TROPHON TENUISCULPTUS.

T. testa *T. barvicensi* simili, sed sculptura minus extante; vertice nucleoso minimo; anfractibus uno et dimidio lævibus, apice acuto; normalibus v., tumidis, postice subangulatis, suturis impressis;

costis radiantibus x.–xiv., plerumque xii., haud varicosis. angustis, obtusis; liris spiralibus majoribus, distantibus, quarum ii.–iii. in spira monstrantur, aliis intercalantibus, supra costas radiantes undatim transeuntibus; tota superficie lirulis incrementi, supra liras spirales squamosis, eleganter ornata; canali longiore, subrecta, vix clausa; labro acutiore, postice et intus incrassato, dentibus circ. v. munito; labio conspicuo, lævi: columella torsa.

Hab.—Santa Barbara, Pleistocene formation (Jewett).

This very elegant shell is like the least-sculptured forms of *T. barvicensis*, from which it appears to differ in its extremely small nucleus. It is very closely related to *T. fimbriatulus*, A. Ad., from Japan, but differs in texture, and is regarded by Mr. Adams as distinct. It stands on the confines of the genus, there being a slight columellar twist, as in *Peristernia*.

PISANIA FORTIS.

P. testa *P. insigni* simili, sed solidiore; crassissima, sculptura valde impressa; anfr. norm. v., parum rotundatis, suturis distinctis; costis radiantibus t. juniore circ. xii., obtusis, parum expressis, postea obsoletis; liris spiralibus validis, crebris (quarum t. juniore v., postea x., in spira monstrantur), subæqualibus, anticis majoribus; canali recurvata; lacuna umbilicali magna; labro intus crebrilirato; labio conspicuo, spiraliter rugose lirato.

Hab.—Santa Barbara, Pleistocene formation (Jewett).

Colonel Jewett's single specimen is in very fine condition, and is confirmed by a fragment obtained by Mr. Gabb, the palæontologist to the California State Survey. Although resembling *Purpura aperta* and congeners in the irregular rugose folds of the labium, and *Siphonalia* in the strongly bent canal, Mr. H. Adams considers that its affinities are closest with the *Cantharus* group of *Pisania*. That genus is extremely abundant in the tropical fauna, but does not now live in California. It is the only distinctly tropical shell in the whole collection; and its presence, along with so many boreal species and types, appears somewhat anomalous, like the appearance of *Voluta* and *Cassidaria* in the Crag fauna. It is distinguished from the extreme forms of *P. insignis* by having the spiral liræ pretty equally distributed over the early whorls, by the close internal ribbing of the labrum, by the absence of the stout posterior parietal tooth, and by the great development of the columellar folds.

—————

NOTE.—Unfortunately, during the long interval which has elapsed between the transmission of the MS. and receipt of the proof, the types have been returned to the owner, and (with the remainder of Colonel Jewett's invaluable collection of fossils) have become the property of a college in New York State. As they are packed in boxes, and at present inaccessible, I am unable to give the measurements; but the unique specimens were drawn on wood by Mr. Sowerby for the Smithsonian Institution.— P. P. C., Montreal, February 22, 1866.

MATERIAL TOWARD A BIBLIOGRAPHY OF PUBLICATIONS ON THE POST-EOCENE MARINE MOLLUSKS OF THE NORTHWEST COAST OF AMERICA, 1865–1908.

By William Healey Dall.

The present bibliography is intended to take the subject up where it was dropped by Dr. Philip P. Carpenter in 1864, when he concluded his supplementary report to the British Association, which was reprinted, with a short bibliography, as Smithsonian Miscellaneous Collections No. 252, in 1872.

It has been my object to include all papers published since 1865, bearing on the marine post-Eocene mollusks, whether recent or fossil. I have also included a full and exact reference to certain works issued before 1865, to which Doctor Carpenter did not refer, or to which his references were insufficiently exact.

No attempt has been made to include general monographs, or the like, where the references to western American forms are purely incidental; but a few monographic titles were inserted because they were for some reason exceptionally important for the fauna concerned. Some titles of papers on the tropical west-coast fauna, important for comparative purposes, have been included, though I have not attempted to make the bibliography complete for the Panaman or South American faunas.

When they could be procured, the full name and years of birth and death of the authors referred to precede the list given of their published papers on this region. I shall be glad to receive any additions or corrections to the data of this kind, or references to papers which should be inserted in the list.

(Anonymous.) Preliminary list of Mollusca, etc., of the Seattle district. Puget Sound. Young Naturalists' Association, Seattle, Wash., 4 pp., 8°, 1894.

Arnold, Delos (1830–   ). An interrogation regarding the fossil shells of San Pedro Bay. Nautilus, X, No. 3, pp. 33–34, July, 1896.

Arnold, Ralph (1875–   ). The paleontology and stratigraphy of the marine Pliocene and Pleistocene of San Pedro, Cal. Mem. California Acad. Sci., III, pp. 419, pls. 1–37, June 27, 1903. Also separately. The work includes a lengthy bibliography.

—— Bibliography of the literature referring to the geology of Washington. Washington Geol. Survey, I, Ann. Rept. for 1901, pt. 6, pp. 1–16, Olympia, 1902.

—— Faunal relations of the Carrizo Creek beds of California. Science, n. s., XIX, No. 482, March 25, 1904, p. 503.

—— Coal in Clallam County, Wash. Bull. U. S. Geol. Survey No. 260, pp. 413–421, 1905. Contains list of fossils.

PARTAGEZ LA JOIE

Merci d'avoir magasiné sur indigo.ca.

Recevez une boisson GRATUITE* à l'achat de toute boisson espresso artisanale Starbucks®

Profitez du temps des Fêtes pour partager des moments de bonheur avec ceux que vous aimez.

Du 11 novembre 2013 au 6 janvier 2014

MOKA À LA MENTHE POIVRÉE

LATTE AU CARAMEL BRÛLÉ

Présentez ce bon dans les cafés Starbucks des magasins Indigo et Chapters, ainsi que dans tout autre café Starbucks participant.

!ndigo | **Chapters** | **indigo.ca**

Barista : SVP entrez le code 815

*Achetez une boisson espresso Starbucks® à prix courant du format de votre choix et présentez ce bon pour en obtenir une gratuite de valeur égale ou inférieure. Limite d'un bon par client. Valeur en espèces de 0,01 $. Nul là où la loi l'interdit. Ce bon ne peut être jumelé à une autre offre ni à aucun autre rabais. Toute reproduction est interdite. Ne peut être transféré ou vendu. Bon valide du 11 novembre 2013 à 0 h 01 HNE au 6 janvier 2014 à 23 h 59 HNP pour échange dans les cafés Starbucks des magasins Indigo et Chapters ou tout autre café Starbucks participant du Canada. Indigo, Chapters et indigo.ca sont des marques de commerce d'Indigo Books & Music Inc.

SHARE JOY

Thanks for shopping at indigo.ca.

Purchase any handcrafted Starbucks® espresso beverage
and receive a FREE beverage* to give to a loved one.

'Tis the season to reconnect and share joy.

November 11, 2013 – January 6, 2014

CARAMEL BRÛLÉ
LATTE

PEPPERMINT
MOCHA

Present this coupon at any Starbucks store in Indigo
and Chapters and other participating Starbucks stores.

!ndigo | **Chapters** | **indigo.ca**

Barista: discount code 815

*Get any Starbucks® espresso beverage of any size for the regular price and receive one of equal of lesser value with coupon. Limit one coupon per customer. Cash value 0.01¢. Void where prohibited. Cannot be combined with other offer or discounts. Not valid if reproduced, transferred or sold. Offer valid for redemption at Starbucks stores located at Chapters and Indigo or any participating Starbucks stores in Canada from November 11, 2013 at 12:01am EST to January 6, 2014 at 11:59pm PST. Indigo, Chapters and indigo.ca are trade marks of Indigo Books & Music Inc.

TM/MC

ARNOLD, RALPH (1875–   ). The Tertiary and Quaternary pectens of California. U. S. Geological Survey, Professional Paper No. 47; Series C, No. 76. 53 pls., 2 text figs., 264 pp., 4°. Washington, Government Printing Office. 1906.

———— Geological reconnaissance of the coast of the Olympic Peninsula, Washington. Bull. Geol. Soc. America, XVII, 1906, pp. 451–468, pls. 55–58. Contains list of fossils.

———— New and characteristic species of fossil mollusks from the oil-bearing Tertiary formations of southern California. Proc. U. S. Nat. Mus., XXXII, 1907, No. 1545, pp. 525–546, pls. XXXVIII–LI.

———— Geology and oil resources of the Summerland district, Santa Barbara County, Cal. Bull. U. S. Geol. Survey No. 321, 1907, pp. 93, figs. 1–3, pls. I–XVII. Pls. IX–XVII are devoted to Tertiary fossils.

———— New and characteristic species of fossil mollusks from the oil-bearing Tertiary formations of Santa Barbara County, Cal. Smithsonian Misc. Coll. (quarterly issue), vol. 50, pt. 4, No. 1781, pp. 29, pls. L LVIII, December 13, 1907 (separately paginated).

———— and ANDERSON, ROBERT VAN VLECK (1884–   ). Geology and oil resources of the Santa Maria oil district, Santa Barbara County, Cal. Bull. U. S. Geol. Survey No. 322, 1907, pp. 161, pls. I–XXVI. Pls. XII–XXVI illustrate Tertiary fossils.

———— and ARNOLD, DELOS. The marine Pliocene and Pleistocene stratigraphy of the coast of southern California. Jour. Geology, X, No. 2, February–March, 1902, pp. 117–133, pls. I–IV, figs. 1–7, and correlation table.

———— *See also* Haehl, H. L., and Eldridge, G. H.

ASHLEY, GEORGE HALL. The Neocene of the Santa Cruz Mountains. I. Stratigraphy. Proc. California Acad. Sci., 2d ser., V, pp. 273–367, pls. 22–25, August, 1895. Reprint in Leland Stanford Junior University Pubs., Geol. and Pal., II, 1895.

AURIVILLIUS, CARL WILHELM SAMUEL (1854–1899). Öfversigt öfver de af Vega-expeditionen insamlade arktiska Hafsmollusker. II. Placophora och Gastropoda. Vega Exp. vetensk. arbeten, IV, pp. 313–383, taf. 12–13, 8°. 1885.

BAILY, JOSHUA L., jr. Shells of La Jolla, California. Nautilus, XXI, No. 8, pp. 92–93, December, 1907. Contains additions to the list given in the same periodical, from the same locality, by Maxwell Smith (q. v.).

BAIRD, WILLIAM (1803–1872). Description of some new species of shells collected at Vancouver Island and in British Columbia by J. K. Lord, esq., naturalist to the British North American Boundary Commission in the years 1858–1862. Proc. Zool. Soc. London for 1863, pp. 66–70 (no plate).

———— Descriptions of two species of shells collected by Doctor Lyall of H. M. ship *Plumper* at Vancouver Island. Proc. Zool. Soc. London for 1863, p. 71, May, 1863.

———— and LORD, J. K. Remarks on a species of shell belonging to the family Dentaliidæ, with notes on their use by the natives of Vancouver Island and British Columbia. Proc Zool. Soc. London for 1864, pp. 136–138.

BAKER, FREDERICK (1854–   ). Cruising and collecting on the coast of Lower California. Nautilus, XVI, No. 3, pp. 25–29, July, 1902.

———— List of shells collected on San Martin Island, Lower California, Mexico. Nautilus, XVI, No. 4, pp. 40–43, August, 1902.

BARTSCH, PAUL (1871–   ). New mollusks of the family Vitrinellidæ from the west coast of America. Proc. U. S. Nat. Mus., XXXII, No. 1520, pp. 167–176, figs. 1–11, 1907.

———— A new mollusk of the genus *Macromphalina* from the west coast of America. Proc. U. S. Nat. Mus., XXXII, No. 1522, p. 233, 1907.

———— A new parasitic mollusk of the genus *Eulima*. Proc. U. S. Nat. Mus., XXXII, No. 1548, pp. 555–556, pl. LIII, June 15, 1907.

———— New marine mollusks from the west coast of America. Proc. U. S. Nat. Mus., XXXIII, No. 1564, pp. 177–183, October 23, 1907.

BARTSCH, PAUL (1871–). West American mollusks of the genus *Triphoris*. Proc. U. S. Nat. Mus., XXXIII, No. 1569, pp. 249–262, pl. XVI, December 12, 1907.

BECK. *See* Zeck, M.

BERGH, LUDVIG SOPHUS RUDOLPH (1824–). On the nudibranchiate gasteropod Mollusca of the North Pacific Ocean, with special reference to those of Alaska. Proc. Acad. Nat. Sci. Philadelphia for 1879, pt. 1, pp. 71–132 (129–188), pls. 1–8, May 10, 1879; pt. 2, pp. 40–127 (189–276), pls. 9–16, January, 1880. Also separately as Articles V and VI of Scientific Results of the Exploration of Alaska, edited by W. H. Dall, 1879–1880.

—— Die Gruppe der Doridiiden. Mitth. aus der Zool. Stat. Neapel, XI, pp. 107–135, pl. 8, 1893. *D. purpureum* Bergh, Santa Catalina Islands.

—— Die Gattung Gastropteron. Zool. Jahrb., VII, pp. 281–308, pls. 16–17, December, 1893.

—— Reports on the dredging operations off the west coast of Central America (etc.), by the U. S. S. *Albatross* during 1891. XIII. Die Opisthobranchier. Bull. Mus. Comp. Zool., XXV, No. 10, pp. 125–233, pls. 1–12, October, 1894.

—— Die Opisthobranchier der Sammlung Plate. Zool. Jahrb., 1898, suppl. 4, heft 3, pp. 481–582, pls. 28–33.

—— Ergebnisse einer Reise nach dem Pacific (Schauinsland 1896–1897). Die Opisthobranchier. Zool. Jahrb., XIII, pp. 207–246, pls. 19–21, May 30, 1900.

BERNARD, FÉLIX ÉDOUARD (1863–1898). Anatomie de *Chlamydoconcha orcutti* Dall, lamellibranche à coquille interne. Annales des Sci. Nat., Zoologie, 8th ser., IV, pp. 221–252, pls. 1–2, 1897.

—— Études comparatives sur la coquille des lamellibranches. Les genres Philobrya et Hochstetteria. Jour. de Conchyl., XLV, No. 1, pp. 5–47, pl. 1, November, 1897.

BERRY, SAMUEL STILLMAN (1887–). Note on a new variety of *Cerithidea sacrata* Gould, from San Diego, Cal. Nautilus, XIX, No. 12, p. 133, fig., April, 1905.

—— Molluscan fauna of Monterey Bay, California. Nautilus, XXI, pp. 17–22, June, 1907; pp. 34–35, July, 1907; pp. 39–47, August, 1907; pp. 51–52, September, 1907.

—— *Murex carpenteri*, form *alba*. Nautilus, XXI, No. 9, pp. 105–106, January, 1908.

—— *See also* Dall, W. H.

BERTIN, VICTOR (1850–1880). Révision des Tellinidés. Nouv. Arch. du Muséum, Paris, 2d ser., I, pp. 201–361, pls. 8–9, 1878.

—— Révision des Donacidées du Muséum d'Histoire Naturelle. Nouv. Arch. du Mus., 2d ser., IV, pp. 57–121, pls. 3–4, 1881.

BLOOMER, HARRY HOWARD (1866–). The anatomy of certain species of *Siliqua* (*patula* Dixon) and *Ensis*. Proc. Malac. Soc. London, VI, No. 4, pp. 193–196, pl. 12, March, 1905.

BOYCE, SARAH ELIZABETH (1820–). *Cypræa spadicea*. Nautilus, IV, No. 6, p. 71, October, 1890.

BRADSHAW, Mrs. MARY F. *Haminea virescens*. Nautilus, VIII, No. 9, pp. 100–101, January, 1895.

—— *Megatebennus bimaculatus*. Nautilus, VIII, No. 10, pp. 112–113, February, 1895.

—— Extract from a notebook. Nautilus, X, No. 7, pp. 82–84, November, 1896.

—— Record of a lost year. Nautilus, XI, No. 9, p. 104, January, 1898.

—— Collecting at Laguna and Fishermans Bay, California. Nautilus, XII, No. 1, p. 9, May, 1898.

BÜLOW, C. Einige Seltenheiten, aus meiner Sammlung. Nachrichtsblatt der Deutschen malakozoologische Gesellschaft, XXXVII, p. 78, pls. I–11, 1905.

BURTON, VIRGINIA. Coffee-bean cowries of the California coast. Los Angeles Weekly Tribune, August 16, 1890.

BUSH, KATHARINE JEANNETTE (1855–). Revision of the marine gastropods referred to *Cyclostrema*. *Adeorbis*, *Vitrinella*, and related genera, with descriptions of some new genera and species belonging to the Atlantic fauna of America. Trans. Connecticut Acad. Sci., X, pp. 97–144, pls. 22, 23, July, 1897.

BUTTON, FRED LAWRENCE (1856–). List of Mollusca of the west coast of the United States, for exchange by Fred L. Button, etc., 4 pp., 8°, no date.

—— Note sur l'habitat du *Cypræa spadicea* Gray. Jour. de Conchyl., XXVI, p. 97, January, 1878.

BUTTON, FRED LAWRENCE (1856-   ).   West American Cypræidæ; with a prefatory note by L. St. G. Byne, M. Sc. Jour. Conch., X, pp. 254-258, October, 1902.

—— Note on *Trivia acutidentata* Gaskoin. Nautilus, XIX, No. 11, p. 132, March, 1906.

BYNE, LOFTUS ST. GEORGE. *See* Button, F. L.

CAMPBELL, JOHN H. (1847-1897). Mollusca of the United States; Haliotis. Nautilus, IV, No. 9, pp. 101-104, January, 1891.

CAMPBELL, Mrs. JULIA ELLA (1855-   ).   Marine shells on the southern California coast. Nautilus, X, No. 5, pp. 56-57, September, 1896.

—— Quaternary fossil shells, Long Beach, California. Nautilus, XII, No. 1, pp. 7-8, May, 1898.

CARPENTER, PHILIP PEARSALL (1819-1877). Notice of shells collected by Mr. J. Xantus at Cape St. Lucas. Proc. Acad. Nat. Sci. Philadelphia for 1859, pp. 321-322, 1860.

—— Lectures on shells from the Gulf of California. Smithsonian Institution, Ann. Rept. for 1860 pp. 195-218, 1861. Also separately.

—— Descriptions of new marine shells from the coast of California, I-III. I. Proc. California Acad. Nat. Sci., III, pp. 155-159, July, 1864; II, idem, pp. 175-177, December, 1864; III, idem, pp. 207-208, February, 1865; pp. 209-224, February, 1866. Also separately.

—— Contributions toward a monograph of the Pandoridæ. Proc. Zool. Soc. London for 1864, pp. 596-603, 1865.

—— On the connection between the Crag formations and the recent North Pacific faunas. Geol. Mag., II, No. 10, pp. 152-153, April, 1865.

—— Diagnoses specierum et varietatum novarum molluscorum prope sinum Pugetianum a Kennerlio Doctore, nuper decesso, collectorum. Proc. Acad. Nat. Sci. Philadelphia for 1865, pp. 54-56, April, 1865.

—— On the Acmæidæ of the Vancouver and Californian province. Am. Jour. Conch., II, pp. 332-348, October, 1866.

—— Catalogue of the family Pandoridæ. Am. Jour. Conch., IV, app., pp. 69-71, 1869.

—— The mollusks of Western North America, embracing the second report made to the British Association on this subject, with other papers; reprinted by permission, with a general index. Smithsonian Misc. Coll., X, No. 252, Washington. December, 1872; 8°; pp. xii, 325, and index pp. 13-121; the index covering all the papers, whether reprinted or not, mentioned in bibliography, pp. ix-xii.

COCKERELL, THEODORE DRU ALISON (1866-   ). Pigments of nudibranchiate Mollusca. Nature, XV, pp. 79-80, 1901.

—— Three new nudibranchs from California. Jour. Mal., VIII, pp. 85-87, September, 1901.

—— *Lucapina crenulata* Sowerby, *Navanax inermis* Cooper. Nautilus, XV, No. 6, pp. 71-72, October, 1901.

—— A new *Tethys* from California. Nautilus, XV, No. 8, pp. 90-91, December, 1901.

—— Notes on two California nudibranchs. Jour. Mal., VIII, pp. 121-122, December, 1901.

—— Three new species of *Chromodoris*. Nautilus, XVI, No. 2, pp. 19-20, June, 1902.

—— Note on *Tritonia palmeri* Cooper. 1862. Nautilus, XVI, No. 10, p. 117, February, 1903.

—— California nudibranchs. Nautilus, XVIII, No. 11, pp. 131-132, March, 1905.

—— Mollusca of La Jolla, California. Nautilus, XXI, No. 9, pp. 106-107, January, 1908.

—— and ELIOT, C. N. E. Notes on a collection of Californian nudibranchs. Jour. Mal., XII, No. 3, pp. 31-53, pl. 7-8, September, 1905.

CONRAD, TIMOTHY ABBOTT (1803-1877). Descriptions of new marine shells from Upper California, collected by Thomas Nuttall, esq. Jour. Acad. Nat. Sci. Philadelphia, VII, pp. 227-268, pls. 17-20, 1837.

—— Description of two new genera and new species of recent shells. Proc. Acad. Nat. Sci. Philadelphia, IV, p. 121, December, 1848.

CONRAD, TIMOTHY ABBOTT (1803–1877). Fossil shells from the Tertiary deposits on the Columbia River, near Astoria. Am. Jour. Sci., 2d ser., V, pp. 432–433, 15 cuts, 1848.

—— Descriptions of new fossil and recent shells of the United States. Jour. Acad. Nat. Sci. Philadelphia, n. s., I, pp. 207–209, August, 1849.

—— Notes on shells with descriptions of new genera and species. Jour. Acad. Nat. Sci. Philadelphia, n. s., I, pp. 210–214, 1849.

—— Descriptions of new fresh-water and marine shells. Proc. Acad. Nat. Sci. Philadelphia, IV, pp. 155–156, 1849.

—— Fossils from northwestern America; Mollusca. United States Exploring Expedition during the years 1838, 1839, 1840, 1841, and 1842, under the command of Charles Wilkes, U. S. N. Geology by James Dwight Dana. [4°], with a folio atlas of 21 plates. App. I, pp. 723–729, pls. 17–20. New York, G. P. Putnam, 1849.

—— Descriptions of new fresh-water and marine shells. Jour. Acad. Nat. Sci. Philadelphia, n. s., I, pp. 275–280, pl. 39, January, 1850.

—— Notes on shells, with descriptions of new species. Proc. Acad. Nat. Sci. Philadelphia, VI, pp. 199–200, 1852.

—— Descriptions of new fossil shells of the United States. Jour. Acad. Nat. Sci. Philadelphia, n. s., II, pt. 3, p. 273, January, 1853.

—— Synopsis of the genus *Parapholas* and *Penicilla* (=*Penitella*). Jour. Acad. Nat. Sci. Philadelphia, n. s., II, p. 355, February, 1854.

—— Notes on shells, with descriptions of three recent and one fossil species. Proc. Acad. Nat. Sci. Philadelphia, VII, pp. 31–32, 1854.

—— Note on the Miocene and post-Pliocene deposits of California, with descriptions of two new fossil corals. Proc. Acad. Nat. Sci. Philadelphia, VII, p. 441, 1855.

—— Report on the fossil shells collected in California by W. P. Blake, geologist of the expedition under the command of Lieut. R. S. Williamson, U. S. Topographical Engineers, 1852. 20 pp. 8°. 1855. In Description of the fossils and shells collected in California by W. P. Blake (etc.). Appendix, art. 1, pp. 5–20. House Doc. 129, July, 1855.

—— Descriptions of eighteen new Cretaceous and Tertiary fossils. Proc. Acad. Nat. Sci. Philadelphia for 1855, VII, pp. 265–268.

—— Descriptions of the fossil shells. Pacific R. R. Repts., V, pt. 2, app., pp. 322–329, pls. 2–9, 1856.

—— Descriptions of three new genera, twenty-three new species of middle Tertiary fossils from California, and one from Texas. Proc. Acad. Nat. Sci. Philadelphia for 1856, VIII, pp. 312–316, 1857.

—— Description of the Tertiary fossils collected on the survey. Pacific R. R. Repts., VI, pt. 2, No. 2, pp. 69–73, pls. 2–5, 1857. Appendix to report of Dr. J. S. Newberry.

—— Report on the paleontology of the survey. Pacific R. R. Repts., VII, pp. 189–196, pls. 1–10, 1857. Appendix to report of Thomas Antisell.

—— Descriptions of new genera, subgenera, and species of Tertiary and recent shells. Proc. Acad. Nat. Sci. Philadelphia, 2d ser., VI, pp. 284–291, 1862.

—— Catalogue of the older Eocene shells of Oregon. Am. Jour. Conch., I, pp. 150–154, 1865. The fossils are really Oligocene and Miocene.

—— Paleontological miscellanies. Am. Jour. Conch., III, pp. 5–7, 1867.

—— Description of new genera of fossil shells. Am. Jour. Conch., III, pp. 8–16, 1867.

—— Descriptions of new west coast shells. Am. Jour. Conch., III, pp. 192–193, September, 1867; p. 335, April, 1868.

—— Note on a cirripede of the California Miocene, with remarks on fossil shells. Proc. Acad. Nat. Sci. Philadelphia, 3d ser., VI, pp. 273–275, 1876; cf. also Am. Jour. Sci., 3d ser., XIII, pp. 156–157, 1877.

COOPER, JAMES GRAHAM (1831–1902). Report upon the Mollusca by William Cooper, with notes by J. G. Cooper. Pacific R. R. Repts., XII, pt. 2, pp. 369–386, 1860; also in The Natural History of Washington Territory, by J. G. Cooper and George Suckley, pp. xiv, 497, 4°. New York, 1859.

COOPER, JAMES GRAHAM (1831-1902). On some new genera and species of California Mollusca. Proc. California Acad. Nat. Sci., II, pp. 202-207, 1863.

—— *Strategus* (preoccupied) changed to *Navarchus* Cooper. Proc. California Acad. Nat. Sci., III, p. 8, 1863. *See also* Pilsbry, H. A.

—— On new or rare Mollusca inhabitating the coast of California. Proc. California Acad. Nat. Sci., III, pp. 56-60, fig. 14, 1863.

—— Geographical catalogue of the Mollusca found west of the Rocky Mountains between 33° and 49° north latitude. Geol. Survey of California. 40 pp., 4°. San Francisco, 1867.

—— Notes on Mollusca of Monterey Bay, California. Am. Jour. Conch., VI, pp. 42-70, 1870.

—— Note on *Gadinia* and *Rowellia*. Am. Jour. Conch., VI, pp. 319-320, 1871.

—— Note on *Waldheimia pulvinata* Gould. Am. Jour. Conch., VI, p. 320, 1871.

—— Additions and corrections to the catalogue of Monterey Mollusca. Am. Jour. Conch., VI, pp. 321-322, 1871.

—— Catalogue of California fossils, I-V. Seventh Ann. Rept. State Mining Bureau, pp. 221-308, 1888. See also Bull. No. 4, California State Mining Bureau, pp. 65, pls. 1-6, 1894. Contains a very imperfect bibliography.

—— Pacific coast oysters. Overland Monthly, XXXIII, 2d ser., pp. 648-660, San Francisco, June, 1894.

—— On some Pliocene fresh-water fossils of California. Proc. California Acad. Sci., 2d ser., IV, pp. 166-172, pl. 14, 1894.

—— Catalogue of west North American and many foreign shells, with their geographical ranges. For labels, exchange and check lists, with a supplement. Printed for the State Mining Bureau, April, 1894, 4°. No pagination, and sheets printed on one side only. Sacramento, State Printer, 1894.

—— Lists of fossils from the oil-bearing formations of California. Bull. California State Mining Bureau, No. 3, pp. 7. 10, 25, 38-40, 43, 49. 53-59, 62-65. Sacramento, State Printer, 1894. 8°. *See also* Wall, W. L.

—— Catalogue of marine shells collected chiefly on the eastern shore of Lower California, for the California Academy of Sciences during 1891-92. Proc. California Acad. Sci., 2d ser., V, pp. 34-48, 1895.

—— Lists of fossils from the oil-bearing formations of California. Bull. California State Mining Bureau for 1897, pp. 79-87. Sacramento, State Printer, 1897. *See also* Wall, W. L.

COOPER, WILLIAM (1798-1864). *See* COOPER, J. G., 1859.

CROSSE, JOSEPH CHARLES HIPPOLYTE (1826-1898). Catalogue des mollusques qui vivent dans le détroit de Behring et dans les parties voisines de l'Océan Arctique. Jour. de Conchyl., XXV, pp. 101-128, April, 1877.

DALL, WILLIAM HEALEY (1845-   ). Conchological notes: I. Note on *Octopus punctatus* Gabb. Proc. California Acad. Sci., III, pp. 243-244, 1866.

—— Materials for a monograph of the family Lepetidæ. Am. Jour. Conch., V, pp. 140-150, pl. 15, 1869.

—— On the natural history of Alaska. Proc. Boston Soc. Nat. Hist., XII, pp. 136-138, 143-145, 164, 171, 1869.

—— Materials toward a monograph of the family Gadiniidæ. Am. Jour. Conch., VI, pp. 8-22, pls. 2-4, 1870.

—— Remarks on the anatomy of the genus *Siphonaria*, with a description of a new species. Am. Jour. Conch., VI, pp. 30-41, pls. 4-5, 1870.

—— A revision of the Terebratulidæ and Lingulidæ, with remarks on and descriptions of some recent forms. Am. Jour. Conch., VI, pp. 88-168, pls. 6-8, October, 1870.

—— On the limpets; with special reference to the species of the west coast of America, and to a more natural classification of the group. Am. Jour. Conch., VI, pp. 227-282, pls. 14-17, 1871.

—— Preliminary sketch of a natural arrangement of the order Docoglossa. Proc. Boston Soc. Nat. Hist., XIV, pp. 49-54, 1871; reprinted in Ann. Mag. Nat. Hist., VII, pp. 286-291, 1871.

DALL, WILLIAM HEALEY (1845–   ). Supplement to the "Revision of the Terebratulidæ" with additions, corrections and revision of the Craniidæ and Discinidæ. Am. Jour. Conch., VII, pp. 39–85. pls. 10–11, November, 1871.

——— Descriptions of sixty new forms of mollusks from the west coast of North America and the North Pacific Ocean, with notes on others already described. Am. Jour. Conch., VII, pp, 93–160. pls. 13–16, November, 1871.

——— Note on *Gadinia*. Am. Jour. Conch., VII, pp. 192–193, March, 1872.

——— Notes on California Mollusca. Proc. California Acad. Sci., IV, pp. 182–183, 1872.

——— Preliminary descriptions of new species of mollusks from the northwest coast of America. Proc. California Acad. Sci., IV, pp. 270–271, October, 1872.

——— Preliminary descriptions of new species of mollusks from the northwest coast of America. Proc. California Acad. Sci., IV, pp. 302–303, pl. 4, December, 1872.

——— Preliminary descriptions of new species of Mollusca from the coast of Alaska, with notes on some rare forms. Proc. California Acad. Sci., V, pp. 57–62, pl. 2, April, 1873.

——— Catalogue of the recent species of the class Brachiopoda. Proc. Ac'd. Nat. Sci. Philadelphia for 1873, pp. 177–204.

——— Catalogue of shells from Bering Strait and the adjacent portions of the Arctic Ocean, with descriptions of three new species. Proc. California Acad. Sci., V, pp. 246–253, February, 1874.

——— Notes on some Tertiary fossils from the California coast, with a list of the species obtained from a well at San Diego, Cal., with descriptions of two new species. Proc. California Acad. Sci., V. pp. 296–299. March, 1874.

——— Notes on an examination of four species of chitons with reference to posterior orifices. Bull. Essex Inst., Salem, Mass., VI, 2 pp., 1874.

——— On the marine faunal regions of the North Pacific. Proc. Acad. Nat. Sci. Philadelphia for 1876, pp. 205–208, December, 1876; Sci. Results, pp. 1–4, 1876.

——— On the extrusion of the seminal products in limpets, with some remarks on the phylogeny of the Docoglossa. Proc. Acad. Nat. Sci. Philadelphia, 1876, pp. 239–247, December, 1876; Sci. Results, pp. 35–43.

——— On the Californian species of *Fusus*. Proc. California Acad. Sci., VII, pp. 1–5, March 19, 1877.

——— Preliminary descriptions of new species of mollusks, from the northwest coast of America. Proc. California Acad. Sci., VII. pp. 6–12, March 19, 1877. This and the preceding paper form the only part which was printed of Vol. VII of the first series of the Proceedings.

——— Report on the Brachiopoda of Alaska and the adjacent shores of northwest America. Proc. Acad. Nat. Sci. Philadelphia for 1877, pp. 155–170; Sci. Results, III, pp. 45–62, July, 1877.

——— Note sur la machoire et la plaque linguale du *Liriola peltoides* Carpenter, var. *vernalis*. Jour. de Conchyl., Paris, XXVI, pp. 68–73, January, 1878.

——— Descriptions of new forms of mollusks from Alaska, contained in the collections of the National Museum. Proc. U. S. Nat. Mus., I, pp. 1–3, February, 1878.

——— Post-Pliocene fossils in the Coast Range of California. Proc. U. S. Nat. Mus., I, p. 3, February, 1878.

——— Fossil mollusks from later Tertiaries of California. Proc. U. S. Nat. Mus., I, pp. 10–16, February, 1878.

——— Note on shells from Costa Rica kitchen midden, collected by Drs. Flint and Bransford. Proc. U. S. Nat. Mus., I, pp. 23–24, March, 1878.

——— Distribution of Californian Tertiary fossils. Proc. U. S. Nat. Mus., I, pp. 26–30, March, 1878.

——— Descriptions of new species of shells from California in the collections of the National Museum. Proc. U. S. Nat. Mus., I, pp. 46–47, March, 1878.

——— Report on the limpets and chitons of the Alaskan and Arctic regions, with descriptions of genera and species believed to be new. Proc. U. S. Nat. Mus., I, pp. 281–344, pls. 1–5, February, 1879; Sci. Results, IV, pp. 63–126, 1879.

——— On the genera of chitons. Proc. U. S. Nat. Mus., 1881, pp. 280–291. January 20, 1882.

DALL, WILLIAM HEALEY, (1845–   ). Note on Alaska Tertiary deposits. Am. Jour. Sci., 3d ser., XXIV, No. 139, pp. 67–68, July, 1882.

—— Species in *Buccinum*. Nachrichtsbl. d. Deutsch. Mal. Ges., 1882, pp. 118–121.

—— Notes on the Pacific coast trade in shells, shrimps, cod, and salmon, during the year 1882. Bull. U. S. Fish Comm., III, p. 425, 1883.

—— Trade in California invertebrates. Science, I, p. 78, 1883.

—— Notes on fishing products exported from San Francisco, Cal., during the year 1883. Bull. U. S. Fish Comm., IV, pp. 125–128, 1884.

—— Report on the Mollusca of the Commander Islands, Bering Sea, collected by Leonhard Stejneger in 1882 and 1883. Proc. U. S. Nat. Mus., VII, pp. 340–349, pl. 2, September, 1884.

—— A remarkable new type of mollusks. Science, IV, No. 76, pp. 50–51, July 18, 1884. Describes *Chlamydoconcha orcutti*.

—— The arms of the octopus, or devilfish. Science, VI, No. 145, p. 432, November 13, 1885.

—— Mollusks from near Point Barrow. Rept. Pt. Barrow Exp. under Lieut. P. H. Ray, pp. 177–184, plate, 1885.

—— Notes on the mollusks of the vicinity of San Diego, Cal., and Todos Santos Bay, Lower California (by C. R. Orcutt, with notes and comments by W. H. Dall). Proc. U. S. Nat. Mus., VIII, pp. 534–552, pl. 24, September 30, 1885.

—— Contribution to the natural history of the Commander Islands. VI. Report on Bering Island Mollusca collected by Mr. Nicholas Grebnitzki. Proc. U. S. Nat. Mus., IX, pp. 209–219, October 11, 1886.

—— Supplementary notes on some species of mollusks of the Bering Sea and vicinity. Proc. U. S. Nat. Mus., IX, pp. 297–309, pls. 3–4, October 19, 1886.

—— Notes on *Lophocardium* Fischer. Nautilus, III, No. 2, pp. 13–14, June, 1889.

—— On the genus *Corolla* Dall. Nautilus, III, No. 3, pp. 30–31, July, 1889.

—— On a new species of *Tylodina*. Nautilus, III, No. 11, pp. 121–122, March, 1890.

—— Scientific results of explorations by the U. S. Fish Commission steamer *Albatross*. VII. Preliminary report on the collection of Mollusca and Brachiopoda obtained in 1887–88. Proc. U. S. Nat. Mus., XII, No. 773, pp. 219–362, pls. 5–14, March 7, 1890.

—— Scientific results of explorations by the U. S. Fish Commission steamer *Albatross*. XX. On some new or interesting west American shells obtained from the dredgings in 1888, and from other sources. Proc. U. S. Nat. Mus., XIV, No. 849, pp. 172–192, pls. 5–7, June, 1891.

—— Conchological notes from Oregon. Nautilus, IV, No. 8, pp. 87–89, December, 1890.

—— Notes on some recent brachiopods. Proc. Acad. Nat. Sci. Philadelphia, for 1891, pp. 172–175, pl. 5.

—— and PILSBRY, H. A. On some Japanese Brachiopoda, with a description of a species believed to be new. Proc. Acad. Nat. Sci. Philadelphia for 1891, pp. 165–171, pl. 4.

—— —— *Terebratulina* (*unguicula* Cpr. var.?) *kiiensis* Dall and Pilsbry. Nautilus, V, No. 2, pp. 18–19, pl. 1, June, 1891.

—— On a new species of *Yoldia* from California. Nautilus, VII, No. 3, pp. 29–30, July, 1893.

—— On the species of *Mactra* from California. Nautilus, VII, No. 12, pp. 136–138, pl. 5, April, 1894.

—— On some species of *Mulinia* from the Pacific coast. Nautilus, VIII, No. 1, pp. 5–6, pl. 1, May, 1894.

—— Monograph of the genus *Gnathodon* Gray (*Rangia* Desmoulins). Proc. U. S. Nat. Mus., XVII, No. 988, pp. 89–106, pl. 7, July, 1894.

—— Synopsis of the Mactridæ of North America. Nautilus, VIII, No. 3, pp. 25–28, July, 1894, and No. 4, pp. 39–43, August, 1894.

—— Description of a new species of *Doridium* from Puget Sound. Nautilus, VIII, No. 7, pp. 73–74, November, 1894.

—— A new chiton from California. Nautilus, VIII, No. 8, pp. 90–91, December, 1894.

DALL, WILLIAM HEALEY (1845–   ). Scientific results of explorations by the U. S. Fish Commission steamer *Albatross*. XXXIV. Report on Mollusca and Brachiopoda dredged in deep water, chiefly near the Hawaiian Islands, with illustrations of hitherto unfigured species from northwest America. Proc. U. S. Nat. Mus., XVII, No. 1032, pp. 675–733, pls. 23–32, July, 1895.

—— On some new species of *Scala*. Nautilus, IX, No. 10, pp. 111–112, February, 1896.

—— Diagnoses of new species of mollusks from the northwest coast of America. Proc. U. S. Nat. Mus., XVIII, No. 1034, pp. 7–20, April, 1896.

—— New species of *Leda* from the Pacific coast. Nautilus, X, No. 1, pp. 1–2, May, 1896.

—— Report on the mollusks collected by the International Boundary Commission of the United States and Mexico, 1892–1894. Proc. U. S. Nat. Mus., XIX, No. 1111, pp. 333–349, pls. 31–33, January, 1897.

—— Editorial correspondence. Nautilus, XI, No. 6, p. 66, October, 1897.

—— New West American shells. Nautilus, XI, No. 8, pp. 85–86, December, 1897.

—— Notice of some new or interesting species of shells from British Columbia and the adjacent region. Bull. Nat. Hist. Soc. British Columbia, II, pp. 1–18, pls. 1–2, 1897.

—— Synopsis of the recent and Tertiary Psammobiidæ of North America. Proc. Acad. Nat. Sci. Philadelphia for 1898, pp. 57–62, May, 1898.

—— On a new species of *Fusus* from California. Nautilus, XII, No. 1, pp. 4–5, May, 1898.

—— On a new species of *Drillia* from California. Nautilus, XII, No. 11, p. 127, March, 1899.

—— A new species of *Pteronotus* from California. Nautilus, XII, No. 12, pp. 138–139, April, 1899.

—— Synopsis of the American species of the family Diplodontidæ. Jour. Conch. (Leeds), IX, No. 8, pp. 244–246, October, 1899.

—— Synopsis of the recent and Tertiary Leptonacea of North America and the West Indies. Proc. U. S. Nat. Mus., XXI, No. 1177, pp. 873–897, pls. 87–88, June, 1899.

—— Synopsis of the Solenidæ of North America and the Antilles. Proc. U. S. Nat. Mus., XXII, No. 1185, pp. 107–112, October, 1899.

—— The mollusk fauna of the Pribiloff Islands. The Fur Seals and Fur Seal Islands of the north Pacific Ocean, pt. 3, pp. 539–546 and map, November, 1899.

—— Note on *Sigaretus oldroydii*. Nautilus, XIII, No. 8, p. 85, December, 1899.

—— A new species of *Capulus* from California. Nautilus, XIII, No. 9, p. 100, January, 1900.

—— Note on *Petricola denticulata* Sowerby. Nautilus, XIII, No. 11, pp. 121–122, March, 1900.

—— A new species of *Lima*. Nautilus, XIV, No. 2, pp. 15–16, June, 1900.

—— A new *Murex* from California. Nautilus, XIV, No. 4, p. 37, August, 1900.

—— Synopsis of the family Tellinidæ and of the North American species. Proc. U. S. Nat. Mus., XXIII, No. 1210, pp. 285–326, pls. 2–4, November, 1900.

—— On a genus (*Phyllaplysia*) new to the Pacific coast. Nautilus, XIV, No. 8, pp. 91–92, December, 1900.

—— A new species of *Pleurobranchus* from California. Nautilus, XIV, No. 8, p. 92, December, 1900.

—— Synopsis of the family Cardiidæ and of the North American species. Proc. U. S. Nat. Mus., XXIII, No. 1214, pp. 381–392, January, 1901.

—— A new *Lyropecten*. Nautilus, XIV, No. 10, pp. 117–118, February, 1901.

—— A new species of *Subemarginula* from California. Nautilus, XIV, No. 11, pp. 125–126, March, 1901,

—— A new *Pinna* from California. Nautilus, XIV, No. 12, pp. 142–143, April, 1901.

—— Synopsis of the Lucinacea and of the American species. Proc. U. S. Nat. Mus., XXIII, No. 1237, pp. 779–883, pls. 39–42, August, 1901.

—— and BARTSCH, PAUL. A new California *Bittium*. Nautilus, XV, No. 5, p. 58, September, 1901.

—— On the true nature of *Tamiosoma*. Science, n. s., No. 366, pp. 5–7, January 3, 1902.

—— A new species of *Volutomitra*. Nautilus, XV, No. 9, pp. 102–103, January, 1902.

DALL, WILLIAM HEALEY (1845–   ). Illustrations and descriptions of new, unfigured, or imperfectly known shells, chiefly American, in the United States National Museum. Proc. U. S. Nat. Mus., XXIV, No. 1264, pp. 499–566, pls. 26–40, March, 1902.

——— Note on the names *Elachista* and *Pleurotomaria*. Nautilus, XV, No. 11, p. 127, March, 1902.

——— Notes on the giant Limas. Nautilus, XVI, No. 2, pp. 15–17, June, 1902.

——— New species of Pacific coast shells. Nautilus, XVI, No. 4, pp. 43–44, August, 1902.

——— Note on viviparity in *Corbicula* and *Cardita*. Science, n. s., XVI, No. 410, pp. 743–744, November 7, 1902.

——— Synopsis of the family Veneridæ and of the North American recent species. Proc. U. S. Nat. Mus., XXVI, No. 1312, pp. 335–412, pls. 12–16, December, 1902.

——— On the genus *Gemma* Deshayes. Jour. Conch. (Manchester), X, No. 8, pp. 238–243, December, 1902.

——— and BARTSCH, PAUL. A new *Rissoa* from California. Nautilus, XVI, No. 8, p. 94, December, 1902.

——— Synopsis of the Carditacea and of the American species. Proc. Acad. Nat. Sci. Philadelphia for 1902, pp. 696–716, January, 1903.

——— Review of the classification of the Cyrenacea. Proc. Biol. Soc. Washington, XVI, pp. 5–8, February, 1903.

——— Note on the name *Miodon*. Nautilus, XVI, No. 12, p. 143, April, 1903.

——— and BARTSCH, PAUL. Pyramidellidæ. Mem. California Acad. Sci., III, pp. 269–285, pls. 1–2, 1903. [The portion of Mr. Arnold's memoir relating to the Pyramidellidæ.]

——— Two new mollusks from the west coast of America. Nautilus, XVII, No. 4, pp. 37–38, August, 1903.

——— A new species of *Metzgeria*. Nautilus, XVII, No. 5, pp. 51–52, September, 1903.

——— Diagnoses of new species of mollusks from the Santa Barbara Channel, California. Proc. Biol. Soc. Washington, XVI, pp. 171–176, December, 1903.

——— and BARTSCH, PAUL. Synopsis of the genera, subgenera, and sections of the family Pyramidellidæ. Proc. Biol. Soc. Washington, XVII, pp. 1–16, February, 1904.

——— A new species of *Periploma* from California. Nautilus, XVII, No. 11, pp. 122–123, March, 1904.

——— Neozoic invertebrate fossils, a report on collections made by the expedition. Harriman Alaska Expedition, IV, pp. 99–122, pls. 9, 10, March, 1904.

——— An historical and systematic review of the Frog-shells and Tritons. Smithsonian Misc. Coll. (quarterly issue), XLVII, No. 1473, pp. 114–144, August, 1904.

——— Note on *Lucina* (*Miltha*) *childreni* Gray, and on a new species from the Gulf of California. Nautilus, XVIII, No. 10, pp. 110–112, February, 1905.

——— New species of mollusks from California. Nautilus, XVIII, No. 11, pp. 123–125, March, 1905.

——— Two undescribed California shells. Nautilus, XIX, No. 2, pp. 14–15, June, 1905.

——— Notes on a variety of *Crepidula nivea* C. B. Adams, from San Pedro, Cal. Nautilus, XIX, No. 3, pp. 26–27, July, 1905.

——— Thomas Martyn and the Universal Conchologist. Proc. U. S. Nat. Mus., XXIX, No. 1425, pp. 415–432, October, 1905.

——— Land and fresh-water mollusks. Harriman Alaska Expedition Repts., XIII, pp. i–ix, 1–171, pls. 1–2, text figs. 1–118, November, 1905. Inserted on account of the references to such forms as *Siphonaria* and *Arctonchis*, as well as for the Pleistocene fossils.

——— Note on some names in the Volutidæ. Nautilus, XIX, No. 12, pp. 143–144, April, 1906.

——— Early history of the generic name *Fusus*. Jour. Conch. (Leeds), XI, pp. 289–297, April, 1906.

——— and BARTSCH, PAUL. Notes on Japanese, Indopacific, and American Pyramidellidæ. Proc. U. S. Nat. Mus., XXX, No. 1452, pp. 321–369, pls. 17–26, May, 1906.

——— A new *Scala* from California. Nautilus, XX, No. 4, p. 44, August, 1906.

DALL, WILLIAM HEALEY (1845-   ). A new *Cardium* from Puget Sound. Nautilus, XX, No. 10, pp. 111–112, February, 1907.

—— A review of the American Volutidæ. Smithsonian Misc. Coll. (quarterly issue). XLVIII, pt. 3, No. 1663, pp. 341–373, February, 1907. Reviewed by Burnett Smith, Nautilus, XX, No. 11, pp. 129–131, March, 1907.

—— Notes on some Cretaceous Volutidæ, with descriptions of new species and a revision of the groups to which they belong. Smithsonian Misc. Coll. (quarterly issue), L, pt. 1, No. 1704, pp. 1–23, figs. 1–13, March, 1907.

—— Three new species of *Scala* from California. Nautilus, XX, No. 11, pp. 127–128, March, 1907.

—— Correspondence [American Volutidæ]. Nautilus, XX, No. 12, pp. 142–143, April, 1907. A response to a review by Burnett Smith of the above-mentioned paper on Volutidæ.

—— On climatic conditions at Nome, Alaska, during the Pliocene, and on a new species of *Pecten* from the Nome gold-bearing gravels. Am. Jour. Sci., n. s., XXIII, June, 1907, pp. 457–458, fig. 1 in text.

—— Descriptions of new species of shells, chiefly Buccinidæ, from the dredgings of the U. S. S. *Albatross*, during 1906, in the northwestern Pacific. Bering, Okhotsk, and Japanese seas. Smithsonian Misc. Coll. (quarterly issue). L, pt. 2, No. 1727, pp. 139–173, July 9, 1907.

—— On the synonymic history of the genera *Clava* Martyn and *Cerithium* Bruguière. Proc. Acad. Nat. Sci. Philadelphia for 1907, pp. 363–369, September, 1907.

—— Supplementary notes on Martyn's Universal Conchologist. Proc. U. S. Nat. Mus., XXXIII, No. 1565, pp. 185–192, 1 text figure, October, 1907.

—— On a *Cymatium* new to the California fauna. Nautilus, XXII, pp. 85–86, December, 1907. See also note on *Ilyanassa obsoleta* in San Francisco Bay, page 91.

—— and BARTSCH, PAUL. The pyramidellid mollusks of the Oregonian faunal area. Proc. U. S. Nat. Mus., XXXIII, No. 1574, pp. 491–534, pls. XLIV–XLVIII, December, 1907.

—— A new species of *Cavolina*, with notes on other pteropods. Smithsonian Misc. Coll. (quarterly issue), L, No. 1785, pp. 501–502, January, 1908.

—— Subdivisions of the Terebridæ: Nautilus, XXI, No. 11, pp. 124–125, March, 1908.

—— Note on *Turbonilla castanea* and *Odostomia montereyensis*. Nautilus, XXI, No. 11, p. 131, March, 1908.

—— Some new Californian shells. Nautilus, XXI, No. 12, pp. 136–137, April, 1908.

—— A revision of the Solenomyacidæ. Nautilus, XXII, No. 1, pp. 1–2, May, 1908.

—— Descriptions of new species of mollusks from the Pacific coast of the United States, with notes on other mollusks from the same region. Proc. U. S. Nat. Mus., XXXIV, No. 1610, pp. 245–257, June, 1908.

DANA, JAMES DWIGHT (1813–1895). *See* Conrad, T. A.

DAVENPORT, CHARLES BENEDICT (1866-   ). A comparison of some pectens from the east and the west coasts of the United States. Mark Anniversary Volume, art. 6, pp. 121–136, pl. 9, 1903.

DAWSON, GEORGE MERCER (1849–1901). *See* Whiteaves, J. F.

DE FOLIN, LÉOPOLD GUILLAUME ALEXANDRE (–1896). Les Méléagrinicoles, espèces nouvelles. Lepelletier, Havre, 1867, 8°, pp. 1–74, pls. 1–6.

—— Descriptions des espèces nouvelles de Cæcidæ. Jour. de Conchyl., XV, pp. 44–58, 1867.

—— Les fonds de la mer. Paris, Savy, 1867–1880, Vols. I–IV, 8°; Vol. I, pp. 6–12, 1868; pp. 130–136, 166–174, 1869; pp. 262–263, 1871; II, pp. 163–168, 1873; pp. 250–251, 1874; IV, p. 37, 1880.

DESHAYES, GERARD PAUL (1796–1875). [Descriptions of shells from California, etc.]. Rev. Zool. Soc. Cuvierienne, 1839, pp. 324, 357, 358–360; 1841, pls. 25–29, 34–40, 43, 45, 47, 48; 1843, pl. 82.

—— Description de deux espèces nouvelles de *Jouannetia*. Jour. de Conchyl., X, pp. 375–376, October, 1862.

D'ORBIGNY, ALCIDE DESSALINES (1802–1857). Voyage dans l'Amérique méridionale, III, Mollusques. 4°, 2 vols. [Vol. V of the series, published in fasciculi as follows: pp. 1–48, 1835; pp. 49–184, 1836; pp. 185–376, 1837; pp. 377–408, 1840; pp. 409–488, 1841; pp. 489 to end, 1846. The date on the title-page is 1835–1843, and it is frequently cited as 1847.]

DORE, HARRY E. Mollusks in the Portland, Oreg., market. Nautilus, V, No. 5, pp. 58–59, September, 1891.

DRAKE, Mrs. MARIA. Marine shells of Puget Sound. Nautilus, IX, No. 4, pp. 38–42, August, 1895.

———— Notes on some shells of Puget Sound. Nautilus, X, No. 6, pp. 68–70, October, 1896.

DUNN, GEORGE WASHINGTON. Coleoptera and Mollusca of the ocean beach at San Francisco. Zoë, II, pp. 310–312, January, 1892.

ELDRIDGE, GEORGE HOMANS, and ARNOLD, RALPH. The Santa Clara Valley, Puente Hills, and Los Angeles oil districts, southern California. Bull. U. S. Geol. Survey No. 309, pp. xii, 266, figs. 1–17, pls. I–XLI, 1907. Pls. XXV–XLI illustrate Tertiary fossils.

ELIOT, Sir CHARLES NORTON EDGCUMBE (1864–   ). Notes on a remarkable nudibranch from northwest America. Proc. Malac. Soc. London, IV, pp. 163–165, fig., 1901.

———— See also Cockerell, T. D. A., and Eliot, C. N. E.

EVANS, JOHN (1812–1861). See Shumard, B. F.; also Am. Jour. Sci., 2d ser., XXXII, pp. 311–318, 1861, and Rept. U. S. Nat. Mus. for 1904, pp. 455, 696, 1906.

FISCHER, PAUL HENRI (1835–1893). Mollusques marins des îles Aléoutiennes provenant du voyage de M. A. Pinart. Jour. de Conchyl., XXI, pp. 243–248, July, 1873.

———— Remarques sur la coloration générale des coquilles de la côte occidentale de l'Amérique. Jour. de Conchyl., XXIII, pp. 105–112, April, 1875.

———— Des anomalies de l'opercule dans les genres *Volutharpa* et *Buccinum*. Jour. de Conchyl., XXIII, pp. 112–114, April, 1875.

———— Invertébres marins des îles Aléoutiennes; mollusques et cirripèdes. In Pinart, A. L., Voyages à la côte nord-ouest de l'Amérique; Zoologie, pp. 37–39, pl. E, 1875.

———— Sur un nouveau type de mollusques (*Chlamydoconcha*). Jour. de Conchyl., XXXV, pp. 201–206, 1887.

———— and CROSSE, H. Note sur *Neritina picta* Sowerby. Jour. de Conchyl., XL, pp. 292–293, 1892.

FISCHER, PIERRE-MARIE HENRI (1865–   ). Découverte d'un nouveau type de mollusques gastropodes entoparasites (*Entocolax*). Jour. de Conchyl., XXXVII, pp. 101–105, 1889.

FISHER, WALTER KENRICK (1878–   ). The anatomy of *Lottia gigantea* Gray. Zool. Jahrb., XX, I, pp. 1–66, pls. 1–4, 1904.

FOLIN, L. G. A. See De Folin.

FORD, JOHN (1827–   ). Description of a new species of *Ocinebra* (*michaeli*). Proc. Acad. Nat. Sci. Philadelphia for 1888, p. 188, cuts.

— A new variety of *Olivella*. Nautilus, VIII, No. 9, pp. 103–104, January, 1895.

GABB, WILLIAM MORE (1839–1878). Descriptions of new species of American Tertiary fossils and a new Carboniferous cephalopod from Texas. Proc. Acad. Nat. Sci. Philadelphia, 2d ser., V, pp. 367–372, 1861.

———— Descriptions of two new species of cephalopods from the Museum of the California Academy of Natural Sciences. Proc. California Acad. Nat. Sci., II, pp. 170–173, September, 1862.

———— Description of new species of marine shells from the coast of California. Proc. California Acad. Nat. Sci., III, pp. 182–190, January, 1865.

———— Paleontology of California, I, II. Geol. Survey of California. Paleontology, I, 1864, pp. xx, 243, pls. 1–32; II, 1869, pp. xiv, 38 (issued February, 1866), pp. 39–299, pls. 1–36 (issued December, 1868).

GOULD, AUGUSTUS ADDISON (1805–1866). Report on shells from California. Am. Jour. Sci., XXXVIII, p. 396, 1840.

GOULD, AUGUSTUS ADDISON (1805–1866).   On the relation of shells from the east and west coasts of
    America.   Proc. Boston Soc. Nat. Hist., IV, pp. 27–28, 1851.

────── Descriptions of shells from the Gulf of California and the Pacific coasts of Mexico and California.
    Boston Jour. Nat. Hist., VI, pp. 374–408, pls. 14–16, October, 1853; also in Otia Conchologica, pp.
    184–188, 1862; also issued in advance of the Journal, separately. April, 1852.

────── Descriptions of California shells collected by Maj. William Rich and Lieut. Thomas P. Green.
    Proc. Boston Soc. Nat. Hist., IV, pp. 87–93, 1851; also in Otia Conchologica, pp. 210–215, 1862.

────── Catalogue of shells collected in California by William P. Blake, with descriptions of the new
    species.   House Ex. Doc. 129, art. 2, pp. 22–28, Washington, D. C., July, 1855.

────── Catalogue of the recent shells with descriptions of the new species.   Pacific R. R. Repts., V,
    pt. 2, app., art. 3, pp. 330–336, pl. 11, 1856.

────── Description of shells collected in the North Pacific Exploring Expedition under Captains Ring-
    gold and Rodgers.   Proc. Boston Soc. Nat. Hist., VI, pp. 422–426; VII, pp. 40–45, 138–142, 161–166,
    1859; pp. 323–340, 382–389, 1860; pp. 400–409, 1861; VIII, pp. 14–40, 1861.   Reprinted in Otia
    Conchologica, pp. 101–178, 1862.

GRAY, JOHN EDWARD (1800–1875).   On a recent species of the genus *Hinnita* of De France.   Annals of
    Philosophy, XXVIII, pp. 103–106, 1826.

GREWINGK, CONSTANTINE.   Die an der Westküste Nord-Amerika's und auf den Aleutischen Inseln
    bisher gefundenen Fossilen Thier- und Pflanzen-Reste.   Verh. der Russ. Kais. min. Ges. St. Peters-
    burg, Jahrg. 1848–49, pp. 343–366, with 3 plates, 1850.

────── Beitrag zur Kenntniss der orographischen und geognostischen Beschaffenheit der Nordwest-
    küste Amerika's mit den anliegenden Inseln, 8°, pp. 351, pls. 1–4, St. Petersbourg, 1850.

GRIFFIN, BRADNEY B.   Adaptation of the shell of *Placunanomia* to that of *Saxidomus*, with remarks on
    shell adaptation in general.   Trans. New York Acad. Sci., XVI, pp. 77–81, February, 1897.

────── *See also* Harrington, N. R.

HAEHL, HARRY LEWIS, and ARNOLD, RALPH.   The Miocene diabase of the Santa Cruz Mountains in
    San Mateo County, Cal   Proc. Am. Philos. Soc., XLIII, No. 175, pp. 15–53, figs. 1–25, 1904.

HANKS, HENRY G.   Catalogue of the State Museum of California, 350 pp., 8°, Sacramento, 1882.

HARRINGTON, N. R., and GRIFFIN, B. B.   Notes upon the distribution and habits of some Puget Sound
    invertebrates.   Trans. New York Acad. Sci., XVI, pp. 152–165, March, 1897.

HEATH, HAROLD (1868–   ).   External features of young *Cryptochiton*.   Proc. Acad. Nat. Sci.
    Philadelphia for 1897, pp. 297–302, pl. 8, 1897.

────── and SPAULDING, M. H.   *Cymbuliopsis vitrea*, a new species of pteropod.   Proc. Acad. Nat. Sci.
    Philadelphia for 1901, pp. 509–511, October, 1901.

────── The function of the chiton subradular organ.   Anat. Anzeiger, XXIII, pp. 92–95, 1903.

────── The larval eye of chitons.   Proc. Acad. Nat. Sci. Philadelphia for 1904, pp. 257–259, figure.

────── The habits of a few Solenogastres.   Zool. Anzeiger, XXVII, No. 15, pp. 457–461, April, 1904.

HEILPRIN, ANGELO (1853–1907).   North American Tertiary Ostreidæ.   Fourth Ann. Rept. U. S. Geol.
    Survey, app. 1, pp. 309–316, pls. 62–72, 1883.

HEMPHILL, HENRY (1830–   ).   Catalogue.   Land, fresh-water, and marine shells of California and adja-
    cent States.   For sale by Henry Hemphill, San Diego, Cal.   Leaflet of 2 pp., 8°, no date.

────── Edible mollusks of western North America.   Zoë, II, pp. 134–139, July, 1871.

────── Catalogue.   Land, fresh-water, and marine shells of California (etc.).   San Diego, Cal., the
    author, 12°, 8 pp., 1875.

────── Catalogue of North American shells collected and for sale by Henry Hemphill, San Diego, July,
    1890. 8°, 26 pp.

────── *Haliotis rufescens* Swainson.   Nautilus, IV, No. 5, p. 59, September, 1890.

────── Studies among mollusks.   Instinct and genera.   Zoë, II, pp. 312–318, 1892.

────── Note on a Californian *Loligo* (*stearnsii* n. sp.).   Zoë, III, pp. 51–52, 1892.

HEMPHILL, HENRY (1830-   ). A new species of *Bulimulus* (*Eulimella occidentalis*). Zoë, IV, pp. 395–396, March 12, 1894.

——— Notes on *Haliotis rufescens* Swainson. Nautilus, XVI, No. 7, p. 84, November, 1903.

——— A second contribution to west coast conchology, I, II. Nautilus, XIX, No. 1, pp. 5–8, May, 1905; No. 2, pp. 19–24, June, 1905.

——— Note on the genus *Haliotis*, with a description of a new variety. Trans. San Diego Soc. Nat. Hist., I, No. 2, pp. 56–60, 1907.

HERZENSTEIN, SALOMON. Aperçu sur la faune malacologique de l'Océan Glacial russe. Proc. Soc. Imp. des Amis d'Hist. Nat. (Moscow), pp. 1–21.

HOYLE, WILLIAM EVANS (1855-   ). Reports on the dredging [etc., of the U. S. S. *Albatross*, 1891–1900] off the west coast of Central America. Reports on the Cephalopoda. Bull. Mus. Comp. Zool., XLIII, No. 1, pp. 1–83, pls. 1–12, March, 1904.

IHERING, H. VON. Ein vermeintliches Mollusk (*Entocolax*). Nachrichtsbl. d. Deutsch. Mal. Ges., XXII, pp. 46–48, 1890.

ISBISTER, A. K. On the geology of the Hudsons Bay territories and of portions of the Arctic and northwestern regions of America, with a colored geological map. Quart. Jour. Geol. Soc., XI, pp. 497–520, 1855. The Miocene beds of Oregon are especially referred to, with their fossils.

JACKSON, CHARLES THOMAS (1805–1880). On the Miocene and Cretaceous formation at Santa Barbara, Cal. Proc. Boston Soc. Nat. Hist., X, pp. 262–263, 1866.

JEFFREYS, JOHN GWYN (1809–1885). Notes on the Mollusca in the Great International Fisheries Exhibition, London, 1883. Ann. Mag. Nat. Hist., 5th ser., XII, p. 119, 1883.

JENSEN, ADOLPH SEVERIN (1866-   ). Studier over Nordiske Mollusker. I. *Mya*. Vidensk. Meddel. Naturh. Foren. i Kjöbenhavn, 1900, pp. 133–158, figs., June, 1900.

——— Studier over Nordiske Mollusker. III. *Tellina* (*Macoma*). Vidensk. Meddel. Naturh. Foren. i Kjöbenhavn, 1905, pp. 21–52, tab. 1, 1904; pp. 149–152, 1905.

JONAS, J. H. Molluskologische Beiträge. 4°, pp. 1–30, taf. 7–11. Abh. aus d. Gebiete d. Naturwiss. Hamburg, I, pp. 99–130, taf. 7–11, 1846. (Cf. also Proc. Zool. Soc. London, XIV, pp. 34–36, 1846, and Ann. Nat. Hist., XVIII, pp. 121–123, 1846.

KEEP, JOSIAH (1849-   ). Common sea shells of California. San Francisco, 1881, 64 pp., 95 figs.

——— West coast shells: A familiar description of the marine, fresh-water, and land mollusks of the United States found west of the Rocky Mountains. San Francisco, Bancroft Bros., 1887: sq. 16°, 230 pp., 182 cuts, 1 col. plate.

——— Cabinet notes. Conchologists' Exchange, II, pp. 107, February, 1888.

——— The *Haliotis*. Nautilus, IV, No. 2, pp. 13–15, June, 1890.

——— Mollusks of the San Francisco markets. Nautilus, IV, No. 9, pp. 97–100, January, 1891.

——— West coast species of *Haliotis*. Nautilus, IX, pp. 129–132, March, 1896.

——— Exotic mollusks in California. Nautilus, XIV, No. 10, pp. 114–115, February, 1901.

——— Shells and sea life. San Francisco, 1901. 200 pp., 16°, illustrated.

——— West American shells. A description in familiar terms of the principal marine, fresh-water, and land mollusks of the United States found west of the Rocky Mountains, including those of British Columbia and Alaska. San Francisco, Whitaker & Ray Co., 1904, sm. 8°, 360 pp., 1 pl., 303 cuts in text.

KELSEY, FREDERICK WILLIS (1858-   ). San Diego, California, as a collecting ground. Nautilus, XII, No. 8, pp. 88–89, December, 1898.

——— Dredging in San Diego Bay. Nautilus, XIII, No. 9, pp. 101–102, January, 1900.

——— *Serridens oblongus* Cpr. Nautilus, XV, No. 12, p. 144, April, 1902.

——— A peculiar *Haliotis*. Nautilus, XVIII, No. 6, p. 67, October, 1904.

——— Mollusks and brachiopods collected in San Diego, Cal. Trans. San Diego Soc. Nat. Hist., I, pp. 31–55, 1907.

KING, Mrs. ENSIGN H. Collecting in Monterey Bay. Nautilus, XI, No. 2, pp. 23–24, June, 1897.

—— Collecting in southern California. Nautilus, XIII, No. 2, pp. 23–24, June, 1899.

KOBELT, WILHELM (1840–   ). Dall, einleitende Bemerkungen über die Provinzen der marinen Fauna im nord-pacifischen Ocean. Nachrichtsbl. d. Deutsch. Mal. Ges., IX, pp. 33–35, 1877.

—— *Neptunea* et *Siphonalia*. Syst. Conchylien Cabinet, ed. Küster, pt. 281, pp. 89–136, pls. 11–46, 1879.

—— Zur Synonymie der nordischen *Buccinum*. Nachrichtsbl. d. Deutsch. Mal. Ges., XIII, pp. 18–22, 1881.

—— Die Buccinen des Petersburger Museums. Jahrbuch d. Deutsch. Mal. Ges., IX, pp 229–235, 1882.

KRAUSE, ARTHUR. Ein Beitrag zur Kenntniss der Mollusken-Fauna des Berings-Meeres, I, II. Arch. für Naturgesch. LI, heft 1, pp. 14–40, pl. 3, 1885; heft 3, pp. 256–302, pls. 16–18, 1886.

LAWRENCE, Mrs. ELIZABETH ANN. Seeing eyes. Nautilus, XI, No. 4, pp. 42–43, August, 1897.

LECHE, JAKOB WILHELM EBBE GUSTAF (1850–   ). Öfversigt öfver de af Vega-expeditionen insamlade arktiska Hafsmollusker. I. Lamellibranchiata. Vega Exped. vetensk. iakt., III, pp. 433–453, pls. 32–34, 1883.

LOCKINGTON, W. N. Rambles around San Francisco. Am. Naturalist, XII, pp. 505–512, 1878.

LORD, JOHN KEAST (1817–1872). List of shells taken on the eastern side of Vancouver Island, dredged in 10 fathoms water and collected from rocks between tide marks. The Naturalist in British Columbia and Vancouver Island, II, appendix, pp. 356–370, London, R. Bentley, 1866.

LOWE, HERBERT NELSON (1879–   ). My first year collecting and studying shells. Nautilus, IX, No. 7, pp. 80–81, November, 1895.

—— Cuttlefishes washed ashore in San Pedro Bay. Nautilus, X, No. 1, pp. 11–12, May, 1896.

—— Collecting during the summer of 1896. Nautilus, XI, No. 7, pp. 80–81, November, 1897.

—— Dredging off San Pedro. Nautilus, XIII, No. 3, pp. 27–30, July, 1899.

—— Notes on the mollusk fauna of San Nicholas Island. Nautilus, XVII, No. 6, pp. 66–69, October, 1903.

—— A dredging trip to Santa Catalina Island. Nautilus, XVIII, No. 2, pp. 18–20, June, 1904.

LUBOMIRSKI, Prince L. Notice sur quelques coquilles du Pérou. Proc. Zool. Soc. London for 1879, pp. 719–728, pls. 55–56.

MABILLE, JULES FRANÇOIS (1831–1904). Mollusques de la Basse Californie recueillis par M. Diguet. Bull. Soc. Philomathique de Paris (8), VII, pp. 54–76, 1895.

MACFARLAND, FRANK MACE (1869–   ). A preliminary account of the Dorididæ of Monterey Bay, California. Proc. Biol. Soc. Washington, XVIII, pp. 35–54, February 2, 1905.

—— Opisthobranchiate mollusca from Monterey Bay, California, and vicinity. Bull. Bureau Fisheries, XXV, pp. 109–151, pls. 18–31, 1906.

MARRAT, FREDERICK PRICE (1820–1904). List of shells from Fuca Straits and Cape Flattery, collected and presented to the Liverpool Free Public Museum, by Dr. David Walker. Proc. Lit. and Phil. Soc. of Liverpool, XXXII, pp. xcix–ci, 1878.

MARTENS, CARL EDUARD VON (1831–1904). Conchylien von Cook's Reisen. Malak. Blätt., XIX, pp. 1–48, 1872.

—— Conchylien aus Alaschka. Malak. Blätt., XIX, pp. 78–99, taf. 3, 1872.

—— Schnecken aus dem Tschuktschen lande. Nachrichtsbl. d. Deutsch. Mal. Ges., XIV, pp. 43–44, March, 1882.

—— Krause's shells. Sitz.-Ber. der Ges. naturf. Freunde zu Berlin, No. 9, 1882, pp. 138–143.

—— Conchologische miscellen. II. Ueber einige Olividen. Arch. für Naturg., I, heft 2, pp. 157–180, taf. 16–17, 1897.

—— Purpur-Färberei in Central America. Nachrichtsbl. d. Deutsch. Mal. Ges., XXXI, pp. 113–122, 1899; *also* Verh. des Berliner anthrop. Ges., Sitz. vom 22 October, 1898.

—— Die Meeres Conchylien der Cocos-Insel. Sitz.-Ber. der Ges. naturf. Freunde zu Berlin, 1902, No. 6, pp. 137–141.

MEEK, FIELDING BRADFORD (1817–1876). Descriptions and illustrations of fossils from Vancouver and Sucia islands, and other northwestern localities. Bull. U. S. Geol. and Geogr. Survey Terr., II, No. 4, pp. 351–374, 6 pls., 1876.

MELVILL, JAMES COSMO. Description of a new species of *Mitra (idæ)*. The Conchologist, II, pp. 140–141, fig., 1893.

—— The genera *Pseudoliva* and *Macron*. Jour. Conch. (Leeds), X, No. 11, pp. 320–330, July, 1903.

MENKE, KARL THEODOR (1791–   ). Verzeichniss einer Sendung von Conchylien von Mazatlan, mit einingen kritischen Bemerkungen. Zeitschr. für Malak., IV, pp. 177–191, December, 1847.

—— Conchylien von Mazatlan, mit kritischen Anmerkungen. Zeitschr. für Malak., VII, pp. 161–173, 177–190, April, 1851; VIII, pp. 17–25, May, 1851; pp. 33–38, July, 1851.

MERRIAM, JOHN CAMPBELL (1869–   ). A list of type specimens in the Geological Museum of the University of California which have served as originals for figures and descriptions in the paleontology of the State Geological Survey of California under J. D. Whitney. Berkeley, the Unversity, 1895. 3 pp., 8°.

—— Note on two Tertiary faunas from the rocks of the southern coast of Vancouver Island. Univ. California, Bull. Dept. Geol., II, pp. 101–108, 1896.

—— The distribution of the Neocene sea urchins of middle California, and its bearing on the classification of the Neocene formations. Univ. California, Bull. Dept. Geol., II, pp. 109–118, 1898.

—— The fauna of the Sooke beds of Vancouver Island. Proc. California Acad. Sci., 3d ser., I, No. 6. pp. 175–180, pl. 23, March, 1899.

—— Lists of fossils in the oil and gas yielding formations of California. Bull. California State Mining Bureau, No. 19, pp. 218–224, Sacramento, State Printer, 1900.

—— A note on the fauna of the lower Miocene in California. Univ. California, Bull. Dept. Geol., III, No. 16, pp. 377–381, March, 1904.

MICHAEL, GEORGE WILFRED, jr. On collecting and preserving chitons. Conchologist's Exchange, II, No. 1, p. 8, July, 1887.

—— Shells collected at a point on the coast of San Luis Obispo County, Cal. Conchologist's Exchange, II, No. 5, p. 68, November, 1887.

MICHELIN, HARDOUIN. *Venericardia flammea*. Mag. de Zool., I. p. 6, May, 1830.

MIDDENDORFF, ALEXANDER THEODOR VON (1815–1894). Beitrage zu einer Malacozoologia Rossica. Mém. Sci. Nat. de l'Acad. Imp. des Sci. de St.-Pétersbourg, VI, pt. 1, pp. 1–151, pls. 1–14, 1847; pt. 2, pp. 1–187, pls. 15–21, 1849; pt. 3, pp. 1–94. 4°.

—— Vorläufige Anzeige einiger neuen Arten und Synonymien, nebst einer neuen ausgezeichneten Varietät, aus dem Geschlechte *Patella* L. Bull. Classe phys.-math., de l'Acad. des Sci. de St. Pétersbourg, VI, No. 20, pp. 1–5, April, 1847.

—— Beschreibung von zehn neuen Arten aus dem Geschlechte *Chiton*. Bull. Classe phys.-math., de l'Acad. des Sci. de St.-Pétersbourg, VI, No. 8, 1847; No. 11. 1847.

—— Vorläufige Anzeige einiger neuer Konchylien aus den Geschlechtern: *Littorina*, *Tritonium*, *Bullia*, *Natica*, und *Margarita*. Bull. Classe phys.-math., de l'Acad. Imp. des Sci. de St.-Pétersbourg, VII, No. 16. pp. 1–7, October, 1848.

—— Vorläufige Anzeige einiger neuer Konchylien Russland's, aus den Geschlechtern: *Scalaria*, *Crepidula*, *Velutina*, *Trichotropis*, *Purpura*, und *Pleurotoma*. Bull. Classe phys.-math., de l'Acad. des Sci. de St.-Pétersbourg, VIII, No. 2, pp. 1–4, December, 1848.

—— Grundriss für eine Geschichte der Malako-Zoographie Russlands. Bull. der Naturf. Gesellschaft in Moskau, XXI, pp. 424–476, 1848.

—— Die Meeresmollusken Russland's in ihren Beziehungen zur zoologischen und physicalischen Geographie. Bull. Classe phys.-math., de l'Acad. des Sci. de St.-Pétersbourg, VIII, No. 5, pp. 1–21, May, 1849.

—— Sibirische Reise, Bd. II, th. I: Mollusken, pp. 163–508, pls. 8–30, St.-Pétersbourg, Kais. Akad. Wiss., 1851, 4°.

MÖRCH, OTTO ANDREAS LOWSON (1828–1878). Diagnoses Molluscorum novarum littoris Americæ occidentalis. Medd. fra d. naturh. Foren. i Kjöbenhavn, 1857, No. 18–21, pp. 340–342. Summary in Jour. de Conchyl., VII, p. 103, 1858.

MÖRCH, OTTO ANDREAS LOWSON (1828-1878).   Description de nouveaux mollusques de l'Amérique centrale. Jour. de Conchyl., VI, pp. 281-282, 1857.

———— Note on the genus *Volutharpa* Fischer. Jour. de Conchyl., VII, pp. 40–44, 1858.

———— Novitates Conchologicæ. Mollusca Marina. Cassel, Theodor Fischer, 1858, pp. 1-8, pls. 1-2: p. 103, pl. 34 (Herausg. von Wilhelm Dunker, 1809–1885).

———— Beiträge zur Molluskenfauna Central Amerika's. Malak. Blätt., VI, pp. 102–126, 1860; VII, pp. 66–106, 170–213, 1861.

MONKS, SARAH PRESTON. San Pedro as a collecting ground. Nautilus, VII, No. 7, pp. 74–77, November, 1893.

NELSON, EDWARD T. On the molluscan fauna of the later Tertiary of Peru. Trans. Connecticut Acad. Arts and Sci., II, pp. 186–206, pl., 1871.

NEWBERRY, JOHN STRONG (1822–1892). On the flora and fauna of the Miocene Tertiary beds of Oregon and Idaho. Am. Naturalist, III, pp. 446–447, 1870.

NEWCOMB, WESLEY (1808–1892). Description of a new species of *Pedicularia*. Proc. California Acad. Nat. Sci., III, p. 121, March, 1864; IV, pl. 1, fig. 9, January, 1873.

———— Description of a new species of shell from San Francisco Bay. Proc. California Acad. Sci., V, p. 415, December, 1874.

NEWCOMBE, CHARLES F. Preliminary check-list, marine shells of British Columbia. R. Wolfenden, Victoria, B. C., 1893, 8°, 13 pp.

———— Report on the marine shells of British Columbia. Bull. Nat. Hist. Soc. British Columbia, I, art. 5, pp. 31–72, February, 1894.

———— New or rare species of marine Mollusca recently found in British Columbia. Nautilus, X, No. 2, pp. 16–20, June, 1896.

———— A preliminary catalogue of the collections of natural history and ethnology in the Provincial Museum, Victoria, British Columbia. R. Wolfenden, 1898, 8°, 196 pp. Cf. pp. 83–107.

NIERSTRASZ, H. F. Bemerkungen ueber die Chitonen-Sammlung im Zoologisches Museum zu Leiden. Notes Mus. Leiden, XXV. pp. 141-159. pls. 9-10, 1905.

OLDROYD, Mrs. TOM SHAW. *See* Shepard, I. M.

ORBIGNY. *See* D'Orbigny, A. D.

ORCUTT, CHARLES RUSSELL (1864-   ). Notes on the mollusks of the vicinity of San Diego, Cal. and Todos Santos Bay, Lower California. Proc. U. S. Nat. Mus., VIII, pp. 534–552, pl. 24, 1885. Edited, with notes, by W. H. Dall, q. v.

———— Mollusks of San Diego. West American Scientist, II, No. 1, pp. 3–4, January, 1886.

———— Some notes on Tertiary fossils of California. West American Scientist, VI, No. 45, p. 70; No. 46, p. 84, 1890.

———— California pearl shells (*Haliotis*). West American Scientist, X, No. 5, pp. 30–31, March, 1900.

———— West American Mollusca, I–XIII (reprints), 8°, pp. 1–36, subsequently paginated by columns 37–67, 1900. Continued, West American Scientist, XI, pp. 27–34, 41–49, 63–69, 74–76, 78–80, 1901.

OSMONT, VANCE C. Areas of the California Neocene. Univ. California Bull. Dept. Geol., IV, No. 4, pp. 89–100, pls. 8–11, 1904.

PEASE, WILLIAM HARPER (-1872). Remarks on marine Gasteropoda inhabiting the west coast of America: with descriptions of two new species. Am. Jour. Conch., V, pt. 2, pp. 80–84, October 7, 1869.

PECK, JAMES I. Scientific results of explorations by the U. S. Fish Commission steamer *Albatross*. XXVI. Report on the pteropods collected by the U. S. Fish Commission steamer *Albatross* during the voyage from Norfolk, Va., to San Francisco, Cal., 1887–88. Proc. U. S. Nat. Mus., XVI, No. 943. pp. 451–466, pls. 53–55, September 30, 1893.

PERRIER, EDMOND, and ROCHEBRUNE, A. T. DE. Sur un *Octopus* nouveau (*O. digueti*) de la basse Californie, habitant les coquilles des mollusques bivalves. Comptes Rendus de l'Acad. Sci., CXVIII, pp. 770–773, 1894.

PETIT DE LA SAUSSAYE, SAUVEUR (1792–1870). Notice sur le genre *Trichotropis* Sowerby, et description de coquilles appartenant probablement à ce genre. Jour. de Conchyl., II, pp. 17–24, May, 1851.

—— Description d'un genre nouveau, genre *Recluzia*, appartenant à la famille des Janthinidées. Jour. de Conchyl., IV, pp. 116–120, May, 1853.

PHILIPPI, RUDOLF AMANDUS (1808–1904). Kritische Bemerkungen über die von Eschscholtz aufgestellten Arten von Acmæa. Zeitschr. für Malak., III, pp. 106–108, July, 1846.

PILSBRY, HENRY AUGUSTUS (1862–   ). *Lucapinella*, a new genus of Fissurellidæ. Nautilus, IV, No. 8, p. 96, December, 1890.

—— Monographs of the Acmæidæ and Lepetidæ. Man. Conch. Struct. and Syst. (Acad. Nat. Sci. Philadelphia), XIII, pp. 1–76, pls. 1–40, 1891.

—— and JOHNSON, C. W. Catalogue of Fissurellidæ of the United States. Nautilus, V, No. 9, pp. 102–107, January, 1892.

—— On *Acanthopleura* and its subgenera. Nautilus, VI, No. 9, pp. 104–105, January, 1893.

—— Notes on the Acanthochitidæ, with descriptions of new American species. Nautilus, VII, No. 3, pp. 31–32, July, 1893.

—— A synonym of *Leptothyra* (*Petropoma* Gabb). Nautilus, VII, No. 7, p. 84, November, 1893.

—— Monograph of the Polyplacophora. Man. Conch. Struct. and Syst. (Acad. Nat. Sci. Philadelphia), XIV, pp. xxxiv, 350, pls. 1–68, 1892–93; XV, pp. 133, pls. 1-17, 1894.

—— On *Chiton hartwegii* Cpr. and its allies. Nautilus, VIII, No. 4, pp. 45–57, August, 1894.

—— *Trachydermon raymondi* in British Columbia. Nautilus, VIII, No. 5, p. 57, September, 1894.

—— *Navarchus* (preoccupied) changed to *Navanax*. Nautilus, VIII, p. 131, March, 1895. *See also* Cooper, J. G.

—— On *Dolabella californica* Stearns. Nautilus, IX, No. 7, pp. 73–74, November, 1895.

—— Notes on some west American chitons. Nautilus, X, No. 5, pp. 49–51, September, 1896.

—— Manual of Conchology. Scaphopoda. Man. Conch. Struct. and Syst., XVI, pp. i-xxxii, 1–280, pls. 1–34, 1897–98.

—— Note on *Halistylus*. Nautilus, XII, No. 4, pp. 46–47, August, 1898.

—— Notes on a few chitons. Nautilus, XII, No. 5, p. 51, September, 1898.

—— Note on the subgenus *Eucosmia* Cpr. (*Eulithidium* Pilsbry). Nautilus, XII, No. 5, p. 60, September, 1898.

—— *Haliotis cracherodii* variety *californiensis* Swainson. Nautilus, XII, No. 7, pp. 79–80, November, 1898.

—— Chitons collected by Dr. Harold Heath at Pacific Grove, near Monterey, California. Proc. Acad. Nat. Sci. Philadelphia for 1898, pp. 287–290.

—— *Margarita sharpii*, a new Alaskan gastropod. Proc. Acad. Nat. Sci. Philadelphia for 1898, p. 486, fig. 1.

—— and RAYMOND, W. J. Note on *Septifer bifurcatus* Conrad. Nautilus, XII, No. 6, pp. 69–71, October, 1898.

—— *See also* Dall, W. H.

PINART, ALPHONSE LOUIS. *See* Fischer, Paul Henri.

RANDOLPH, PEYTON BROOKS. Collecting shells in the Klondike country. Nautilus, XII, No. 10, pp. 109–112, February, 1899.

RAYMOND, WILLIAM JAMES (1865–   ). The Californian species of the genus *Nuttallina*. Nautilus, VII, No. 12, pp. 133–134, April, 1894.

—— A new *Dentalium* from California. Nautilus, XVII, No. 11, pp. 123–124, March, 1904.

—— Two new species of *Pleurotoma* from California. Nautilus, XVIII, No. 1, pp. 1–3. May, 1904.

—— A new species of *Pleurotoma* from the Pliocene of California. Nautilus, XVIII, No. 2. pp. 14–16, June, 1904.

RAYMOND, WILLIAM JAMES (1865–   ). The west American species of *Pleurotoma* subgenus *Genota*. Nautilus, XX, No. 4, pp. 37–39, pl. 2, August, 1906.

REDFIELD, JOHN HOWARD (1815–1895). Description of some new species of shells. Annals New York Lyc. Nat. Hist., IV, pp. 163–168. pl. 10, 1846.

RÉMOND, AUGUSTE. Description of two new species of bivalve shells from the Tertiaries of Contra Costa County. Proc. California Acad. Nat. Sci., III, p. 13, 1863.

RIVERS, JOHN JAMES (1825–   ). Occurrence of a Miocene shell in the living state (*Nassa californiana* Conrad). Zoë, II, pp. 70–72, fig., April, 1891.

——— A new volutoid shell from Monterey Bay. Proc. California Acad. Sci., 2d ser., III, August, 1891 (per separate). Reprinted, Nautilus, V, No. 10, pp. 111–112, February, 1892. The shell is really from Magellan Straits.

——— *Pandora (Kennerlia) grandis* Dall. Bull. Southern California Acad. Sci., I, No. 6, p. 69, June, 1902.

——— Descriptions of some undescribed fossil shells of the Pleistocene and Pliocene formations of the Santa Monica Range. Bull. Southern California Acad. Sci., III, No. 5, pp. 69–72, 1 pl., May, 1904.

ROCHEBRUNE, ALPHONSE TRÉMEAU DE (1836–   ). Diagnose d'espèces nouvelles de la famille de Chitonidæ, premier supplement. Bull. Soc. Philom., 7th ser., VI, pp. 190–197, 1882.

——— Note sur les mollusques recueillis par M. Diguet en Basse Californie. Bull. Mus. d'Hist. Nat. de Paris, I, p. 36, 1895.

——— Sur les propriétés toxiques du *Spondylus americanus* Lamarck. Bull. Mus. d'Hist. Nat., de Paris, I, pp. 151–156, 1895. *See also* Revue Scientifique, LV, p. 728, and Jour. Roy. Micros. Soc., 1895, p. 621.

——— Diagnoses de mollusques nouveaux provenant du voyage de M. Diguet en Basse-Californie. Bull. Mus. d'Hist. Nat., de Paris, I, pp. 239–243, 1895.

ROEMER, EDUARD (1819–1874). Ueber *Saxidomus*. Malak. Blätt., VIII, pp. 63–70, April, 1861.

ROUS, SLOMAN (1838–1907). *Cancellaria obtusa* Deshayes. Nautilus, XXI, No. 9, p. 105, January, 1908.

SCHRENCK, LEOPOLD VON (1826–1894). Les diagnoses de quelques nouvelles espèces de mollusques trouvées dans le détroit de Tartarie et dans la mer de Japon. Bull. de l'Acad. Imp. des Sci. de St.-Pétersbourg, IV, pp. 408–413, November, 1861.

——— Remarques sur la faune de Sakhaline et des isles Kouriles. Bull. de l'Acad. Imp. des Sci. de St.-Pétersbourg, IV, pp. 413–433, 1861.

——— Reisen und Forschungen im Amurlande. II (III). Mollusken des Amur-landes und des Nord-japanischen Meeres, 40, pp. 259–974. pls. 12–30, October, 1867.

SHEPARD, IDA MARY (1853–   ). With a dredge. Nautilus, IX, No. 6, pp. 71–72, October, 1895.

SHUMARD, BENJAMIN FRANKLIN (1820–1869). Descriptions of new fossils from the Tertiary formation of Oregon and Washington territories and the Cretaceous of Vancouver Island, collected by Dr. John Evans, U. S. geologist, under instructions from the Department of the Interior. Trans. St. Louis Acad. Sci., I, pp. 120–125, 1858.

SIMPSON, CHARLES TORREY (1846–   ). The molluscan fauna of the Galapagos Islands. Am. Naturalist, XXVIII, No. 327, pp. 255–257, March, 1894. [Review of Stearns's paper on this subject.]

SMITH, EDGAR ALBERT (1847–   ). Remarks on several species of Bullidæ, with descriptions of some hitherto unknown forms and of a new species of *Planaxis*. Ann. Mag. Nat. Hist., 4th ser., IX, pp. 344–355, May, 1872.

——— Remarks on the genus *Alaba*, with the description of a new species. Proc. Zool. Soc. London for 1875, pp. 537–540.

——— Account of the zoological collection made during the visit of H. M. S. *Peterel* to the Galapagos Islands. Proc. Zool. Soc. London for 1877, pp. 69–73, pl. 11.

——— Descriptions of twelve new species of shells. Proc. Zool. Soc. London for 1880, pp. 478–485, pl. 48; cf. p. 481, pl. 48, fig. 6.

SMITH, EDGAR ALBERT (1847-   ). Descriptions of six new species of shells from Vancouver Island. Ann. Mag. Nat. Hist., 5th ser., VI, pp. 286–289, October, 1880.

——— Observations on the genus *Astarte*, with a list of the known recent species. Jour. Conch. (Leeds), III, No. 7, pp. 196–232, July, 1881.

——— Diagnoses of new species of Pleurotomidæ in the British Museum. Ann. Mag. Nat. Hist., 6th ser., II, pp. 300–317, 1888.

——— Descriptions of new species of shells from the *Challenger* expedition. Proc. Zool. Soc. London for 1891, pp. 436–438, pl. 34, figs. 5–6.

——— Descriptions of new species of shells from Mauritius and California. Ann. Mag. Nat. Hist., 6th ser., IX, pp. 255–256, March, 1892.

——— Description of a new species of *Nucula* and a list of the species belonging to the subgenus *Acila*. Jour. Conch (Leeds), VII, pp. 110–112, October, 1892.

——— Observations on the genus *Sphenia*. Ann. Mag. Nat. Hist., 6th ser., XII, pp. 277-281, October, 1893.

——— A list of the recent species of the genus *Pirula* Lamarck, with notes respecting the synonymy. Jour. Mal., III, pt. 4, pp. 64–69, December, 1894.

——— On some Mollusca from Bering Sea, with descriptions of two new species of Trochidæ. Proc. Malac. Soc., III, pt. 4, pp. 205–207, figs. 1-2, March, 1899.

——— Note on the genera *Callocardia* and *Vesicomya*. Proc. Malac. Soc. London, IV, pt. 2, pp. 81–83, August, 1900.

SMITH, JAMES PERRIN (1864-   ). Studies for students. Geologic study of migration of marine invertebrates. Jour. Geol., III, No. 4, pp. 481–495, 1895.

——— Periodic migrations between the Asiatic and American coasts of the Pacific Ocean. Am. Jour. Sci., 4th ser., XVII, No. 99, pp. 217–233, March, 1904.

SMITH, MAXWELL. Annotated list of the Mollusca found in the vicinity of La Jolla, San Diego County, Cal. Nautilus, XXI, pp. 55–59, September, 1907; pp. 65–67, October, 1907.

——— *Triton gibbosus* Broderip in California. Nautilus, XXI, No. 9, p. 106, January, 1908.

SOPER, EMMA CATHERINE. Notes on shells. Nautilus, IX, No. 6, pp. 69–71, October, 1895.

SOWERBY, GEORGE BRETTINGHAM, sr. (1783–1854). A descriptive catalogue of the species of Leach's genus *Margarita*. Mal. and Conch. Mag., I, pt. 1, pp. 23–27, 1838.

SOWERBY, GEORGE BRETTINGHAM (3d) (1843-   ). Descriptions of two new species of shells from Japan. Ann. Mag. Nat. Hist., 7th ser., IV, pp. 370–372, figs., 1899.

STEARNS, ROBERT EDWARDS CARTER (1827-   ). Conchological memoranda. I, July 16, 1866; II, August 20, 1866; III, December 2, 1867; VI, May 18, 1871; VII, August 28, 1871; IX, September 4, 1871; X, June 5, 1872; XII, April 7, 1873. [Referred to below as C. M.]

——— List of shells collected at Baulinas Bay, California, June, 1866. (C. M., I.) Proc. California Acad. Nat. Sci., III, pp. 275–276, January, 1867.

——— List of shells collected at Santa Barbara and San Diego, by Mr. J. Hepburn in February-March, 1866. (C. M., I.) Proc. California Acad. Nat. Sci., III, pp. 283–286, January, 1867.

——— Additional shells from Baulinas Bay. (C. M., II.) Proc. California Acad. Nat. Sci., III, p. 291, January, 1867.

——— Shells collected at Santa Barbara, by W. Newcomb, M. D., in January, 1867. (C. M., II.) Proc. California Acad. Nat. Sci., III, pp. 343–345, September, 1867.

——— List of shells collected at Purissima and Lobitas, California, October, 1866. (C. M., II.) Proc. California Acad. Nat. Sci., III, pp. 345-346, September, 1867.

——— List of shells collected at Bodega Bay, California, June, 1867. (C. M., III.) Proc. California Acad. Nat. Sci., III, pp. 382–383, May, 1868.

——— Shells collected by the U. S. Coast Survey expedition to Alaska, in the year 1867. (C. M., III.) Proc. California Acad. Nat. Sci., III, pp. 384–385, May, 1868. Also in U. S. Coast Survey, Ann. Rept. for 1867, app. 18, pp. 291–292.

STEARNS, ROBERT EDWARDS CARTER (1827-   ).   The *Haliotis* or pearly ear-shell.   Am. Naturalist,
III, No. 5, pp. 250-256, figs., July, 1869.

——— Preliminary descriptions of new species from the west coast of America.   Conchological Memoranda, VI, 1 lf., May 18, 1871.

——— Descriptions of new marine mollusks from the west coast of North America.   Conchological Memoranda, VII, August 28, 1871.   Also Proc. California Acad. Sci., V, pp. 78-82, pl. 1, May. 1873.

——— On the habitat and distribution of the west American species of Cypræidæ, Triviidæ, and Amphiperasidæ.   (C. M., IX.)   Proc. California Acad. Nat. Sci., IV, pp. 186-189, January, 1872.

——— Description of a new species of *Monoceros* from California, with remarks on the distribution of the North American species.   Am. Jour. Conch., VII, pp. 167-171, pl. 14, fig. 16, March, 1872.

——— Descriptions of new California shells.   Am. Jour. Conch., VII, pp. 172-173, pl. 14, figs. 14, 15, March, 1872.   (Cf. also C. M., VI, May, 1871.)

——— The California *Trivia* and some points in its distribution.   Am. Naturalist, VI, pp. 732-734, figures, December, 1872.

——— Description of a new Mangelia from California.   (C. M., X.)   Proc. California Acad. Nat. Sci., IV, p. 226, pl. 1, fig. 10, January, 1873.

——— Remarks on marine faunal provinces on the west coast of America.   (C. M., X.)   Proc. California Nat. Sci., IV, p. 246, January, 1873.   *See also* Ann. Mag. Nat. Hist., 4th ser., XII, p. 185, 1873.

——— Description of new species of shells from California.   (C. M., X.)   Proc. California Acad. Nat. Sci., IV, p. 249, pl. 1, January, 1873.

——— Notes on *Purpura canaliculata* of Duclos.   (C. M., X.)   Proc. California Acad. Nat. Sci., IV, pp. 250-251, January, 1873.

——— A partial comparison of the conchology of portions of the Atlantic and Pacific coasts of North America.   (C. M., X.)   Proc. California Acad. Nat. Sci., IV, pp. 271-273, pl. 1, January, 1873.

——— The pectens, or scallop shells.   Overland Monthly, April, 1873, 4 pp.

——— Remarks on xylophagous marine animals, or marine animals which destroy wood.   California Horticulturalist and Floral Magazine, May, 1873, 4 pp. with figures.

——— Descriptions of a new genus and two new species of nudibranchiate mollusks from the coast of California.   (C. M., XII.)   Proc. California Acad. Sci., V, pp. 77-78, figs. 1-2, May, 1873.

——— Description of new marine mollusks from the west coast of North America.   (C. M., VII, XII.)   Proc. California Acad. Sci., V, pp. 78-82, pl. 1, May, 1873.

——— Remarks on the nudibranchiate or naked-gilled mollusks.   California Horticulturalist and Floral Magazine, July, 1873, 2 pp. with figures.

——— Shells collected at San Juanico, Lower California, by William M. Gabb.   Proc. California Acad. Sci., V, pp. 131-132, July 21, 1873.

——— Shells collected at Loreto, Lower California, by William M. Gabb, in February, 1867.   Proc. California Acad. Sci., V, p. 132, July 21, 1873.

——— Description of new fossil shells from the Tertiary of California.   Proc. Acad. Nat. Sci. Philadelphia for 1875, pp. 463-464, pl. 27, November 23, 1875.

——— Description of a new species of *Dolabella* from the Gulf of California, with remarks on other rare or little-known species from the same region.   Proc. Acad. Nat. Sci. Philadelphia for 1878, pt. 3, pp. 395-401, pl. 7.

——— *Mya arenaria* in San Francisco Bay.   Am. Naturalist, pp. 362-365, May, 1881.

——— Verification of the habitat of Conrad's *Mytilus bifurcatus*.   Proc. Acad. Nat. Sci. Philadelphia for 1882, pp. 241-242.

——— The edible clams of the Pacific coast and a proposed method of transporting them to the Atlantic coast.   Bull. U. S. Fish. Comm., III, No. 23, pp. 353-362, October 19, 1883.

——— The giant clams of Puget Sound.   Forest and Stream, May 28, 1885.

——— The teredo or shipworm.   Am. Naturalist, XX, pp. 131-136, February, 1886.

——— On certain parasites, commensals, and domiciliars in the pearl oysters, Meleagrinæ.   Rept. Smithsonian Inst. for 1886, pt. 1, pp. 339-344; plates 1-3, June, 1889.

STEARNS, ROBERT EDWARDS CARTER (1827–   ). Scientific results of explorations by the U. S. Fish Commission steamer *Albatross*. XVII. Description of new west American land, fresh-water, and marine shells, with notes and comments. Proc. U. S. Nat. Mus., XIII, No. 813, pp. 205–225, pls. 15–17, September 16, 1890.

—— Edible mollusks, etc. Here and there. Nautilus, V, No. 1, pp. 2–4, May, 1891.

—— Edible shell notes for "The Nautilus." Nautilus, V, No. 3, pp. 25, 26, July, 1891.

—— List of shells collected on the west coast of South America, principally between latitude 7° 30′ S. and 8° 49′ N., by Dr. W. H. Jones, surgeon, U. S. Navy. Proc. U. S. Nat. Mus., XIV, No. 854, pp. 307–335, 1891.

—— Preliminary descriptions of new molluscan forms from west American regions, etc. Nautilus, VI, No. 8, pp. 85–89, December, 1892.

—— Description of a new species of *Nassa* from the Gulf of California. Nautilus, VII, No. 1, pp. 10–11, May, 1893.

—— On rare or little-known mollusks from the west coast of North and South America, with descriptions of new species. Proc. U. S. Nat. Mus., XVI, No. 941, pp. 341–352, September 28, 1893.

—— Scientific results of explorations by the U. S. Fish Commission steamer *Albatross*. XXV. Report on the mollusk fauna of the Galapagos Islands, with descriptions of new species. Proc. U. S. Nat. Mus., XVI, No. 942, pp. 353–450, September 29, 1893.

—— On recent collections of North American land, fresh-water, and marine shells received from the U. S. Department of Agriculture. Proc. U. S. Nat. Mus., No. 971, pp. 743–755, February 9, 1894.

—— *Urosalpinx cinereus* in San Francisco Bay. Nautilus, VIII, No. 2, pp. 13–14, June, 1894.

—— The shells of the Tres Marias and other localities along the shores of Lower California and the Gulf of California. Proc. U. S. Nat. Mus., XVII, No. 996, pp. 139–204, July 19, 1894.

—— A new variety of *Ocinebra circumtexta* Stearns. Nautilus, IX, No. 2, p. 16, June, 1895.

—— *Uvanilla regina*, a new locality. Nautilus, XI, No. 1. p. 1, May, 1897.

—— Description of a new species of *Actæon* from the Quaternary bluffs of Spanish Bight, San Diego, Cal. Nautilus, XI, No. 2, pp. 14–15, June, 1897.

—— Description of a species of *Actæon* from the Quaternary bluffs at Spanish Bight, San Diego, Cal. Proc. U. S. Nat. Mus., XXI, No. 1145, pp. 297–299, 1 fig., November 2, 1898.

—— Notes on the *Cytherea (Tivela) crassatelloides* Conrad, with descriptions of many varieties. Proc. U. S. Nat. Mus., XXI, No. 1149, pp. 371–378, pls. 23–25, November 10, 1898.

—— Preliminary description of a new variety of *Haliotis*. Nautilus, XII, No. 9, pp. 106–107, January, 1899.

—— *Urosalpinx cinereus* Say, in San Francisco Bay. Nautilus, XII, No. 10, p. 112, February, 1899.

—— *Crepidula convexa* Say, variety *glauca* Say, in San Francisco Bay. Nautilus, XIII, No. 1, p. 8, May, 1899.

—— Natural history of the Tres Marias Islands of Mexico. Nautilus, XIII, No. 2, pp. 19, 20, June, 1899.

—— Natural history of the Tres Marias Islands, Mexico. Science, new ser., X, No. 239, July 28, 1899.

—— *Donax stultorum* Mawe=Conrad's species *Cytherea crassatelloides*. Nautilus, XIII, No. 7, pp. 73–75, November, 1899.

—— Abalone fishery in California. Protective regulation. Nautilus, XIII, No. 7, pp. 81, 82, November, 1899.

—— *Modiola plicatula* Lamarck, in San Francisco Bay. Nautilus, XIII, No. 8, p. 86, December, 1899.

—— Description of a new variety of *Haliotis* from California, with faunal and geographic notes. Proc. U. S. Nat. Mus., XXII, No. 1191, pp. 139–142, April 7, 1900.

—— Exotic Mollusca in California. Science, new ser., XI, No. 278, pp. 655–659, April 27, 1900.

STEARNS, ROBERT EDWARDS CARTER (1827–   ).   Notes on the distribution of and certain characteristics in the Saxidomi of the west coast.   Nautilus, XIV, No. 1, pp. 1–3, May, 1900.

——— The fossil shells of the Los Angeles tunnel clays.   Science, new ser., XII, pp. 247–250, August
17, 1900.

——— An abnormal chiton.   Nautilus, XV, No. 5, pp. 53–54, September, 1901.

——— Fossil shells of the John Day region.   Science, new ser., XV, No. 369, pp. 153–154, January
24, 1902.

——— Mollusks occurring in southern California.   Nautilus, XVI, No. 12, pp. 133–134, April, 1903.

——— Abalones and the earthquake.   Nautilus, XX, No. 12, pp. 135–136, April, 1907.

——— In re *Cytherea petechialis* of Carpenter's Mazatlan catalogue.   Nautilus, XXI, No. 3, p. 29,
July, 1907.

STIMPSON, WILLIAM (1832–1872).   Review of the northern Buccinums, and remarks on some other northern marine mollusks.   Canadian Naturalist, new ser., II, pp. 362–388, October, 1865.

STOUT, ARTHUR B. (1814–1898).   Remarks on *Octopus punctatus* Gabb.   Proc. California Acad. Sci.,
IV, pp. 30–31, November, 1868.

STUXBERG, ANTON JULIUS (1849–1902).   Evertebratfaunan i Sibiriens ishaf.   Vega Exp. vetensk.
iakt., I, pp. 695–715, 756, 766, 793–810, 1882.

TAYLOR, GEORGE WILLIAM (1854–   ).   Notes of a collecting trip to Departure Bay, Vancouver
Island.   Nautilus, VII, No. 9, pp. 100–102, January, 1894.

——— Preliminary catalogue of the marine Mollusca of the Pacific coast of Canada, with notes upon
their distribution.   Trans. Royal Soc. Canada, 2d ser., I, pp. 17–100, 1895.

THIELE, JOHANNES.   Bemerkungen über die Gattung *Photinula*.   Nachrichtsbl. Deutsch. malacozool.
Gesellsch., heft 1, 1906, pp. 12–15.

THOMPSON, D'ARCY WENTWORTH (1860–   ).   On a rare cuttlefish, *Ancistroteuthis robusta* (Dall)
Steenstrup.   Proc. Zool. Soc. London for 1900, pp. 992–998, figs., 1901.

THROCKMORTON, SAMUEL R.   Eastern oysters in California waters.   Proc. California Acad. Sci., V, p.
306, December, 1874.

TRASK, JOHN BOARDMAN (1824–1879).   Descriptions of fossil shells from the Tertiary deposits [of
Santa Barbara, Cal.].   Proc. California Acad. Sci., I, pp. 41–43, April 9, 1855.   [Describes *Chem-
nitzia papillosa*, *Tornatella elliptica*, *Murex fragilis*, *Fusus barbarensis*, *F. robustus*, and *F. rugosus*,
from the Pliocene of Santa Barbara, as new.]

TROWBRIDGE, LAURA HELEN.   Collecting at Ballast Point.   Nautilus, XI, No. 6, pp. 67–69, October,
1897.

VANATTA, EDWARD G.   West American Eulimidæ.   Proc. Acad. Nat. Sci. Philadelphia for 1899, pp.
254–257, pl. 11.

VERKRUZEN, T. A.   Zusammenstellung der Buccinen der nördlichen Hemisphaere.   Nachrichtsbl. d.
Deutsch. Mal. Ges., XIII, pp. 42–44, March, 1881 (cf. pp. 18–22, January, 1881); Jahrb. d. Deutsch.
Mal. Ges., XI, pp. 203–229, 356–365, 1882; Nachrichtsbl., XIV, pp. 161–172, December, 1882; XV,
pp. 144–150, October, 1883; XVI, pp. 98–103, July, 1884; XVII, pp. 85–88, June, 1885.

VERRILL, ADDISON EMERY (1839–   ).   Contributions to zoology from the museum of Yale College.
VI.   Descriptions of shells from the Gulf of California.   Am. Jour. Sci., 2d ser., XLIX, pp. 217–227,
March, 1870.

——— North American cephalopods.   Trans. Connecticut Acad. Sci., V, pp. 245–252, pls. 23–24,
February, 1880.

——— Descriptions of two species of *Octopus* from California.   Bull. Mus. Comp. Zool. at Harvard
College, No. 6, XI, pp. 117–124, pls. 4–6, 1883.

VOGDES, ANTHONY WAYNE. (1843–   ).   A bibliography relating to the geology, paleontology, and
mineral resources of California.   Bull. California State Mining Bureau, No. 30, Sacramento, State
Printer, 1904, 290 pp., 5 pl., 8°.

WATTS, W. L.   The gas and petroleum yielding formations of California.   Bull. California State Mining Bureau, No. 3, Sacramento, State Printer, 1894, pp. 1–65.   [Contains lists of fossils by J. G. Cooper.]

———   Oil and gas yielding formations of Los Angeles, Ventura, and Santa Barbara counties.   Bull. California State Mining Bureau for 1897, XI, pp. 1–94, Sacramento, State Printer, 1897.   [Contains lists of fossils.]

WASHBURN, FREDERICK LEONARD (1860–   ).   Present condition of the eastern oyster experiment and the native oyster industry.   Rept. State Biologist, Salem, Oreg., State Printer, 1900, 8°, pp. 1–13.

———   Notes on the spawning habits of the razor clam, *Machæra patula* Dixon.   Recommendations regarding protective measures.   8°, 6 pp., 2 pls., Eugene, Oreg., April, 1900.

WHITE, [Mrs. G. W.] LETTIE HUTCHINS.   Collecting in southern California.   Nautilus, IX, No. 9, pp. 102–104, January, 1896.

WHITEAVES, JOSEPH FREDERICK (1835–   ).   On some marine Invertebrata from the west coast of North America collected by Mr. J. Richardson.   Canadian Naturalist, new ser., VIII, pp. 464–471, December 20, 1878.

———   On some marine Invertebrata from the Queen Charlotte Islands.   Rept. Progress, Geol. Survey Canada, 1878–79, pp. 190B–205B. 1880.

———   On some marine Invertebrata, dredged, or otherwise collected, by Dr. G. M. Dawson in 1885, on the coast of British Columbia [etc.].   Trans. Royal Soc. Canada, IV, sec. 4, for 1886, pp. 111–135, 1887.

———   Notes on some marine Invertebrata from the coast of British Columbia.   Ottawa Naturalist, VII, No. 9, pp. 133–137, December, 1893.

WHITNEY, JOSIAH DWIGHT (1819–1896).   *See* Gabb, W. M.

WILLCOX, MARY ALICE (1856–   ).   A revision of the systematic names employed by writers on the morphology of the Acmæidæ.   Proc. Boston Soc. Nat. Hist., XXIX, No. 11, pp. 217–222, April, 1900.

WILLIAMSON, MARTHA BURTON.   Leaves from a diary.   Nautilus, III, pp. 143–144, April, 1890.

———   Collecting chitons on the Pacific coast.   Nautilus, IV, No. 3, pp. 32–33, July, 1890.

———   An annotated list of the shells of San Pedro Bay and vicinity, with a description of two new species.   Proc. U. S. Nat. Mus., XV, No. 898, pp. 179–220, pls. 19–23, 1892.

———   On *Clementia subdiaphana* Cpr. in San Pedro Bay.   Nautilus, VI, No. 10, p. 116, February, 1893.

———   Edible mollusks of southern California.   Nautilus, VII, No. 3, pp. 27–29, July, 1893.

———   Abalone or *Haliotis* shells of the Californian coast.   Am. Naturalist, XXXII, pp. 849–852, October, 1894.

———   Conchological researches in San Pedro Bay, including the Alamitos oyster fishery   Ann. Pub. Hist. Soc. Southern California, III, pp. 10–15, 1894.

———   An interrogation in regard to *Septifer bifurcatus* Reeve and *Mytilus bifurcatus* Conrad.   Nautilus, XII, No. 6, pp. 67–68, October, 1898.

———   How *Potamides* (*Cerithidea*) *californica* travels.   Nautilus, XV, No. 7, pp. 82–83, November, 1901.

———   A monograph on *Pecten æquisulcatus* Cpr.   Bull. Southern California Acad. Sci., I, No. 5, pp. 51–61, pls. 4–6, May, 1902.

———   New varieties of *Crepidula rugosa* Nuttall, found on *Natica* and *Norrisia*.   Nautilus, XIX, No. 5, pp. 50–51, September, 1905.

———   West American shells, including a new variety of *Corbula luteola* Cpr. and two new varieties of gastropods.   Bull. Southern California Acad. Sci., IV, No. 8, pp. 118–129, November, 1905.

———   Abalones and the penal code of California.   Nautilus, XX, No. 8, pp. 85–87, December, 1906.

———   West American Mitridæ north of Cape St. Lucas, Lower California.   Proc. Biol. Soc. Washington, XIX, pp. 193–198, December 31, 1906.

———   The *Haliotis* or abalone industry of the Californian coast: preservative laws.   Ann. Hist. Soc. Southern California, VII, pp. 22–30, 1907.

WIMMER, AUGUST. Zur Conchylien-Fauna du Galápagos Inseln. Sitzb. der K. Akad. der Wiss.,
    LXXX, 1st Abth., pp. 1–50, December, 1879.

WOOD, WILLIARD M., and RAYMOND, WILLIAM J. Mollusks of San Francisco County. Nautilus, V,
    No. 5, September, 1891, pp. 54–58; No. 8, p. 94, December, 1891.

——— On a collecting trip to Monterey Bay. Nautilus, VII, No. 6, pp. 70–72, October, 1893.

——— Bolinas, Cal., the conchologist's paradise. Nautilus, XI, No. 5, pp. 49–54, September, 1897.

WOODWORTH, FREDERICK AUGUSTUS (1858–   ). See Dall, W. H.

YATES, LORENZO GORDIN (1837–   ). The Mollusca of Santa Rosa Island, California, U. S. Quart.
    Jour. Conch. (Leeds), I, No. 10, pp. 182–185, 1877.

——— Stray notes on the geology of the Channel Islands. The Mollusca of the Channel Islands of
    California. Ninth Ann. Rept. California State Mining Bureau, pp. 171–178, 1889.

——— The Mollusca of Santa Barbara County, Cal., and new shells from the Santa Barbara Channel.
    Santa Barbara Soc. Nat. Hist., Bull. No. 2, pp. 37–48, pls. I, II, August, 1890.

——— *Cypræa spadicea.* Nautilus, IV, No. 5, p. 54, September, 1890.

——— Shells of the Santa Barbara Channel. Overland Monthly, August, 1897.

ZECK, Mrs. MATILDA (misprinted Beck). Morning tides. Nautilus, XI, No. 8, pp. 89–90, December,
    1897.

PLATES II TO XXIII.

PLATE II.

(All species from the Miocene of Coos Bay, Oregon.)

218

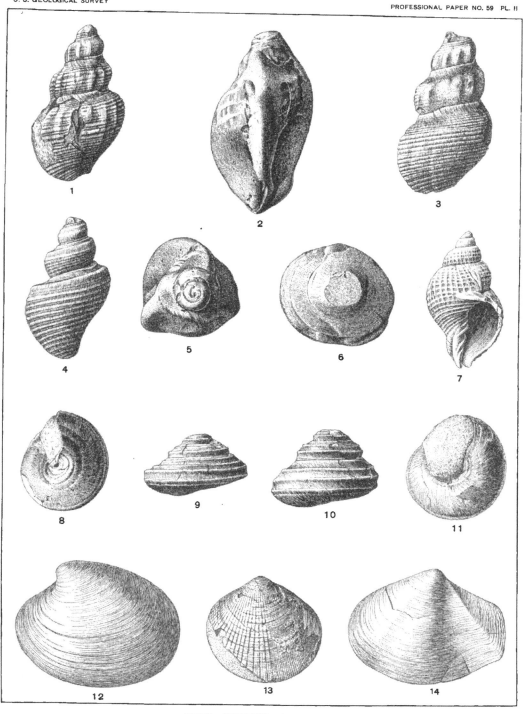

FOSSIL INVERTEBRATE FAUNA.

PLATE III.

220

FOSSIL INVERTEBRATE FAUNA.

PLATE IV.

222

FOSSIL INVERTEBRATE FAUNA.

PLATE V.

224

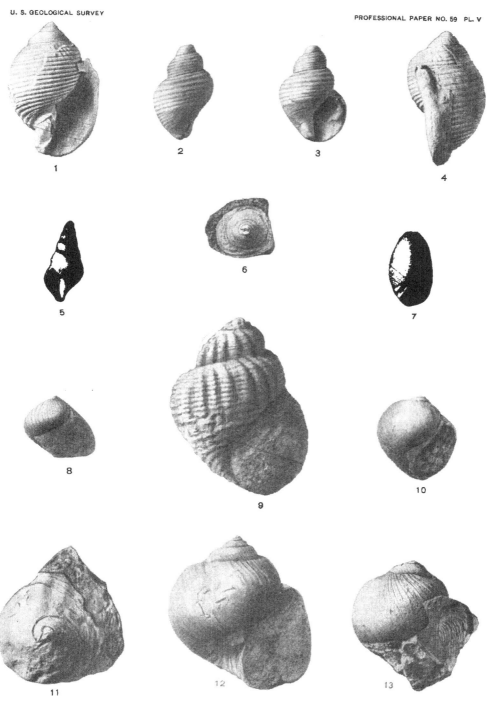

FOSSIL INVERTEBRATE FAUNA.

PLATE XX.

1

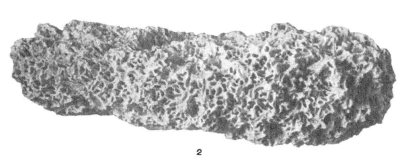

2

FOSSIL INVERTEBRATE FAUNA.

PLATE XXI.

256

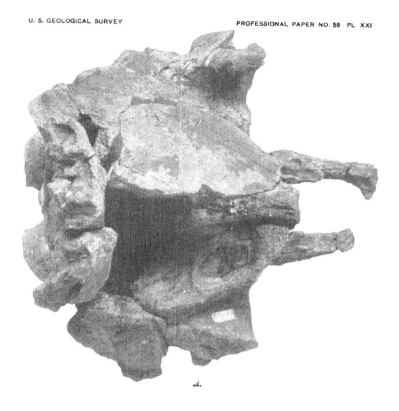

A.

B.

THE FOSSIL SEA LION PONTOLIS MAGNUS.

258

A.

B.

THE FOSSIL SEA LION PONTOLIS MAGNUS.

PLATE XXIII.

260

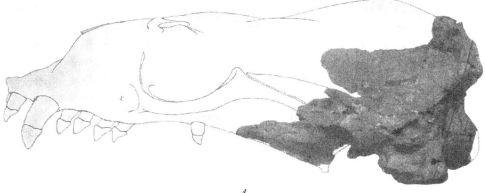

A.

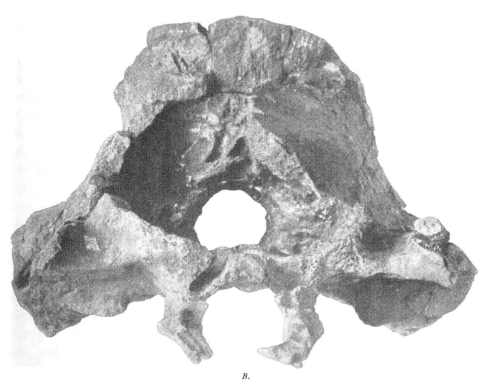

B.

THE FOSSIL SEA LION PONTOLIS MAGNUS.

INDEX.

[Names in *italic* are those of new species and genera. Figures in **bold-face** type denote descriptions. Figures in *italic* denote illustrations.]

O

CPSIA information can be obtained at www.ICGtesting.com
Printed in the USA
LVOW03s0505101213

364648LV00005B/70/P